Missing Links

Missing
Links

Gender Equity in Science and Technology
for Development

Gender Working Group,
United Nations Commission on Science
and Technology for Development

INTERNATIONAL DEVELOPMENT RESEARCH CENTRE
in association with
INTERMEDIATE TECHNOLOGY PUBLICATIONS
and
UNIFEM

Published in Canada by
International Development Research Centre
PO Box 8500, Ottawa, ON, Canada K1G 3H9

and

in the United Kingdom by
Intermediate Technology Publications Ltd
103-105 Southampton Row, London WC1B 4HH, UK

and

in the United States by
UNIFEM (United Nations Development Fund for Women)
304 East 45th Street, 6th Floor, New York, NY 10017, USA

United Nations Commission on Science and Technology Development,
Genève CH. Gender Working Group

Missing links: gender equity in science and technology for development.
Ottawa, ON, IDRC, 1995. xv + 376 p.

/Women's role/, /women's rights/, /science and technology/, /sustainable
development/, /developing countries/ — /indigenous knowledge/, /food
security/, /energy/, /health/, /decision making/, /science education/,
/technology assessment/, /entrepreneurship/, /information/, /UN/,
/recommendations/, references.

UDC: 396:600

A CIP record for this book is available from the British Library.

A microfiche edition is available.

All paper used is recycled as well as recycleable. All inks and coatings are
vegetable-based products.

ISBN 0-88936-765-5 (IDRC)
ISBN 1 85339 289 8 (IT Publications)
ISBN 0-912917-37-7 (UNIFEM)

DISCARD

Contents

Foreword

Since Galileo Galilei, the world has learned about the close connection between science and liberty. Now, as we approach the dawning of the third millenium, nobody can deny how much technology has contributed to the well-being of humankind and to the spread of freedom around our planet.

Science has given us muscles to move machines, telescopic views of the origins of our universe, and additional years to our brief existence. It has multiplied memories and opened our eyes and ears to different cultures. But, much more importantly, science has given us the means to liberate slaves and colonies and has made the attainment of global equity a real possibility, for the first time in history.

All of us may now be connected by electronic pulses, but we are truly united by a common destiny. Wherever there is life, there is also knowledge that could make our lives better; wherever there is pain, it is felt by each of us. All of us share the same home, and the challenges we face are multiplying. In responding to these challenges and building for this and future generations, science provides us both vision and powerful tools.

After centuries of action, research, and development, the gap between science and liberty has almost vanished. However, what of the gap between science and justice? What of equality of opportunity and access to knowledge, which is now our most precious resource? Closing this gap remains an enormous task.

Recognizing this, the United Nations, with the wisdom of its members, created the Commission on Science and Technology for Development. Its novel working style, created during the first session of the Commission, relied on the full participation of members, governments, and partner organizations. Social, geographical, and gender differences were gradually cast aside as ideas and efforts were merged to form the Commission's final report and this publication.

Now we pass our work on to you, the reader. By opening this book, you too have become an actor in bridging justice and science. The proof, the means, and the ways are now in front of us. All that is left is to act.

Oscar Serrate
*Chair, United Nations Commission on Science
and Technology for Development*

Preface

In April 1993, the newly established United Nations Commission on Science and Technology for Development (UNCSTD) met for the first time. Held in New York, this meeting focused on the criteria for selecting the topics on which the Commission would work over the next 2 years. One suggestion was to address the science and technology dimension of the major UN conferences that would be held in the year the Commission next reported: 1995 would be the year of the World Summit on Social Development in Copenhagen and the 4th World Conference on Women and Development in Beijing.

From my time with the Science Policy Research Unit at the University of Sussex, I was aware that there were important science and technology policy issues relating to the impact of technical change on women's lives, especially as it affected employment. I therefore formally proposed that "Gender, Science, Technology, and Development" be one of the topics that the Commission address. I was unprepared for the reaction of my fellow delegates. Although some supported the proposal, many others thought that the issue of gender had little to do with science and technology. Only after a great deal of debate was it finally agreed that gender be one of three topics that the Commission would address over the next 2 years.

Eight national delegates — from Burundi, Costa Rica, the Netherlands, the People's Republic of China, Romania, Saudi Arabia, Tanzania, and the United Kingdom — volunteered to serve on the Gender Working Group. All of them were men; not surprising, as 51 out of the 52 governments who had nominated delegates to the Commission had nominated men! This (all-male) Gender Working Group realized at its first meeting that, no matter how incisive its study and subsequent report, it would be bound to be rejected by at least half the world's population as lacking validity. Our first decision therefore was to "coappoint" eight women, all experts in the field, to work with us as equal members of the Working Group. We then undertook to prepare a consensus report.

The Working Group first met in conjunction with an "expert group meeting" on gender in science and technology convened by UN Development Fund for Women (UNIFEM). At this meeting, some 50 experts debated the issues of gender, science, and technology to generate ideas for the 1995 Beijing Conference. In this atmosphere, the Gender Working Group reached agreement on the nine themes for its analysis and appointed a Director of Studies.

In all, the Working Group met four times, and all those involved — delegates, advisors, experts, and volunteers — can testify to the remarkable process that took place. Over a 14-month period, Working Group members sought to understand one another's points of view and identify issues that warranted change and the attention of governments, the scientific community, nongovernmental organizations (NGOs), and individuals. The delegates learned a great deal about the gender-specific nature of development; the advisors, I believe, became more aware of political realities. It was certainly one of the most intensive learning experiences of my life.

The "esprit de corps" that developed does not mean that there were no differences of opinion or tensions within the Working Group. They tended to crystallize around questions such as "How much evidence is required before an hypothesis can be considered proven, at least to the point where it is reasonable to make policy proposals?" and "How much emphasis should be given to extending the field by defining a new research agenda and how much should be given to influencing policy?" There was also a split between those who wanted to stress the potentially liberating opportunities generated by modern science and technology and those who felt that sustainable human development would be achieved faster if more attention was given to the local knowledge held by women in rural areas. Finally, there was tension between those who wanted to take a more pragmatic incremental approach to recommending policy changes and those who favoured a more radical approach.

For me, and I suspect for most of the other delegates, the biggest surprise was recognizing the extent to which development is gender specific. I have spent a great deal of my life working in, and on, the problems of developing countries. I should have recognized that the science and technology projects and programs that I was involved with would likely have a different impact on the lives of men and women; but I had not. Neither had most of the other delegates. Yet, the strong evidence of differential impact convinced all of us of the need for science and technology programs to consider explicitly their gender impact.

The other dimension we considered was the issue of education and barriers to career development for women scientists and engineers. These were not new topics — many other groups had explored them before us. Now, we were able to build on this previous work. There are substantial variations between countries and cultures regarding most dimensions of this topic, but there is one dimension that is common to all countries: the absence of women from top decision-making positions. This becomes a particularly serious defect when we recognize the gender-specific nature of development. It means that the needs and aspirations of women rarely get fully articulated in decision-making bodies.

The overriding concern of the Gender Working Group was to move toward a situation where there would be gender equity. We wanted this because of our belief in human rights and because we thought that sustainable human development would occur faster if equity existed. Some scholars argue that if there were more women scientists there would be a different sort of science, that more women research directors would mean different management styles, and that more women scientists in decision-making positions would lead to different research priorities and the development of different sorts of technology. Of these three suppositions, the Working Group accepted the validity of only the last one; many members believed that the first two needed further testing.

A major objective of the 1995 Beijing Conference is to identify ways in which women can be empowered. One of the most effective tools for empowerment is knowledge. As such, the Gender Working Group has tried to identify specific ways in which women can be empowered by gaining access to scientific and technological knowledge.

This book largely consists of essays commissioned to distinguished scholars and experts by the Gender Working Group. Each contributor was asked to explore the issues related to science, technology, and gender in her own area of expertise. In particular, they were asked to give examples where technical change had differentially affected the lives of women and men. The topics chosen by the Gender Working Group reflected an early decision to focus its work primarily on the basic needs of people in rural areas of the developing world (a few essays, however, do also explore the wider impact of new technologies on the lives of women in both urban and rural environments and the relationship between gender and science in the developed world).

Indeed, in these rural areas of the developing world, science and technology has tended to benefit men more than women. A prime reason for this is the dominance of men in the decision-making chain.

There are many links in this chain: from the science and technology institutions that generate the technology, to the mediating institutions that transfer it, to the societal institutions that use it. However, there are missing links in that chain. These are the women scientists, entrepreneurs, and community leaders, who can best reflect the needs and aspirations of women. The sooner these missing links are in place, the sooner science and technology will serve all of society, and the stronger the chain will be.

The Gender Working Group has built on the wealth of information and ideas contained in the essays of this book to identify a set of common themes. For each of those themes, the Working Group proposed transformative actions that, if implemented, would have a major impact in bringing about greater gender equity in science and technology for sustainable human development.

The final report of the Gender Working Group is presented (in a modified form) as Chapter 1. The original report was transmitted to the Second Session of the UN Commission on Science and Technology for Development in May 1995, where all of its recommendations were endorsed, with only minor modifications, and transmitted to the Economic and Social Council. In addition, its main findings were communicated to five of the Preparatory Committee meetings of the 4th World Conference on Women to be held in Beijing in September 1995.

Many academics have been involved in the preparation of this book. However, the principal objective was not to generate new knowledge or to prepare an academic book. It was to persuade governments, the United Nations, the scientific community, donors, and NGOs of the need for change. It is clear that more work is needed to understand better the links between gender, science, technology, and sustainable human development. But enough is known to warrant action now. My hope is that this book will help stimulate both action and research for a more equitable world.

Geoffrey Oldham
Chair, Gender Working Group
United Nations Commission on
Science and Technology for Development

Acknowledgments

This book is the result of 2 years of intensive of work by many individuals and many organizations. Acknowledgment is made to all who have participated in the process. In particular, thanks are due to all the members of the Gender Working Group (see Appendix A) for their expertise and commitment. Special thanks are extended to Shirley Malcolm, Farkhonda Hassan, Sonia Correa, and Marilyn Carr for serving as the informal editorial board for this publication, and to the contributors, who were willing to set aside other intentions and divert their efforts to the work of the UN Commission on Science and Technology for Development.

The work was made possible through generous financial contributions from the Netherlands Ministry of Foreign Affairs, the International Development Research Centre (Canada), the United States Agency for International Development, the Swedish Agency for Research Cooperation with Developing Countries, the United Nations Development Fund for Women (UNIFEM), the Carnegie Corporation of New York (USA), the World Women's Veterinary Association, and Mr William Hewlett. In addition, the following organizations made substantial nonfinancial contributions in time, and their substantive assistance is deeply appreciated: the Gender, Science, and Development Programme of the International Federation of Institutes for Advanced Study, the Board on Science and Technology for International Development (US National Academy of Sciences), and the Third World Organization of Women in Science. Thanks are due also to the Government of the Netherlands, the Government of Costa Rica, and the Inter-American Institute for Cooperation on Agriculture for hosting the meetings of the Working Group.

The review of the United Nations system was carried out by UNIFEM, which responded positively and enthusiastically to the Commission's request that it act as the "lead agency" in this review. UNIFEM's contribution, both in conducting the review and in helping to host and organize the initial meeting of the Gender Working Group, is deeply appreciated.

Finally, I would like to acknowledge the work of the Secretariat in facilitating all the activities of the Gender Working Group. In particular, I thank Elizabeth McGregor, the Director of Studies, for her professional contribution and personal support and enthusiasm throughout the 2-year process.

Geoffrey Oldham
Chair, Gender Working Group
United Nations Commission on
Science and Technology for Development

Chapter 1

Taking action

Conclusions and recommendations of the Gender Working Group[1]

Introduction

The overlap of science and technology, sustainable human development, and gender is an area of human activity that has never been deeply explored, until now. But what are the essential elements of each of these three domains? Knowing this will enable you, the reader, to identify the common perspectives shared by all members of the Gender Working Group and understand the basis for the analysis, diagnosis, and prescriptions presented in this book.

Science and technology

A distinction was made by the Gender Working Group between the development, diffusion, and use of modern science-based technologies, and the local knowledge and traditional technologies that have evolved within communities over many years of trial and error. Both knowledge systems are important for sustainable human development, but science-based technologies have formed the basis for industrialization of the more developed countries over the past

---

[1] This chapter is a modified version of the final report of the Gender Working Group — as presented to the United Nations Commission on Science and Technology for Development — entitled *Science and Technology for Sustainable Human Development: The Gender Dimension* (Gender Working Group, February 1995).

century. Those developing countries that have invested in their own modern scientific and technical capabilities have been able to join the industrialization process. Several East Asian countries have experienced remarkable economic growth rates over the past 20 years with this strategy.

Developing countries that have not been able to make comparable investments in their own scientific and technical capabilities have not shared these successes, and current trends in "globalization" render these countries increasingly marginalized. There now exists a wide spectrum of developing countries, ranging from those with little capability in science and technology, which are all but excluded from the global economy, to those with advanced capabilities and whose economic growth rates are outstripping many of the older developed countries.

It is not only in economic growth and wealth creation that science-based technologies have made substantial contributions; there have also been major transformations in agricultural practices made possible by new technologies. Perhaps most dramatic has been the contribution of modern science to the eradication and amelioration of diseases and the improvement of health care worldwide.

The impact of science and technology on society has not been uniformly beneficial. Not all members of society have shared in the benefits; and the development of weapons of mass destruction and growing pollution and environmental degradation demonstrate the flip side of the coin, as do the social problems of alienation, unemployment, and increased crime, which often seem to follow in the wake of technical change.

Technological change, for good or bad, does not automatically follow from the results of scientific research. It is a consequence of countless decisions made by scientists, engineers, corporations, and governments, which collectively govern the impact of science and technology on all of our lives. It must be an objective of science and technology policy to maximize the benefits to be derived from science and technology and to minimize its harmful effects, for all members of society. This objective underlies the Gender Working Group's approach to examining the gender dimension of science and technology.

Sustainable human development

Sustainable human development emphasizes people rather than economic growth, per se. It seeks to improve the quality of life of all people today without harming the prospects of future generations. It is a concept that has been elaborated at length by the United Nations

Development Programme (UNDP) in its annual *Human Development Report* and is the type of development to which the Gender Working Group subscribes. As described in a speech by James Gustave Speth, the Administrator of UNDP, to the April 1994 UN Global Conference on Sustainable Development and Small Island Developing States:

> Sustainable human development brings together the vision of sustainable development at the Earth Summit with the vision of human development we expect from Cairo, Copenhagen, and Beijing.... Sustainable human development is a powerful concept of a new type of development. It is development that not only generates economic growth but distributes its benefits equitably; that regenerates the environment rather than destroys it; that empowers people, enlarges their choices and opportunities, and provides for their participation in decisions which affect them, rather than marginalising them.... It is development that is pro-poor, pro-nature, pro-women, and pro-jobs. It stresses growth, but growth with equity.

Gender

Gender refers to the distinct roles that men and women are assigned in any society. As a result, women and men assume distinct socially and culturally defined responsibilities and tasks both within the household and in the wider community. The knowledge and experience gained from undertaking these tasks, as well as their requirements, lead women and men to have different needs and aspirations. This concept of gender differentiation underpins the conviction that "science and technology for development" must systematically and purposefully recognize the gender-specific nature of development and respond to the concerns, needs, and aspirations of both women and men appropriately and equitably.

The Working Group accepted the conclusions of previous studies that had demonstrated that development itself is gender specific. As well, all studies point to the fact that women are among the poorest of the poor and are notably disadvantaged. As described in the 1993 *Human Development Report* (UNDP 1993, pp. 16–17):

> In industrialized countries, gender discrimination...is mainly in employment and wages, with women often getting less than two-thirds of the employment opportunities and about half the earnings of men. In developing countries the great disparities, besides those in

the job market are in health care, nutritional support and education. For instance, women make up two-thirds of the illiterate population. And South and East Asia, defying the normal biological result that women live longer than men, have more men than women. The reasons: high maternal mortality and infanticide and nutritional neglect of the girl-child.

Mandate: the overlap

Within the area defined by the overlap of these three domains, the Gender Working Group was required to

+ Make science and technology policy recommendations to national governments;

+ Review the performance of the United Nations system and suggest improvements; and

+ Provide advice to "other relevant organizations."

In fulfilling its mandate, the Working Group was hindered by the paucity of available data.[2] What data that do exist, however, strongly suggest that, within the area of concern, women are more disadvantaged than men.

Particular attention was paid to the gender dimension of science and technology for basic needs in developing countries. It was hoped that this approach would complement the recommendations of the Basic Needs Working Group of the United Nations Commission on Science and Technology for Development (UNCSTD). It became apparent, however, that the fundamental issues were germane to all countries. They differed between countries often only in context, scale, and scope. Thus, although the primary focus of this report is on transformative actions for developing countries, it ends with a challenge to all governments to sign a "Declaration of Intent" regarding a set of goals that should underlie every country's approach to gender and science and technology for development.

---

[2] More attention must be paid in the future to the collection of data both on "participation rates of women" in science and related decision-making bodies and on the "differential impact of technical change" on the lives of men and women. Interestingly, there is substantially more data available on the impact of science and technology on the lives of poor women than on the lives of poor men.

The Diagnosis

At the close of the 20th century, women in the rural areas of developing countries are still experiencing serious difficulty in meeting their own basic needs and the basic needs of their households. Scientific and technological interventions have improved many aspects of women's lives, allowing for important declines in both maternal and infant mortality. However, over the last three decades, women in the developing countries have also become disproportionately poor in relation to men in their own communities.

Several recent United Nations reports, produced at the highest levels of expertise, have documented women's differential poverty as a significant phenomenon requiring policy attention and intervention. This well-defined difference between men and women worldwide cannot be understood without explicit reference to the gender-specific nature of development, including scientific and technological contributions to the development process.

This book focuses primarily on the basic needs of men and women in rural areas in developing countries. This is where most of the poorest people live and where there is strong evidence, collected over the past two decades, that development itself is gender specific. It was recognized that there are also gender, science, and technology issues in the urban areas of developing countries and in the developed countries. Some reference is made to these issues, but they were not so fully explored as those related to basic needs in rural areas.

To assist the Working Group, essays were commissioned from leading experts to diagnose the ways in which science and technology have differentially affected the lives of men and women in various key sectors: environment, health, agriculture, energy, information, education, employment, small and medium-sized enterprises, and indigenous knowledge systems. These essays are presented in the pages of this book, and, from them, the Working Group drew two key observations.

I. Gender inequity in education and careers in science and technology

In most developing countries, there are serious obstacles to girls and women receiving science and technology education and in pursuing scientific and technical careers. Similar obstacles also exist for women in developed countries, particularly with regard to advanced science and technology training and education. These obstacles, which extend beyond those faced by boys and men, prevent women from fully contributing to scientific and technological advances, including ones that could better meet women's basic needs and support their hopes and aspirations for the future.

More girls remain marginalized from the mainstream of education than boys. Girls do not enjoy equal access to the formal education system. Outside the education system, this disparity between women and men in terms of literacy and access to science and technology training is pronounced. Among girls who do gain entry to school, fewer study science and fewer advance to high levels in science and technology, where women are clearly under-represented. Girls and women are disadvantaged compared with boys and men both in acquiring a scientific and technical education and in entering and staying in scientific and technical careers. This conclusion is not new.

A recent series of national government task forces, regional workshops on gender in science and technology, and international reviews have analyzed the evidence and reached similar conclusions (for example, Ellis 1990; APPROTECH Asia 1992; AAAS 1993; Logue and Talapessy 1993; NABST 1993; Baringa 1994; Office of Science and Technology 1994). Many of the observations made about education and careers apply to all countries, although some aspects are culture and country specific. All agree that, in most developing countries,

- ✦ Cultural attitudes and gender stereotyping are obstacles to education and careers for girls and women;

- ✦ More boys than girls receive basic education;

- ✦ Among those who receive education, more boys than girls study science and technology;

- ✦ There are more men than women in scientific and technical careers; and

- ✦ There are very few women in science and technology policy and decision-making positions or on advisory boards.

In many regions of the world, there have been substantial improvements in the gender balance of students studying science and technology subjects in tertiary education. The exceptions are Africa, where the ratio of women to men has remained around 10% over the last two decades, and Eastern Europe where the ratio has declined over the past 10 years (APPROTECH Asia 1992).

There are compelling reasons to create policy and institutional environments that foster and promote gender equity in education, careers, and decision-making in science and technology. Beyond the moral force of fairness, there is also the need for nations to succeed in the global marketplace. Governments of developed and developing nations alike recognize the need to maximize the creativity and ingenuity of all available human resources. Marginalization of one half of the pool of national talent does not make good sense.

The Gender Working Group explored the reasons why there is such pronounced under-representation of girls in technical education and women in scientific careers. Although there is considerable variation between countries and cultures, and although improvements have occurred in some countries over the past two decades, there appeared to be a set of common characteristics that contribute to the persistent under-representation of women in science.

The Working Group identified a range of factors that serve to mitigate against young girls gaining access to the school system and continuing in the science and technology stream:

- ✦ Social conditioning and gender stereotyping, particularly of young children worldwide;

- ✦ Lack of national government resources to support education for all and, in some cultures, a national bias favouring the education of boys over the education of girls;

- ✦ Parental preference favouring the education of boys over girls because of cultural reasons and economic constraints, resulting in young girls assuming family and household responsibilities early in their lives;

- ✦ The misleading perception of parents, some teachers, and guidance counsellors that science and mathematics are "difficult subjects" and not as suitable for girls as for boys;

- ✦ Curricula and textbooks that do not relate science to everyday experiences of both boys and girls, contain gender-biased language, fail to give due recognition to the contributions to women scientists, and do not promote women role models for girls; and

- ✦ The fact, in some countries, that girls' schools are not as well equipped with laboratories and equipment as boys' schools.

Among the many factors that explain why women are under-represented in scientific careers are the following:

- ✦ The challenge of combining family responsibilities with professional careers where household responsibilities are not equitably shared;

- The pace at which science advances makes it difficult to re-enter a scientific career once it is interrupted to raise a family or for other reasons;

- The difficulty of breaking into the formal and informal scientific networks that characterize the workings of the scientific community and which have been largely male dominated; and

- The reluctance of some employers to invest in training women due to the perceived likelihood of their leaving the organization to raise a family.

2. The gender-specific nature of technical change

Technical change aimed at benefiting people in rural areas in developing countries has, in fact, tended to benefit men more than women. This is because science and technology programs have not explicitly recognized the gender-specific nature of development. As a result, technical change offered to women has often been inappropriately formulated and designed. Also, although women in the rural areas of developing countries have the most significant difficulties in meeting their basic needs, in the urban areas, women are also poorer than men and are affected differentially by technical change.

The Rural Impact

The conclusion regarding the impact of technical change in rural areas has a number of components. Although some members of the Working Group considered them to be firm conclusions, others viewed them as hypotheses that require further testing.

- The potential of science and technology to effect changes in the lives of rural women and meet their basic needs has not been fully realized.

- Most science and technology programs oriented toward addressing basic needs in rural areas of developing countries have failed to recognize the gender-specific nature of development.

- Most technical change appears to have been oriented to the tasks that men perform and to men's interests and needs in the development process.

- Although some technical advances clearly benefit society as a whole, other scientific and technological activities may cause harm for some groups of people or some aspects of the natural environment. Individuals may lose income, jobs, or status. There may be unwanted environmental impact, such as the spread of pollution or toxic contamination. Women have been differentially and, in many cases, more adversely affected by negative consequences in the sectors investigated by the Working Group.

✦ A substantial amount of local traditional knowledge is held by women in the areas of agriculture, environmental resource management, and health. This knowledge is often different from that held by men in the same areas. There is a need to find more effective ways of recognizing the value of this gender-specific knowledge and to integrate it with modern science and technology for more sustainable development.

The Urban Impact

The only aspects of sustainable development that were examined in urban areas were income generation and employment. Within these areas, the main focus was on the employment impact of new technologies, especially information technology. The main conclusion derived from this study was the following:

✦ New information technologies have increased employment opportunities for women, especially in service-sector occupations such as banking and finance. But the new technologies have also made many existing jobs in manufacturing redundant or obsolete. These changes have affected men and women differently; but, overall, female labour has been displaced more than male labour. New jobs are more skill intensive than old ones, and women have been at a disadvantage because of limited training opportunities compared with men.

Most studies of women's needs and aspirations identify income generation as a basic need. This has led to increased interest in the role of women as entrepreneurs in small and medium-sized enterprises in the formal sector and in microenterprises in the informal sector. Many efforts are underway to encourage and facilitate women's participation in such enterprises. Most factors that facilitate this participation are not science or technology based. They have more to do with access to credit and other necessary resources. However, technical and managerial training and access to both local and new technologies — including information and technology management and marketing training — are important factors that influence the success of these enterprises.

The impact of technical change on the lives of men and women is different. Sometimes men benefit, other times women benefit. The implication is that a "gender impact analysis" — to identify the nature of the differential impact — should accompany the development of all new technologies. This would enable the introduction of supportive policies, which would lessen the negative impacts on disadvantaged parties.

If the objective of science and technology policy is to maximize the benefits from science and technology for all members of society, then ethical considerations must be part of the policy process. This is especially true for gender-related issues, which often cut across the rural–urban and the developing–developed divides. Specific examples in the health sector include the application of amniocentesis and ultrasound to determine fetal sex for the purpose of selective abortion of the girl child. Another example is the testing of drugs on Third World women without their informed consent. These examples underline the need for both the scientific community and governments to develop ethical guidelines for the conduct of research and the application of research results, with particular emphasis on the gender dimension.

Transformative Actions

Each contributor to this book was asked to identify recommendations for change within her sector of study. As a result, dozens of ideas and recommendations are presented in the following pages. From these recommendations, the Gender Working Group identified seven key issues that it considered to be particularly important and for which transformative actions were both necessary and feasible.

These issues are presented here. Each section states the issue and outlines policy and program options for the consideration of national governments and science and technology bodies and agencies. It has not been possible to estimate the costs of implementing these transformative actions. Some will be easy and cost little to implement; others will take a long time and be costly. It will be necessary for each country to determine its own priorities and implement what it can within its own financial situation.

Issue 1: Gender Equity in Science and Technology Education

Fewer girls than boys are given the opportunity to obtain formal education. Of the girls who do gain access to schools, a smaller proportion than boys obtain training in science and technology. This limits girls' and women's opportunities to meet their basic needs and improve the quality of their lives and those of their families; gain access to employment; create businesses; and acquire skills for citizenship. It also deprives nations of the contribution of many highly talented citizens. The extra barriers and obstacles confronting girls who seek training in science and technology subjects must be removed. *The following transformative actions are recommended:*

Equity in gaining access
+ Provide the same opportunities for access to formal education to girls and boys.

Equality of opportunity within schools
+ Ensure literacy and basic instruction in science and technology for all boys and girls.

+ Ensure that the infrastructure, laboratories, and equipment in schools are equally available for girls and boys.

+ Ensure that teaching materials in science and technology are sensitive to gender concerns in terms of language and illustrations. Where possible, these materials should also illustrate the link between the subject matter and everyday lives of girls and boys.

+ The teaching of science should be broadened to include elements addressing the economic, social, and ethical implications of science and technology.

+ Recognize the importance of mentors and role models by women science teachers and provide rewards to those who devote substantial time to this activity.

Opportunity for distance education and re-entry to schools
+ Provide multiple opportunities for re-entering school, especially for young mothers (in some cultures, early marriage and teenage pregnancy are major reasons for girls leaving school).

- ✦ Introduce education programs with flexible locations and times to enable more students, especially girls, to acquire scientific literacy.

- ✦ Introduce new approaches to science and technology education, such as distance learning, making optimal use of both old (radio) and new (multimedia) technologies.

Issue 2: Removing Obstacles to Women in Scientific and Technological Careers

In many countries, there are few women in scientific and technological careers. In addition to considerations of equity no country can afford to lose up to one half of its pool of creative and innovative human resources. The obstacles to greater participation of women in scientific and technical careers need to be addressed and overcome. *The following transformative actions are recommended:*

Specific measures for all employers

Recent national government task forces and reports have explored options for removing barriers to women in science and technology careers (for example, Ellis 1990; APPROTECH Asia 1992; AAAS 1993; Logue and Talapessy 1993; NABST 1993; Baringa 1994; Office of Science and Technology 1994). These include general policies and policies to support the professional, personal and family needs of all employees and ensure that the employees are able to balance family responsibilities with professional ones and career development. For example:

- ✦ Alternative work arrangements such as flexible hours, flexible locations, and job-sharing opportunities, and commitment to on-site child-care facilities;

- ✦ Maternity and paternity leave policies, and hiring and promotion criteria and processes to allow for family responsibilities so that maternity, paternity, and parental leaves do not jeopardize career progression;

- ✦ Commitment to the hiring, promotion, and career development of women in science and technology, while adhering to the merit principle; and

- ✦ Policies against discrimination and harassment in the workplace.

Policy tools for governments

Tax relief for payment of "child-minders"; pay equity legislation; legislation against discrimination; directives for collection of gender-disaggregated statistics; establishment of focal points for advice on gender in science and technology; and an increase in the number of women appointed to policy-advisory and decision-making bodies.

Initiatives in academia and the school system

Establish networks of female professionals in science and engineering; enhance mentoring, role-model, and career advisory programs; provide flexible tenure criteria to accommodate family roles and responsibilities; and provide refresher courses and re-entry scholarships for women returning to careers in science.

Issue 3: Making Science Responsive to the Needs of Society

Most professionals working in science and technology are insufficiently aware of the needs of their society and the impact of their work on these needs. Equally, citizens are insufficiently aware of the positive potential of science and technology to meet these needs. In particular, the gender-specific nature of the needs and the differential impact of science and technology on the lives of men and women are inadequately recognized by either science and technology professionals or citizens. *The following transformative actions are recommended:*

✦ Improve the decision-making mechanisms within the science system to ensure clear articulation of the gender-specific needs and goals of society by incorporating end-user opinions, both those of women and men. Use decision-making techniques, such as technology assessment and decision framework analysis, that make the gender implications of the decisions explicit.

✦ Encourage political parties and governments to be more explicit in their policy platforms about how they intend to use "science and technology" to meet the basic needs of both men and women equitably in society.

✦ Encourage public media to sponsor popular science programming, including reports on the potential of science to serve the goals of society and the basic needs of people; promote reporting on the impact of science on people's lives and, in particular, the differential impact of science and technology on men and women.

✦ Support nongovernmental organizations (NGOs) working at the interface of gender in science and technology for development.

Issue 4: Making the Science and Technology Decision-Making Process More "Gender Aware"

Current structures and processes for decision-making in science and technology for development do not systematically take into account the needs and aspirations of both women and men in a gender-disaggregated manner. Women's needs and interests have been relatively neglected. *The following transformative actions are recommended:*

✦ Increase the number of women on science and technology decision-making and policy-advisory bodies. Set targets for representation on these bodies with schedules and strategies to ensure adherence.

✦ Establish databases of professional women to provide institutions with a pool of names of qualified women to be considered for appointment to policy and advisory bodies.

✦ Increase the understanding of all decision-makers about the gender implications of their decisions through explicit training programs.

✦ Involve end users, men and women equally, in the determination of research priorities and in the design and implementation of technology and development programs. This will require explicit attention to the participation of women.

✦ Subject all development programs with a high science and technology component to "gender impact analysis" before initiation. Gender analysis should be included in the design and the subsequent monitoring and evaluation. Technology-assessment techniques and decision framework should incorporate a gender dimension.

✦ Governments should establish a focal point of expertise in gender, science, and technology to be available to advise government departments, facilitate training sessions, and monitor and report on the implementation of government strategies in gender, science, and technology.

Issue 5: Relating Better with Local Knowledge Systems

Modern science and technology has inadequately addressed the potential of local knowledge systems, especially women's knowledge, in the design and implementation of development programs. There is a need to develop new methods of interaction between the two systems for their mutual benefit. Local knowledge is frequently not recorded and is in danger of being lost. *The following transformative actions are recommended:*

✦ Ensure the preservation of local knowledge systems with specific attention to its gendered nature.

✦ Development agencies should give full consideration to the contributions of local knowledge systems, giving specific recognition to the gendered nature of these systems.

✦ Make greater efforts to find creative ways to promote mutually beneficial exchanges between modern and traditional knowledge systems and technologies for the benefit of both women and men in rural areas.

✦ Bodies engaged in the study and promotion of intellectual property rights should address the capability of the current system to protect local knowledge owned by communities, paying special attention to its gendered nature. When external agencies exploit this knowledge for commercial gain, mechanisms should be found for compensating the men and women in the communities where the knowledge originated.

Issue 6: Addressing Ethical Issues in Science and Technology

Ethical issues associated with both the conduct of scientific research and the application of the results of research frequently have a gender dimension that has not been sufficiently recognized or addressed. *The following transformative actions are recommended:*

✦ National and international scientific organizations, both governmental and nongovernmental, should develop international conventions, declarations, or ethical codes of conduct to provide clear boundaries of acceptable practice both in research and in application pertaining to their fields of responsibility. These should be widely promulgated.

✦ National governments should consider whether legislation is needed to enforce adherence to these codes of conduct. The use of technical procedures to identify fetal sex when the purpose is to abort the girl child is a case where some national governments have taken action to legislate the boundaries of unacceptable practice. Other examples include testing of drugs on underprivileged groups, particularly women, and the exploitation of local knowledge for commercial gain by outside organizations without appropriate acknowledgment or compensation.

✦ In determining the ethical issues on which guidelines and codes of conduct are to be developed, there should be wide consultation and involvement of stakeholders and end users.

Issue 7: Improving the Collection of Gender-Disaggregated Data for Policymakers

There is a paucity of data available at the national and international levels on the participation rates of men and women in scientific and technological education and careers. There still is no systematic approach or coordinated method for ensuring the systematic collection of gender-disaggregated data on science and technology. Of equal importance for policymakers is the unavailability of data on the differential impact of technical change on men's and women's lives. *The following transformative actions are recommended:*

✦ An international meeting of statisticians, and science, technology, and gender specialists from national and international bodies should be convened by the UN — possibly by Unesco (the United Nations Educational, Scientific and Cultural Organisation) — to identify the critical statistics necessary for policy purposes, to designate responsibility centres, and to establish mechanisms for coordination and collaboration. Methods and common approaches should be decided on to permit cross-culture comparisons over time and to ensure the best use of resources.

✦ National governments and the United Nations system should revise statistics data-collection methods to ensure gender-disaggregated statistics are systematically and regularly collected both on participation rates and on differential impact. These bodies should coordinate efforts to ensure the collection of complementary sets of data using common methods.

✦ Data collected by national governments should be made available to both local and international bodies to ensure their maximum use in policy and program formulation and to ensure their aggregation at the regional and international levels.

✦ Scientific bodies, universities, and academies should also collect relevant gender-disaggregated data.

Performance of the UN System

The Gender Working Group was asked to review the performance of UN agencies in the domain of gender, science, and technology. This task was to include an assessment of interagency coordination.

At the request of the Working Group, UNIFEM (the United Nations Development Fund for Women) undertook a review of 24 multilateral organizations in Bangkok, Geneva, New York, Paris, Rome, Vienna, and Washington in early 1994.[3] The result was detailed information relating to the policies, structure, staffing, programming, and evaluation activities of the agencies concerned, as well as information on interagency coordination and relations with NGOs. A written and oral report summarizing the UNIFEM exercise was presented to the Gender Working Group in April 1994.

Based on this report and subsequent discussion, the Working Group drew the following conclusions:

✦ Most agencies have a commitment to gender equity that is often enshrined in policy resolutions and have created gender departments, programs, or focal points; many also have a strong commitment to science and technology. However, only four agencies had clearly identifiable gender, science, and technology focal points and, in all cases (except UNIFEM and INSTRAW), corporate-level recognition and promotion of gender, science, and technology issues did not exist.

---

[3] The 24 agencies were UNDP, Unesco, UNIFEM, the Consultative Group on International Agricultural Research (CGIAR), the Economic and Social Commission for Asian and the Pacific (ESCAP), the Food and Agriculture Organization of the United Nations (FAO), the Inter-American Development Bank (IDB), the International Atomic Energy Agency (IAEA), the International Labour Office (ILO), the International Research and Training Institute for the Advancement of Women (INSTRAW), the International Trade Centre (ITC), the UN Children's Fund (UNICEF), the UN Conference on Trade and Development (UNCTAD), the UN Environment Programme (UNEP, Europe Office, Geneva), the United Nations Fund for Population Activities (UNFPA), the UN High Commissioner for Refugees (UNHCR), the UN Industrial Development Organization (UNIDO), the UN Research Institute for Social Development (UNRISD), the UN Secretariat, UN Volunteer (UNV), the World Bank, the World Food Program (WFP), the World Health Organization (WHO), and the World Intellectual Property Organization (WIPO).

✦ In most agency program and project work, the concern is to help women gain equal access to improved technologies. There is less emphasis on involving women in the process of technology development and little attention to promoting the increased involvement of women in science and technology decision-making or the systematic incorporation of women's perspectives into the formal science and technology system.

✦ Intra-agency mechanisms for appraising, monitoring and evaluating gender, science, and technology projects and programs is very weak for a variety of structural, staffing, and financial reasons. The result of this is that gender perspectives have not been integrated effectively into science and technology activities within the UN system.

✦ Although there is some evidence of interagency collaboration on these issues, it takes place on an ad hoc rather than in a coordinated, strategic way. Although there is increased recognition of the importance of learning from NGOs, few agencies have developed mechanisms for supporting NGOs and working effectively with them.

The Working Group also requested a follow-up review by an independent consultant. Accordingly, and within budgetary limitations, selected agencies[4] were visited in May 1994 and a draft report was presented to the Working Group in July. A matrix was prepared comparing policies across agencies.

Based on this report, the Gender Working Group drew the following conclusions:

✦ Most UN agencies perceive the theme of gender, science, and technology as marginal to the main mandate of their individual organizations. Promoting an awareness of the relations between gender, science, and technology should include the provision of practical examples of how current programs can contain a gender bias and how "gender analysis" can help to overcome obstacles by incorporating gender analysis in the design of science and technology policies and programs. Governing councils, which represent the member states of the UN agencies, should recognize the importance of gender issues and require monitoring and regular reporting of agency actions addressing the incorporation of gender

---

[4] IAEA, ILO, UNCTAD, Unesco, UNHCR, UNIDO, UNIFEM, UNRISD, and WHO.

analysis and assessment into science and technology policies, programs, and projects.

✦ Although there is some evidence to suggest that the positioning of high-level women professionals in key technical posts can assist in "engendering" science and technology policies and programming, and there is evidence of improvements in some agencies (such as UNHCR and WHO) in recent years, there are still very few women in senior management or technical advisory positions. Although the gender balance should continue to improve in response to resolutions by governing councils, agencies should be required to report regularly on progress in the recruitment and promotion of women professionals.

✦ There is little collaboration between gender focal points and science and technology focal points within agencies with respect to the design, monitoring, and evaluation of policies, programs, and projects. There is a lack of specific guidelines to assist scientific and technical staff to undertake this task. Recent attempts by agencies such as UNIDO and the Women, Science and Technology program of Unesco to introduce agency-wide programs aimed at integration among units should help promote awareness.

✦ Although there are a few examples of studies on the "impact of technology projects" on women, there is a general lack of gender-disaggregated "impact assessment" data available to improve programming. The problem of undertaking impact assessments is a generic one, but there are no guidelines on how to build specific gender, science, and technology questions into routine monitoring and evaluation.

✦ UN agencies tend to work in isolation; in part, this is due to their perceived separate mandates and to difficulties in communication (lack of travel budgets, e-mail networking, etc.). Although instituting formal mechanisms for coordination would not necessarily promote better exchange of information, methods should be supported to promote and sustain exchange between gender focal points and science and technology focal points on an agency-wide basis.

✦ Although there is a general trend among UN agencies to work with NGOs, only some organizations (such as ILO, UNHCR, UNICEF, UNIFEM, and WHO) have established formal relations with NGOs at both the policy and field (project) level. This trend reflects the heightened awareness in recent years of the capabilities of NGOs to contribute to development policy, including their ability to deliver cost-effective programs and their detailed knowledge of local communities. The experiences of IFAD (the International Fund for Agricultural Development), ILO, UNIDO, UNIFEM, and others testify to the effectiveness of UN–NGO collaboration. Agencies that have not yet fully supported NGOs in their activities should be required to build these partnerships. A 1994 survey of UNIFEM identified some 650 NGOs active in the field of gender, science, and technology. A consortium of these NGOs — the Once in Future Action Network — is actively planning input into the UN's 4th World Conference on Women in Development (Beijing, 1995) to ensure a high profile for issues of gender in science and technology in Beijing and beyond.

In light of these many conclusions, the Gender Working Group makes the following recommendations to the United Nations.

Recommendation I

The United Nations should be required to review its current corporate policy to ensure that gender, science, and technology is formally incorporated. As a means to successful implementation of such policy, gender, science, and technology specialists within each agency should be required to prepare case studies and training materials. Monitoring and evaluation and statistical divisions within each agency should establish a process for the systematic collection of gender-disaggregated data. Agencies should collaborate to ensure common methods, progress should be assessed on an on-going basis, and a relevant specialized agency should be requested to assist UN agencies in this task, with the UNCSTD Secretariat responsible for overseeing initiation and monitoring progress.

Time frame: Policies to be reviewed and action taken on implementation by September 1996.

Recommendation 2

United Nations agencies should actively respond to policies calling for recruitment of professional women by establishing clear targets and timelines for recruitment of women into high-level professional posts with strategic importance for science and technology. There should be explicit proactive recruitment, retention, and re-entry programs with supporting policies for high-level professional women in science and technology. Agencies should be required to report regularly to their governing bodies on the progress achieved and specific constraints encountered. Agencies should review some early successful experiences, such as that of CGIAR and WHO, in this regard.

Time frame: Progress to be reported through the UNCSTD Secretariat by September 1996.

Recommendation 3

United Nations agencies should use accessible and practical guidelines for incorporating gender analysis and assessment into the design of science and technology policies, programs, and projects. Although each agency has a distinct mandate and programming approach and guidelines will have to be specific to individual agencies, a set of general guidelines that could be adapted to specific circumstances could be useful. The guidelines developed by UNIFEM could be built upon for this purpose.

Time frame: Specific guidelines in place by September 1996 with briefing to relevant staff on implementation of policies. Progress to be reported annually through the UNCSTD Secretariat.

Recommendation 4

The United Nations should establish procedures to research, document, monitor, and evaluate the gender impact of their science and technology programs, including regular reporting of results and lessons learned to its various governing councils. Experience of such agencies as ILO, UNIDO, and UNIFEM, could be built upon to develop general guidelines for adaptation by other agencies. Gender, science, and technology specialists in each agency should work together with monitoring and evaluation units to implement this process.

Time frame: Specific guidelines in place by September 1996 with evidence of incorporation in at least one project document. Progress to be reported regularly through the UNCSTD Secretariat.

Recommendation 5

The United Nations should give its full support to strengthening and sustaining informal methods of interagency networking on gender, science, and technology issues. The UNCSTD should interact with this network in an on-going way to ensure gender perspective and mutual support in achieving goals. The United Nations should investigate alternative methods of increasing intra- and interagency communication in this area by, for example, establishing an electronic network link on gender, science and technology. This could be linked to existing NGO networks. The process could be facilitated by UNIFEM and UNIDO in conjunction with the UNCSTD Secretariat.

Time frame: Progress on the role of the UNCSTD in this collaboration and cooperation to be reported at its third session (May 1997).

Recommendation 6

UN agencies, particularly those reviewed by the UNCSTD Gender Working Group as having functions at the interface of science and technology, should incorporate "gender and science and technology" analysis into all regular programs and, through redistribution of agency funding priorities, provide increased regular budgetary allocations to gender units. Technically based agencies should support adequate staffing of gender experts and require training of all staff in gender analysis to ensure full incorporation of gender into their regular work programs.

Time frame: Progress to be reported through the UNCSTD Secretariat by September 1996.

Recommendation 7

The United Nations should recognize the value of collaboration with NGOs and expand its formal partnership with, and support for, these organizations both at the level of implementing field projects and also obtaining policy advice and assistance with the design, implementation, and evaluation of gender-sensitive technical cooperation programs. Partnership with the over 650 NGOs active in gender, science, and technology should be forged. Models such as those being developed by UNHCR could be explored and approaches suitable for each agency identified.

Ongoing UN support for the NGO science and technology consortium — the Once and Future Action Network — would assist in this process. Relevant UN staff focal points for gender, science, and technology should be supported to participate in the on-going activities of this NGO consortium.

Time frame: Agencies to explore options and begin to implement plans to enhance cooperation and support to NGOs by September 1996. Progress to be reported through UNCSTD Secretariat. Up to

10 of the most relevant agencies should be active participants in the NGO consortium by September 1996.

Recommendation 8

The Gender Working Group recommends the establishment of an Advisory Board on Gender to the UNCSTD for 4 years to ensure that gender issues are adequately addressed in all future deliberations of the UNCSTD. The Advisory Board should consist of seven international gender experts, appointed by the Secretary General. Among its initial responsibilities will be the task of monitoring implementation of the above recommendations. The UNCSTD Secretariat would support the Advisory Board in its activities.

Time frame: Advisory Board to be set up at the second session of UNCSTD (May 1995).

Conclusion: A Declaration of Intent

The recommendations and conclusions presented here could be the basis for reform of both the current science and technology system and the ways in which the output of that system is used to contribute to sustainable human development for the benefit of both men and women. The specific measures adopted by each government will necessarily depend on the national context. The transformative actions, therefore, are provided as a list of possible actions that each country may adopt according to its own local situation.

Two recommendations, however, apply to all countries and a third is directed at donor governments. The **first recommendation** is that all governments agree to adopt a Declaration of Intent on Gender, Science, and Technology for Sustainable Human Development. This Declaration consists of important goals toward which each country should move.

It is not the job of the Gender Working Group to suggest specific ways in which each country should implement this Declaration of Intent. The **second recommendation**, therefore, is that each country establish an ad hoc committee to make recommendations to its own government on how the goals in the Declaration might be implemented under the specific conditions of that country. The Working Group recognizes that, to implement the recommendations of its own ad hoc committee, each government will need to pass appropriate legislation and establish regulatory policy frameworks.

Declaration of Intent on Gender, Science, and Technology for Sustainable Human Development

All governments agree to work actively toward the following goals:

1. To ensure basic education for all, with particular emphasis on scientific and technological literacy, so that all women and men can effectively use science and technology to meet basic needs.

2. To ensure that men and women have equal opportunity to acquire advanced training in science and technology and to pursue careers as technologists, scientists, and engineers.

3. To achieve gender equity within science and technology institutions, including policy- and decision-making bodies.

4. To ensure that the needs and aspirations of women and men are equally taken into account in the setting of research priorities and in the design, transfer, and application of new technologies.

5. To ensure all men and women have equal access to the information and knowledge, particularly scientific and technological knowledge, that they need to improve their standard of living and quality of life.

6. To recognize local knowledge systems, where they exist, and their gendered nature as a source of knowledge complementary to modern science and technology and valuable for sustainable human development.

The **third recommendation** is directed to donor countries and agencies. Donor agencies may help each "National Ad Hoc Committee on Gender and Science and Technology" to obtain access to relevant information and should target financial support to projects that enable recipient countries to implement the recommendations of their own ad hoc committee.

The manner in which governments adopt strategies to achieve these goals will depend on the national context. It is, therefore, recommended that:

+ Each country establish an ad hoc committee to review the national situation regarding gender, science, and technology and to devise action plans and timelines to achieve the goals stated in the Declaration of Intent;

+ These ad hoc committees be constituted with equitable participation of women and men and with involvement of end users and stakeholders; and

+ Country reports on progress in achieving the goals of the Declaration of Intent be published.

Finally, for donor agencies, it is recommended that:

+ Financial support be targeted at projects that enable recipient countries to implement the recommendations of their own ad hoc committee on gender, science, and technology.

Chapter 2

Key paths for science and technology

On the road to environmentally sustainable and equitable development

Bonnie Kettel

In many communities in developing countries — rural and urban — women and men continue to have different needs and interests in the natural environment (Dankelman and Davidson 1988). They arise out of particular cultural traditions, various experiences of colonial rule, specific impacts of the global economy, and other locally relevant factors, such as climatic patterns (Stamp 1989). They are reflected in the prevailing gender-based division of labour; in the various responsibilities and rights that women and men have in the use and ownership of land, trees, animals, plants, and water; and in the different knowledge that women and men may have about the sustainable management of particular natural resources and ecological zones. As a result of all of these factors, women's and men's environmental perceptions, their interests and rights in the natural environment, and their environmental awareness and knowledge may differ significantly from one another, and from one cultural or ecological context to another, even in the same country.

"Gender and environments analysis" is an emerging area that is reshaping research and policy formulation on "women, environment, and development" (Kettel 1995; see also Braidotti et al. 1994; Harcourt 1994). This new conceptual framework emphasizes the gendered nature of women's and men's environmental perceptions, their knowledge of environmental management and conservation, and, therefore, the potentially negative effect on women, their families, and the natural environment of science and technology (S&T) interventions that address men's environmental needs and interests in an exclusive or superior manner.

In general, gender and environments analysis addresses the promotion of sustainable livelihoods, the protection of the natural environment, and women's equitable participation and "conceptual authority," in environmental decision-making (Kettel 1995). The intention is not to exclude men, but to understand how the gender-based rights and responsibilities of women and men in relation to the natural world shape their varying goals and interests with regard to the natural environment and, therefore, their goals and interests with regard to the use of S&T for development. In this paper, a gender and environments approach is used to highlight the significant overlap of issues of gender equity, environmental sustainability, and S&T for development, and to outline the possibilities for a renewed, gender-sensitive approach to the use of S&T in development policy and action in developing countries.

The focus on the participation and conceptual authority of women in developing countries in environmental decision-making is not a plea for a romantic reliance on existing methods of natural resource management or for preservation of the inequities that deny such women access to the many S&T benefits available to those of us who live in developed countries. It is a plea for recognition of the fundamental importance of informed choice — on the part of women and men at the local community level — based on their own individual and community-based awareness of the potential environmental benefits, costs, and risks of all S&T interventions in the development process.

Understanding of the terms "science" and "technology" is deliberately broad, including both the Western ideal of systematized and exact knowledge and technological application, and the culturally derived, non-Western systems of knowledge and know-how that are held by women — often predominately by women — in local communities of developing countries. No claim is made about the intrinsic superiority of either of these very different sources of knowledge. Instead, my initial purpose is to assess how the use and imposition of these knowledge frameworks have affected women's lives, their families, and the natural environment and to establish a sound basis for a new, gender-sensitive approach to the use of S&T for sustainable development. Five key areas are outlined, in which gender-sensitive research and policy formulation can begin to establish significant paths for S&T interventions that will lead to sustainable development. They are environmental health, poverty alleviation, employment and entrepreneurship, environmental literacy, and women's participation in environmental policy formulation and decision-making at the national level.

The invisibility of women in the development process

The process of "modern technological development" described in the UN's Vienna platform of action (UN 1979b), which has centred on the introduction of Western S&T knowledge into developing countries, has also been premised largely on the cultural aspirations and gender ideologies of the developed world, especially the ideal of the male "breadwinner" and the home-based "housewife." As a result, S&T interventions for local-level development have focused on meeting men's income needs as the presumed "breadwinners" for their families. Women's access to income, and their direct contributions to the sustenance of their households through food production and gathering water and fuelwood, have everywhere been treated as secondary and insignificant issues, if they have been recognized at all.

The prevalence of gender-discrimination in the use of S&T for development is well documented (Mies 1986; Sen and Grown 1987; Moser 1993). As Jacobson (1992, p. 12) suggests:

> Development programs have been built on the premise that what is good for men is good for the family. But in many areas, this is patently not the case, because women effectively provide the largest share of the family's basic needs.

Despite cultural, regional, and local differences, there are clear commonalities in women's needs and interests in the natural environment that provide an important baseline for gender-sensitive and culturally appropriate S&T development. Two decades of "women in development" research have demonstrated that women are central in the production of food and the provision of energy, water, health-care, and income in the developing world (Dankelman and Davidson 1988). They produce at least 80% of all food crops in sub-Saharan Africa, 70–80% in south Asia, and 50% in Latin America and the Caribbean (Jacobson 1992). They also provide at least 50% of the labour necessary for cash-crop production and contribute substantially to animal husbandry. Women are usually the major providers of water for people and livestock, and biomass fuels and fodder for domestic use (Muntemba 1989b). They are also heavily involved in gathering and processing medicinal plants, oils, and resins (Jacobson 1992). Furthermore, access to the natural environment is often crucial for women's income generation, especially in the informal economy.

As producers of food, energy, fodder, water, medicines, and income, women rely heavily on cropland, animals, trees, and common property resources in forests, rangelands, rivers, and lakes. Even urban women may continue to rely on natural resources in the city (especially in the form of urban agriculture) and from the countryside (fuelwood and charcoal) to meet their basic household needs (Lee-Smith and Trujillo 1992). In their involvement with the natural environment, women act as local environmental managers and decision-makers, and they have a keen interest in, and often substantial knowledge of, strategies for environmental conservation and protection (Kettel 1995). However, until 1987, with the publication of *Our Common Future* (WCED 1987), women's needs and interests in the use and management of the natural environment were largely invisible as an issue for scholarly research, or for development policy and planning.[1]

This invisibility is not surprising, given that the importance of women's work is often unrecognized in their own households. Jacobson cites a study by Joke Schrijvers of the Mahaweli River Development Scheme in Sri Lanka. Although women had as many agricultural responsibilities as men, far more domestic duties, and worked longer hours, men's beliefs that "women work less hard ... [were] so dominant that they seem[ed] to blur observed reality" (Jacobson 1992, p. 17). This misperception of the scale and importance of women's work, including their use of natural resources, has been broadly shared by development planners and policy analysts.

Women's access to the natural environment, especially the resources that they use to provide food, shelter, health maintenance, and income, has been jeopardized by many S&T interventions, and the well-being of their husbands and children, who typically benefit from the use and cash value of women's environmental activities, has also been undermined. In addition, women's lack of access to development planning and policy formulation has also had a negative effect on the effective, long-term management and protection of the natural environment and the promotion of sustainable development (Dankelman and Davidson 1988).

Following *Our Common Future* (WCED 1987), some important community-based strategies for environmental management and decision-making, such as "participatory rural appraisal," were introduced (Kenya 1990; Kabutha et al. 1991). However, women are still

---

[1] The only significant exception to this lack of attention has been the path-setting work on women's use of fuelwood and other forest resources (Fortmann and Rocheleau 1985; see also Ubochi 1988).

seldom identified as legitimate and necessary participants in such community-based activities (Ford and Lelo 1991).

In the early 1980s, an integrated rural development project, the Plan Sierra, was implemented in the Dominican Republic (Fortmann and Rocheleau 1985). The project, which was intended to remedy the extensive deforestation and soil degradation in the region, introduced several S&T interventions focused on agroforestry and reforestation. Although the agroforestry component emphasized coffee production, in which both men and women were involved, the design of the reforestation program did not consider whether women's forest needs were different from men's. Tree planting emphasized indigenous and exotic pines for watershed management and timber production. Hundreds of men were hired to construct tree nurseries and participate in soil conservation and forestry training, extension, and construction. Women were hired initially as home-economists, secretaries, cooks, and cleaners. However, eventually some women were also hired as "budders and grafters" for plant propagation, because they were considered to be more patient and efficient.

Although women were also actively sought out as volunteer labourers, "it was the project not the women themselves who benefited." Women were not consulted about the agroforestry and reforestation aspects of the plan until a mid-project evaluation took place. At that time, they requested help in developing fuelwood supplies, patio gardens, and cottage industries, all of which would involve agroforestry. The scarcity of fuelwood was having a significant impact, especially on poor families, and was forcing some women to close down their cassava-bread processing operations. Because fuelwood was not recognized as a priority in the design of the project, when the issue did arise, the technical staff did not have the expertise to address the problem. As a result, "a major opportunity to involve and serve local women in agroforestry and reforestation was lost" (Fortmann and Rocheleau 1985, pp. 259–260).

As this example illustrates, any failure to recognize women's environmental needs and interests in S&T interventions for sustainable development is likely to have a negative impact on their ability to provide food, household needs, and income for themselves and their families, on their ability to use and manage the natural environment in a sustainable manner, and on their equitable participation as environmental decision-makers in their own communities. Unfortunately, the gender insensitivity of the Plan Sierra is not unique. Examples still abound in every region of the developing world (Dankelman and Davidson 1988).

Discovering women and the environment

With the publication of *Our Common Future* (WCED 1987), women, environment, and development suddenly became a key topic for scholarly research and development policy analysis. In response, the UN Environment Programme (UNEP) set up a Senior Women's Advisory Group on Sustainable Development (SWAG). SWAG organized four regional "women and environment" assemblies in Harare, Tunis, Bangkok, and Quito, culminating in the Global Assembly of Women and Environment in 1991 (UNEP and WorldWIDE 1991).

During the same period, donor institutions such as the World Bank (Stone and Molnar 1986), the Food and Agriculture Organization of the United Nations (FAO 1987), and the Canadian International Development Agency (Thompson 1987) began to develop women-and-environment perspectives and programs. These early United Nations (UN) and donor policy initiatives demonstrate a prevalent tendency to merely "involve" (and even to "manage") women as a "human resource" for sustainable development rather than recognizing women as legitimate and necessary environmental decision-makers. They were also commonly based exclusively on prevailing Western perceptions of the appropriate role of S&T in environmental management, excluding the S&T knowledge and expertise of women as local environmental managers.

The policy dilemmas inherent in this "involvement" approach were apparent at the African Women's Assembly on Sustainable Development, held in Harare in 1989. The impetus and organization for the event stemmed ultimately from SWAG, with the assistance of an international women and environment organization called WorldWIDE, and personnel from the International Union for the Conservation of Nature (IUCN) and the Zimbabwe Ministry of Natural Resources. This top-down approach addressed the goal of "empowering" African women, especially rural women, in the quest for sustainable development.

Not surprisingly, given its institutional origins, the assembly's deliberations were organized around a Western "resource management" view of the sustainable development agenda and not from the perspective of women who actually use the natural environment for subsistence and income. Workshops were based entirely on resource zones or sectors: forests and woodlands, deserts and arid lands, rivers and lake basins, and seas (Loudiyi et al. 1989). As a result, issues arising from women's gender-based activities in the use and management of the natural environment, and their knowledge of environmental conservation and protection, were marginalized and distorted. The overall result was a notable element of confusion in the structure of the assembly, the discussions at the workshops, and the initial outcome of the deliberations.

Despite inadequacies in their organization, the four regional assemblies and the Global Assembly were crucial to the emergence and formulation of a new, gender-sensitive perspective on women's involvement in the quest for sustainable development (Ofusu-Amaah and Philleo 1993). The Global Assembly recommended, "The needs and views of women must be incorporated in the establishment of priorities in the management of human and natural resources" and "women should also be involved in setting priorities" (WorldWIDE 1991, pp. 5–6).

These events also helped make clear that the goals and priorities that women are likely to set for their own participation in sustainable development initiatives may be very different from those formulated by donor institutions and national governments. Indeed, policy frameworks that encourage the use of Western-derived S&T in the development process may be viewed, at least initially, by women in developing countries as part of the problem, not the solution to meeting their environmental needs and interests (Shiva 1988). At the African Women's Assembly, participants from rural Zimbabwe expressed their belief that the environmental problems that confront them are a direct result of the failure to consider their environmental interests and knowledge, and the imposition of inappropriate, Western technology and environmental management systems. According to the Zimbabwe national report (Zimbabwe 1989):

> One of the strange and frustrating paradoxes of rural life is that as western technology and management techniques have increased, food surpluses in the rural areas have decreased and a pattern of sustained starvation ... has been ushered in.... Unless the rural farmers (the women) are ... given their rightful recognition then what they are capable of will remain a mystery.

The price of complacency and gender bias[2]

Although Western ideas about S&T can be used for great good in the development process, they can also bring about profound human and environmental damage, especially when they are implemented in a gender-insensitive and culturally inappropriate manner. Unfortunately, it is often the populations that are most vulnerable and

---

[2] Material in this section is reprinted with permission from Apex Publishing Corporation.

impoverished, and least politically powerful, who are likely to experience these significantly negative outcomes.

In eastern Africa, indigenous herding systems were based largely on supplying milk, the primary element in the local diet. Responsibility for various aspects of the milk production process was allocated on the basis of gender: men managed the herd, while women focused on the milk supply (Dahl 1987). In the 1970s, commercial meat production, for urban markets and for export, was introduced to protect the rangelands from overgrazing and to increase the cash incomes of men in nomadic communities. The new approach, which was supported by considerable scientific knowledge, was based on the American "cattle-ranching" model.

This transformation, which took place over several years, quickly led nomadic populations to settle in rural villages, with livestock now kept in distant camps. From an ecological point of view, meat production has been a disaster. According to Timberlake (1985, p. 93), "Africa is littered with examples of arrogant and failed attempts 'to rationalise' pastoralism, which have often caused desertification and bloodshed." Nor have these initiatives led to a broad improvement in living standards. Instead, "the picture that emerges is one of almost unrelieved failure. Nothing seems to work ... there is no evidence of increased production of milk and meat, the land continues to deteriorate, and millions of dollars have been spent" (Goldschmidt 1981, p. 116).

Generally, environmental deterioration has been caused by the breakdown of community-based resource-management systems (in which women played a significant role), overstocking, and the clustering of animals around bore holes, which is a significant source of local desertification. The failure to involve herders in project design was a crucial factor behind this dismal outcome. Herder participation in the design, implementation, and assessment of livestock sector projects was marginal; the participation of women was nonexistent (Horowitz 1981). Women's interests and rights to milk production were almost totally ignored.

Today, little of the cash income that men acquire from the sale of animals reaches women in households. With the replacement of milk by grain in the daily diet, women's time and labour spent in collecting water and fuelwood and preparing food has been substantially increased. The change to a sedentary life-style along with the addition of maize to the daily diet increased women's efforts to collect fuelwood by 1 300% (Ensminger 1987). Because older men tend to protect their incomes, young men no longer have access to the cattle (or money) they need to establish a household. Many young men and women are leaving the rangelands, but urban opportunities are few for former nomads, and many young women have turned to "cash gathering of firewood ... small handicraft trades, employed housework or concubinage, prostitution or begging" (Dahl 1987, p. 272).

More recent research has shown that milk production in this setting is actually likely to be more sustainable than meat production. Worldwide, milk production systems can actually support about 2.5 times as many people per hectare as meat production. When they are not clustered around bore holes, a herd of milking stock can actually promote sustainable rangeland use by maintaining a useable plant cover (Bates and Conant 1981, pp. 90–92). Based on this assessment, Kerven (1987, p. 33) suggests that herders could obtain much-needed income through informal-sector sales of seasonally available milk. Such milk sales are the traditional income domain of women.

In this case, a well-intended S&T intervention went badly wrong for two primary reasons. First, the "science" was culturally biased and inadequate. Range-management systems that work in the environmental and social conditions of the American southwest simply cannot be transferred wholesale to another ecological and cultural zone. A thorough understanding of the nature and significance of community-based resource management systems is essential for the success of any S&T intervention. Second, the entire agenda was gender insensitive. The important roles that women played in milk production, which allowed them to meet the nutritional needs of their families and sell the surplus, were totally disregarded. Except for a few wealthy older men, everyone has paid dearly for this well-intended intervention.

Shaping a gender-sensitive agenda for sustainable and equitable development

The dismal outcomes of gender-biased and culturally inappropriate S&T interventions have not gone unnoticed by women in developing countries. The best known response at the community level is the "Chipko Movement." It began in 1972–73, when people in the Chamoli District of India protested the sale of trees to a sports manufacturer, after the local cooperative had been refused permission to cut a few trees to make agricultural implements for local use (Agarwal 1992a). Women have been involved in the Chipko Movement together with men to oppose exploitation of the forests by outside commercial interests and against local men, who were willing to cut trees for cash. A "holistic understanding" of the environment in general, and trees in particular, is implicit in women's participation in the Chipko Movement (Agarwal 1992a, p. 148).

In Africa, extensive research of the Women, Environment and Development Network (WEDNET) has also demonstrated that women's technical environmental knowledge is best understood as an aspect of broader indigenous knowledge systems. In addition to their cultural and religious elements, these indigenous knowledge systems contain a great deal of precise and useful S&T information, which for centuries has been the basis of successful environmental management (Kettel 1995). Indigenous knowledge systems are central to women's understanding of their social roles, their participation in the production of food, shelter, energy, medicines and income, and their interests in environmental care and protection.

Ironically, men's indigenous perceptions of the natural environment and their traditional roles in environmental protection in the developing countries are mainly ignored, except through the recent introduction of "participatory rural appraisal." Instead, cash has been used to entice men in developing countries into accepting Western S&T interventions. As the history of east African rangelands project illustrates, men in developing countries have also sometimes paid an unintended price for these interventions. Part of this price has been the eradication of the aspects of indigenous knowledge systems traditionally assigned to men. Although women's indigenous knowledge of environmental management has been marginalized by the Eurocentrism and gender-bias of S&T, men's traditional environmental knowledge has frequently been wiped out completely. In many communities of developing countries, women are the primary holders of indigenous knowledge and know-how about sustainable environmental use and management.

In the community of Kathama, Kenya, more than a third of the households are headed by women; another third are managed by women on behalf of husbands who have moved to cities (Rocheleau 1992). In 1981, the International Council for Research in Agroforestry (ICRAF) and Wageningen University initiated an agroforestry research project in the area. A rapid (nonparticipatory) rural appraisal identified two problems in local farming: a shortage of dry-season fodder and a low level of production.

Farm trials, focused on "alley cropping," were carried out on 10 farms: nine with male heads of households (despite the prevalence of female-headed households) and one managed jointly by a married couple. The trials were evaluated in 1983 by a team of social and ecological scientists, who discovered two problems. First, although some men wanted to expand the alley cropping, their attempts to grow their own seedlings were failing because of insufficient water.

Women, who were responsible for providing the water, had not been consulted in the initial decision to establish seedlings at the household level. Second, although the alley crops were intended to meet women's fuelwood needs, they were not producing enough biomass. Because men's need for timber and poles had not been addressed, they were using the fuelwood trees.

During the next planting season, the women asked the research team to help them establish group-run tree nurseries. These nurseries were a success from both the gender and the S&T point of view. During their creation, women participants developed alternatives to existing systems and to prepackaged agroforestry technologies by evaluating the "package" and altering specific elements according to their own needs and interests. They also introduced aspects of local practice and innovation that better suited the objective of improved soil fertility. Women demonstrated a clear tendency to experiment to find the best results and to involve themselves in activities that were traditionally "male domains," such as tree planting on local homesteads.

In 1984, Kathama was faced with drought, and residents began to experience serious shortages of food, water, and fodder. Entire extended families began to search the remaining woodlands, scrub, fence rows, and stream banks for useful wild species. Every available fragment of knowledge, from old people and young, women and men, had to be put to use to ensure the survival of people and livestock. Witnessing the considerable reliance of local residents on wild species, the research team suggested to local women's groups that these species should be deliberately protected, managed, and even domesticated through on-farm agroforestry. After displaying some shock at this proposed return to "primitive practices," the women responded with enthusiasm. They also insisted on the inclusion of medicinal plants commonly used by women herbal specialists.

Together, the women and men of Kathama identified 118 species that could be used for medicine and 45 species for food. Women and men tended to know and use different species, and prepare different products from the same species. Some men also knew a considerable amount about specialized uses of particular plants. However, both general and specific knowledge were dispersed and fragmented among the men in the community. Furthermore, young men knew very little. Among women, however, knowledge was widely shared, and the generation gap was less pronounced. As a result, the community's survival of the drought depended on the women. The famine also raised a healthy skepticism about the importance of cash income. In keeping with traditional custom, the women gave the famine a name: "I shall die with the money in my hand."

Key policy themes and suggestions for future research

In 1984, the Ad Hoc Panel of Experts on Science and Technology and Women (UN 1984, para. 6) stated that:

> There was remarkable consensus among the panelists concerning general principles.... In particular, they wanted men and women to work together to ensure that science and technology in development would ... heal rather than harm ... the panelists felt that ... issues of importance to women and their families had never been placed in a level of priority above those that were considered "broader" or at least "more quantifiable", a term which, however, did not translate into "more important."

Muntemba (1989a) offers a revealing comment about S&T for environmental management and development that would allow women and men to work together and that would "heal rather than harm."

> Central to the issue of management ... are questions of who conceptualizes and designs patterns of management.... As the major users and traditional resource managers, would more successes be recorded with longer-term implications if greater focus was turned on women? The answer is pointing to the loudest .YES

This does not imply that women are necessarily better at conserving the natural environment than men nor that women in developing countries should be denied access to the benefits of Western S&T approaches to environmental management. However, women have been denied the opportunity to participate in the conceptualization and design of patterns of environmental use and management that make sense to them. As a result, women's environmental needs and interests, and their indigenous S&T knowledge, have been undermined (Kettel 1995).

Although recognition of the importance of women's conceptual authority and their equitable participation in community-based decision-making with regard to S&T interventions in environmental management is an important base-line for future research and policy formulation, there are five key areas where S&T policy formulation, together with new research, can begin to create pathways for sustainable development that will "heal rather than harm." These five areas — The environment and women's health, Alleviating the poverty of women, Women, technology, and entrepreneurship, Environmental literacy and access to information, and National-level participation and decision-making — are outlined in greater detail below.

The environment and women's health[3]

Women's health and the health of the natural environment are intimately linked. The link arises from women's activities as users and managers of the natural environment, as well as from their role as health managers and caregivers. In both developing and developed countries, women protect their own health and that of their families by cleaning, sweeping, drawing water, washing clothes and children, and preparing food. In addition, women in developing countries provide a range of remedies for various illnesses — including tonics, extracts, ointments, and oils (MacCormack 1988). Many of the remedies are found in the natural environment, and women also have considerable knowledge about how to use their environments in a healthy manner. Therefore, as environmental managers, they are also important agents of disease control.

Until recently, the health risks arising from S&T interventions in the use and management of the natural environment have been almost totally neglected, both in medical research and in development policy formulation (Kettel 1993). Greater attention to environmental health, especially women's environmental health, in all S&T development interventions, is essential for sustainable development.

It is surprising how little is known generally about women's health compared with the health of men, even in developed countries (Payne 1991; Lewis and Kieffer 1994). One of the most surprising omissions is research and health-policy formulation in relation to women's menstrual health. Women's menstrual status affects issues as disparate as their recovery from breast cancer, cardiovascular health, and risk of osteoporosis. Yet, we simply do not know how diverse women's menstrual experiences are from one neighbourhood or region to another, or how variations in women's menstrual health

---

[3] Material cited in this section is reprinted with permission from the Commonwealth Secretariat.

affect their long-term risk of cancer, heart disease, or other illnesses (Koblinsky et al. 1993, pp. 50, 55).

Women's bodies, like those of all plant and animal species, are permeable. Pollutants and toxins flow from the air and water into women's bodies where they remain, sometimes for the entire life cycle. However, new research suggests that, due to the nature of women's hormonal production, such pollutants remain in women's bodies far longer than they do in men's, thereby increasing the potential effect of diseases such as cancer and heart disease on women's well-being (Koblinsky et al. 1993). For this reason, women's environmental health is a key diagnostic indicator of the health of local environments, and the appropriateness of S&T interventions that involve changes in the use and management of the natural environment.

Potential health risks arising from women's use of the natural environment include respiratory conditions such as bronchitis and pneumonia; diseases such as diarrhea, typhoid, malaria, and schistosomiasis; and possibly some life-threatening forms of cancer, such as breast and ovarian cancer (Clorfene-Casten 1993). Changes to women's local environments — resulting from the introduction of irrigation systems, hydroelectric dams, monocropping, pesticides and herbicides, and various kinds of cottage and factory production, for example — can transform their healthy balance and establish "disease environments" (Akhtar 1987) that sustain conditions directly hazardous to women's health. Such environmental diseases may be new, furthered, or reintroduced by the disruption of equilibrium in the environments that people occupy (Forget 1992).

Data on the gender-specific incidence of environmental diseases in developing countries are almost totally lacking (Raikes 1989). In developed countries, the absence of research on women's menstrual cycles and their possible susceptibility to environmental impact, also makes it difficult to identify the environmental factors that are damaging to women's well-being. There is also little information about women's occupational health and safety as home-based workers, as participants in microenterprises, or as factory workers (see Packard 1989). Thus, there is a critical need for new S&T research and policy formulation, regarding women's environmental health, at both the international and national levels.

This issue is crucial, especially as Western S&T has caused enormous environmental disruption and harm. Taking women's environmental health as a starting point for ensuring the appropriateness of all S&T interventions that involve the use of the natural environment is, therefore, the first step in assuring the use of S&T for sustainable and equitable development.

Alleviating the poverty of women

As the 20th century ends, it is increasingly clear that any effective framework for sustainable development will have to address the one fact that currently appears most insignificant at the level of international policy formulation: everywhere on this planet and in every social category, there are now more poor women than men. The feminization of poverty has not appeared as a global phenomenon by accident. Women's differential impoverishment is a direct result of the kinds of gender bias and cultural inappropriateness in research and policy for the use of S&T for development that has been discussed above.

Several factors are important in explaining the poverty of women, including position in the global and national economy, race and ethnicity, education and literacy, and age. Three-quarters of the world's women live in countries where the per-capita gross domestic product either declined or increased only marginally during the 1980s. Women in female-headed households, which now represent one-quarter to one-third of all households, are particularly vulnerable to differential impoverishment (Jacobson 1993, pp. 4, 7).

Five major international reports, including the *Human Development Report 1990* (UNDP 1990), demonstrate that everywhere "being a woman means being poorer than a man" (Ahooja-Patel 1992). "The interesting and significant point of these reports produced at the highest level of expertise is that despite significant differences in approaches, methodologies and ideologies, the conclusions point in the same direction" (Ahooja-Patel 1992, p. 32). However, although there is growing awareness of the worldwide feminization of poverty at the international level, women's disproportionate impoverishment has so far received no significant policy attention.

Not only are women, especially in developing countries, disproportionately poor, they are also more likely than men to experience the daily demands and personal consequences of local environmental degradation. One reason for this differential exposure is that, although they play a central role in the use of the natural environment to provide for themselves and their families, women rarely have the same level of ownership of the natural environment as men. Women have been particularly discriminated against in the widespread privatization of land and other common-property resources that has taken place in the last three decades, often as the basis for S&T interventions in environmental management supported by bilateral donor institutions and multilateral organizations such as the World Bank. Today, "discrimination against female farmers in access to land is virtually universal"; in many developing countries, women can acquire access to land only through their male relatives (Jacobson 1992, p. 27). Women's ability to contribute to the sustainable environmental management of privately owned land and the remaining common lands has been seriously undermined by these transformations in resource ownership.

As a result of spreading environmental degradation, women in developing countries also experience extreme demands in terms of labour and time. The local environmental destruction that results from deforestation and desertification often forces women to walk long distances, taking up to 17 hours a week, for water and fuelwood. As obtaining food, water, and energy becomes more time-consuming, women commonly reduce the amount of clean water and cooked food that they serve their families. Recent WEDNET research in Africa shows that women faced with environmental destruction may also use the natural environment in an increasingly unsustainable manner, violating their own environmental knowledge and interests, merely to maintain themselves and their households on a day-to-day basis (Kettel 1995).

Despite these difficulties, indeed because of them, there is considerable opportunity for S&T to contribute to the alleviation of women's poverty and experience of environmental degradation, and the enhancement of their potential contributions to sustainable development. At the international level, policy formulation, rather than research, is needed as the overall parameters of women's differential poverty and exposure to environmental degradation are now clear. However, there is considerable need for participatory research at the national and local community levels to allow women to identify their particular environmental perceptions, needs, and interests, and the way in which these needs, as well as their income needs, might be met through appropriate, gender-sensitive S&T. There is also a related need for national governments to protect women's access to natural resources, including land, forests, water sources, domestic and wild animals, and medicinal plants through appropriate legislation and the establishment of gender-sensitive mechanisms for planning and intervention.

In the area of wasteland reclamation, for example, several projects in India were funded by the International Labour Organisation (ILO). In Rajasthan, people were experiencing drought and a shortage of fuelwood (ILO 1991a, pp. 5–6, 41–42). In 1987, over 3 000 women attended a meeting specifically to discuss women's social and environmental problems. Women from three villages requested assistance in reforesting the remaining local common lands, which were largely wasteland. At first, the reclamation proposal met considerable male hostility, not only from men in the region, but also from men in the People's Environment and Development Organization (PEDO), the nongovernmental organization (NGO) involved in the project. However, much of this hostility was defused during a workshop held by PEDO. At a national technical workshop organized by the ILO in 1991, representatives of the NGO identified two additional problems associated with wasteland reclamation initiatives that deserved closer scrutiny: the legal implications of the use of common land, particularly the need to protect women's access to such lands once they were restored; and the need for careful consideration of related technical problems.

This project illustrates the important role of NGOs as a liaison between women at the local level and the S&T community. PEDO had previously trained local women to build and repair stoves (ILO 1991a, pp. 41–42). In the wasteland reclamation initiative and the ILO workshop, the NGO introduced the desired S&T expertise and promoted the participation of women in environmental reclamation and, more generally, in environmental decision-making. At the ILO workshop, representatives from PEDO reported that where either the opportunities for exposure or input by the women staff of PEDO had been weak or limited, village women's participation in decision-making has also remained weak. It was not until women's self-confidence had been built up through a range of other activities that they really participated in the project. However, once women crossed a certain threshold in breaking with their traditional roles, their commitment and involvement proved far greater than that of men (ILO 1991a, p. 42).

Using S&T in a gender-sensitive manner to alleviate women's poverty through research and policy to meet their expressed environmental perceptions, needs, and interests is the second key path to sustainable and equitable development.

Women, technology, and entrepreneurship

The importance of women's access to "appropriate technology" is well-established (Carr 1985). In addition to their interests in environmental management, women have significant S&T interests that are centred in the household and in microenterprises in the informal economy. Although considerable attention has been devoted to improving cookstoves as a strategy for reducing household fuel consumption, little research or policy attention has been devoted to a range of microenterprise activities with environmental relevance, such as the sale of medicinal plants, fuelwood and charcoal, water harvesting, and recycling waste. Areas that deserve further research and policy analysis include: facilitating the use of renewable and recyclable materials; labour-saving strategies for the management of household and community waste; avenues for microenterprise production based on innovative technology; and avenues for larger-scale production and entrepreneurship especially by local women's groups.

The community of Jhilimili in the Bankura District of West Bengal offers an example of the potential benefits of a gender-sensitive approach to the creation of environmental microenterprises (ILO 1991b). Although the area was once heavily forested, much of the land had gradually been privatized. The poorer residents of the region gradually lost their access to the forests, which had been the major source of their livelihoods. As a result, they had become highly dependent on women's wage labour on private farms some distance away. In 1980, the minister for land reform met with a group of women agricultural labourers. Although government officials suggested that the women might earn income from bee-keeping or tailoring, the women made it clear that they wanted land and trees that would provide fodder, fruit, and fuelwood, rather than the "dead wood" of the new eucalyptus plantations.

With the support of a research centre in Delhi, women from Jhilimili and two other villages organized into local "samities" (advancement societies) and sold leaves and seeds to a local cooperative. About the same time, poor people in the three villages decided to donate their remaining small plots to the local samities to grow indigenous species that would allow them to raise silk worms. After their initial success, the samities looked for other income-generating opportunities. They began to make traditional tableware with a new polythene lining. Later, they also produced rope, traded in seeds, and on an individual basis purchased paddy for rice husking. As a result of these varied activities, the women considerably improved their financial situation, learned skills, and attained a sense of self-worth; they also reclaimed 100 ha of land.

Supporting women's income goals through appropriate S&T can produce impressive results, both for women, and for the environment. There is ample opportunity, particularly when it is supported by enlightened government, NGOs, and research contributions, to make important steps toward further alleviating women's differential poverty in developing countries. Supporting women's microenterprises through environmentally sound and relevant S&T innovations and interventions is, therefore, the third important path to sustainable development.

Environmental literacy and access to information

Full "environmental literacy," of women and men, is a precondition for sustainable development in all countries. Environmental literacy involves three necessary elements: a strong foundation in relevant local knowledge and experience, including indigenous environmental knowledge; access to appropriate and relevant S&T knowledge through informal and formal education; and open communication and access to information with regard to all potential environmental risks and benefits of particular S&T interventions. Women's central role in environmental use and management in developing countries, and their disproportionate lack of access to formal education and to Western S&T expertise, make improving their access to environmental knowledge and information especially important.

The relevance of women's indigenous environmental knowledge to the development process has been noted (Thomas-Slayter et al. 1991; Kettel 1995). An important new intervention, participatory rural appraisal (PRA), resulted from considerable soul-searching within the development community in response to the litany of project failures and ensuing environmental degradation that marked development experience, especially in Africa, over the previous three decades (Kabutha et al. 1991). "The PRA approach assumes that popular participation is a fundamental ingredient in project planning and that locally maintained institutions and technologies as well as sustainable economic, political and ecological inputs are fundamental to reverse Africa's decline" (Kabutha et al. 1991, p. 6).

A technical survey is an integral aspect of the PRA process. It is carried out by technically trained members of the research team, who determine various environmental and agricultural potentials in the area. In a case study in Mbusyani, Kenya, although residents knew a great deal about their local environment and, indeed, had an "intimate awareness" of several important environmental issues, there were also some gaps in their information (Kabutha et al. 1991). Generally, they were unaware of the kind of quantifiable data needed to document their concerns, such as the rate of soil loss on local farm plots. They were also not fully capable of assessing the likely economic and technical feasibility of some of the solutions they proposed (p. 24):

> After doing several PRAs, it has become clear that: (a) the technical data are among the most important to integrate into the villages' socio-economic and institutional capabilities; (b) villagers are the key agents, in cooperation with technical extension and NGO officers, to do the implementation; and (c) the technical

interventions that work best are those that community leaders can understand and manage with very little external help.

In its initial formulation, the PRA approach was not explicitly gender sensitive, and women were usually underrepresented (Kenya 1990). In Mbusanyi, the PRA team developed several "clearly focused strategies to draw out women's participation and to incorporate priorities of women's groups into the village actions plans" (Ford and Lelo 1991, p. 12). A follow-up study was carried out to discover whether any of the plans developed at the community level had been put into effect. Although several initiatives had been undertaken, local women's groups had been central to many of the most important ones. Women's groups rehabilitated a reservoir infested with bilharzia; brought a steep, severely eroded hillside under control and reclaimed the hilltops for production (with technical advice from the Ministry of Agriculture); and raised money for a maize-grinding mill. However, more work is needed to ensure the participation of "underrepresented elements of rural society," including women, generally in future PRA applications (Ford and Lelo 1991, p. 13).

Although gender-sensitive PRA is beginning to ensure women's participation, at least at a modest level, in the formulation of community-based environmental action plans, considerable gaps remain in local women's access to various national-level technical services and scientific information that would support their activities. These gaps are sustained by women's disproportionate illiteracy (Jacobson 1993), by the failure of extension agents and other technical experts to take women's environmental interests and needs seriously (Staudt 1978), and by the failure of national and international research centres to address adequately the S&T problems that are particularly relevant to women's environmental perceptions, needs, and interests at the local level (Feldstein and Poats 1990). Ensuring women's full environmental literacy by increasing their access to informal and formal environmental education, and to relevant S&T expertise and information, as a basis for their increased participation in community decision-making is the fourth key path to sustainable and equitable development.

National-level participation and decision-making

In most developing countries, key policies and plans for the use of S&T for development are formulated at the national level. Thus, increasing the participation of women at that level is also essential. In 1980, the IUCN, UNEP, and the World Wide Fund for Nature

(WWF) issued a joint report that offered a coherent new look at the *World Conservation Strategy* (IUCN et al. 1980). Since then, corresponding national and subnational conservation strategies have been established in over 50 countries.

The new report, *Caring for the Earth: A Strategy for Sustainable Living* (IUCN et al. 1991), sets out nine principles, each with relevant action objectives, several of which relate to the use of S&T for development and to gender equity, both as an aspect of sustainable living and as a basis for sustainable development. The strategy also identifies 12 key steps to "help women to improve their status" as a basis for greater self-fulfillment and contribution to the community. One step involves "instituting reforms to give women a full voice in political, bureaucratic, and economic decision-making at every level" (IUCN et al. 1991, p. 23).

The difficulty in implementing this worthy recommendation is illustrated by the experience of several countries. In 1991–93, an implementation plan for Pakistan's national conservation strategy was developed with funding from the Canadian International Development Agency (CIDA). The role of women is given special attention in the report on the implementation process. "This subject came up in all the workshops," and "there was unanimous agreement that an enhanced respect for women's work and greater support for their training and education lies at the heart of all effort in Pakistan" (Schwass et al. 1992, p. 42).

However, much of this issue was beyond the terms of reference of the national conservation strategy, which was based on the 1980 report. As a result, although the implementation design report lists 68 "critical and important tasks for NCS [national conservation strategy] implementation," only 12 require the "involvement of women in development," and in only two of these is their involvement considered to be critical: energy-efficient cooking and the development and deployment of biogas units (Schwass et al. 1992). Their involvement was considered important, but not critical, in implementing an "intensive population programme in fragile areas with high fertility rates"; yet, even in these fragile areas, it is still only women who actually give birth to children. How could their involvement in such a program and in environmental management, in general, be anything less than critical?

Although the new strategy for sustainable living (IUCN et al. 1991) emphasizes the importance of gender equity as a basis for sustainable development, national-level decision-makers involved in formulating agendas for the use of S&T for environmental management must also be sensitized to the importance of women's participation in these arenas. There is much diverse information on "gender training" for national-level policy analysts and decision-makers and the personnel of major bilateral and multilateral donor institutions (Aklilu 1991). However, much of this material, with the exception of a recent volume from the Commonwealth Secretariat (1992b), is "environment-blind" (see also Commonwealth of Learning 1994).

Moser's (1993) recent work on "gender planning" moves the issue of gender training into the much larger, and more significant, domain of women's political empowerment. "Gender planning is not an end in itself but a means by which women through a process of empowerment can emancipate themselves." This empowerment is best achieved through a process of "negotiated debate about the redistribution of power and resources within the household, civil society and the state" (Moser 1993, p. 190). In the context of this negotiated debate, NGOs, including women's NGOs, occupy a crucial middle ground between individual women at the local level and state institutions at the national level. The importance of effective NGO involvement in increasing the participation of women in decision-making at the local level has been demonstrated, especially in the wasteland-reclamation initiative. Such involvement can also be undertaken, effectively, by nongovernmental research centres and research teams involved in action-oriented activities in local communities. Although, at one time, NGOs were typically highly individualized organizations, working primarily at the local level, today there is also a proliferation of NGO networks, councils, and federations within countries and working internationally (Moser 1993, p. 193). These new networks and coalitions have a crucial role to play in bringing about women's increased participation in national and international decision-making for S&T in development.

Can S&T, and scientists and technologists, support these national and international women's organizations and networks in this process of negotiated debate at the national level? And how can they do it? One crucial avenue for such support is through further, and more gender-sensitive, approaches to the development of new information technologies. Communications technologies, such as electronic mail and electronic conferencing, have already made possible links between NGOs. There is also a crucial need for the development of feasible and inexpensive communication networks between national-level NGOs and the S&T policy and research community, and between national level NGOs and women and women's groups at the local level.

New communications links are particularly vital to make use of such information sources as Geographic Information Systems (GIS), a computer-based system for gathering, manipulating, and analyzing environmental data. GIS databases are commonly established with information obtained from remote surveys via satellite and a variety of atmospheric and ground level surveys (Christopherson 1990, pp. 49–51). GIS software packages and data-bases, which have almost unlimited applications, have a crucial rele-vance for national and local environmental management and learning.

However, although GIS allows for the simulation of hypo-thetical models of environmental management and can demonstrate how subtle changes in one element of a landscape may have a pow-erful effect elsewhere, no attempt (at least none known to this author) has been made to establish a GIS software package that would allow for gender sensitivity in environmental modeling. Given the considerable difference between women's and men's environmental needs and interests in many developing countries, this is a critical gap. In the absence of gender sensitivity, information sources such as GIS are unlikely to be used in a manner that supports women's envi-ronmental perceptions, interests, and needs at the community level, or their empowerment, locally or nationally, in environmental deci-sion-making. Instead, such S&T contributions, which could benefit women's lives, might become yet another, even more influential, source of harm and disruption. Supporting women's participation in national level environmental decision-making through the develop-ment of gender-sensitive information technologies and approaches for environmental management is the fifth key pathway to sustain-able and equitable development.

The role of the United Nations

A number of UN agreements are relevant to the quest for a gender-sensitive, culturally appropriate approach in the use of S&T for sus-tainable and equitable development. The *Convention on the Elimination of All Forms of Discrimination Against Women* (UN 1979a), which has been adopted by fewer than 100 countries, contains some important baseline directives: equal access to formal and informal education and technical training; the right to health and safety at work; the right of rural women to participate in the elaboration and implementation of development planning at all levels; and the right to adequate living conditions, particularly in relation to housing, san-itation, electricity, water supply, transport, and communications.

The *Vienna Programme of Action on Science and Technology for Development* (UN 1979b) contains a number of relevant directives: institutional arrangements to ensure the full participation of women in the S&T development process; integrated use of natural, human, and other national resources, with due regard to the need to protect resources of the biosphere; potential limits on research on chemosterilants and pesticides in developing countries; and potential use of environmental impact assessment in donor-funded projects. However, the last two directives ultimately depend on decisions and environmental standards adopted by the developing country concerned.

The Nairobi Forward-Looking Strategies for the Advancement of Women (UN 1985b), adopted by 157 countries, is somewhat limited in its approach to environmental issues. However, recommendations include a directive regarding the participation of women in national ecosystem management and control of environmental degradation, and a directive that "women should be included ... in all policy planning, implementation and administration of water supply projects and trained to take responsibility for the management of hydraulic infrastructures and equipment and for its maintenance."

Agenda 21 (UN 1992a) is remarkable in that an entire chapter (chapter 24) is devoted to women as a "special group" in relation to the environment. If implemented, many of its recommendations would certainly bring increased benefit to women and to the natural environment. However, objectives are "proposed" for governments to consider, listed as activities where they "should" take action, or conventions that they are "urged" to ratify. There is, therefore, an element of tentativeness in many of the recommendations, such as the "proposed" objective which suggests that governments work to eliminate "by the year 2000" all "constitutional, legal, administrative, cultural, behavioral, social and economic obstacles" to women's full participation in sustainable development.

In addition to these UN agreements, the NGO community has produced a key document emerging from the women's caucus at the NGO Forum at the UN Conference on Environment and Development (UNCED) and the World Women's Congress for a Healthy Planet (WEDO 1992). It pledges the commitment of the 1 500 participants at the World Women's Congress "to the empowerment of women, the central and powerful force in the search for equity between and among the peoples of the Earth and for a balance between them and the life-support systems that sustain us all" (WEDO 1992, p. 16).

Under the leadership of the Women's Environment and Development Organization, the women's caucus had a large impact on the policy formulation process at UNCED. A similar effort was undertaken in relation to women's issues at the recent UN Conference on Human Rights in Vienna, and is being undertaken in relation to the upcoming Fourth World Conference on Women in Beijing. As a result of these ongoing activities, there is increasing political sophistication on the part of international women's NGOs and networks about how to have an effect on the international policy-formulation process. Other key international NGOs involved in the quest for research and policy for S&T for sustainable and equitable development include the International Women's Tribune Center (IWTC), the Intermediate Technology Development Group (ITDG), the Third World Organization for Women in Science and Technology (TWOWS), the World Women's Veterinary Association, and the Gender, Science and Development Programme of the International Federation of Institutes for Advanced Studies (IFIAS). Many of these international organizations have been involved in collaborative planning for a "Once and Future Pavilion," intended to demonstrate the importance of women's participation in S&T policy, research, and application, in the past and in the future, at the Fourth World Conference on Women in Beijing in 1995. Gender-sensitive S&T for sustainable and equitable development will certainly continue to be a key issue for international discussion and policy formulation in the foreseeable future.

The five key pathways

This paper has identified five key pathways for S&T research and policy formulation in support of women's environmental perceptions, needs, and interests. They address the overall goals of chapter 24 of *Agenda 21* and the *Women's Action Agenda 21* in the specific context of S&T for environmental management and development, and they centre on the importance of women's equitable participation and conceptual authority in agenda-setting for the use of S&T for sustainable and equitable development. The five pathways are:

+ .Taking women's environmental health as a starting point for ensuring the appropriateness of all S&T interventions;

+ Using S&T in a gender-sensitive manner to alleviate women's poverty through research and policy to meet their expressed environmental perceptions, needs, and interests;

+ Supporting women's microenterprise activities through environmentally sound and relevant S&T innovations and interventions;

+ Ensuring women's full environmental literacy through their increased access to formal and informal environmental education, and to relevant S&T expertise and information, as a basis for their increased participation in community-based environmental decision-making; and

◆ Supporting women's participation in national-level environmental decision-making through the development of gender-sensitive information technologies and approaches to environmental management.

The implementation of these recommendations will be largely a matter of negotiated debate and political will, in this case the political will of the S&T policy and research community, which is represented at the international level by the UN Commission for Science and Technology for Development. In this international debate on the use of S&T for development, the question that must ultimately be addressed is: Are women's environmental perceptions, needs, and interests critical for our common future, for their lives, the lives of the men and children in their households, and for the future of the global environment? How can the answer be anything but yes?

In conclusion, here are two images of the Karamoja region of Uganda, separated by 30 years and by the use of S&T in war and peace. In Karamoja today (IIED 1992, p. 17):

> The district's residents suffer from a lack of basic infra-structure, chronic poverty and famine.... Despite the creation of the Karamoja Development Agency and a few initiatives by local missions and NGOs, little has been achieved in the way of sustainable development, and few ideas have emerged for improving conditions in the district.

However, 30 years ago, a different image of social life, based on women's work in food production and environmental management, is clear (Marshall-Thomas 1965, p. 15):

> Later in the day ... the women of the house, their many metal earrings chiming ... would go to the fields.... They had many acres under cultivation and many different crops. They grew a type of corn that stands ten or fifteen feet high and bears huge ears.... They grew finger millet, which bears small tender heads of grain and bulrush millet.... They grew sorghum, the stalks of which are sweet and wet and can be eaten like sugar-cane, while the heads, large clusters of round kernels in beautiful combinations of red, orange, purple, and white, can be ground into flour. Among the grain crops,

pumpkins grew, and gourds, and many types of beans and squashes.

In this and in many communities in developing countries, rural and urban, the road toward this bright image of abundance created and nourished by women will now be a long one. However, the five key pathways identified in this paper offer us all, women and men, in developing and developed countries, our shared best hope for a sustainable and equitable future.

Chapter 3
Claiming and using indigenous knowledge

Helen Appleton, Maria E. Fernandez,
Catherine L.M. Hill, and Consuelo Quiroz

Knowledge is generated by communities, over time, to allow them to understand and cope with their particular agroecological and socioeconomic environment (Brouwers 1993). Such knowledge — referred to as "local," "indigenous," or "traditional" — can be termed science, because it is generated and transformed through a systematic process of observation, experimentation, and adaptation.

Local knowledge systems are geared to dealing with diversity, in both the natural environment and social organization and continue to evolve over time. Like other scientific systems, local knowledge systems develop technology and management practices to improve the quality of life of people. However, local knowledge systems differ fundamentally from those based on modern science and technology (S&T) in that they are managed by the users of the knowledge and they are holistic. Although both "bodies of knowledge" — traditional and modern — are structured by systems of classification, sets of empirical observations about local environments, and systems of self-management that govern resource use (Johnson 1992), they differ in their capacity to deal with local problems and in the degree to which they are accessible to the members of the social group charged with resource management and production.

Because the primary social differentiation among adult, economically active members of a society is based on gender, specific spheres of activity become the domains of different genders as they increase their knowledge and skill over time. As a result, local knowledge and skills held by women often differ from those held by men. For example, in certain parts of the Andes, women have much more knowledge of livestock management practices than men, whereas men know much more about soil classification than women. This specialization is publicly recognized: women are consulted when decisions about health and breeding strategies have to be made; men are consulted when the appropriateness of a particular field for a crop is being weighed (Fernandez 1992). Relations between men and women in a culture will affect hierarchies of access, use, and control resulting in different perceptions and priorities for innovation and their use of technology (Appleton 1993a, b).

Full recognition of local knowledge systems is central to the issue of sustainable and equitable development. Until recently, they have been viewed as "backward," "static," and a "hinderance" to modernization. This negative view has been fostered by a tradition of Western science, which has resulted in today's highly specialized disciplines such as cell biology, molecular biology, and epidemiology (Hill 1994). Although the idea of scientists and technologists working together globally to find solutions to the world's problems is inspiring, the reality is many different units racing independently toward goals that are defined principally in terms of the profit potential (Appleton 1993b).

The view that modern science is capable of providing the solution to "underdevelopment" is also responsible for the depreciative view of indigenous and local knowledge systems. Furthermore, the focus on objectivity, rigor, control, and testing has helped to develop the perception that S&T are value-free, and that they operate outside of the societies in which they are based. Unfortunately, given the tremendous influence of S&T, this attitude has undermined the capacity of local knowledge systems to innovate and has lowered the status of the innovators themselves, especially women whose contribution to technological development has been historically undervalued.

For example, in a study in semi-arid areas of western India, researchers set out to establish the degree of knowledge scientists had about farmers' practices and to highlight the importance of understanding scientists' assumptions about local knowledge (Gupta 1989). The scientists, from various scientific backgrounds, were working for the All India Coordinated Research Project on Dryland Agriculture (AICRPDA), Haryana Agricultural University, Hissar, and the University's Dryland Research Station at Bawal. The study concluded (Gupta 1989):

> These scientists have rarely investigated the reasons for the practices they mentioned. Thus the science underlying the rational practices and the myths behind not-so-scientific practices have not been understood. We want to state unambiguously that the mere documentation of peasant practices is not enough. We have to identify the scientific basis of peasant practices and link it with their rationality.

Gupta (1989) also set out to test the validity of biologists' assumptions about women's homestead gardens. At a meeting, the scientists revealed that they believed the homesteaders used space inefficiently; that the vegetation was planted randomly or left to chance; and that trees were grown for only a single purpose, fuel or fruit. The validity of these assumptions was then tested by a team of women scientists working through maps of homesteads with local women. They discovered a complex system of planning, indicating some order in the apparent disorder. It also emerged that responsibilities for the homestead were divided among the men and women, and did not rest solely with the women as had been previously assumed.

The women scientists concluded that greater emphasis had to be placed on women's knowledge and practices: "The role of women in the homestead needed to be understood in terms of their own specialist knowledge and not just by regarding them as exploited workers who contribute to post-harvest chores" (Gupta 1989).

If a productive structure, based on the satisfaction of basic human needs and collective rather than individual consumption, is concomitant with sustainable development, the need for imported technology must be replaced by increased demand for local S&T innovation. However, the development of endogenous S&T capabilities should not necessarily follow the route of S&T in Western industrialized nations (Sagasti 1979). In Sagasti's view of resources, S&T systems focus on control and utilization, whereas local knowledge systems focus on usufruct and management. The generation of S&T is directly linked to centralized control over the distribution of information; information in local knowledge systems is the common property of integrated social groups.

Recognition and reinforcement of local knowledge systems can be the basis for an alternative development model. The capacity of these systems to integrate multiple disciplines, and the resultant synergism, are beginning to demonstrate higher levels of efficiency, effectiveness, adaptability, and sustainability than many conventional technologies. If they are to continue to contribute to sustainable development, however, local knowledge systems must be respected for what they are.

Currently, the United Nations (UN) agenda includes two interrelated issues that have to do with the interface of gender, S&T, and respect and recognition of local knowledge systems in their own right:

◆ Conservation and reproduction of the natural environment for use by future generations; and

◆ The intellectual property rights (IPRs) of local groups who have been responsible over time for the construction and conservation of biodiversity.

These issues directly affect the rights of women and men to manage resources critical to their innovative capacity and, therefore, their ability to contribute to a sustained development from which future generations may benefit.

Gender, biodiversity, and new agrotechnologies

Although women have long been key food producers and "managers" of their environments and play a central role in the sustainable use of biological resources and life support systems, especially in the conservation and enhancement of genetic resources, their work remains relatively unnoticed by researchers and development workers (Shiva and Dankelman 1992, p. 44). In Dehra Dun, India, for example, local women were able to identify no fewer than 145 species of trees and their uses; forestry "experts" were familiar with only 25 species (Shiva and Dankelman 1992). The stability and sustainability of the intricately interwoven ecosystem of forest, crops, and livestock depended on the practices and knowledge systems of the local women. Their collection of fodder, fuel, and other forest material was vital to the continued flow of resources that maintained the local economy in a sustainable way (Shiva and Dankelman 1992, p. 46).

The introduction of new agricultural technologies is resulting in women increasingly losing control in areas where they once had considerable control. In India, for example, the shift from subsistence to commercial agriculture has led to a reduction of women's sphere of influence. Women are shown to be increasingly dependent on men for extension services, purchase of seeds, and handling of tools and money (Indian Institute of Management 1992, p. 47). These problems have been exacerbated by the fact that outside "experts" have tended to interact with men in rural communities. Women, who are often not directly represented in local political decision-making structures become increasingly disadvantaged, because they lose both their knowledge and their status derived from their control over resources and knowledge. As Shiva and Dankelman (1992) argue, this situation breaks "women's sense of dignity, self-respect and self-determination." There is then the immediate danger that women's ecological knowledge will be "packaged as a product to be collected, owned, and sold in the marketplace of ideas of the scientific community" without them being compensated in any way (Shiva and Dankelman 1992).

Women's knowledge systems tends to be holistic and multi-dimensional. The introduction of agricultural technologies usually results in "resource fragmentation, undermining the position of women. The flows of biomass resources, that is, plant material for food, fodder and fuel, as well as animal wastes traditionally maintained by women, are disturbed and the different linkages between the agriculture, forest and livestock sectors of the system break down" (Shiva and Dankelman 1992, p. 48). In addition, inputs and outputs become completely dependent on external markets. Within this environment, the "women's role becomes more and more that of a labourer as she loses her control over production and access to resources" (Shiva and Dankelman 1992, p. 47).

Gender and intellectual property rights

IPRs refer primarily to international and national legal mechanisms used to protect primarily corporate and individual interests within a profit-motivated S&T system. The term is ineffective when applied to local knowledge as it does not recognize its status as a community responsibility rather than "private" property.

For thousands of years, plant genetic material has been collected, initially by local communities, then by colonizers, and later by botanists, plant breeders, and biotechnologists. Over the last 20 years, germplasm has been systematically collected from and stored in "genebanks." There has been much debate over the "ownership" of these collections as well as the safety of the material, the development of national laws restricting the availability of germplasm, and IPR to new varieties.

Because of the recent practice of "biodiversity prospecting," IPRs focus disproportionately on protecting corporate or individual knowledge in the area of biological products, leaving a whole range of cultural or community knowledge open to exploitation. Genetic resources are often incorrectly referred to as the "raw materials" for biotechnology, whereas in reality they are the products of the intellectual, cultural, and environmental contributions of local innovators, both women and men. Describing them as raw materials allows dominant S&T systems to exploit not only the matter, but also the people, as they are seen to belong to "no one in particular."

An exploitive asymmetry is thus created. When information is collected from Andean women peasants and Amazonian native peoples, for example, scientists consider it to be the "common heritage" of humanity, a public good for which no payment is appropriate or necessary. However, when the information is processed and transformed in the laboratories or factories of so-called "developed" nations, its value is enforced by legal and political mandate.

In the era of biotechnology, all biological "products" and processes could become patentable material, and countries such as the United States could be in a position to act against any country that did not provide exclusive opportunities for their corporations protected by their national laws. As Greaves (1994, p. ix) argues,

> [Local knowledge] now far more than in the past, is under real or potential assault from those who would gather it up, strip away its honoured meanings, convert it to a product, and sell it. Each time that happens the heritage itself dies a little, and with it its people.

Acquirers of local knowledge have power, technology, "inside" information, and sophisticated economic systems that allow them to take unfair advantage of knowledge innovators, particularly women, who have less access to power structures.

Currently, there are few provisions for the protection of local knowledge systems from outside exploitation. Applying existing patent and copyright laws to local knowledge is not only impossible, but also impractical for various reasons: there is no identifiable inventor; all traditional culture is already in the "public domain"; and the protection would, at best, last only a finite number of years. Furthermore, the present purpose of patent and copyright protection is to encourage profits for a few, not to sustain a community and environment as a living system.

A new legal instrument is needed — one that confers ownership and control of local knowledge on those who create, develop, and enhance it and that recognizes the differential access of women and men to political decision-making structures. This instrument would include ownership of, and control over, knowledge that is commonly held rather than individual. This kind of instrument cannot be developed without the active participation of those who possess the knowledge — both men and women.

The work of governments, universities, nongovernmental organizations, and local groups

Few programs have focused specifically on women's indigenous S&T knowledge. To obtain information in this area, it is necessary to examine a range of relevant programs and research that fall into three broad categories: S&T programs with women; general women's programs; and programs focused on indigenous knowledge. However, these categories are self-limiting in terms of adding to knowledge about women's existing S&T capacities. Also, information derived from an activity-specific approach encourages a focus on particular areas of work rather than general issues around women's indigenous technical knowledge. There is little analysis of how information contributes to a broader understanding of the issues or, at a strategic level, about the implications of this information for the design of policies and strategies.

S&T programs generally focus on integration of women into S&T activities. Women are viewed as the recipients of knowledge, rather than the generators, and the focus is on transfer of technologies to women through "training" and equipping women with the "necessary skills." This emphasis on delivery *to* women of the necessary opportunities, technologies, and management skills detracts from examination of existing capacity.

Women's programs tend to focus on improving women's status, access to resources, education, training, decision-making, and empowerment *in relation to men*. There is little critical examination of the value of women's knowledge in relation to identified problems and available resources in the wider environment, or of the integrity of women's knowledge as a sphere of knowledge in its own right. The identification of "women" as a group "in need" further militates against recognition of existing strengths, as does the view of S&T as a "male" area of expertise.

Indigenous knowledge programs are not always clear about their approach, either in relation to indigenous knowledge as a system or in relation to the gender-based nature of indigenous knowledge. "Researchers ... need to be clear in their own minds about whether they aim to legitimize local knowledge solely in the eyes of the scientific community, by picking out the 'tit-bits' of practical information, or whether they are trying to strengthen and maintain its cultural integrity" (Chambers et al. 1989). Knowledge is evaluated in terms of how well it correlates to orthodox scientific and technological thought, rather than in terms of the belief system that supports it (Last and Chavunduka 1986). Even when the system as a whole is examined, differences in type, status, and classification of women's and men's knowledge, which are fundamental to understanding the contributions and priorities of both sexes within a system, are ignored.

In the following sections, we provide examples of research and projects related to women's S&T knowledge. Much existing information is based on work in agriculture or food processing, where the essential contributions of women are finally being recognized; activities and programs in "hard" technology are less evident.

Work designed to strengthen women's indigenous skills is often carried out in teams comprising nongovernmental organizations (NGOs), research institutes, local groups, and universities at local national and international levels. It reflects two main areas of interest: the collection of information about indigenous knowledge systems, that is, their content, validity, and integrity; and the examination and development of suitable participatory research techniques for improving understanding of and working with local knowledge systems. Some universities and academic networks have also attempted to create links between formal research and development (R&D) and local experimentation (see, for example, Chambers et al. 1989, p. 165).

Gender and indigenous knowledge systems

Between 1990 and 1993, offices of the Intermediate Technology Development Group (ITDG) in Asia, Africa, Central and South America, and the United Kingdom carried out research designed to focus on women as technology users, producers, and innovators. The project (IWTC n.d.), called *Do It Herself*, was based on the hypothesis that women's technological capacities are less visible than men's and that a different approach to research would, therefore, be needed. This was achieved by working with researchers (mainly women) from organizations that had established links with women technology users at the community level. Because most of the researchers were relatively inexperienced, they were taught the necessary skills — methods of research and analysis — through a series of group workshops.

The program attempted to build understanding of the existence of women's technical knowledge, and constraints to its recognition, through communication with regional audiences of NGOs, government personnel, and academic networks. After analyzing 22 case studies across a range of technical areas, researchers concluded that the invisibility of women's technology is linked to the domestic nature of their work (which denies its technical content) and the fact that women's techniques tend to focus on processes and organization of production rather than "hardware" and are, therefore, less prestigious and have a lower profile. However, at the community level, it was clear that women's technical skills are critical in survival responses to crises and problems, and that the safety nets created by these responses may be destroyed by insensitive, uninformed policies. The potential contribution that existing skills and knowledge could make to tackling problems is ignored rather than built upon.

For example, in Sudan, as many as 60 fermented food products prepared by women form an important part of people's diet (Dirar 1991). The most complicated, a clear beer called *assaliya*, is the result of a 40-step process, starting with germinated sorghum grain; it takes 3 days to produce.

Fermentation is a complex chemical process that is still not fully understood. Variations in temperature and time during the different stages, affect the quality of the final product. Fermentation adds to the nutritional content of food. Using this process, women have been able to produce nutritious food from such substrates as bones, leaves, caterpillars, and cow urine.

Because fermentation increases nutritional value and preservative qualities, the process has played an important role in enabling people to cope with food shortage and famine in the past. Unfortunately, international drought and famine relief operations have been based on supplying imported foods rather than building capacity to produce local foods. This capacity is beginning to diminish as older women die without passing on their knowledge.

The information derived from the *Do It Herself* study has been disseminated to policymakers in NGOs and governments nationally and internationally. However, an important element of research is the feedback of information to the owners of knowledge. Therefore, the program includes the repackaging of information for women technology-users to build up their own knowledge and awareness of the skills and techniques that they are using (see Appleton 1993a,b).

Chambers et al. (1989) document a wealth of evidence of S&T knowledge, innovation, and activities of farmers in the South. The paper sets out "flexible research processes" to facilitate interaction between farmers and scientists and develop or adapt existing methods and technologies. The editors advocate a "complementary relationship" between knowledge possessed by scientists and technical experts and farmers' indigenous S&T knowledge. Although the message is not new, the approach is particularly helpful in bridging the gap between theoretical and abstract literature, and providing actual case material from which practical methods can be developed.

The editors stress the role of women farmers as a group who possess a wealth of often neglected knowledge. For example, the On-Farm Seed Project (OFSP), was a collaborative program of the Peace Corps Senegal, the African Food Systems Initiative, a Senegalese rice agronomist and plant breeder from Institut Sénégalais de Recherches Agricoles, and women rice farmers in the Casamance (southern Senegal). Individual interviews revealed that the women farmers were knowledgeable about the varieties of rice they grow and are using methods best adapted to the local environment. "Rice projects have found it impossible to improve on this indigenous kajando technology" (Chambers et al. 1989, p. 15).

Women promoting diversity

Several programs have highlighted the importance of recognizing gender issues in the maintenance of diversity. Women and men have different roles and areas of knowledge in relation to seed selection, for example. A further factor is that women depend on environments rich in diversity to ensure household and community survival during periods of crisis.

Curators of diversity: A few of the old women farmers in the Quechua communities of the Andes possess rare knowledge of plant breeding, which is probably a legacy of the ancient Inca civilization (Ojeda 1994). Potatoes are normally propagated by asexual reproduction, that is, by planting whole potatoes or sections. The resulting plants are, therefore, clones, genetically identical to the parent plant. However, the wise women gather potato seeds from the fruit of the potato — a practice which has been all but abandoned.

Because potatoes were first cultivated in the Andes, there are countless varieties of the crop, and people have different uses for each type. Gathering seeds enables the women to breed new varieties with characteristics they prefer. The process includes collecting the fruit, storing it outside until the following season to promote the production of the chemicals that activate the dormant seeds, planting the seeds just before the rains, harvesting tiny tubers and hiding them until the following year, then planting them to produce first generation tubers. The "tuber seed" products of this harvest, "grandchildren" of the original seeds, are sorted by shape, colour, and other characteristics. The various types are usually distributed among the woman's children to be planted to produce food crops. So far, younger generations have not taken on this role of "curator of diversity."

Developers of a new crop: In 1957, the Tonga of northwestern Zimbabwe were moved to Matabeleland, because their valley was to be flooded during the Kariba hydroelectric scheme (Mpande and Mpofu 1991). Soil conditions at the new site were poor, rainfall low, and hunting was prohibited. People could not produce enough to feed their families and became dependent on government handouts. To survive, Tonga women have invented and adapted food production and processing technologies and have identified new sources of food — 47 indigenous plants whose leaves are used for relish and over 100 tree species with a variety of edible parts.

One of these plants is the tamarind, *Tamarindus indica.* Although tamarind is widely used throughout the world for many purposes from medicine to fish preservation, it is relatively unknown in Zimbabwe, except among the Asian population. Women store the fruit for up to 12 months. It has some nutritional value and does not rot, making it especially valuable during famine. Tamarind is processed and used:

+ As a flavouring agent in sorghum or millet porridge — the fruit or, in times of shortage, the leaves are soaked and boiled;

+ As a substitute for commercial beverages such as tea and coffee, which are expensive or unavailable — ripe or unripe fruits are used, the acidity of the latter being neutralized with ash;

+ As a snack — the seeds, which have a high protein content, are fried;

+ As a substitute for or supplement to scarce maize, sorghum, or millet meals — the seeds are soaked, boiled, pounded, and added to cereals;

+ As a medicine — concentrated tamarind juice is used to cure gastrointestinal disorders and may also be added to animal drinking water as it is thought to cure sleeping sickness; and

+ As a coagulant — the juice is used to curdle fresh milk.

Tonga women have begun to realize the commercial potential of tamarind and other wild fruits, and are trading the fresh fruit for clothing from agents outside the area. The women are aware of the market, but have not yet developed strategies for dealing with it. They are afraid that large-scale commercialization will cause them to lose control over the source of the fruit, and that it will no longer be available to them as a subsistence crop.

The comparative advantage of indigenous knowledge

The assumption that technology introduced from the outside is more cost-effective or more productive has begun to be challenged. Various studies highlight the necessity of evaluating existing indigenous technologies, with full understanding of local conditions and local priorities, *before* introducing new ones. Other work demonstrates how interventions can build on the comparative advantages of existing systems, providing an interface between external and internal knowledge.

Traditional processes versus mechanization: The aim of one study (Luery et al. 1992) was to "analyse the effect of innovation on rural women, with particular reference to *gari* processing in the Ibaden area of south-western Nigeria" — cassava processed into *gari* is the most important staple food in most of Nigeria. The study focused initially on obtaining estimates of costs, returns, and amount of labour involved in processing from the 105 women participants. The women were asked to suggest solutions to problems they had identified, and traditional production processes were compared with those used by the "mechanized" cooperative and a nearby factory. The most significant finding was that the traditional *gari*-processing system is more efficient than mechanized systems, in terms of cost, returns, and relevance to the needs of the village economy.

Governments using indigenous medicine: In China, traditional medicine has been practised for about 3 000 years and has developed into a complex system of methods, including acupuncture, herbal medicine, moxibustion, massage, and deep-breathing exercises. Chinese medicine is low cost and accessible. From the early 1950s, the integration of Chinese and Western medicine was encouraged, and the practice was officially recognized in the Chinese constitution of 1982. Today, hospitals and research institutes incorporate both systems. Results have been impressive: major breakthroughs have been achieved in medicines for the treatment of certain types of cancer, hepatitis B, lupus erythematosus, leukemia, bone fracture, acute abdominal disease, and coronary heart disease. Among those who practise integrated medicine, 26% are women; women make up 22% of doctors working in Chinese medicine and 46% of those working in Western medicine.

In its development plan, the Government of Ghana identified as a national priority the need for

> a thorough investigation of the processes and techniques involved in all the important traditional economic activities in farming, processing of agricultural products.... This will help evolve and develop the

appropriate technology which can help create reasonably self-reliant communities enjoying progressively better standards of living.

With financial support from the Dutch government, a project was launched, under auspices of the International Labour Organisation (ILO), to place special emphasis on improving the status, education, development, and employment of women and to improve their living and working conditions. The specific objectives were to promote the use of appropriate technologies by rural women; arrange the local and indigenous manufacture of the necessary tools and equipment; and strengthen the technological capabilities of indigenous R&D institutions (Ewusi 1987).

For example, soap-making (*alata* and *amonkye*) has been a traditional activity among rural women in Ghana long before the introduction of bar soap (Ewusi 1987). *Alata*, in particular, is used by women who like its mildness and cosmetic properties. However, the commercial value of light-coloured bar soap has prompted many women to produce it rather than the traditional soaps, even though problems were associated with its production: they were not able to produce enough pale soap to make the enterprise commercially viable; foaming during the boiling stage constituted a health hazard; and caustic soda had to be imported.

At Essam, women use a combination of traditional methods of soap-making and technology developed by the Technical Consultancy Centre (TCC) to overcome these problems. They have also been able to combine palm-oil processing with soap production. The palm oil can be used either for home consumption or in soap-making. The work is carried out by a cooperative. Different members with varying levels of experience are involved at different stages. As a woman gains experience, she takes on different responsibilities; thus, skills are shared within the group.

Overall, the initiative created a valuable contact between individual women's cooperatives and R&D institutions, particularly the TCC, and local manufacturers. The women were able to identify and relay their concerns about the technology and highlight safety, resource, and sociocultural constraints. Because of their experience, they were able to contribute ideas to improve the process. Where the technology proved inadequate or inappropriate, they were able to compensate with traditional methods. The skills that women already possessed contributed to the overall success of the introduction of the technology. Women were also able to suggest enhancements, such as perfumes and alternative oils, to increase the commercial value of the soap.

The role of NGOs and networks

Indigenous knowledge is often passed informally by word of mouth from generation to generation. People's ability to gain access to information or to pass it on vary according to, among other things, the amount of time available, literacy rates, access to written material, ability to travel, and control over household media (such as radio or television).

Formal S&T information is shared in high-profile, widely recognized forums such as academic journals and national or international conferences. Communications networks are thus developed on the assumption that such knowledge has global relevance and applicability; there is an internationally understood language and symbolism, and although scientists may argue about the hypotheses or findings of a piece of work, they do not question the knowledge system that has produced it.

Networks specializing in indigenous knowledge face different challenges. First, they are working with information derived from many different systems that may not be comparable. Second, the information may be geographically limited, that is, its applicability in other conditions cannot be assumed. Third, indigenous knowledge, skills, and information are strongly gender-based. Fourth, networks specializing in indigenous knowledge have an interest in sharing information outward from a knowledge system, repackaging information so that it can be used by people within a knowledge system, and facilitating the exchange of information between people in the same knowledge system.

Indigenous Peoples' Biodiversity Network (IPBN): The IPBN is a growing global network of indigenous peoples' organizations working on biodiversity issues and the protection of local knowledge systems and genetic material. It was established by indigenous peoples who acted as observers at the initial meeting of the Intergovernmental Committee on the Convention on Biological Diversity (ICCBD), held in Geneva, Switzerland, in October 1993, to give such groups influence over policy development and access to information on biodiversity and IPR issues.

The IPBN has a Women and Biodiversity Working Group, which acknowledges that women have special knowledge of biodiversity and a crucial role in its maintenance. Noting that women's needs and perspectives are not currently addressed in biodiversity-related agreements and actions, the IPBN plans to address the effect of the Convention on Biological Diversity on women and their potential role in policy development in the area.

World Council of Indigenous Peoples (WCIP): The WCIP facilitates communication among individual communities, participates in workshops, seminars, and conferences on topics of concern to indigenous peoples, and encourages the enactment of legislation that recognizes the reality of indigenous peoples in different countries. In 1992, the Council established an Indigenous Women's Commission and it has also worked on environmental issues of relevance to indigenous peoples, including biodiversity. WCIP is interested in looking at local and indigenous knowledge systems, particularly in terms of gender. It recently endorsed a project to explore the gender perspectives of indigenous and local knowledge in animal health and production systems.

Indigenous Knowledge and Development Monitor: This publication is produced by the Centre for International Research and Advisory Networks (CIRAN), with cooperation from the Centre for Indigenous Knowledge for Agriculture and Rural Development (CIKARD), the Leiden Ethnosystems and Development Programme (LEAD), and the national and regional indigenous knowledge resource centres. The *Monitor* is published three times a year and is aimed at "the international community of people who are interested in indigenous knowledge." Recognizing that formal S&T knowledge is disseminated through a variety of well established channels, the *Monitor* aims to provide a route for less-formal knowledge. An issue on women's indigenous knowledge is being prepared for late 1994.

International Federation of Institutes for Advanced Study (IFIAS): IFIAS is an association of independent research institutions that collaborate to address global, long-term issues. In 1991, a Gender, Science, and Development Programme was launched to further the "contributions and well-being of women in the process of scientific and technological changes for just development." IFIAS has tended to focus on formally trained women scientists, and an attempt has been made to broaden this to include grassroots knowledge and skills by joining other organizations in the "Once and Future" Consortium. IFIAS's activities include: a working paper series, with titles on energy, health, trade, and environment issues; workshops on science at the service of women; and a symposium on "mainstreaming" women in S&T.

Third World Organisation of Women in Science and Technology (TWOWS): TWOWS's overall objective is to promote the role of women in S&T development in the South. It conducts surveys to analyze the status and potential for women in S&T, to improve access to training and education, and to increase the scientific productivity of women scientists in the South. TWOWS produces a newsletter and a database directory of Southern women scientists.

The International Women's Tribune Center (IWTC): Based in New York, IWTC works with women's and community groups in the areas of community economic development, women organizing, S&T, and communications networking. Its newsletter *The Tribune*, which is written in simple language and well illustrated and with names and addresses of contacts, is published in English, French, and Spanish three times a year. IWTC is a key player in preparations for the Beijing conference in 1995 as it publishes a regular "roadmap" to Beijing.

Center for Indigenous Knowledge for Agricultural and Rural Development: CIKARD and several other indigenous knowledge centres around the world support R&D efforts in indigenous knowledge systems. CIKARD has long been involved in research into local knowledge systems, particularly with respect to agriculture, agroforestry, and other related areas. It is based at Iowa State University, with offices scattered throughout Africa, Asia, and Latin America. The global network is well-placed to conduct further research in the area of gender, local knowledge systems, and S&T.

Work of the United Nations and its agencies

For the most part, policy recommendations and technical applications regarding gender, S&T for development, and indigenous knowledge are uncommon within the UN system. "Indigenous (or) traditional knowledge as 'science' ... has only been marginally conceived," but accords such as the *Draft Declaration of Rights of Indigenous Peoples* and other arenas within the UN system offer opportunities for change (Posey and Goeldi 1994, p. 240). Gender concerns and women's local knowledge remain invisible in agreements on indigenous peoples.

S&T agreements

Throughout most of the following documents, a common theme prevails — one that emphasizes women's access to Western-developed technology, education, extension, and credit and their subsequent impact on women. More specifically, these resolutions are often made in relation to men's main areas of concern. Although there is call for protection of traditional sciences, conspicuously lacking are resolutions and recommendations calling for the strengthening, exploration, and support of women's locally developed technologies, initiatives, and inventions in all sectors.

The *Vienna Programme of Action on Science and Technology for Development* (UN 1979b) acknowledges that men and women can contribute constructively to the realm of S&T for the enhancement of development (UN 1979b, p. 1). Recommendations with particular relevance include: the stimulation of demand for indigenous research and technology (para. 21.g); the protection of traditional S&T bases and upgrading such knowledge to use it fully (para. 21.m); and the call to ensure women's full participation in the S&T development process (para. 23.g).

The *Report of the Ad Hoc Panel of Experts on Science and Technology and Women* (UN 1984) highlights the area of endogenous research and development. It recommends that national governments and scientific communities listen to the needs of the average (woman) user in setting research and development priorities (Recommendation 33). This suggests possible exchange of local indigenous expertise and so-called "scientific" expertise. Likewise, Recommendation 58 promotes joint technology projects between scientific groups with urban and rural women in the development of scientific education and training techniques and materials.

Women and gender

General agreements on gender issues also tend to ignore women's local initiatives, innovations, inventions, and processes. These agreements again focus on the improvement of women's status and access to "modern" technologies, education, and decision-making processes rather than on the value, promotion, and strengthening of their local knowledge systems.

Support for women's rights to administer property, act as signatories on contracts, and hold land and other means of production is important in terms of women's control and use of their local knowledge systems. However, the emphasis remains on the rights of the individual rather than both individual and collective, or community, rights.

Although the *Convention on the Elimination of All Forms of Discrimination Against Women* (UN 1979a) does not specifically mention "indigenous" women or women's indigenous knowledge systems, it recommends that "State Parties ... take into account the particular problems faced by rural women and the significant roles ... [they] play in the economic survival of their families, including their work in the non-monetized sectors of the economy" (Article 14.1). The convention also recommends that all parties ensure the rights of rural women to access to all types of training and education, including access to appropriate technology (Article 14.2). Perhaps, most importantly Article 15 recommends that state parties "accord to women equal rights to administer property and conclude contracts."

The Nairobi Forward-Looking Strategies for the Advancement of Women (UN 1985b) was the first agreement to provide specific recommendations for indigenous women. Paragraph 303 calls for governments to ensure that all fundamental human rights and freedoms enshrined in international conventions be guaranteed for women belonging to minority groups and indigenous populations. Regarding S&T, it recommends that governments "ensure respect for the economic, social and cultural rights of these women ... [and provide] vocational, technical ... and other training ... [with] access to all services in their own language" (UN 1985b, para. 303).

Paragraph 26 suggests that a "new international economic order" should include, "self-reliance, collective self-reliance, and activation of indigenous human and material resources." Of particular significance to women's indigenous knowledge systems, a directive on agrarian reform measures suggests that "reforms should guarantee women's constitutional and legal rights in terms of access to land and other means of production and should ensure that women will control the products of their labour and their income, as well as benefits from agricultural inputs, research, training, credits and other infrastructural facilities" (UN 1985b). Finally, drawing two systems together, the document calls for an improvement of traditional knowledge and the introduction of modern technology for food production (para. 179), a recommendation particularly pertinent to women as they are intensely involved in this realm.

Agenda 21 (UN 1992a) refers to women throughout. Chapter 24 is completely devoted to women and their particular role in, and relation to, the environment. However, there are no particular recommendations directed at "indigenous women" or women's indigenous knowledge systems per se. This is possibly due to the continued confusion over the term "indigenous."

Improvement of the Situation of Women in Rural Areas: The report of the Secretary-General (1993) on women in rural areas repeats much of what has been said in previous UN documents. Given the post-Rio climate and the *International Year for the World's Indigenous Peoples*, it is unfortunate that it does not address some of the issues raised in the areas of women's local knowledge systems, the protection of that knowledge in light of the "bio-gold rush" in which Northern companies and researchers are engaged to exploit the natural resources of the South. This trend has grave implications for rural women as keepers of much agricultural and health-related knowledge.

The *Draft Platform for Action* (ECOSOC 1994) for the 4th World Conference on Women is a rather innocuous document with few far-reaching recommendations. Rather, it calls for the ratification of past agreements, aims for women's equality with men, and reiterates that women are not a homogeneous mass. Like past agreements, its approach to gender and S&T is to promote women's increased access to, and control over, "modern" technology, capital, land, and so forth (para. 29). Only one paragraph (74) mentions the specific promotion of women's indigenous knowledge. It suggests that NGOs "might include non-formal health education and advisory services for women and girls at the community level, giving particular emphasis to women's traditional health knowledge." The draft rarely mentions rural women, let alone women's indigenous knowledge or sciences. General comments on "critical areas of concern and action to be taken" mention indigenous women in general (para. 17) and reiterate interest in promoting traditional health (para. 33).

The Food and Agriculture Organization (FAO) of the United Nations' plan of action for women (FAO 1990b) focuses on engaging women in new practices and incorporating "modern" techniques in agriculture rather than promoting and strengthening their local, indigenous techniques and innovations. However, examples of the increasing interest in the gendered nature of local knowledge systems are found in various areas, including forestry and animal-production systems.

The World Health Organization's (WHO's) office for traditional medicine has a particular concern with traditional birth attendants; other areas of gender, indigenous knowledge, and health concerns are lacking (WHO 1991c). At a Pan American Health Organization (PAHO 1993, p. 7) workshop on indigenous peoples and health, several recommendations were tabled regarding indigenous women's position in the family as well as their relation to the dominant sectors of local and national society. Some of the concerns were problems related to reproduction and child care; mental health; sexual abuse; working conditions in agriculture; and cultural discrepancies between home-based and hospital care.

Indigenous people, biodiversity, and intellectual property rights

Work in the area of indigenous people, biodiversity, and intellectual property rights tends to focus on the concerns of indigenous people, per se, not specifically indigenous knowledge systems. Many people associate the term "indigenous" only with *specific* ethnic, religious, or cultural peoples or populations occupying ancestral lands. Indigenous knowledge systems, however, encompass *local* as well as *indigenous* communities, their experiences, their environment, and their processes of innovation. Furthermore, indigenous (or local) knowledge systems are, by their very nature, gender-related. Although many agreements on indigenous peoples recognize the special nature of these knowledge systems, they do not acknowledge the gendered nature of these systems.

The various forums on indigenous peoples note the importance of recognizing the individual and the collective. In pointing out the inadequacies of current intellectual property agreements for addressing indigenous peoples' concerns, they also acknowledge the necessity for linking "content" and "context." In addition, current IPR agreements recognize only new knowledge. Old knowledge, or that which would normally be generated in local communities, cannot be protected under current international IPR agreements. Moreover, none of the forums currently include a gender focus.

In 1972, a special subcommission to address discrimination against indigenous peoples was formed under the Commission on Human Rights and authorized by ECOSOC. In 1982, the Working Group on Indigenous Populations emerged out of the subcommission to become the focal point for the efforts of indigenous peoples working for international legal recognition of their human rights (Suagee 1994, p. 197). Annual meetings bring together indigenous representatives, NGOs, and state representatives. Actions of national governments and transnational corporations are examined to see how they conflict with the rights and interests of indigenous peoples.

Several organizations of indigenous people are questioning the values and approaches of the dominant science systems and struggling with the impact of these systems on their own communities and environments. Their views are reflected in the report of the Working Group on Indigenous Populations (ECOSOC 1993). Focused on the protection of cultural and intellectual property, the report highlights the importance of addressing the concerns of indigenous peoples, particularly with respect to their sciences in light of the "renewed interest in acquiring indigenous peoples' arts, cultures, and sciences" (ECOSOC 1993, para. 19).

Some of the critical issues for women's control over, access to, and potential compensation for their indigenous knowledge systems emerge out of the debate over IPRs. As mentioned earlier, women have long been, and remain, key actors in seed and animal selection. The *Study on the Protection of the Cultural and Intellectual Property of Indigenous Peoples* (ECOSOC 1993, para. 99) notes that, "in principle, the industrial property laws of most countries only protect 'new' knowledge. 'Old' knowledge, such as the herbal remedies used by traditional healers for centuries, has generally been regarded as not patentable". Yet, as the World Intellectual Property Organization (WIPO) maintains, much of the world's diversity is still only known to local peoples, and incompletely understood by outsiders (ECOSOC 1993). Because of current international legal mechanisms and the accelerating profit-driven race for genetic resources in the North, local and indigenous women are at risk of losing further control over their knowledge systems and resource base.

So-called "modern" science has long depended on, although not credited or adequately compensated, the innovations of local communities (ECOSOC 1991, para. 22).

> World food systems, textile industries, medicine and pharmacology still rely heavily on plant and animal varieties selected and modified by pre-industrial societies, including the isolation, modification and creative use of micro-organisms. Fermentation and the production of wine, beer, breads and cheese employs ... specialized strains of yeasts and molds. Staple foods [such as] maize, potatoes and rice were significantly improved by selective cultivation long before the discovery and commercial application of genetic chemistry.

Current international agreements on IPRs do not provide coverage for indigenous knowledge and sciences, due in large part to an "artificial distinction between cultural and intellectual property" (ECOSOC 1993, para. 21).

> The distinction between cultural and intellectual property is from indigenous peoples' viewpoint, an artificial one and not very useful. Industrialized societies tend to distinguish between art and science, or between creative inspiration and logical analysis. Indigenous peoples regard all products of the human mind and heart as interrelated, and as flowing from the same source: the relationships between the people and their land, their kinship with the other living creatures that share the land, and with the spirit world. Since the ultimate source of knowledge and creativity is the land itself, all of the art and science of a specific people are manifestations of the same underlying relationships, and can be considered as manifestations of the people as a whole.

It is more appropriate to refer to "collective heritage" (ECOSOC 1993, para. 23) than to distinguish between "cultural" and "intellectual" property. "Collective heritage" includes human thought and ingenuity, songs, arts, stories, and *scientific knowledge*. Heritage is not seen in terms of "property" with a specific owner, but rather a community responsibility and "a bundle of relationships, rather than a bundle of economic rights" (para. 26). It is "inappropriate to try to subdivide the heritage of indigenous peoples into separate legal categories such as 'cultural,' 'artistic,' or 'intellectual,' or into separate elements such as songs, stories, *science*, or sacred sites" (para. 31).

In 1993, the International Year for the World's Indigenous Peoples was declared; it led to the International Decade for the World's Indigenous Peoples (1995–2005). Although there is no particular gender focus in the Working Group on Indigenous Populations, it has suggested that 1996 be dedicated to indigenous women and that there is much interest in promoting women's indigenous S&T in that year.

The Working Group has developed a draft declaration that, if approved by the General Assembly, unfortunately holds the status of a Statement of Principles and is, therefore, not binding or justiciable (Suagee 1994, p. 198). However, it is an important document that sets out recommendations pertinent to the process of recognizing indigenous people and knowledge as legitimate and critical.

Although specific gender issues are not addressed, Article 41 notes that "all the rights and freedoms recognized herein are equally guaranteed to male and female indigenous individuals." Article 22 mentions women as one subgroup requiring specific attention regarding vocational training. Article 23 recommends that indigenous peoples have the right to "determine and develop all health, housing and other economic and social programmes ... and to administer them through their own institutions." Article 24 also supports indigenous peoples' "right to their traditional medicines and health practices, including the right to the protection of vital medicinal plants, animals, and minerals."

This could mean increased support for traditional health systems as practised by indigenous peoples and would have particular relevance for indigenous women, who are in many places, the health-care givers and traditional birth attendants. Article 24 also holds implications for the protection of intellectual and cultural property within these communities. Particularly applicable to the focal point of gender, indigenous knowledge, and S&T for development is Article 29 which states that

> indigenous peoples are entitled to the recognition of the full ownership, control and protection of their

cultural and intellectual property. They have the right to special measures to control, develop and protect their sciences, technologies and cultural manifestations, including human and other genetic resources, seeds, medicines, knowledge of the properties of fauna and flora, oral traditions, literatures, designs and visual and performing arts.

Agenda 21 (UN 1992a) recognizes the role of indigenous communities in relation to the environment. Women are mentioned infrequently: for example, the last line of chapter 26 urges that "particular attention ... be given to strengthening the role of indigenous women." Suggested activities propose that UN bodies and other international development and finance organizations and governments should "incorporate (indigenous peoples') values, views and knowledge, including the unique contribution of indigenous women, in resource management and other policies and programmes that may affect them" (UN 1992a, para. 26.5).

Perhaps, most importantly, chapter 26 acknowledges, as a basis for action, generations of holistic traditional scientific knowledge about land, natural resources, and environment held by many indigenous peoples (para. 26.1). Disappointingly, however, the chapter lacks any concrete recommendation and remains a shadow of a potentially strong document.

The *Convention on Biological Diversity* (UN 1992b, p. 19), developed to "curb the destruction of biological species, habitats and ecosystems," was signed by 157 countries. For it to become law, it must be ratified by at least 30 countries, most likely through national legislation. It is seen by many indigenous groups as one of the best forums for expressing their concerns about their sciences, knowledge, and cultural and IPRs as biodiversity, being a local concern requires local participation (Appleton 1994). However, many indigenous groups are apprehensive about the degree to which national and international laws will "adequately recognize and protect their knowledge, innovation and practices" (Posey and Goeldi 1994, p. 234). As an ongoing global process, and recognizing both indigenous peoples' and women's vital roles in conservation and sustainable use of biological diversity, the convention provides an important entry point for addressing indigenous knowledge, gender, and S&T.

Article 8 on in-situ conservation calls for the respect, preservation, and maintenance of indigenous and local knowledge, innovations, and practices in biological diversity conservation and sustainable use, as well as the wider application of such knowledge and practices "with the approval and involvement of the holders"; however, women are not specifically mentioned (UN 1992b, article

8.j). Article 17.2 calls for the exchange of indigenous and traditional knowledge with other systems, whereas article 18.4 encourages methods of cooperation for developing and using technologies, "including indigenous and traditional technologies." Again, women, their ways of communication exchange, and their development of knowledge and technologies are left out of the equation.

Posey and Goeldi (1994, p. 227) note that the ILO was the first UN organization to deal with the concerns of indigenous peoples, having first established standards for the "protection of native workers" as early as 1926. It developed a *Convention [107] Concerning the Protection and Integration of Indigenous and Other Tribal and Semi-Tribal Populations in Independent Countries* (ILO 1957) and revised it in Convention 169 in 1989 (ILO 1989a).

Importantly, Convention 169 recognizes the collective aspects of indigenous cultures and values, which is critical in appreciating women's and men's indigenous knowledge systems in the holistic community sense in which they are based. Unfortunately, few countries have ratified it, and its provisions are not applicable to nonsignatories (Chapman 1994, p. 218).

The UN system with its associated agreements and conventions has worked within, rather than across, sectors. Subsequently, gender, local knowledge systems, and S&T have been addressed, for the most part, as separate spheres, rather than as an intersection, resulting in the marginalization, circumvention, or outright subjugation of many of the world's peoples and their indigenous knowledge systems.

Particularly problematic is the disaggregation of documents and programs between women or gender, on the one hand, and indigenous peoples, on the other. Furthermore, because of the continuing confusion around, and interpretation of, the term indigenous and its association with certain groups of people, other local knowledge systems are rendered invisible in UN documents. Local knowledge systems do not fit into documents on indigenous peoples, and documents focusing on women in general tend to promote modern S&T. Recommendations have focused on improving women's access to "modern" technologies, education, and credit based on men's prioritized needs and in relation to often alien, inappropriate modern expressions of need. They have also tended to focus on the "content" or "hardware" of science, rather than its "context" or "software."

Certain forums, including the Working Group on Indigenous Populations, the *Draft Declaration on the Rights of Indigenous Peoples*, and the ongoing processes for the *Convention on Biological Diversity*, provide particularly valuable entry points for future considerations of gender and indigenous knowledge systems within the UN and other international systems.

Recommendations and agenda for future research

In this paper, we have addressed the nature of indigenous knowledge systems, their potential role in sustainable and equitable development, and possible strategies for creating an interface that promotes mutually beneficial interactions between local and S&T knowledge systems. Local knowledge systems have evolved from ongoing experimentation to resolve agricultural, environmental, health, and other social problems in a particular agroecological and sociocultural context. Only recently have researchers acknowledged that men and women may have different knowledge about materials, their environment, or processes; and that they may also have very different ways of organizing, maintaining, and transferring their systems of knowledge. Western S&T systems have stereotyped men's and women's roles and social relations and in doing so have, for the most part, marginalized women and their local knowledge systems. However, case studies demonstrate that it is often local women, not foreign scientists or "experts," who have the "expertise" in their environment.

Women's local knowledge is crucial to the maintenance of biodiversity. The introduction of new biotechnologies and biodiversity prospecting threatens women's control over and access to the very materials necessary for them to sustain the multidimensional knowledge systems and environments on which they depend for their livelihood and survival.

Most research, policy directives, and programs have tended to disembody local knowledge systems. Rather than providing an interface, research and policy efforts have developed three separate spheres: S&T related to women; general studies of gender or women; and programs and policies on indigenous knowledge.

A critical area of concern is the current view of knowledge as individual or corporate property rather than community held and a community-regulated responsibility. This perspective, grounded in a market-driven political, economic, and social context, is generally alien to peoples who see their local knowledge as something to be shared with others for the good of their society and their environment.

To counteract the existing exploitive asymmetry between the different systems of knowledge (S&T and local), policy initiatives and programs concerned with IPRs should recognize and support concepts of knowledge that are more holistic, community-held, and "old" in contrast to the present acceptance of rights to knowledge protection only for "new" knowledge held by individuals or corporations.

Given the current attitudes of scientists to local knowledge systems and the resulting invalidation of those systems or their exploitation for the "good of "humanity," efforts should be made both at the policy level and in training syllabi to counter these attitudes and develop in scientists a respect for local knowledge systems, encompassing both holistic and gender perspectives. At all levels of education, efforts should be made in culturally appropriate and respectful ways to include local knowledge in syllabi to ensure that it continues to be reproduced by communities.

National and international bodies should develop mechanisms to promote respect for local knowledge systems and community-based technical processes.

At all levels of policy and programming, the UN system should make concrete efforts to create an interface among S&T, women and gender issues, and indigenous knowledge. UN bodies should develop mechanisms to ensure that gender expertise is spread across sectors and through technical divisions and enable two-way dialogues.

National and international governments should support the research and advocacy efforts of NGOs and indigenous organizations working to protect their local knowledge systems and their social and environmental spheres. Organizations, such as the IPBN, that are centrally involved in the ongoing conferences on the *Convention on Biological Diversity* should be supported financially and in terms of supporting research.

International bodies should also elevate the concerns of indigenous organizations such as the WCIP and incorporate their suggestions on gender and indigenous women's and men's needs and interests including their holistic knowledge systems.

An International Year for Indigenous Women should be proclaimed by the UN, possibly as early as 1996, to highlight the concerns of indigenous women.

All UN and other international agreements and all working documents and amendments should include statements supporting the enhancement and protection of indigenous knowledge systems.

A monitoring system should be implemented to monitor and evaluate the interface of gender, indigenous knowledge systems, and S&T in the UN system.

As has been shown, little research has been undertaken around the area of gender and local knowledge systems. More research is needed in this area to address the implications of biodiversity prospecting and the introduction of new agrotechnologies on the people's control of and access to local knowledge systems.

Research should address the specific social, political, economic, and environmental effect of current IPRs on local knowledge systems and the consequences of ignoring "old" knowledge.

Every effort should be made to promote research by indigenous people and local communities and opportunities created for their input into local, national, regional, and international decision-making processes, policy directives, implementation, and evaluation processes.

Chapter 4

Women spearhead food security

Science and technology an asset?

Shimwaayi Muntemba and
Ruvimbo Chimedza[1]

Historically, women have evolved systems of relating to and managing the resource base and have developed technologies to assist
them. Their science and technology (S&T) was locally oriented and
location specific. Their knowledge base provided them with diverse
ways of meeting their food needs. Disruptions to this knowledge base
have threatened household food security. In addition, gender relations at the household, institutional, and national levels; approaches
of modern S&T; land dispossession; and structural constraints that
resource-poor communities face have all converged to undermine
food security. However, a ray of hope may be seen in the shifts occur-
ring within governmental organs, among nongovernmental organizations (NGOs), and within poor communities themselves.

We define food security as maintaining desirable nutritional
levels (quality) and staving off the pangs of hunger (quantity). We
focus on the household, while acknowledging the importance of sufficient food stocks at the national level. Food security means desirable consumption levels not only for families and households, but
also for their most vulnerable members — young girls, the elderly,
and women. Food security depends on who controls access to available food at the household level. Central to the issue of household
food security, then, are issues of gender and intergenerational equity.

There are two ways to get food — producing it (physical
access) and buying it (economic access). At the heart of physical
access is the question of who controls the means of production.

[1] We thank Perpetua Kalala, an intern at the International Development Research Centre and a member of the Gender Working Group Secretariat, for her assistance in obtaining
necessary background information that was not readily available in our countries of residence.

Resource-poor farmers often have limited land; most women neither own nor have direct rights to use land. Food security implies agricultural systems that ensure high yields and sustainable productivity. Labour and S&T are critical to ensuring this productivity, but must also protect and enhance the resource base. Food security includes knowledge of good land and crop "husbandry." Gender and intra-household relations determine access to and control over these factors, and their control has implications for availability of food stocks at the household level. In most cases, women have limited access but no control.

Economic access is the ability of people to purchase food from national stocks or other sources. It depends on the availability of opportunities for off-farm activities or wage work. Factors such as access to credit, mobility, and location of markets all affect the ability of rural families to raise their incomes. Economic access, then, must be seen within the broad context of rural development.

For the urban poor, formal and informal employment opportunities are essential, but economic access is related to gender. Women, although central actors in food provision, have less access to income-generating activities. Household food security is thus compromised. In much of the Third World, policies reinforce this prejudice.

Households experience food insecurity as a result of several factors:

+ "Hunger months" within the normal agricultural cycle (Richards 1932; Agarwal 1992b);

+ Natural calamities such as droughts, leading to famine;

+ Human-caused crises such as civil wars;

+ Severe ecologic degradation that diminishes land productivity; and

+ Policy-led choices about what crops to grow and where.

However, there need not be "hunger months" if sufficient levels of productivity can be reached. The effects of natural calamities need not be disastrous if nations have sufficient reserve stocks, and households have the income to purchase food. However, coping with normal shortfalls and disaster-driven calamities reveal relations among household members within the context of gender. Gender and intergenerational equity are challenged as households cope with food deficits. Women make most of the adjustments, as they and girl children are the first to forgo most of their nutritional needs. Although technologies have been developed or enhanced in response to recurring calamities, they do not build on existing technologies, allow for local participation, or reach the major custodians of food security — women.

As the ranks of the hungry increase, food security has become an issue of basic human rights. The United Nations (UN) has focused global concerns over food security. Initially, efforts of such agencies as the Food and Agricultural Organization (FAO) of the United Nations and UN commissions on women, S&T, and gender were unintegrated. However, from the 1970s, some issues began to converge. Interlinkages between gender, enduring food security, S&T, and a healthy environment have emerged. In this paper, we examine what changes various UN declarations have brought about in terms of shifting access and control of the means and factors of production; in changing policies and attitudes; and in empowering the most vulnerable social groups and households.

Food security is closely linked to environmental issues and its sustainability. Some countries have attained short-term food security by importing, but others look to increased domestic production. In many countries, smallholder producers meet the bulk of national food needs through sale of their surpluses. However, the land and water resource base, on which rural production depends, have been coming under mounting stress: desertification, deforestation, soil erosion, and sinking water tables are widespread and this stress has further challenged food security.

Relation of food security to sustainable livelihood security

Lasting food security is based on sustainable livelihood security. Sustainable livelihood security is defined as (Advisory Panel on Food Security, Agriculture, Forestry and Environment 1987):

> Adequate stocks and flows of food and cash to meet basic needs. Security refers to secure ownership of, and access to, resources and income-earning activities, including reserves and assets to offset risk, ease shocks and meet contingencies. Sustainable refers to the maintenance or enhancement of resource productivity on a long term basis. A household may be enabled to gain sustainable livelihood security in many ways — through ownership of land, livestock, or trees; rights to grazing, fishing, hunting or gathering; through stable employment with adequate remuneration; or through varied repertoires of activities.

Achieving food security challenges us to create an environment that enables and facilitates an increase in productivity and in the incomes of those who are poor in resources. Sustainable livelihood security requires the reversal of the trends to marginalize the poor as a prerequisite to food security.

Sustainable livelihood security automatically raises gender issues, because it requires that we answer the questions who owns what, and who controls what. Various studies in Asia, the Middle East, Africa, and parts of Latin America (FAO 1990a) show women as the majority of agricultural workers (70% in Asia and 30–90% in Africa), as livestock tenders and managers (in the Middle East), and as food producers (73% in sub-Saharan Africa, Colombia, and the Caribbean). In all cases, women are the hewers of wood and drawers of water. The quest for sustainable livelihood security enables us to address issues of their rights to ownership and use of the means and factors of production. It challenges governments to come up with policies and action plans to make enduring food security a reality, in both rural and urban areas.

Sources of food security

Agriculture

Food security is intimately tied to sustainable agriculture. Three production systems dominate world agriculture:

+ Industrial agriculture, which is capital and input intensive, is practiced in temperate zones of Europe, North America, Australasia, and their enclaves in the Third World.

+ "Green Revolution" agriculture is more widespread in Asia and in parts of Latin America and North Africa. Resource-rich farmers in these areas enjoy the benefits of this system.

+ Resource-poor agriculture uses rain-fed systems and is practiced in diverse, complex, and vulnerable conditions. Farmers tend to be resource-poor in all ways except perhaps in terms of human resources. This type of agriculture predominates in much of sub-Saharan Africa and in the hinterlands of Asia and Latin America. This system also includes the agriculture practiced by the urban poor.

Gender plays an important role in agricultural production systems, and questions pertaining to food security must consider such gender-determined factors as who enjoys property rights; who has control; who has access to what; and who does what work.

Ownership of land eludes over 90% of women in resource-poor agriculture systems. The majority of the 70% landless people in Asia are women. In parts of Africa and the Caribbean where women have traditionally held land rights, they have been losing these rights progressively to men.

In many countries of Asia, Africa, and Latin America, privatization of land has accelerated the loss of women's land rights. Titles are reallocated to men as the assumed heads of households even when women are the acknowledged household heads. Women's knowledge, which is critical to S&T and food security, becomes irreparably disrupted or irrelevant as a result of the erosion or denial of their rights (Muntemba 1988; Okuneye and Nwosu 1988).

Equally important is the quality of land. In some countries, peasants are being forced onto poor quality land as better areas are allocated to cash crops. The problems of the (mainly) women who are left to produce food crops in marginal areas are compounded by land and water degradation, particularly through soil erosion and deforestation.

Soils have also been affected negatively by the inappropriate use of fertilizers. To increase production, chemical fertilizers have been sold to farmers without information on possible adverse consequences of overuse and how to minimize them. In 1987, Muntemba interviewed a peasant woman farming on the central plateau of Zambia. This head of a household of seven described the acidification of her land due to overuse of fertilizer. Her urgent appeal was for information on technology to help her reclaim her source of livelihood, and she was prepared to sell her cattle to make this possible.

Control of land is the most basic requirement for food security. However, its productivity is imperative. In resource-poor systems, producers have to manage not only with land of poor quality, but with a scarcity of resources. Historically, such producers have experimented with and implemented innovations to match their food requirements to supply, without undermining the productivity of their resource base. Swaminathan (1981) succinctly captured a critical element in S&T when he wrote, "Agriculture starts moving forward only when appropriate packages of technology, services and public policies are introduced in a symbiotic manner."

Fisheries

Fish and other aquatic products provide about 6% of the protein consumed by the world's population; they account for about 17% of all animal protein. In some countries, however, over a third of people's animal protein comes from fish, and in some African countries the proportion is half or more (Advisory Panel on Food Security, Agriculture, Forestry and Environment 1987). Fisheries are also important as a source of employment and income necessary for food security. Fishing for sale and trade is often dominated by men, whereas women concentrate on fishing for domestic consumption (Muntemba 1977). However, women's fish-processing activities for local and urban markets have been a major source of income in some countries (Steady 1985).

Fish farming is proving to be another cost-effective source of food. Because fish farms can be established at a relatively low cost and are easy to manage, they can be maintained as a small-scale activity. Fish farming can be a means to rehabilitate ecosystems and exploit agriculturally less-productive soils. Thus, some individual farmers and countries are making use of their wastelands in this way. Additionally, because fish-farming is a low-cost operation, it is less-susceptible to gender biases.

Household incomes

The increasing numbers of landless people in Asia and parts of Africa and Latin America and the growing rate of urbanization mean that problems of economic access to food are becoming acute. At the height of the food crisis of the 1980s in Africa, it was noted that there were enough food stocks in the world to feed the planet's populations, but only those with economic power could obtain food. Even in countries in crisis, the rich never go hungry. During the famines of Bengal in 1943, Ethiopia in 1973, and Bangladesh in 1974, the amount of food consumed per capita was no less than in previous years. Those who died did so because they could not obtain food (Agarwal 1992b).

As landless people turn to wage work, the gender factor also comes into play. Women seem to generate less income than men even though they work as hard or harder. Studies from India and Kenya reveal that the family income of female-headed households is 50% less than that of male-headed families (FAO 1990a). Increasingly, as wage employment opportunities decrease and wages become inadequate, many turn to other nonfarm activities. West African women can be seen in capitals away from their own countries trading various wares and providing services, especially food-related. Regional cooperation and liberal laws governing cross-border movement have made this possible. As entrepreneurs, women have become increasingly innovative, adopting and adapting tools to increase their output. A visit to any West African capital will reveal a diversity of food-processing technologies.

Wildlife resources

For resource-poor households, "commons" have been a good source of food security. In Zambia in 1976, many farmers denied that they experienced "hunger months" in their agricultural cycle, because they relied on food gathered from the forest at these times (Muntemba 1977). Collected tubers supplied them with starch and carbohydrates, wild vegetables and leaves were gathered for relishes, and fruit was picked. The onset of rains brought other wild foods rich in protein, such as flying termites, caterpillars, and locusts (Chimedza 1993). To many poor households, wild foods remain an integral component of food security. Yet proponents of modern S&T have regarded some of these resources as pests.

Collection of wild foods for domestic consumption has been the responsibility of women. They have developed precise knowledge of the biodiversity and chemical composition of local plants to avert any danger of poisoning, and have passed this knowledge to younger generations in informal but systematic ways. This chain of knowledge has been disrupted as poor farmers and other rural dwellers are forced into foreign ecosystems.

Many communities in developing countries have been moved, sometimes several times, to make way for development projects, sometimes during the most inconvenient period in the agricultural cycle. Colson (1971) followed the fate of people moved from the neighbourhood of the Kariba Dam, constructed on the Zambezi River to provide electric power to Zambia and Zimbabwe. In the first few years of resettlement, a significant number of these people were killed and many others suffered from various forms of food poisoning because they were dealing with an unfamiliar ecosystem.

Gender issues in the S&T of food security

Women's roles have been pivotal in achieving food security for their families and communities, but their efforts are beset by structural and societal constraints. In this section, we explore the processes that have undermined women's knowledge systems and frustrate their participation in modern S&T systems.

Women's knowledge

Women relate to the various sources of food security as part of their daily work. They manage soils and other land-based resources and have accumulated intimate knowledge of their ecosystems, developing strategies for managing change. Women have amassed valuable knowledge in such areas as plant genetics, pest manage-ment, and soil conservation. For example, in Zimbabwe, women farmers do not buy seed to grow basic foods: millets, sorghum, peanuts, groundnuts, and sweet potatoes. They *select* seed, looking for particular traits, such as stability, disease resistance, drought tol-erance, palatability, and storage potential.

Women have determined which plants to grow where to con-trol pests. They are particularly well informed about intercropping, mingling plants that complement each other, and have developed ways of storing produce from one agricultural season to the next. Their role in conservation and utilization of plant genetic resources is valuable. Women continue to develop genetic diversity. Through their creative practices, they preserve cultivars that are environmen-tally sustainable and socially acceptable.

However, this knowledge base has been upset be develop-ment factors and processes that include forced population move-ments to unfamiliar ecosystems; breakdowns in the transmission of knowledge, resulting from disruption in social organization; inter-generational breakdown as younger people leave rural for urban areas; and new systems of education that require physical absence from traditional sources of knowledge. In some cases, the break from the familiar base has not led to positive adjustment and innovation, as producers attempt to follow technological practices without suffi-cient scientific support.

Women and S&T

New technologies have not built on women's rich knowledge base. The social (colonial) and cultural (male) milieux in which technology and modern science were introduced in the colonies did not acknowl-edge the existence of practical S&T among the conquered. For a long time, researchers failed to recognize that, in most African and Asian smallholder agriculture, women have been the key actors in food-technology development.

In many quarters, it is now accepted, although not yet acted on, that technology can be of sustainable use if it is compatible with prevailing systems, management skills, acceptable cultural practices, and the prevailing socioeconomic resource base. If these factors had been taken into consideration, women, as custodians of local knowl-edge and food-production technology, would have been strengthened by new S&T. Sustainable agriculture and food security demand strate-gic interaction between traditional and modern systems.

The shift of agriculture to men's control

Official colonial and postcolonial agricultural policy viewed men as "the farmers," thus marginalizing women. New technologies were accompanied by the introduction of cash crops, which, destined for the market, were regarded as farmers', and therefore men's, crops. Often, because these crops were not native, they were outside women's knowledge base.

Cash crops also compete with food crops and receive priority in terms of land and capital investment and labour. Although men have been assumed to be responsible for cash-crop production, the input of women's labour remains high, actually increasing in households that use low technology. Men take full responsibility for marketing, and they control agricultural income. This income is not necessarily used to improve food technology or significantly increase access to food. An important element in improved food technology and economic access to food is who controls the income. Women do not.

Lack of local participation in S&T

To make a sustainable contribution to food security, S&T must start with local communities, building upon their existing knowledge and practices. S&T must use the local communities' capacities and strengthen them to meet the challenges of sustainable livelihood security. This approach identifies useful elements of both local and mainstream S&T, combining them to produce effective solutions. It uses both human capital and local natural resources to allow development of more location-specific, and therefore relevant, solutions through collaborative efforts by women at the grassroots level, modern scientists, and technologists.

Currently, scientists and technologists, tied to their laboratories, set research agendas and develop technologies without consulting the end-users. Often, they do not know in what social context the technology will be applied and whether it is men, women, or children who will apply it. To find lasting solutions to the challenges of sustainable livelihood and food security, a reversal must occur, placing the people and not technology at the centre.

The origins of technology, who owns it, who controls it, and whose interest it serves are relevant questions. Over half of all scientific research is carried out in developed countries by multinational companies and international research centres. Even scientists working at research centres in developing countries tend to be removed from the situation for which they are producing the technology, and technologies are seldom modified to suit local conditions.

Dissemination of modern technology

The dominant route for technology development and transfer puts women at the end. Extension workers, most of whom are still males in most countries, have been responsible for the transfer of technology from international or national centres to the end-users. Generally, they direct information about innovations at men who selectively pass it along to women, often in diluted forms. Where women have been contacted directly, they have received unclear and incomplete messages. Assuming limits on women's capacity to absorb information, extension workers leave out points that they (not the women) consider too technical.

Because of sociocultural barriers, male extension workers sometimes find it difficult to reach women farmers on an individual basis. Most women farmers contact extension services through groups and get little individual attention (Rathgeber 1990). Admitting the error of this approach, E.R. Nyirenda, an agricultural officer in charge of a training institute in Zambia, remarked, "The exclusion of women was a great mistake made by the Department [of Agriculture]. Agricultural production could have increased enormously if women were taught the modern technical know-how" (Muntemba 1977).

An additional problem lies in inadequate links between technology developers and extension workers. Technologies are developed without consultation with those who deliver it to end-users. Some national research institutions have attempted to establish links with extension workers, but frequently such efforts come at the end of the research cycle when it is too late to benefit from their suggestions. The absence of linkages among these key actors compounds the problem of matching technology to local conditions and results in the development and dissemination of inappropriate technologies.

Purpose and target audience for S&T

Much of today's technology is supply-led. It is developed and ascribed to a problem that is described in terms of its already-defined solution. Technology comes first, then it is applied to a problem. In the transition to enduring food security, however, technologies are required that farmers will use, not ones that are abstractly effective in reaching certain production goals. Desirable technology, which reflects concrete situations, can only be developed with the full participation of the end-users.

Driven by the profit motive, technology is largely designed for large-scale commercial farmers who produce primarily for markets. Because they control better-quality land, the focus of innovations has been on improving crops produced on good soil with abundant water supplies. Little attention has been paid to problems associated with rain-fed agriculture on marginal soils. Although not strictly profit-motivated, by focusing on industrial agriculture, international research centres have also tended to neglect rain-fed agriculture, the system in which most women are involved.

Control of technology

Modern technology is completely owned and controlled by powerful multilateral companies based in the North. Although ownership and control of knowledge are protected through patents, most local knowledge is open to international piracy. Knowledge and the material for technology development have been expropriated from the South without compensation. Companies from the North collect plant genetic material from the Third World and use it to develop new varieties protected through patent law. It is estimated that 25% of all genetic material in North American wheat comes from Mexico. Most areas of Europe could not grow tomatoes commercially if they did not contain genetic material from the South. That technologies relying on material from the South are protected whereas local knowledge, of which women have largely been custodians, is not is an area of concern (Brouwer et al. 1992).

Policy to regulate technology

Multinational corporations and international research centres have continued to dominate in the development and transfer of agricultural technology in developing countries, particularly those in Africa. No alternatives have been suggested, even when negative effects have been observed, because policymakers have been conditioned not to think in terms of alternatives. Heads of local research institutions and senior civil servants play key roles in policy formulation without consulting those affected by the policies. Policymakers support the production of export crops to generate revenues. In many cases, they do not fully appreciate the problems facing smallholder producers, particularly women. Thus, they often support technologies that are inappropriate for small-scale production, especially growing food.

Links between policymakers and extension workers are also weak. Without sufficient feedback, policies do not promote technologies that are suited to local situations. In many cases, they actually create an environment that favours the dissemination of technologies that are harmful to ecological systems. For example, government policies in many African countries have supported plant protection methods that are harmful to the environment in the long run (Gata 1992). The exclusion of women from the policy formulation and monitoring has contributed to negative results.

Impact of inappropriate technology

In Africa, some development change agents have criticized the appropriate technology approach. They have raised the questions: appropriate for whom? who benefits? and why do African women now need appropriate technology? Originating in the North, "appropriate" technology continues to be designed with little or no consultation with, let alone participation from, end-users. Because the technology is not designed, owned, or controlled by its users, it cannot contribute significantly to sustainable livelihood security, including food security.

Most externally driven technologies have ignored the existing gender-based division of labour and have not accounted for the physical, social, and cultural differences in various localities. Research has revealed that female labour becomes displaced with mechanization, because men as the focus of technology take over the related tasks. Technologies have made men's work lighter, while in many cases actually increasing women's work burden. For example, many water and sanitation programs have introduced water pumps designed for the physique of male users. The fact that women and girls are responsible for fetching water in many societies does not appear to have been considered. Therefore, many pumps remain unused, while women continued to walk long distances to fetch water from rivers and wells (authors' observations).

In theory, the search for appropriate technology has inherent merits because it views technology as a social process. Thus, its intention is to facilitate access to, use of, and control over technologies in food production and processing by resource-poor women, making "women's projects" its key target. However, the promoters of such technology, including — sometimes mainly — women from the North, did not consider women as farmers. The cook stove gained much attention, although its value could not be understood by women farmers. According to one woman farmer (in 1976):

> Men have always been going for agricultural training. Very few of us went between 1964 and 1970. Never before that date. What they taught us cannot help us much. Our friends [men] were taught piggery, how to use tractors, etc. We were taught how to make scones, how to cook and with what tools. How can that help us with our farming?

Research approaches

In the last two decades, international and national research institutions have made special efforts to address the problems of smallholder producers who depend on rain-fed agriculture in marginal areas. Inclusion of social scientists on research teams is a positive step toward making such research more people-centred. However, these efforts have not adequately integrated women farmers in the research cycle, because of the approaches adopted.

The "farming systems research" approach was a direct response to the need to focus on smallholder agriculture under varying conditions. This method recognized the importance of location specificity in the development of solutions. It promotes technology-sharing as opposed to technology transfer. Participatory methods in particular have the potential for putting local knowledge in its rightful place. In addition to learning from and appreciating the local physical and social situation, researchers start with local resources and capacities and, together with end-users, develop technologies that meet the needs of communities.

Participatory research empowers resource-poor farmers because it gives them a sense of ownership and control over technology. In Nepal, for example, a local farmer took over the work of a scientist after the latter had left (Biggs 1989). The farmer pulled together a team of colleagues to test varieties of a particular tree species for use in intercropping. The project was a success. The formal scientist had used a consultative approach, but the participatory approach of the farmers deepened their sense of ownership of the results. In Zambia, farmers in Luapula and Lusaka provinces had been testing various methods of agriculture and pest control. When the Adaptive Research Planning Team from the national central research station focused on this area — perhaps because of the farmers' efforts — they found a rich source of scientific knowledge. The team drew on some of the farmers' experiments and built on their results.

More emphasis on beginning with the local resources would shift attention back to women farmers, as custodians of a large body of local knowledge.

Constraints persist

Policies that militate against food security seem to persist despite governments' continuing expression of support to smallholder farmers. Although government structures, policies, and attitudes have been the major factors causing the marginalization of women, social organization has also played a decisive role. The last few years have seen shifts in attitudes; however, national intent remains confined to declarations, decrees, expressions of sympathy, acknowledgement of women's worth, and political rhetoric.

In Asia and Latin America, governments have lauded the roles of women's groups and farming families in bringing about the Green Revolution. In Africa, at the height of the food crisis of the 1980s, government organs were urged to invest in women's activities. Women were specifically mentioned and their problems addressed in some national plans.

At the international level, relevant organizations within the UN system have been calling on national governments to acknowledge women. At the World Conference on Agrarian Reform and Rural Development (FAO 1979), participants recommended the establishment of "special recruitment and training schemes for women extension workers" (IV.A.ii); expansion of extension services "to specifically include those tasks involving women" (IV.A.iii); and the promotion by governments of "collective action by rural women to enhance their opportunities to participate in activities on an equal footing with men" (IV.C.iii).

In 1984, the Advisory Committee on Science and Technology for Development (UN 1984, para. 69) stated, "Where new technologies displace women, alternatives, including retraining where necessary, should be included in the project proposal."

At the end of the UN's decade for women, women still appeared to be marginalized: "Also important are the dissemination of information to rural women ... using all available media and established women's groups; ... the participation of women farmers in research and information campaigns; and ... in technical co-operation among countries" (UN 1985b, para 181).

In 1987, pushing for sustainable livelihood security, the World Commission on Environment and Development's (WCED's) advisory panel on food security called for a focus on women, a theme that was adopted and promoted by WCED (1987). At the Earth Summit in 1992, women were singled out in the search for solutions to global threats to environmental sustainability — a basis for food security (UN 1992a).

Some organizations, such as the FAO, have made it a policy to recruit as many women as possible and encourage national governments to do the same (FAO 1990b). The Consultative Group on International Agricultural Research (CGIAR) is urging international agricultural research centres to identify women scientists in the Third World and make use of their expertise (Gapasin 1993).

Systemic barriers

Despite these recommendations and many more, women's control over, involvement in, and access to S&T remain problematic. Established institutions seem to maintain barriers for a variety of reasons. First, S&T institutions and actors have inadequate accountability to those who bear the consequences of their decisions and actions. Second, S&T as a discipline is too narrowly defined; it seldom extends to the social consequences of technology. Third, mainstream S&T activities are generally planned and implemented in a top-down manner, omitting the views of end-users. Fourth, the nature of training for and the practice of S&T tend to isolate the field from the people and, because it is male dominated, communication with women is particularly constrained.

Shortage of gender-sensitive scientists

Gender-sensitive technology requires clearly set out research priorities and agendas. This calls for gender sensitivity at the policymaking and technology development levels. However, women's representation in these areas is extremely limited. In sub-Saharan Africa, for example, women constitute about 3.4% of professionals in agriculture (Winrock International 1988). The few women who are involved in research and technology development do not demonstrate much gender sensitivity. The figure is even lower at policymaking levels. Women continue to lag behind in training institutions, such as university and agricultural colleges. In sub-Saharan Africa, they constitute fewer than 18% of all students enroled in agricultural training institutions.

The pattern is the same in most Asian countries (APPRO-TECH Asia 1992). In 1990 in Indonesia, women constituted only 16% of professionals in the Ministry of Agriculture; in Vietnam, only 24% of agriculture scientists working at major research centres were women. In the same year, fewer than 3% of the students enroled at the agricultural university in Bangladesh were women. Women have not established a critical mass necessary for bringing about change. Although creating this critical mass is desirable, however, it must be accompanied by gender sensitization if women are to make an impact.

The lack of gender-sensitive scientists presents a fundamental problem in that changes cannot be initiated from within the discipline itself. If such scientists took the lead in accepting and using local S&T, it would quickly gain recognition and, therefore, value. This would encourage more participatory approaches to technology development.

The process of establishing a new vision of S&T has led to various initiatives that recognize women's contributions. The collection of gender-disaggregated data on S&T undertaken by UNIFEM (1993a) for volume 2 of *The World's Women*, for example, is useful in presenting evidence of what women are doing. Many researchers are also documenting local knowledge systems and acknowledging women innovators. Such international recognition of women's achievements and the trend toward networking are helping to increase women's professional visibility in the traditionally male domain.

Inadequate support systems

Most smallholder producers in rain-fed agricultural areas have not benefited much from the new farming systems because of inadequate support. For example, where smallholdings require irrigation to sustain production using biological technologies, it has either not been forthcoming or men, the assumed market producers, have taken charge of them. A number of irrigation schemes have not only not benefited women, they have increased their labour input, further threatening food production and security.

Policymakers have paid some attention to women farmers as a result of donor pressure; some projects require that a portion of the funding be targeted at women. Women are often included in these programs haphazardly or as appendices rather than as an integral part of national development plans.

Some governments are taking positive steps to redress gender imbalances. However, results have not been encouraging, for lack of adequate support systems. For example, a presidential decree might call for equal access to the means and factors of production, processing, or credit by women, but it might not be backed up by legislation and structures to make implementation possible. For example, such a decree in Kenya in 1988 prohibited disposal of land without consultation with spouse or other female family members. It has failed to have the desired effect, because it is not yet enacted in legislation.

Inequitable allocation of resources

Public investment in agriculture, particularly smallholder agriculture, remains low. At a meeting in April 1994, 22 ministers of agriculture from east and southern Africa ranked agriculture sixth on a list of priority areas for resource allocation and the smallholder sector received one-fifth of the resources allocated to agriculture (Rukuni 1994). In 1990, the agricultural loans disbursed by the Agricultural Finance Corporation of Zimbabwe amounted to 200 million ZWD,[2] of which only 17% (34.5 million ZWD) went to smallholder producers; of that portion, less than 5% went to women farmers (AFCZ 1991).

Government institutions spend less time on research on resource-poor agriculture systems and subsistence food crops. The bulk of funded research is on cash crops, generally grown by farmers who already have substantial resources. Despite its potential for improving resource-poor systems and food production, the thrust of research has been on crops destined for the market. Those for domestic consumption are frequently ignored by plant breeders. Food security will require policies and approaches that increase food production by rural and urban women.

Lessons from the field

It appears that most countries are caught up in a top-down syndrome: we know, you learn; we have, you lack. However, in the last few decades, changes have occurred, partly as a result of the failures that litter the development scene. In the late 1970s and early 1980s, some organizations within the UN system shifted from being informed by failures to being guided by successes. In 1981, for example, the then

[2] In February 1995, 16 Zimbabwean dollars (ZWD) = I United States dollar (USD).

Rural Employment Policies Branch of the International Labour Organisation's (ILO's) World Employment Programme commissioned a study that focused on successful initiatives for improving the working conditions of rural women in Africa and Asia (Muntemba 1985). Twenty-five projects were identified; the following four illustrate how a local group, an NGO, and a government initiative have contributed to food security.

Increasing agricultural productivity through cooperation

In central Zambia, a group of village women responded to "conscientization" seminars by forming a cooperative to focus on increasing their crop yields (Stjernstedt 1985). By the end of the second year, cooperative members began realize impressive returns from the sale of produce and could generate and control enough income to meet household needs. Elements contributing to the success of this project included:

✦ A tenurial system that enabled women (married or single) to secure land to grow crops under their own control.

✦ An enabling political climate. The political party in power had a women's section (Women's League) charged with reporting women's aspirations to the central body. Village women used this avenue to obtain leadership training to help them in aspects of group organization and operating the group's credit facility.

✦ Available credit. Although the district had been producing food for the market much longer than other parts of the country, capital accumulation, especially by women, remained low, impeding access to more productive technology. With the support of the Ministry of Agriculture, women were able to secure a credit facility.

✦ Access to more efficient technology. The district had been exposed to modern technology since the 1910s, but it had benefited men. To increase output and because women's labour remained critical in the agricultural system, men taught women in their families how to use the machinery and modern methods. When the cooperative was formed, women were able to use some of this technology.

✦ Availability of markets. Clearly, women's first priority was household food security. However, group solidarity enabled them to demand that enough food be reserved from the family plot (under their husbands' control). To meet their secondary aim of income creation, they sold fresh produce in the nearby town, Mumbwa. They also marketed maize (grown commercially) alongside the family produce, with the clear understanding that the cooperative would get all the proceeds from these sales.

This case demonstrates the successful implementation of the *Nairobi Forward-Looking Strategies* recommendation: "Women's participation in programmes and projects to promote food security should be enhanced by providing them with opportunities ... to receive training in leadership, administration and financial management" (UN 1985b, para. 179).

Empowerment to achieve livelihood security

The Working Women's Forum (WWF) acknowledged powerlessness as an acute malaise afflicting rural and urban poor women in India and reinforcing their vulnerability (Azad 1985). This NGO aimed to increase the collective power of self-employed slum women, peasants, and fisherwomen to allow them to operate in the market and negotiate with money lenders, middlemen, and landlords for access to land and credit. In 1984, WWF had mobilized over 16 000 petty traders, 5 000 rural workers, 1 500 Agarbathi rollers, and 2 000 beedi workers. The income of these women buys 60% or more of their household needs including food. In addition to joining a union, the women were extended credit through the Working Women's Credit Society. The success of this project has been facilitated by several factors.

- ✦ The organizational structure, which allows groups to elect their own leaders who work with WWF officers to identify the services, tools, and training they need in their various occupations and pass the information along to WWF's head office. Leaders act as guarantors for the borrowers and are responsible for collection of repayments and subscriptions.

- ✦ Reinforcement of a sense of belonging through activities that build solidarity, such as support in times of need and visits to each other's workplace.

- ✦ Availability of credit.

- ✦ Access to more efficient, more productive, and less labour-intensive technologies, such as grinding machines for sellers of rice-cakes, push carts for vendors, and solar dryers for fish sellers. Women are able to obtain this equipment on credit.

◆ Conscientization seminars addressing such issues as civil rights, physical abuse, and dowries. These helped women place their struggle within the broader context of inequity, oppression, and gender relations.

The approach WWF adopted in helping these workers was to adapt technology to the women's own activities rather than the other way around. It practiced what others were warned against at the Nairobi conference: "Appropriate food processing technologies ... should be designed and introduced ... in a manner that ensures women's access to the new technology and to its benefits and does not displace women from means of livelihood when alternative opportunities are not available" (UN 1985b, para. 184).

Livestock production for food and income

Another of WWF's rural activities — the Livestock-for-Landless Project to allow women to establish milk production and sales enterprises — demonstrates the value of NGO–government collaboration (Azad 1985).

"We do not starve any more," reported women who, before the project, had earned 60 rupees[3] a month, working 8–10 hours a day. With cattle obtained through the scheme, they made up to 100–200 rupees a month. Success was made possible by:

◆ An open organizational structure that enabled women to express their needs freely;

◆ WWF solidarity with the poor in negotiations for a credit facility with a local national bank;

◆ Availability of a market for the milk they produced through a local dairy farm;

◆ Support from the national government through the Indian Council of Agricultural Research — Scientists visited the area for rural orientation training. Then, they offered training to 60 members in simple technology of animal husbandry. The trainees shared the information with their colleagues in the project. Thus, a nonofficial, nonintimidating extension system was created. A veterinarian was always present to advise on the health of cows before they were purchased.

---

[3] In February 1995, 30 Indian rupees (INR) = 1 United States dollar (USD).

+ Conscientization seminars that have enabled women to with-
stand overtures from male relations wishing to undertake
selling on their behalf.

Adopting and adapting technology for food processing

Fisherwomen in Sierra Leone adopted, adapted, and experimented
with fish-processing technology until more efficient, cost-effective,
and durable equipment was developed (Steady 1985). Initially, the
women used simple methods such as open smoking, solar drying,
grilling, frying, and salting to preserve their fish. They began using a
simple smoking oven. In the 1950s, fishermen from Ghana introduced fishing and processing technology that the women adapted to
create a much more efficient oven that allowed them to handle big-
ger catches and take advantage of a growing urban market within
Sierra Leone and in neighbouring Liberia.

In the 1980s, the Federal Republic of Germany supported a
government project to introduce a more efficient oven. Women were
attracted to it because it reduced fuel consumption by 60%; repair
costs were lower, resulting in an overall saving of 160–200 leones a
month in operating costs; it saved time; it was easier and safer to use;
and it lasted twice as long as the type they were using. Despite the
need for two people to handle a drying tray, the overall performance
of the new style of oven has been significantly better and has resulted
in higher incomes for participating households. The adaptation of
this technology was possible mainly because:

+ Women acted collectively in experimentation and in bargaining with shrewd fishermen on the one hand and more
sophisticated women from towns and Liberia on the other.

+ Women interacted with neighbouring communities and were
willing to learn from them.

+ The project staff worked with the women to produce an
acceptable design. In consultation with the women, they
developed a prototype oven for experimentation and demon-
stration. The women were able to alter the design so that the
final product was the result of interaction between them as
"beneficiaries" and project staff.

+ Local materials and human resources were used, reinforcing
a sense of ownership of the technology by the village
women.

Government efforts

In some countries, governments have initiated measures to increase access to and control over factors of production by the producers themselves. For example, the Africa Party for the Independence of Guinea and Cape Verde (PAIGC) began by tackling ideological conflicts to make reforms equitable (Urdang 1979). Its approach comprised the following steps: teaching about ideological conflicts; promoting changes in the gender-determined division of labour in households; socializing production at the household level; and, finally, moving on to structural reorganization. By 1978, there were indications of a social reorientation and agricultural systems were being reshaped.

India presents an interesting case regarding the use of S&T. Once a country of famines and food imports, government policy after independence was aimed at establishing food security, at least at the national level, through investment in S&T. Steps were taken to strengthen the scientific base of productivity. A team of scientists was mobilized and research centres strengthened, laying the ground for the Green Revolution.

India has a large population of landless people and, therefore, food insecurity among the poor. It has recorded national food surpluses, while many of its citizens are chronically hungry. The Green Revolution technology has had negative social, economic, and environmental impacts, but the country also sets an example of sufficient productivity founded on a solid S&T base. Perhaps the social questions raised by this national S&T success story demonstrate innate shortcomings of today's S&T.

In the Philippines, the government has invested in women's scientific education (Gapasin 1993). As a result, the country boasts one of the highest proportions of women physical and natural scientists (50%) in the world.

Recommendations

We have described the paradox that lies in the fact that the number of those threatened by food insecurity is increasing despite international pledges to "end hunger." Although national governments acknowledge the need for food self-sufficiency, most of the poor continue to be marginalized as assets, information, and technology pass into the hands of the financially and politically powerful.

Male-dominated power structures fail to relate to women at a time of acclaimed acknowledgement of the latter's contribution to agricultural, specifically food, production. At the household level, women lack access to productive technology. At the institutional and national levels, policies continue to discriminate against women in terms of access to and control over land, trees, technology, credit, markets, and so forth. Determining how to build on and use women's knowledge base so that modern S&T can benefit from it and strengthen women's efforts remains a problem..

Establishing food security calls for strategies in which grass-roots communities own, control, and play effective roles in technological choices and development. We recommend the following:

✦ A reversal of the trends that marginalize women to achieve food security and improve gender relations. To do this, national governments must allocate 10% of their national budgets to food production, storage, and processing technology as defined in consultation with rural and urban women — the end-users.

✦ Appropriate organs within the UN system, especially FAO, CGIAR, and UNIFEM, should set up a 5-year grant to enable researchers from five developing countries to work with NGOs and communities to develop and test people-centred, women-friendly, research methods, specifically geared toward empowering resource-poor female food producers.

✦ International and national research centres should set specific annual targets for the recruitment of women scientists so that a critical mass is reached by the year 2000. These scientists should be trained in gender issues so that they bring gender sensitivity to food technology.

Chapter 5
A crisis in power

Energy planning for development

Judi Wangalwa Wakhungu
and Elizabeth Cecelski

Events of the past 20 years have transformed energy from a little-known technical issue into a matter of prominent civic and political concern. Dramatic increases of oil prices in 1973 and 1974 and the subsequent changes in the international oil market resulted in a proliferation of policies and publications on the subject of energy resources management. *The Limits to Growth* (Meadows et al. 1972) and *A Blueprint for Survival* (Goldsmith et al. 1972) warned of the consequences of industrial society's excessive use of natural resources such as oil. Eckholm (1975) compared diminishing oil resources with accelerated deforestation in Africa, Asia, and Latin America. This gave birth to the household energy sector as a legitimate concern in energy-policy analyses, and with it a focus on women. In 1981, the United Nations (UN) held a conference to examine the relevance of small-scale renewable energy technology for developing countries (Foley 1991). In the rush to address such problems, socioeconomic issues such as gender roles, which ought to have been useful in guiding policy formulation, were not fully appreciated (Leach and Mearns 1988). According to Sontheimer (1991, p. 83):

> New agricultural technologies often make life even harder for women. When a male head of the household is given credit to buy a cultivator or share a tractor, he soon begins to cultivate more land. His wife and his daughters must then weed a larger area in the same time. When fast-growing "improved" tree species are introduced, they usually provide a cash crop, often at the expense of multipurpose species that are used by women for food and fodder production [as well as] a source of income.... In timber-rich Borneo, men and women have traditionally worked at wood-cutting as family teams. When heavy chain saws were introduced to improve productivity, women were effectively

excluded from an activity that had valuable social as
well as fiscal functions.

Participants at the UN Conference on Science and Technology for Development acknowledged that the rewards of modern science and technology (S&T) were not enjoyed equally by all groups of
society (UN 1979b). They may in fact have adverse effects on the
socioeconomic status of women and their contribution to the development process. In addition, disparities are much more acute in
developing countries than in developed ones (Sontheimer 1991). This
viewpoint was reiterated in *The Nairobi Forward-Looking Strategies for
the Advancement of Women* (UN 1985b), which stated that both the
potential and actual impact of S&T on factors affecting women's integration into various sectors, their health, and socioeconomic status
should be assessed.

However, conventional energy planning, which relies heavily on S&T developments, is based on the premise that the effects of
energy technologies are gender neutral. This situation has been exacerbated by the fact that, until recently, we lacked information about
women's active and productive roles in energy matters. Cecelski
(1992) argues that this cursory approach has been inadvertent; not
only women, but also socioeconomic issues, have on the whole been
omitted from the energy paradigm.

For no cogent reason, prominent positions in society, as well
as within S&T and hence the energy sector, are the exclusive
province of men (Overholt 1984; Rothschild 1988; Østergaard 1992).
The goals of S&T reflect the goals of society as well as the political
structures in which S&T are set (Morin 1993). In this way, S&T as
enterprises comprise both subjective (through value judgements) and
objective elements (Bleir 1984). These influence the direction of scientific inquiry and its application to practical matters in energy:
which energy problems are addressed, which experiments are performed, and which energy research is supported. The implication is
not that S&T are inherently masculine, but, because S&T evolved
within a patriarchal society, women's knowledge was excluded and
the practical outcomes of these disciplines had a masculine bias
(Harding 1986; Schiebinger 1989; Noble 1992).

Thus, energy means work, kinetic energy, potential energy,
mass-equivalent energy, and heat. Energy technologies, for example,
engines, breeder reactors, and turbines, harness energy in service-
able forms, such as useful heat, mechanical work, and electricity.
Work done using metabolic energy and small-scale energy technologies based on biomass are considered peripheral. The status quo is
biased toward the socioeconomic groups that have access to "high
tech" energy resources and technologies and discriminates against

the vast majority of the world's population who cannot afford these technologies. This situation is especially acute in the South where a large proportion of the "poorest of the poor" are rural and urban households headed by women (Sontheimer 1991).

Energy and development

Energy is an essential component of a modern economy. A significant proportion of the global economy is dedicated to providing energy services in the form of cooking, heating, lighting, motors, appliances, and industrial processes. Nearly all available energy — fossil fuels, biomass, wind, and incoming radiation — can be traced to the sun or, as in the case of nuclear power, to the process of cosmic evolution that preceded the origin of the solar system. Smaller amounts of energy are derived from lunar motion (tidal power) or from the earth's core (geothermal power). Fossil fuels currently provide 78% of the energy consumed globally; renewable energy, including hydropower and biomass, account for 18%, and nuclear power provides 4% (Davis 1990).

Countries in the South depend largely on noncommercial energy. Therefore, their per-capita energy consumption is much lower than that of the North, which, however, uses two-thirds of the world's energy. Technological advances allow industrialized countries to employ more efficient means of energy consumption. Because of widespread inefficiency, developing countries require 40% more energy than developed ones to produce the same value of goods and services (Lenssen 1993). This gross inefficiency — of cement plants, light bulbs, vehicles, stoves, and so forth — offers untold opportunities to reduce the amount and cost of energy while expanding the services it provides (Wakhungu 1993).

In their efforts to improve the lives of people in the South, multilateral and bilateral energy planners have clung to a questionable assumption: a growing energy supply is requisite to raising standards of living. Because high energy use is a conspicuous trait of most developed countries, this assumption seems logical. In practice, however, the fallacy of equating energy consumption with economic performance has become more apparent. In the past 30 years, countries in the South have more than quadrupled their energy consumption. Yet the energy policies that have facilitated this growth have left these countries staggering from oil-price shocks, grappling with foreign debt, and suffering from environmental and health problems, while still facing severe energy shortages (Lenssen 1993).

A new model for energy use is needed. The emerging belief is that the links between energy, the environment, and social welfare are inextricable. Although energy is an integral component of development, increasing energy supplies (for example, through large-scale energy projects) does not guarantee improved social welfare. The energy services, not energy per se nor "techno-fixes," satisfy people's needs (Wakhungu 1993). Focusing on people, who must be empowered with know-how and access to resources, makes the issue of energy and development much more receptive to gender considerations.

Empirical knowledge about gender and energy issues

Substantive interest in gender and energy can be traced back to the fuelwood crisis during the 1970s in many countries in the South. Although a substantial body of research developed (see Cecelski 1992) and UN initiatives to explore women's role in energy issues intensified, most of this work focused on fuelwood and stove programs. In the 1980s, energy-policy initiatives identified and described the critical role played by women in the household energy and forestry sectors. They portrayed women variously as:

- ✦ Victims of energy scarcity and related ecological problems, which were manifested by a decline in the standard of living of women and their families;

- ✦ Managers of energy and other natural resources in the household, agricultural, and small-industry sectors;

- ✦ Marginalized by development programs on the whole, including those related to energy, and having less access to credit, technology, education, land, and services; and

- ✦ Actors instrumental in developing innovative energy strategies, in taking remedial action, and in disseminating new ideas at all levels from global to local.

Cecelski's (1992) literature review, in particular, is a stark reminder that the nuances involved in factoring gender into energy and development have yet to be fully understood. For example, research on the implications of S&T know-how, S&T advancements, and modern energy-sector policies on women's livelihoods is urgently needed (Sontheimer 1991, pp. 83–84):

> For example, shea butter is the major cooking oil used in many semi-arid areas of Africa. It is processed from

the nut of the tree *Butyrospermum parkii* by women who sell the surplus. The process, however, requires heating and prolonged whipping. Women have often requested labor- and energy-saving technologies for the job, but these have yet to be developed.

Nevertheless, the foundation for future initiatives that put S&T and gender issues on the energy agenda has been laid and has potential for helping to solve many of our current energy problems. Will women increasingly be able to participate in shaping our future energy agenda? How can organizations such as the UN be instrumental in facilitating this process? Women have contributions to make to energy policymaking at every level: R&D, implementation, and leadership in international forums.

Key policy themes and suggestions for future research

Although S&T are essential ingredients for innovation in energy, substantive efforts devoted to ameliorating women's subordinate position in the energy policymaking arena by making explicit use of S&T knowledge are minimal. Gender aspects of issues affecting innovation and diffusion within the energy sector are discussed here in relation to

+ Education and training in energy resources management;

+ Global energy policy;

+ Small- and medium-scale enterprises; and

+ Poverty and basic needs.

Regarding the first two themes, there are no exemplary models to evaluate per se, but suggestions for future research are highlighted. This oversight illustrates the lacuna between policies and substantive action, as well as the paucity of information on women's issues in the prevailing energy sector. The other two themes are well documented. Significant strides have been made in improving the basis for policy formulation as well as the nature of policies themselves. However, much remains to be done, especially mobilizing and integrating, more effectively, women's concerns in energy policymaking and planning and making more effective use of S&T to further this process.

Education and training in energy resources management

In the prevailing S&T model, energy is a highly technical field and, therefore, dominated by practitioners of the basic sciences, engineering, mathematics, and economics, as well as political scientists, sociologists, and lawyers. These areas, especially basic sciences, engineering, and mathematics, remain male bastions. For example, in the United States, only 16% of employed scientists and engineers are female. Despite efforts to redress this imbalance, worldwide attrition rates of women in the sciences and engineering — especially in physics, geology, and engineering — are high (Holloway 1993). This situation is compounded by the fact that male scientists have great difficulty understanding the obstacles that women must overcome to pursue careers in science, mathematics, and engineering (Lane 1994). As reported by Kammen and Lankford (1991):

> In their commentary on solar cooking, Kammen and Lankford gave pride of place to the box-type-cooker. But this design suffers from several drawbacks.... [They] require that cooking be done in direct sunlight and during the middle of the day ... [and] they lack storage facilities and have no provision for frying.
>
> In a bid to overcome some of these problems, a cooker with fresnel lens was designed. A large fresnel lens is used to heat a container surrounded by an annular cavity filled with ammoniated salts of magnesium chloride and calcium chloride. Heat is stored chemically in these compounds and is released on demand at 300°C.
>
> Another system that has storage but is less expensive than the above, uses heat pipes for parabolic as well as flat-plate collectors. In this arrangement, an evaporator with minimum shading effect is placed at the focus of the solar collector. The energy reaching the evaporator is conveyed rapidly to the condenser end of the heat pipe. The condenser, in the form of cooking chamber, is located in the shade or inside the kitchen. As the shaded cooking chamber is well insulated, pot losses associated with wind will not arise. This system uses energy from sunshine and will not allow reverse circulation losses, due to its diode-like operation. Because of the unique feature of isothermal operation of heat pipes, temperatures on a flat-plate collector equipped with a heat pipe will be forced to follow the temperatures in the condenser section. A. Jagadeesh,

Society of Science for the People, 2/210, Nawabpet, Nel-
loore-524002, Andhra Pradesh, India.

[K & L reply] Jagadeesh's letter is similar to several that we have received in response to our article. It
describes technically sophisticated designs for solar
cookers that will achieve higher temperatures than our
simple box cooker. The question is whether they will
be used or not.

Not only are the designs technically complex and
rather expensive, but one of them uses magnesium
chloride battery salts that could be harmful to livestock
or children if the batteries were dumped or broken and
the salts consumed.

We strongly support the notion that a diversity of
solar and other renewable technology systems is necessary to support energy self-sufficient development,
but we feel that Jagadeesh has missed the essential
point concerning ovens. We have found that when the
end-user (nearly always a woman) makes her own
oven, her interest in using it is very high. If someone
else makes and donates the oven or significant components, her interest is substantially less. For this reason
we believe that until solar cooking equipment has
become commonplace a design that can be made
locally is essential for widespread acceptance of this
technology.

Examples of the ramifications of male bias in the household-
energy sector of developing countries are well known. They include:

+ Designing stoves that were incompatible with end-users'
  (primarily women) needs;

+ Disregarding women's knowledge about the properties of
  various fuels; and

+ Assuming that energy efficiency was the predominant
  household concern.

Ramifications, if any, of male bias in the modern energy sector of various countries remain unexplored.

Neglect of appropriate education and training can seriously
hinder energy-development efforts as well as undermine the full participation of women in the development process. Too often, women
are perceived as not having the ability to apply relevant knowledge
to their energy issues, and as lacking the negotiating skills that are
essential for designing and implementing energy-policy reforms.

A host of documents recommend policy formulation in this domain. For example, *The Nairobi Forward-Looking Strategies* (UN 1985b) stated that women should be offered more opportunities and be encouraged to pursue studies in the sciences, engineering, and mathematics. It called for "the full and effective participation of women" in all decisions about and implementation of S&T.

However, the relevant knowledge and skills that women require to improve their effectiveness in energy-policy analysis have not been fully defined. In turn, it is difficult to devise curricula and design associated teaching materials without a clear view of training needs. The gap between discourse and action, in the energy context, is most evident here; efforts to educate women in the S&T of energy are few despite attempts by the UN and other international agencies to improve this situation.

The sole exception is the work of the International Research and Training Institute for the Advancement of Women (INSTRAW), which, in cooperation with Volunteers in Technical Assistance (VITA), is implementing a project to "improve linkages between women and energy sector policies, programs and projects with special reference to new and renewable sources of energy." Funded by the UN Development Programme's (UNDP's) Office for Project Services, the project seeks to

> Develop a systematic approach to integrating women fully into the mainstream of energy planning and programming for energy development by demonstrating through pilot projects how women can be drawn into participating fully in these sectoral issues. The project will also contribute to redirecting, refocusing and orchestrating the imperfectly coordinated efforts existing in different ministries, departments and agencies to secure the more efficient involvement of women in energy programs and projects [INSTRAW mandate, para. 60].
>
> The expected output for the first year of the project includes a situational analysis, draft methodological approach, framework and plan of operations for involving women more effectively in the energy sector activities, preparation of a national high-level consultative meeting and preparation of prototype training curricula [para. 62].
>
> The major constraints to involving women more effectively at various levels in the energy sector, as indicated from the situational analysis for the two project countries, included lack of education, lack of participation or consultation of women in energy projects,

energy projects that did not target women, lack of information and training, lack of involvement of women [para. 65].

The few other initiatives, although worthy, emphasize women's prominent role in the household energy and informal sectors. For example, the food technology source books developed by the UN Development Fund for Women give women instructions for labour-saving food technologies (see, for example, UNIFEM 1993b). The Intermediate Technology Development Group (ITDG) and the Stockholm Environment Institute (SEI) have developed instructional materials on a range of renewable energy technologies for a variety of sectors (Kristoferson and Bokalders 1991). The Economic Development Institute (EDI) of the World Bank conducts energy policy and planning seminars for senior staff (some of whom are women) of various energy agencies (Siddayao 1990). However, these do not highlight women per se.

Because energy issues affect virtually every sector of society, the scope for energy education and training programs is large. It covers universities, research institutes, technical training institutes, formal and informal programs for energy policymakers and planners, and activities designed to improve the general public's understanding of energy issues (Unesco 1981). Research should focus on finding the pedagogical approach needed to equip women from all walks of life with the skills required to make informed energy choices. This entails expanding on INSTRAW's initiative and monitoring the results of the pilot projects in Burkina Faso, Malawi, Mali, and Zambia.

Women must develop a better understanding of energy issues: where we are headed with current policies and where we ought to go. Globally, some difficult choices — forced by economic, political, and environmental considerations — will have to be made soon. Eventual solutions will rely on conservation (the cheapest alternative in the short run) and alternative energy supplies. Alternatives will include those currently in use, such as hydropower, but a greater role will be played by renewable sources such as the sun and wind. Many energy resources must be used; research conducted by both men and women is needed so that the best options will be available when we need them. Areas where women's input is currently lacking include:

✦ Long-term energy planning, coordination of education among all sectors, and international cooperation to deal with problems of future supply and global ecology that stem from current practices;

- ✦ R&D on long-term energy alternatives: sunlight, wind, bio-mass, geothermal energy, fission breeder reactors, and fusion;

- ✦ Development of national and international standards for energy use in all sectors;

- ✦ Information concerning the state of the art in pertinent energy technologies;

- ✦ Increasing the energy efficiency of end-use technologies;

- ✦ R&D on alternatives to petroleum for transportation, for example, electric and hydrogen-powered vehicles; and

- ✦ Energy conservation for buildings, appliances, windows, and lighting.

How can women's participation in energy policymaking be expanded? If energy education and training for women were pursued, what form would this training take? How can gender considerations be represented in teaching methods? The following study areas are suggested.

Long-term education and training: Explore how long-term education and training for both men and women can be conducted by introducing energy considerations into the curricula of all relevant disciplines. It is worth investigating whether there is a niche for energy education throughout the schooling process, from primary and secondary schools to technical institutions and universities. Investigate how the training of teachers at each of these levels can be conducted, as well as the preparation of curricula and teaching materials dealing with energy. Energy issues can be presented as part of a complete picture (for example, from energy resources to technologies to power generation) and in the context of development.

In rural areas of developing countries, focusing on energy issues at the primary level may be particularly important as this may be the only formal education most girls receive. Moreover, attitudes about energy inculcated at this time could have a profound effect, not only on the students but also on their parents. This may enhance energy awareness in the general public (for example, of energy-efficiency techniques). Curricula might include the maintenance and repair of energy devices and adaptation of nonlocal designs to local needs and materials (Unesco 1981).

Short-term education and training: To disseminate the latest developments in energy, short courses for energy planners at all levels, teachers, civil servants, private-sector personnel, and extension agents have been developed in many countries (Unesco 1981). Research on updating course materials to include gender considerations is warranted. At local, national, and international levels, priorities for research and action should be

+ Assessing specific education and training needs and the capability of existing institutions to meet these needs;

+ Establishing or strengthening formal and informal training programs for policymakers and energy-planning specialists, technical specialists, fieldworkers, extension workers, local administrators, and teachers;

+ Establishing programs to promote and improve public understanding of energy, preferably within a broader program of understanding of the role of energy-resources development;

+ Developing and distributing appropriate curricula and teaching materials to facilitate training; and

+ Reviewing and, where appropriate, increasing scholarships and fellowships for in-country and foreign study and exchange of students and faculty.

Gender issues and global energy policy

Although a forum for articulating a uniform global energy policy does not exist, multilateral and bilateral policies have widespread effects on energy availability, environmental quality, and the social welfare of a cross-section of people — especially in developing countries (Cecelski 1992). To further compound the issue, energy planners at the international level have not paid much attention to the relations between gender roles, energy-resource management, and social welfare.

Increasing women's participation in energy policymaking is consistent with *Agenda 21*'s (UN 1992a) call for engaging all relevant stakeholders, especially women, in the development process and in managing technological change. Yet women's substantive participation is minimal. For example, the UN has yet to fulfill its promise to promote women to fill 25% of its decision-making positions (Cecelski 1992).

What ramifications does energy decision-making at the global level have on local environments, women's livelihoods, and other marginalized groups in both the North and South? What mechanisms link these issues at the international level to the local level? Who makes these decisions?

These issues were the subject of an expert meeting *Women and Energy: New Directions for Policy Research* held in Dakar, Senegal, in January 1994 (IFIAS and IFAN 1994). The objective of the meeting was to explore a phenomenon that has been given little attention: the critical analysis of global energy issues; the politics that shape these issues; and the political, social, and economic implications of these issues for women and for society as a whole. Another goal was to identify prime areas for future research (such as energy pricing and energy policy and planning) and to establish an informal network of researchers, organizations, and donors interested in furthering this agenda.

Some of the recommendations made by workshop participants include the following research:

✦ A review of existing regional mechanisms for energy policy in the Americas, Asia, and Africa;

✦ Including women in regional institutions concerned with S&T education;

✦ Including women in national institutions that make energy-policy decisions;

✦ Devising criteria for energy policymaking that incorporate the allocation of resources to benefit people rather than simply using financial and technological criteria;

✦ Promotion of S&T research grants for documentation of successful energy technology interventions; and

✦ Getting beyond the "stove" mentality concerning energy issues in Africa and Asia.

Outside the household energy sector in developing countries, little effort is made to correlate women's command of energy issues with the successful identification of women's needs and effective diffusion of new energy technologies. Therefore, it is unclear to what degree the absence of women energy planners impedes the resolution and identification of women's energy requirements. The increased representation of women will not automatically make energy organizations function differently. Research on the attitudes of professional women in energy-planning institutions is needed.

Gender-disaggregated information is also required on where women stand in relation to men regarding energy decision-making; how various energy policies affect women and men; and how women are affecting these energy policies. Can a cadre of women energy planners and policymakers bring a distinctive perspective to energy policymaking?

Small- and medium-sized enterprises

Women play a dominant role in many energy-intensive small- and medium-sized enterprises and home industries, especially in food and beverage processing (see also Marcelle and Jacob, this volume). Women's roles in the energy sector have been viewed almost exclusively in relation to domestic energy use. Relatively little research has been carried out on energy use in small- and medium-sized enterprises, generally, and even less on *women's* roles in productive energy uses (Gordon 1986; Carr and Sandhu 1987; de Treville 1987). For example, participants at the 1981 UN Conference on New and Renewable Sources of Energy adopted the *Nairobi Program of Action* (UN 1981), which recognized energy as a women's issue; however, the focus was primarily on subsistence uses.

Traditional biomass production, that is, collection and transport of firewood and charcoal production, and its sale are a major source of employment for women. In Fazoum, Egypt, 48% of women worked in minor forest industries of one kind or another. In Sierra Leone, 80% of urban fuelwood sellers are women. Some 250 000 women are employed in collecting forest products in Manipur, India (FAO 1991). In Gujarat, India, most of the income earned by women fuelwood carriers was used for buying food (FAO 1989).

Home-based industries often depend on biomass as a source of energy. These industries tend to be low paying and labour intensive; the work is tiring and sometimes dangerous to women's health. As much as 106 hours are required to process 30 kg of shea nuts. Preparing palm and other oils requires lifting and moving heavy containers of hot liquid. Women in industries using biomass as an energy source are exposed to burns and smoke, even more than the well-documented exposure of women using biomass as domestic fuel. Operators are exposed to smoke, other harmful emissions, furnace heat, and steam, often for long periods (RWEDP 1988).

The energy consumed by these industries, both in human labour and fuel, is not insignificant. An estimated 816 865 t of fuelwood is consumed annually by hotels, restaurants, guest houses, and tea shops in Nepal, nearly half the total consumption by rural industries. In Mopti, Mali, fish processing uses 40 000 t of wood each year. In Abidjan, street food vendors, fish smokers, and restaurants were estimated to consume 60% of wood fuel and 26% of the charcoal used in the city. On average, small industries probably use 10–50% of fuelwood in rural areas and about the same proportion in biomass-using urban areas.

Efforts to adapt traditional technologies or introduce imported ones are aimed at saving women's time and effort, releasing labour for other uses, increasing incomes, increasing profits and yields, saving fuelwood and reducing deforestation, increasing safety, and improving health. Many activities carried out in small and medium-sized enterprises use a disproportionate amount of fuel. Most of the fuel is used by a relatively small number of entrepreneurs, many of whom are already members of organized groups, making dissemination and marketing of new techniques promising (Cecelski 1992).

However, inadequate needs assessment and lack of attention to local knowledge has frequently resulted in the transfer of "improved" technologies that are inferior to traditional methods. In Tanzania, for example, preparing flour from maize using an imported hand mill required several siftings and regrindings before the quality was deemed acceptable. Moreover, increasing efficiency usually implies larger-scale production and can easily result in the marginalization of women producers, who often work part time on a small scale, and transfer of control of the production process to male owners who can afford the necessary capital investment. In Indonesia, the government promoted the use of mechanized rice hullers; between 1970 and 1978, 90% of rice hulling was carried out using the new technology, but as many as 1.2 million jobs in Java alone and 7.7 million in all of Indonesia were lost as a result. The loss of income among women handpounders in Java amounted to US$50 million annually, or 125 million woman-days of labour (Cecelski 1990a). In Ghana, a project was aimed at improving the efficiency of charcoal-making from sawmill residues. However, the small-scale itinerant producers were unable to secure land on which to establish fixed kilns, to invest in the new equipment, or to purchase the now more valuable residues. Although only about 300 charcoal-makers would have been affected, most were women (Cecelski 1990b).

Successful projects have paid careful attention not only to technical feasibility but also to factors outside the production process, such as access to raw materials (including land ownership and control over cash crops), access to credit, social and cultural context, management and organization, leadership, and marketing. Extending credit and assisting women's groups in other ways has been one of the most effective strategies to enable women to own and profit from larger-scale, more efficient processing technologies. The Food and Agriculture Organization of the United Nations (FAO) has tried to identify minor industries based on forest products that are economically viable, making them worth supporting and improving (FAO 1991).

Although research and project experience exists, gaps in many areas make setting a future research agenda critical. For example, basic research on women's roles in energy-intensive, informal-sector enterprises is needed. We need to know more, not only about fuel consumption and scarcity and its effects on these enterprises, but also about women's roles in the profitability of enterprises and family income, constraints on improving productivity (such as access to credit and marketing), the organization of the sector, and the effects of the availability of street foods on diet, nutrition, and health (Cecelski 1990b).

Case studies of the choice and use of energy technologies are needed as examples of success and models for replication. These models could be disseminated through an extension of the food technologies source books, as proposed by UNIFEM. Donors supporting relevant small-scale enterprise and energy projects could also identify and document their own cases, especially

+ Case studies and models of energy technologies that have recently been disseminated, that is, new and renewable sources of energy (NRSE); and

+ Case studies of the impact of technological change on women, in terms of use of time, productivity, and economic returns to labour before and after a technology has been introduced, in the same location, or with and without the technology in similar locations (Carr and Sandhu 1987).

Gender issues must be considered in ongoing efforts to develop shorter-term, less-expensive methods to evaluate impact, for use by development projects and agencies, and ways to include informal-sector and unpaid labour in national accounts.

Poverty and basic human needs

Energy is not only a basic need in itself, but is required for services, such as transport, industrialization, education, health, water, and communications, that release people from time- and energy-consuming tasks and allow them to turn to more productive activities. Women's role at the centre of the "rural energy crisis" — as users, producers, victims, and activists — as well as in meeting the family's basic needs has been well documented (Cecelski 1992). However, women are also pivotal in the urban energy situation.

Women have been portrayed as subsistence users of biomass energy in rural and urban stove-improvement programs. In the 1980s, with the realization that household chores, specifically cooking, consume the largest portion of total energy (especially biomass energy) in low-income, developing countries, women became the target group for achieving major fuel savings. Initially, however, many improved-stove programs failed, largely because of the tendency to seek universal "technical fixes" rather than analyzing local and national fuel use and supply conditions. Data were frequently based on the limited knowledge of men, and male engineers designed stoves without consulting the women who would have to use them. Many professional technologists found it difficult to elicit, acknowledge, use, or respect women's traditional knowledge and expertise regarding the properties of fuels, food preparation, stove construction, and community education — all so relevant for successful stove design and dissemination (Kammen and Lankford 1991; McGranahan and Kaijser 1993).

Women's role as collectors of fuelwood and other forest products has also been well documented, together, by extension, with their role as managers of trees and forest resources (FAO 1989):

> Trees are important in rural economies largely as a result of the uses to which they are put by women. In many societies, it is women who must find and transport the fuelwood that their families need. It is often women, not men, who gather wild fruit and nuts, find fodder for their domestic stock, and make medicines and other products from woody materials. Women also earn what little cash income they have from activities that relate, directly or indirectly, to trees and forests. In many rural societies, a special relationship therefore exists between women, the family and trees....
>
> [Nonetheless,] this fact has been only rarely acknowledged in past development programs. As in other areas, too many projects have been unwittingly targeted at men with the result that women have sometimes not only failed to benefit from such projects but even been actively disadvantaged by them.

Women's roles in the modern, urban energy sector have received much less attention, despite their importance. First, energy pricing and availability policies (including those on new energy technologies, electrification, credit, and fuel subsidies) determine women's access to more efficient fuels and appliances, and hence a significant part of their time and budgets. Energy costs affect family budgets (accounting for as much as 20% in African cities) and can decrease the amount of money available for other items such as food and education. Women can provide valuable input into energy pricing policy: their preferences, real costs (including labour in searching for fuels, scarcities, and appliances) and real benefits to them as fuel users, and acceptable trade-offs (Cecelski 1992).

Women can also make an important contribution to energy-conservation policies, especially regarding household uses. There is a tendency to believe that women's role in energy use ends once traditional fuels are abandoned and more efficient commercial fuels are adopted. On the contrary, women still play a key role in energy use in modern and modernizing societies, and in particular can make a large contribution to the efficiency of energy use and conservation programs. Women do most of the cooking; have definite preferences for fuel and appliance designs; and purchase or influence the purchase of stoves and other energy-using appliances as well as the procurement of fuels. Women influence their households' direct and indirect energy consumption for heating and air conditioning, hot water, and electrical appliances; when energy is used (therefore, peak use); and household transport. Women are the primary educators and formers of their children's future consumption habits (Cecelski 1992).

Efforts to improve the efficiency of existing technologies (ranging from appropriate technologies, such as grain mills, to more efficient kerosene stoves, to the use of renewable energy) can reduce the drudgery of much of women's work and release time for more productive developmental tasks. For example, the displacement of women from their traditional subsistence responsibilities as men take over more distant fuelwood collection with animals or carts or invest in grain-grinding mills is not necessarily a negative development, if women's labour is reduced and they are able to pay for services that formerly took many hours to perform. Women's traditional knowledge must also be valued and women must be involved in the design, construction, and maintenance of new facilities and services (Sontheimer 1991).

At present, a number of new and renewable forms of energy are technically feasible, but are financially practical in only a limited number of remote or specialized uses (although inclusion of social and environmental costs would make them economically much more attractive). However, rising prices for fossil fuels will eventually make both renewable energies and energy efficiency improvements financially attractive. Questions of centralized versus decentralized application of renewable energy technologies will likely influence the extent to which benefits accrue to women (Cecelski 1992).

One of the most important issues in relation to women, energy, poverty, and basic needs is the increasing activism of local and national women's organizations, and how these efforts can be supported and promoted. Because of their strong interests and distinct perspective, women and their organizations have been active and effective in changing some energy policies. When convinced of the utility and practicality of an energy technology or forestry scheme, women have constituted a powerful lobby to persuade the entire household or community to invest the necessary resources to make the scheme work. When convinced of the negative effects and threat to their livelihoods, on the other hand, women have been equally forceful in blocking supposed "improvements."

Although sufficient research and project experience exists to make many recommendations possible, several gaps make setting a future research agenda critical. Considerable research and experience exists regarding improved stoves, social forestry, and food processing. However, there is still a lack of focused, gender-relevant case studies that can be used as examples and models. Even less research and project experience exists on energy conservation, renewable energy, and energy planning involving women; what is available needs to be documented. Such case studies could be disseminated through an extension of UNIFEM's work in food technologies. Donors funding renewable energy projects could also identify and document their own cases.

Women's less-recognized roles as energy producers, workers, managers, and activists should be better documented. Women's roles in the wider context of changing rural and urban energy and food systems and relations between local, national, and global institutions and actors are also important subjects for research. In particular, the implications for women of the energy transition, NRSE, and global energy policies are largely unexplored.

Gender concerns must be incorporated into implementable, policy-oriented methods for energy policy research; research models that translate women's priorities effectively into energy research methods should be promoted. Some promising areas are total transport demand, including human load carrying; consumer-focused product development and marketing; national accounts including informal sector and unpaid labour; social and environmental cost–benefit analysis; and participatory action research and socio-economic analysis to elicit local knowledge and participation.

The historical context

In 1979, the UN *Convention on the Elimination of All Forms of Discrimination Against Women* (UN 1979a) highlighted the need to enhance women's condition in society by according them equal access in formal and informal education and S&T training; to elicit women's knowledge and promote women's roles in policymaking and

implementation at all levels; and to enhance women's living conditions by promoting the use of clean energy forms such as electricity.
Although the conference on S&T for development (UN 1979b) did not
deal substantively with energy (or natural resources for that matter),
participants identified the disparate effects of S&T on different socioeconomic groups, and on men and women. In addition, conference
deliberations emphasized the urgent need to encourage women to
pursue careers in S&T.

In May 1981, an international workshop on *Non-Technical
Obstacles to the Use of New Energies in Developing Countries* was organized by the UN Educational, Scientific and Cultural Organisation
(Unesco) in cooperation with the Center for Integrative Development, Le Commisariat à l'Énergie Solaire, the Commission of European Communities, the Commonwealth Science Council, the
International Development Research Centre, the Rockefeller Foundation, United Nations University, and the United States Department
of Energy. Participants recognized that the solution of technical problems alone was insufficient to advance the development of new and
renewable sources of energy. Discussions highlighted less tractable
issues such as education and training, information, social and cultural conditioning, institutional structures, costs and financing, environmental impact, and other issues that affect the diffusion of
innovations. Although the condition of women was not identified as
a priority area, the importance of distinguishing among groups
within the society was emphasized as requisite to facilitating the
selection and adaptation of energy technologies to the specific needs
of all people using them — men, women, urban, rural, poor, landlords
(Unesco 1981).

In August 1981, the UN Conference on New and Renewable
Sources of Energy adopted the *Nairobi Program of Action* (UN 1981),
whose main objectives were to promote concerted action for the
development and use of new and renewable sources to help meet
future energy requirements especially in Southern countries.
Women's concerns were articulated in this program of action in a
more positive and integrated manner than in most previous UN documents. However, the focus was primarily on subsistence uses. As
outlined in paragraph 13:

> The successful achievement of the energy transition
> has direct implications for shelter, physical infrastruc-
> ture, health, sanitation, nutrition and general well-
> being in rural and urban communities.... It should
> include, where appropriate, provisions to ensure ade-
> quate supplies of energy in case of acute shortage of
> energy for subsistence. The energy transition must

include consideration of the social dimensions, including the role of women as agents in and beneficiaries of the process of development, in view of their special burdens as producers and users of energy, particularly in the rural areas.

The Nairobi Forward-Looking Strategies for the Advancement of Women (UN 1985b) included a section addressing energy (appendix A) and a paragraph on appropriate food-processing technologies and rural transport (para. 215). The energy section included references to "women as producers, users and managers of energy sources," support to "grassroots participation of women in energy-needs assessment, technology and energy conservation, management and maintenance," "substituting energy for muscle in the performance of the industrial and domestic work of women without loss of their jobs and tasks to men," and in commercialization of fuelwood energy, avoiding "the loss of women's incomes to middlemen and urban industries." There was mention at several points of the need for new energy sources to reduce women's labour demands (para. 219 and 221).

Recommendations concerning the involvement of women as both contributors and beneficiaries in energy measures and training, technology development and improved stoves and farm woodlots, and decision-making and implementation at all levels were also included. Governments and nongovernmental organizations (NGOs) were asked to provide women and women's organizations with information and incentives for training and education. Notably, there was no mention of health issues concerning women in the energy sector; little mention of forestry and environmental issues; and involvement of women in peaceful uses of nuclear energy is mentioned in several places.

In 1992, the UN Conference on the Environment and Development in Rio de Janeiro placed energy concerns mainly in the context of climate change and included a set of program areas as part of *Agenda 21* on protection of the atmosphere (UN 1992a). The major program areas are: promoting the energy transition, increasing energy efficiency, promoting renewable energy sources, and promoting sustainable transport systems. The advancement of women is a cross-cutting issue in *Agenda 21*.

Chapter 24 of *Agenda 21*, "Global Action for Women and Towards Sustainable Development," recommends "programmes to promote the reduction of the heavy workload of women and girl children at home and outside" through several measures, including "the provision of environmentally sound technologies which have been designed, developed and improved in consultation with women, accessible and clean water, an efficient fuel supply and adequate sanitation facilities" (UN 1992a, 24.3(d)).

The *Draft Platform for Action* of the Commission for the Status of Women (1994) does not highlight energy per se, but contains the following recommendations, which if implemented can serve to ameliorate women's position in energy decision making:

+ Training in S&T for women;

+ Promotion of equal access to land, capital, technology, and so forth; and

+ Enhancement of women's position in managing natural resources.

Although worthy in principle, on the whole these UN initiatives and their attendant directives have been ineffective in advancing women's position with respect to energy issues. Despite much debate reality has changed much less than rhetoric — the talk has come to little.

Chapter 6

Looking at health through women's eyes

Soon-Young Yoon

A village woman from Tamil Nadu, India, packed her bag checking to make sure she had enough money to pay the doctor. A bus would take her to a strange city clinic. She had mixed feelings of anticipation and fear. This was the third time she had become pregnant and her husband's family told her that this time she must have a boy. She had prayed to the gods, taken many herbal baths, and did almost everything the old village women told her to do. Had she committed a terrible sin? The last two times she gave birth, her husband had hardly looked at the babies. The family needed a son to keep it from financial ruin, because he would receive a good dowry from a bride. She hoped this new doctor's test worked, but if amniocentesis showed that it was a girl, she would have an abortion and try again.

This story is relived in India, South Korea, and other countries where amniocentesis is used for sex selection. It is a glaring reminder that modern science and technology (S&T) do not necessarily mean better health for women. Indeed, modernization of health technology often replicates rather than challenges gender inequality. Amniocentesis, an advanced medical technique originally used to detect genetic defects in high-risk pregnancies, also reveals the sex of the fetus. In one hospital in West India, 700 people sought prenatal sex determination between June 1976 and June 1977: 250 of the fetuses were male and 450 female. Although all the male fetuses were borne to term, 430 of the 450 females were aborted (WHO/SEARO 1989a).

Why is this happening? One reason is that women are blamed for reproductive "failure." In many countries, infertile women or women without sons become outcasts, even though it is the father, not the mother, whose gametes determine a child's sex.

Many women and health activists think that the United Nations (UN) can influence governments to take action on women's health issues. They also hope that scientists, researchers in women's studies, and scholars will apply their knowledge to help them.

How far has the UN come in meeting this challenge? What can national governments do to improve the situation? What is the role of scientists in dealing with gender and health issues? The purpose of this paper is to address these questions. It deals with the wide range of related issues, such as why gender and health deserve attention within the S&T debate, the issues, and international and national trends. It also contains suggestions for strategic action and where it might lead. Although its main focus is on developing countries, it draws on some global data to illustrate international trends.

Why gender and health?

Why should S&T be concerned about gender and health? Shouldn't development take care of everyone's health problems? There are at least three reasons why this hasn't occurred: women have been victims of health systems, their contributions have been undervalued, and gender has been ignored in general health statistics and research.

Women as victims in the health-care system

Women in industrializing countries are the main health-care providers, caretakers of the aged, and decision-makers about child health. They are vital to national development as producers as well as reproducers. However, their own lives are often considered less valuable than those whom they feed and heal.

Recent studies note that a contributing factor to many adult women's health problems is a lifetime of gender discrimination. The first major review of the health implications of sex discrimination in childhood noted that girls were likely to suffer from a wide variety of discriminatory practices such as differential feeding, care during sickness, and other forms of childhood neglect (WHO 1986). Since then, the evidence has grown, particularly regarding gender differences in nutrition and infant mortality and morbidity. Initially thought to be restricted to northern India where nearly 50% of girls were below 70% of expected weight compared with 14% of boys (WHO 1992), neglect of girl children has now been reported in almost all developing regions.

Male-dominated cultural values are taught in the family and become a way of life. Many girls carry an unequal economic load in family chores; they carry water, gather fuel, take care of younger children, and "fill-in" for their mothers. Girls work longer hours than boys in less productive jobs (Yoon 1982). When times are hard, such as during the recent global recession, they may be taken out of school so that their brothers' school fees can be paid. The UN Childrens Fund (UNICEF), the World Health Organization (WHO), and many governments have tried to draw attention to the health needs of girl children, but these efforts have limited impact if they are not reinforced by changes in economics, education, and elsewhere.

Teenage girls in many industrializing countries are the backbone of modern industries, such as electronics and textiles, and they work in hazardous occupations and sweatshops. In countries such as South Korea, girls aged 16–22 years make up nearly 75% of the labour force in export trade zones (Yoon 1982). Although many suffer from occupational health problems, they often do not report them or ask for treatment because they are afraid of being fired. The most tragic situation, however, is that of the girls who are exploited in the sex and tourism industry. The prevalence of sexually transmitted diseases and AIDS infections (acquired immune deficiency syndrome) is as high as 80% in some countries such as Thailand. Although girls may know that condoms should be used, they are powerless to avoid infection. Meanwhile, younger girls are being drawn into prostitution as male clients seek AIDS-free partners.

In the United States, teenage pregnancies are on the rise, a puzzle because contraception is relatively widely accepted and available. Unwanted teenage pregnancies lead to unhealthy babies and mothers, costing the public US$16–18 billion a year (Carnegie Foundation 1992). In sub-Saharan Africa, teenage pregnancies result in high-cost pregnancies and delivery complications such as toxemia, anemia, premature delivery, prolonged labour, and death. Maternal mortality rates are higher for 15- to 19-year-olds than for women aged 20–34 years (WHO 1992). Such trends mean that young women are more likely to drop out of school and take on the prime responsibility for their children.

Throughout their reproductive years, poor women carry an unequal economic and reproductive burden. As is often noted, women produce 40–80% of the world's food, but own less than 3% of the land. Except in North America, Australia, and western Europe, women still work longer hours per day than men (WHO 1992). In all regions, women still bear the main responsibility for household chores and child care (UNSO 1991). When women are the main wage earners, postpartum recovery periods are shorter and their nutritional and health status declines with each pregnancy (UN 1985a).

The health system's gender bias is also reflected in its concern for women's health only when they are mothers. Their health, according to the WHO definition of "total well-being," is disregarded. Their environmental, occupational, and mental health needs are thus not addressed. However, gender inequality increases health risks for women in many ways. One of the most alarming health problems is violence against women. In the United States, every 15 seconds, a woman is beaten, and four battered women die each day (WHO 1992). Violence may also be related to rape during war, female sexual mutilation, or assaults on aged women. In all cases, the mental as well as physical well-being of women is at risk, and these, not just reproductive health, are equally important in assessing women's health status.

Even with respect to reproduction, it is debatable whether technology has helped women control their bodies. The predominant methods of birth control — pills, intrauterine devices (IUDs), Norplant®, and other injectables — all require acceptance and compliance by women to external control of their normal hormone functions. In target-oriented population-control programs, many family-planning techniques have been aimed solely at women, even though men are often the ones who decide family size. Although women and reproductive-rights activists have protested this gender bias, only recently have researchers and family-planning programs paid more attention to male contraceptives and reproductive responsibility for men.

Although considerable attention has been paid to how gender inequality affects women as health-services users and consumers, less is known about the way it affects women as health-care professionals and providers. In industrialized countries, analysis of gender inequalities among women scientists and researchers, doctors, nurses, pharmacists, and health-services managers (WHO 1982) shows that the health sector is labour intensive and dominated by women, but the women are at the bottom of the hierarchy and pay scales. They are also less likely to exercise authority over others and factors such as race, ethnicity, caste, and class may create further barriers to job mobility.

In many poorer countries, large numbers of women make up the bulk of volunteers and "village health workers." Working conditions vary, and they seldom receive fees for their services and time. Attrition is high and motivation low because of increasing demands on such volunteers without supervision or support from local health clinics. As one woman said, "We have to travel long distances just to inform people about immunization clinics, and we have to pay our own way on the buses. The men get travel money to do government work — why shouldn't we?" (Yoon 1978).

Traditional birth attendants (TBAs), untrained midwives, and indigenous health practitioners are also women who play a variety of roles in health care. Many TBAs and herbalists have high status in the eyes of mothers, but in the overall traditional medical system, their position is not necessarily so favourable. In rural Korea, for example, gender and professional hierarchies exist in both indigenous and cosmopolitan health systems (Yoon 1982). Those most associated with professional health cultures, even within the indigenous system, are mostly men who are literate in Chinese characters — the herbalists, acupuncturists, blind fortune tellers, and geomancers. At a lower level, the population health culture consists mostly of women — the shamans, intuitive fortune-tellers, three-spirit grandmothers (specialists in maternal and child health), and traditional midwives (mostly mothers-in-law).

Although there is much more information about the large numbers of women health care providers within the formal system, more attention should be given to the armies of young (often unmarried) nurse-aids, public hospital nurses, health educators, and nurse–midwives. These workers, who are the backbone of safe motherhood programs and primary health care (PHC) systems, are often overworked, have little voice in the health-care delivery system, and are expected to work miracles with little pay and few supplies.

Gender discrimination combined with age hierarchy, caste, and sometimes racism exacerbated the poor working conditions, barriers to promotion, and even sexual harassment on the job that young female health workers face. In India, for example, nursing students who have night shifts are considered "fair game" for the advances of male interns and are unable to complain to superiors. Because they frequently come into direct contact with blood, they are considered "polluted," unfit for marriage outside their caste. In some societies, they cannot do their job effectively because cultural norms forbid them to ride bicycles, even to visit patients. To understand how gender, race–class, and age structures intersect to define the work status of this category of health personnel, more in-depth research and action are required.

Health for all through gender equality

Rather than dwell on the problems of women as victims, many women and health activists are trying to show how women contribute to development. Women make up the bulk of "invisible" contributors to the economy and managers of natural resources and thus integrate health into all aspects of development.

Although many national policies recognize women as key links in achieving population targets, they do not necessarily provide women with the means to make real reproductive choice possible (Jacobson 1991). Women's groups in industrializing countries are justifiably outraged that some population and environment policies are aimed at controlling women's fertility alone, while ignoring other factors contributing to the depletion of natural resources (Sontheimer 1991), such as excessive consumption especially by the North; unequal distribution of resources so that the landless are forced onto marginal lands; inadequate advances in S&T; poor internal and external migration policies; and insufficient social services, especially for health and family planning.

Women's active involvement in water and sanitation programs has demonstrated that women are not only part of the problem, they are also part of the solution. In Panama, village women helped engineers identify sources of fresh water that had been overlooked in the initial surveys. In Latin America, Africa, and parts of Asia, women volunteered their labour in the construction of a piped water system. In Lesotho and Tonga, they helped build latrines (INSTRAW 1989). Their role in helping to generate new financing for water projects has been shown to be important because women often reinvest in other family basic needs such as better education and improved child nutrition. The women's garden groups in the Casamance of Senegal and rural South Korea, for example, were key links between improved water supplies and income-generation for family welfare.

Gender as a scientific variable

The women's movement has proposed a third reason why "women's issues" must be taken seriously: the gender perspective is simply better "science" in the sense that it has greater heuristic value and generates more useful knowledge than orthodox medical paradigms. In recent decades, the "women's issue" has also become the subject of legitimate academic research. Women scientists and researchers have redefined the concept of gender and applied it to almost every field of science and the humanities, including health.

Often called "women's studies," this new body of knowledge is the scientific study of gender roles and is one of the fastest growing fields of study today. India, for example, has established a national women's studies association to ensure greater cross-fertilization between various fields within women's studies. Although "women and health" courses are only just beginning to appear in medical-school curricula of developing countries, they are common electives in the United States, Canada, and Europe.

In health research and statistics, the gender perspective changes conventional scientific paradigms, introducing gender roles as a new and significant variable. This has led to pioneering research in epidemiologic, biologic, etiologic, and health-behaviour studies.

National averages obscured important differences in statistics, such as the nutritional status of young children noted earlier. Epidemiologic data show gender differences in patterns of AIDS transmission (women are more easily infected than men) and of various noncommunicable diseases, such as lung cancer.

Numerous reports now reveal the fallacy of earlier data, such as cardiovascular information based almost solely on male subjects. Drugs once thought to be safe for women are being reconsidered after investigations showed that original tests were done only on men. In addition, studies of health behaviour and health-systems research are showing that gender roles make a difference in health outcomes. Scientists have noted that the effect of tropical diseases and opportunities for treatment can be quite different for men and women. For example, in Thailand, blood tests done in communities indicated that malaria affected men and women equally, but clinical records showed that more men were treated (WHO 1992). Studies in Colombia showed that women are less likely to assume the "sick role" and that they are slower to seek treatment (Wijeyaratne et al. 1993).

Gender inequality in health is one of the "root causes" of other health problems and is a social variable as significant as age, race, class, or marital status. Like kin status, ethnic identity, or economic conditions, gender roles are among the nonbiomedical factors that determine etiology, progress of illness, and eventual outcome of medical treatment. Through a variety of intermediate institutions such as religion, law, economics, and kinship, gender inequality affects morbidity and mortality rates and life-style differences. Similarly, it is a factor in determining demographic, migration, and fertility trends.

Combined with the other two arguments — that access to and impact of S&T are gender biased and inequitable and that women are a vital resource for the future — scientific emphasis is a powerful argument for focusing on gender issues. In my view, all three are valid and important points of view that can be used in advocacy to create a new ethical basis for health S&T development and assessment.

The issues

Issues specific to technology transfer at the national level can be categorized into three major areas: women's access to health S&T, the impact of S&T on gender equality, and the development of health S&T. A complete situational analysis would require in-depth research of scholarly works, UN data, women's studies reports, bulletins of nongovernmental organizations (NGOs), and other national S&T information. A preliminary review is provided here with suggestions for future policy-related research.

Women's access to health S&T

Women health activists see access to health S&T as a major problem of national health programs. Their views are supported by commonly used national health indicators, such as number of beds per person or patient–doctor ratios, which are designed to monitor progress. More specific gender-related information comes from family-planning services, where the monitoring of access is very refined.

According to national data, it appears that significant progress has been made in reproductive technology research, development, and provision of family planning services. The 1992 *Demographic and Health Surveys and Family Planning Surveys* reports that about one-third of married women in the developing world (excluding China) are currently using modern methods of family planning; since the 1960s, fertility has declined from an average of six children per woman to four (PIP 1992).

Information, education, and communication (IEC) studies measure women's level of access to health information and the "science" of health. Again, family-planning programs have been particularly aggressive in evaluating the extent of women's and men's knowledge of basic reproductive functions and uses of specific contraceptive techniques. Results of the most recent *Demographic and Health Survey* indicate that more than 75% of women in developing countries could name at least one modern method of contraception (PIP 1992). Many also named traditional methods.

Water availability has also increased in both urban and rural areas; in 1990, 82% of the urban and 63% of the rural populations had access to water supplies. Sources and quality vary considerably — from hand-dug shallow wells to clean, potable piped water — but where water and sanitation have improved, there has been a direct impact on women as users and providers of health care.

✦ Stress and fatigue related to carrying water have been reduced;

✦ Women can encourage hygienic practices in the family;

✦ There has been a reduction in some water-borne pathogens (typhoid, cholera, amoebic infections, bacillary dysentery, and diarrheal diseases), thus making it easier for women as health-care providers; and

✦ Many parasitic diseases, which in some countries are reported to be higher for women and girls than for other groups (for example, guinea worm, trachoma, hookworm, and schistosomiasis), are being controlled (Yacoob and Brieger 1991).

Despite these gains, problems surrounding increased access continue to be a focus for health activists, policies, and health services. Those working close to communities have argued that the issue of women's access to health and reproductive technologies is much more complex than currently measured by health statistics. Researchers have confirmed that effective access can only be ensured "if that care is considered affordable, appropriate and acceptable by the women it aims to serve" (Timyan 1993). In other words, it is more than an issue of availability of services or even having services nearby. Women must also find the quality and types of services acceptable and appropriate to their needs.

For example, many rural health clinics have special days set up for maternal and child health (MCH) and family planning services, but women who make long treks to the health clinic find that they cannot treat themselves. Instead, they must come back to the clinic for treatment, paying high costs in time and transportation. In urban settings, a middle-class mother, with a 7-year-old child with strep throat, is frustrated if she must return to the clinic to get treatment from yet another doctor for herself.

Women's general health is often overlooked because their health needs may be channelled through MCH services. Problems, such as reproductive-tract infections and infertility, health care for the elderly, and special care for young women are neglected.

For women who prefer traditional medicine, industrialization and agricultural development has sometimes undermined, rather than improved their access. In many countries, agricultural lands have expanded at the expense of forests that are rich sources of home remedies and herbal medicines. In other countries, such as France, India, Indonesia, and the United States, traditional medicines have been modernized, raising their cost and making them unaffordable — especially as health insurance does not cover many "alternative" medicines.

Critical areas for policy-related research are:

✦ How to improve women's access to health and reproductive technologies beyond MCH–family planning (MCH–FP) services, addressing quality as well as availability;

✦ How women's access to traditional medicine has been affected by its commoditization and lack of local free resources; and

✦ How access differs by subgroup of women: age, economic status, disability, rural or urban residence, and race or ethnicity.

The impact of S&T on women's health

Much less reliable data are available to elucidate the complex issue of the impact of health S&T on women's health status. Generally, it is difficult to isolate medical or health S&T from the effects of other development processes. Generally, it seems some progress has been made. Globally, health conditions around the world have improved more in the past 40 years than in all previous human history. Child mortality fell from 280 to 106 per 1 000 in developing countries and women in developed countries now outlive men, although they suffer more disability (WHO 1992).

Research on this topic involves more than an impact assessment of health S&T. It must entail a gender-specific understanding of basic needs-assessment and impact studies, many of which suffer from lack of adequate health data. The most crucial information needed is an analysis of cases in which there has been a positive, sustainable effect of development on women's health. By looking at these cases, it should be possible to uncover some suggestions for future strategies.

For example, in the newly industrialized countries, such as Korea, Taiwan, and now Thailand, there appear to have been important changes in the overall health status of the population, related as much to improved income distribution and education as to provision of health services. The demographic transitions that occurred are a general indicator that women have gained greater control over their fertility, that there has been a rise in age of marriage, and that the use of effective contraception and other techniques to reduce fertility and space children has increased. Equally important are the development processes that promote access and improve effect — notably women's education, better working opportunities and income, rise in social or legal status, as well as a general improvement in standard of living (World Bank 1993).

Concerning indigenous S&T, a number of policy changes and research are needed. Within the modern health sector, almost nothing is known about the iatrogenic causes of female morbidity and mortality, such as death due to in-hospital infections, malpractice, or severe side effects from overuse of drugs such as antibiotics. Some studies indicate that causes of maternal mortality may actually occur within hospital settings because of delays in treatment, or lack of supplies (Tinker and Koblinsky 1993). The "medicalization" of women's health has also meant that, in many cases, medical procedures like hysterectomies and caesarean births are overused.

In addition to assessments of how the pluralistic health system affects women's health, studies are needed to document women's role in "blending" technologies. For example, Chinese women have had a exceptional opportunity to combine both health systems as government policy has favoured modernization of traditional medicine and provides services as part of the national health services. However, little is known about Chinese women's health behaviour and preferences regarding traditional medicine. Other examples at the community level can also be found. In one area, women leaders initiated a project to build traditional dams, but they used low-cost modern techniques, such as reinforcement with chicken wire, to build the dams larger. Supplementary benefits of the project included fish in the dam waters, vegetable gardens around the dams, water for cattle, and shallow water pumps convenient for washing clothes and personal hygiene.

In the safe-motherhood program, assessments of the TBA training courses are underway, particularly courses that have combined old and new methods. In a highly acclaimed TBA program in Myanmar, most trainees were women over 60 years of age, illiterate, and unaccustomed to modern medical practices. To make the training acceptable, the project head, Dr Tin Hmun, incorporated many of their traditional beliefs. For example, in Myanmar, umbilical cords are cut with a bamboo tool across a coin to bring good fortune to the infant. Dr Hmun tossed a coin into the pot of boiling water along with the rest of the birthing kit instruments so that it would be sterilized.

Another important research topic is how development has affected traditional women healers and their practices. The role of TBAs has been "medicalized" under the PHC–MCH programs. Under the supervision of the modern health system, most TBAs have been trained only to assist in specific areas of MCH; their other practices are either ignored or actively discouraged. In many African cultures, the TBA is actually the family physician, looking after infants as well as the elderly. In central Java, TBAs are more specialized, but they cooperate with other traditional practitioners to provide comprehensive care. Sometimes, integrating TBAs into the modern health-care delivery system actually undermines the TBA's local status. In my own field visits, whenever I asked a TBA if she was training her daughter to take her place, the answer has always been "no." Why?

Because the daughter should take on a more "modern" occupation with better job security and income.

There is also evidence that the general mixing of technologies and uses within indigenous systems is leading in the wrong direction. Colonialism was the first major influence that changed indigenous health systems by waging political battles against "superstitious" health practices. In most instances, this also meant suppression of women's healing practices along with promotion of a patriarchal-biased colonial health system. Today, modern enterprise dominates the health culture. "Quack" healers as well as doctors mix modern drugs with traditional herbs and market them as new wonder drugs. "Injection doctors" take advantage of women's ignorance concerning the use of drugs and provide injections for almost anything at a price.

Women's roles in the development of health S&T

In many ways, women are always involved in the development of health S&T through their many creative approaches to home remedies, management of the environment, and their role as decision-makers in family health. However, their knowledge and methods are informal, outside the world of medical industries, commodities, and technology trade. It is rare for women and health groups to be consulted at the initial stages of developing modern health technologies. Part of this reason may be the general lack of consumer participation in the health industry. Other barriers include a serious communication gap among women as health consumers, researchers, and health-care businesses.

Women health activists have protested this exclusion, particularly with regard to reproductive technologies. For example, they have accused researchers of targeting mainly women as users — resulting in clinical trials hazardous to ill-informed women — while ignoring ways to make men take more responsibility. Women in sub-Saharan African countries would like attention to be paid to helping overcome infertility. Other issues attracting women's attention are the lower-cost women's condom (which can provide effective protection against sexually transmitted diseases (STD) without male knowledge), viricide, biotechnology research, and genetic research related to women's cancers.

New ways are clearly needed to formalize dialogue and involve laypersons, including women, in the development of health S&T. Some positive experiences are reported by WHO's Human Reproduction Program (HRP), in which women's groups were invited to meet with scientists. In 1991, the first meeting to find "common ground" included 14 women's health advocates, representing three regions and four international organizations, who met with scientists and scientific collaborators of the HRP to address the problem of the selection and introduction of fertility-regulation technologies. In 1994, a regional meeting in Asia was based on the same format and recommendations were made concerning policy, research, and services. At both meetings, women's concerns focused on safety and acceptability. Although the discussions were, at times, difficult and heated, all parties agreed that these meetings set a new precedent for a working relationship between scientists and women's health advocates.

Some social scientists and health professionals have argued that radical changes are needed at all stages of technology development. Bonair et al. (1989) have proposed an intriguing alternative model of medical technology innovations in developing countries. They strongly advocate broadening "the research process, by introducing knowledge about the factors influencing sustained use at the earliest possible stage of laboratory research." Applied to gender and health research, this would mean a closer interaction between social issues, such as how women perceive medical technologies and their capability to use them, and the early stages of health technology development. The societal conditions under which women have to use technologies would also be considered in defining preferred conditions, even at the laboratory research stage.

The need for a national S&T policy across sectors

The successful use of S&T to improve women's health depends most on women's ability to decide their own priorities with respect to access, impact, and the development of health S&T. To make these priorities effective, the transfer of health S&T must account for the social, economic, and political policies that support or undermine gender and health programs.

In some newly industrialized countries, economic changes have meant an increase in life expectancy and a decline in infant and maternal mortality, even without widespread access to "high-tech" medical services. Globally, technological progress and expanded health services helped eradicate smallpox in the 1950s. Reproductive technologies have also enabled nearly one-third of married women in the developing world to use modern family planning methods (PIP 1992).

Although these are important gains, there have been unexpected negative effects. In a number of countries, such as Brazil, India, and those of eastern Europe, industrialization and the Green Revolution have created "diseases of development," including upper respiratory infections associated with air pollution. Accurate data are scarce. However, a case study in New Delhi showed that over 30% of females aged 31–40 years suffer from cor pulmonale, thought to be due to kitchen smoke (WHO 1992). Elsewhere, chloroquine-resistant malaria appears as populations increase their intake of chloroquine and an evolutionary process selects for a new genetic strain of parasites. This is of particular concern for pregnant women whose immunity status changes. In the absence of treatment, morbidity and mortality rates are high for this group. In Zambia, many patients experienced abortions or premature labor because of malaria (Wijeyaratne et al. 1993). Dengue hemorrhagic fever, an incurable viral disease with high mortality rates for children 1–5 years of age, spreads as urbanization provides more freshwater containers, such as old tires, and other breeding sites for the mosquito vector.

Health "costs" of development that affect women include the shortened breastfeeding period that often accompanies better work opportunities in cities. Environmental hazards, such as pesticides, seem to increase the prevalence of breast cancer and birth defects. In some cases, environmental health problems caused by development (such as schistosomiasis) were brought under control. In others, industrial and agricultural technologies continue to undermine advances in health. For example, in some Asian countries, water and sanitation programs have trained women to maintain shallow tube wells and repair pumps; however, large-scale agricultural projects divert water in great quantities for cash crops. Deforestation and lack of watershed management have caused watertables to fall so much that the shallow wells have gone dry or become saline (Yoon 1993).

Another set of policies affecting women's health are those concerning traditional or alternative medicine. In most developing countries, a dominant modern medical system exists side by side with indigenous and "alternative" health systems that are widely accepted. Even in the United States, in the 1990s, nearly US$14 billion was spent on alternative health care — an amount equal to that spent on hospitalization. Combined use of technologies, usually does not follow a "rational" order and few practitioners of allopathic medicine are even aware of alternative health practices. In developing countries, colonialism and "cosmopolitan medicine" often undermine the status of the alternative system in which women healers dominate by discouraging their practices or absorb them into the male-dominated modern system. The losers are women health consumers who go back and forth from one system to another.

Closely related to delivery of health services are transportation and infrastructure policies and employment opportunities. These should support rather than undermine national health plans. Studies concerned with social and economic costs to women of gaining access to health have recently recognized that clinic fees were only part of the problem. Lack of communications or high cost of transport can be equally important. In Mexico, the provision of a "good road" was associated with a 30% increase in the use of prenatal care (Timyan 1993). In a Thai village, increases in fuel prices meant an immediate reduction in the number of women and children attending clinics (WHO/SEARO 1989b). Privatization as a response to dwindling public health budgets has put further strains on women whose purchasing power is lowered during recession.

Finally, policies concerning women's access to information and communications should support a national gender and health policy. For example, self-care and prevention along with a more rational use of health services would be an ideal way to reduce costs. Yet, self-reliance in health has become more difficult as the gap between the specialists and the layperson widens.

At one end, sharing of medical knowledge and health information is prevented by medical politics, commercial patents, and lack of attention to public health-information services. At the other end, information systems in developing countries can seldom absorb the quantity of data. Because women have the lowest literacy rates, least mobility, and poorest networks, they are the last to gain access to health knowledge. Although studies show that providing health information is one of the most cost-effective ways of ensuring access to health services, it is low on the list of health spending priorities. Without information about correct use, availability of health technologies does not guarantee healthy people. Mediating institutions decide whether such technology is used to empower or further oppress women.

Health S&T policies alone cannot achieve health for women because of the overwhelming influence of other sectors and development trends. Economic and trade policies affecting alternative medicine, transportation, and infrastructure, along with information and communications policies, all influence the ultimate effect of health-technology transfer on women's welfare. In brief, gender and health concerns must be considered within an overall S&T policy if national health policies are to have any real impact.

Meeting the challenge

The global activities of the UN, women's NGOs, international women and health movements, and other international bodies have increasingly brought national policy issues into the debates over international development. Compared with the those of the 1960s, current women and health issues are less likely to be analyzed as local or national issues. There has been a reemergence of a global consciousness within the women and health movement, encouraged by the last four UN women's conferences and in anticipation of the 1995 conference in Beijing. Through various resolutions and negotiations, governments and women's groups have exchanged experiences and reached consensus.

Women's conferences and NGO forums

At the international level, the UN has a vital role to play in advocacy and financial and technical support to the women's health movement. Through its various bodies, an international exchange of knowledge and information has become possible and national governments have increasingly addressed women's health issues through international conventions and resolutions. In the past 20 years, acknowledgement of the importance of the UN involvement has resulted in "summits" every 5 years to review problems, assess progress, and find new platforms for action. In parallel, NGO forums have brought together individuals and NGOs. Over the years, the forums have been used to apply increasing pressure at the UN meetings for a response to their demands for "democratization" of the UN process and for the UN to widen its political boundaries to include NGO input. Strategies have included confrontation, but more recently, effective lobbying and close interaction in preparatory regional meetings.

It would be timely to conduct in-depth research on the role that the forums and UN conferences have played in the evolution of women's health issues and their impact at the national level. However, in the absence of an intensive study, it is possible to present a general overview of recent conference results and the preparatory documents for the 1995 Beijing women's conference in the area of women's health (see Appendix B).

UN World Women's Conferences of 1975, 1980, 1985, and 1995: In the documents of the world women's conferences of 1975, 1980, 1985, and 1995, health has always been considered a crucial sector. Although emphasis has changed somewhat concerning issues of access to health services to include HIV (human immunodeficiency virus)–AIDS and reproductive health, the recommendations generally reflect a concern for equal access to health technologies. The *Forward-Looking Strategies* from the 1985 conference is exceptional in its broad coverage of issues (UN 1985b). It includes recommendations on women as health-care providers as well as users of health services, the importance of women in managerial positions within the health system, ending stereotypes in health education, and emphasis on prevention and health promotion along with curative services.

Convention on the Elimination of all Forms of Discrimination Against Women: This excellent document does not identify issues by sector alone and, thus, provides a general strategy to protect women's rights that also have a health effect. Articles 5 and 16 are particularly noteworthy (UN 1979a):

> States Parties shall ... modify the social and cultural patterns of conduct of men and women, with a view to achieving the elimination of prejudices and customary and all other practices which are based on the idea of the inferiority or the superiority of either of the sexes or on stereotyped roles for men and women.
>
> States Parties ... shall ensure, on the basis of equality of men and women,... the same rights to decide freely and responsibly on the number and spacing of their children and to have access to the information, education and means to enable them to exercise these rights.

Agenda 21: This document, emanating from the UN Conference on Environment and Development (UNCED) in 1992, was clearly a conceptual as well as political turning point for gender and health. With considerable input from NGOs, *Agenda 21* puts gender and health at the centre of sustainable development issues. With NGO preparations in Miami in the same year and thousands of national and regional conferences, the UNCED "process" culminated in introducing a number of crucial social issues to the international environment discourse. One of the major entry points was the controversial population debate. Men and women advocating women's rights successfully emphasized environmental impact is determined by consumption patterns as well as population size.

Other forums: The preparatory meetings for the 1994 population conference emphasized the importance of women's empowerment as an end in itself and as a means to achieve sustainable development. The draft *Platform for Action for the International Conference on Population and Development,* held in Cairo, Egypt, identified a number of government actions that would contribute to achieving gender equality (UN 1994b). Among them were economic measures such as assuring the end of discrimination in the workplace, as well as health actions such as eliminating violence against women and strengthening grassroots women's organizations.

The draft document for the Social Summit (UN 1994a), similarly, cites gender inequality as a major barrier to "social integration" along with problems of youth and indigenous peoples. Health is expected to be a major topic, although it is unclear what linkages will be made to the issue of gender and S&T.

Although it is easy to be cynical about "yet another UN meeting," the importance of such global exchanges should not be underestimated. They represent a collective working out of a consensus on the ethical basis for S&T policies related to gender and health, even when they do not explicitly mention S&T. Also, such UN conferences have been largely responsible for giving legitimacy to women's efforts at the national level to advocate, institutionalize, and develop strategies. Many national women's bureaus, ministries, and focal points were direct outcomes of the women's conferences. Also, the NGO forums were important meeting places for international women's health networks to form stronger regional and international ties.

However, there is considerable room for improvement. For example, structural position of NGOs has yet to be established. In some instances, such as at the recent preparatory conference for the 1995 population conference, NGO and government delegates were part of the same team, developing joint proposals and negotiating strategies. At the preparatory conference for the 1995 World Women's Conference in Beijing, however, NGOs held a parallel conference with input to the UN proceedings on an ad-hoc basis. The UN has opened its doors to NGOs and has greater understanding of the role they have to play internationally, but the mechanisms are not clear. Should all NGOs be allowed to participate in UN meetings or only those with official UN accredited status? Such questions are still under debate and will affect future interactions between NGOs and the UN.

A general weakness of past conferences has been the lack of attention to youth health issues. Again, UNCED appears to have been a turning point, as youth groups were given their own forums and visibility. In preparations for the 1995 World Women's Conference, for the first time, there is a youth focal point with the secretariats of both the NGO forum and the official UN conference.

Another problem has been a lack of funds for effective information, education, and communications (IEC) after the conferences. Women seldom know what their governments agreed to at the UN meetings concerning gender and health and, thus, there is little chance that constituencies will support policy changes. Media centres, such as the International Women's Tribune Center (IWTC), have made important contributions by translating the turgid language of the UN meetings into concise messages with audiovisual material to reach over 2 000 network organizations.

The World Health Organization

As the lead technical agency in health, the WHO has a special responsibility to advocate and support women's issues. Since the 1980s, its director general's reports on women and health have assessed national progress and suggested policy directions. In 1992, the World Health Assembly took a major step forward when it chose "Women, Health, and Development" as the subject of its technical discussions. Government representatives along with bilateral funders, UN officials, NGOs, and an international panel of experts concluded that a series of proposals for action was required, expanding the mandate of WHO and creating a Women and Health Commission.

In 1989, the 44th World Health Assembly passed a series of comprehensive resolutions to further strengthen previous ones. Resolution 1 (WHO 1989a) urges member states to:

> Accelerate the implementation of the measures for the improvement of the health status of women, their economic and social status, and their quality of life and for their full and equal participation in all aspects of national health and development activities;
>
> Ensure that programs on women, health and development include action to: a) improve female literacy; b) support the role of women as health educators and providers of care; c) promote reproductive health, including family planning and safe motherhood; d) provide in particular for the social, economic and health needs of female children and elderly women; e) provide specifically for the prevention and management of chronic illnesses; f) promote and support women's income-generating opportunities to facilitate their health and development; g) cooperate with voluntary agencies in their activities on behalf of women, health and development.

Resolutions passed in 1992 emphasize the need for better representation of women in ministries of health and improving systems of reporting, coordination, and monitoring of policies.

Although the technical discussions that preceded these meetings emphasized the importance of a "gender" perspective to replace the "women-in-development" framework, the earlier terminology was preferred in resolutions. An expert group panel had emphasized linking gender and health to environment, particularly in areas of reproductive health, cancers, tropical diseases, and occupational health, but these were not specifically highlighted in the resolutions. However, various programs within WHO have taken up these issues.

Like the program on Tropical Diseases Research, the Human Reproduction Program (HRP) has been particularly attuned to the importance of the gender perspective. Although much more needs to be done to integrate gender perspectives into the program, it has established linkages between the basic components of reproductive science, technology, and production. As this involves a complex array of relations with various stakeholders, such as researchers, pharmaceutical companies, and national policymakers, the program has developed internal mechanisms to bring them together. It also has a research section that supports social and economic research on reproductive technology development, transfer, and acceptability.

Another significant thrust as been the promotion of interagency and intersectoral action. "The health problems of women are determined by diverse socioeconomic factors ..." not just health services, concluded expert panelists at the World Health Assembly in Geneva in 1992. Those who drafted the Accra Declaration and participants at the interregional workshops on Women's Participation and Leadership in MCH and Family Planning agreed that health services alone would not create health equality; changes in women's education, economic, and legal status are also required.

Other WHO activities include work carried out by the Intersectoral Action for Health Program. Focusing on the most vulnerable groups, which included women and the poor, research results, meeting reports, and documents point out how the vital health objectives of Health For All can be defined at the outset along with macroeconomic objectives. Such activities are not confined to a few programs. Most WHO programs, such as those on Environment Health, Tropical Diseases Research, Expanded Program on Immunization, Nutrition, and AIDS, promote intersectoral cooperation at the national level to improve women's health.

Internal mechanisms are intended to streamline intrasectoral coordination and planning in the area of women's health. WHO's directorate of Family Health is the main focal point for coordination of activities of regional and national counterparts. At the policy level, a special advisor assists the Director General's office to convene the Global Commission and advise on policy issues. Perhaps the two weak links lie at the regional and national levels.

In reviewing WHO's position, it is important to bear in mind that it is a specialized, technical agency, not a funder. Its main function lies in setting policy direction, providing a neutral zone for S&T knowledge to be pooled, and providing technical guidance to member states. In doing this, it provides a special place for gender and health issues to be discussed and worked out within the UN system. It may also be the appropriate unit to follow-up on the recommendation of the UN Commission on S&T.

UN bodies, funders, and bilateral agencies

The role of donors and other UN agencies is key in providing support to national health programs and WHO. Many health issues require joint actions in health (UN Fund for Population Activities (UNFPA), UNICEF, and UN Development Programme), education (UN Educational, Scientific and Cultural Organization and UNICEF), employment (International Labour Organisation), agriculture (Food and Agricultural Organization of the United Nations and International Fund for Agricultural Development), as well as the UN Development Fund for Women (UNIFEM)). Interagency collaboration on women's issues is already becoming a model of how collective efforts can pay off. The Inter-Agency Statement in preparation for the 1995 World Conference on Women demonstrates the willingness and importance of joint efforts directed toward a common goal. Also, at the WHO regional office for the Americas (Pan American Health Organization), all agencies including UNIFEM will collaborate to review gender training materials and training institutions in the region and prepare a report for the 1995 conference. WHO participation in interagency mechanisms such as the UN Division for the Advancement of Women, Vienna, the UN Commission on the Status of Women, and interagency meetings in preparation for the conferences on human rights (1993), population and development (1994), and women (1995) is also important.

Donors and other UN agencies could use these forums to strengthen interagency cooperation. Also, funders such as the Canadian International Development Agency, the Carnegie Foundation, the Danish International Development Agency, the International Development Research Centre, the Norwegian Agency for Development Cooperation, and the Swedish International Development Authority are seeking to improve interagency coordination at the national level and have valuable experiences to share on the problems and potential of such activity.

Strategic action and recommendations

What action can be taken that is cost-effective, has a long-term effect, and can be implemented immediately? Possibilities exist in four areas: focusing on youth, building on previous successful experiences, emphasizing IEC, and research and development.

A new generation: youth and adolescents

A higher priority should be placed on aiming health programs at young people (WHO/UNFPA/UNICEF 1989). As illustrated by anti-smoking campaigns, one of the most cost-effective strategies is to invest resources in changing the behaviour of the next generation. Young people are at an age when life choices are made. A 15-year-old unmarried mother may be able to continue her schooling, but a 25-year-old married woman may not even be allowed to attend a women's health meeting. In many rural settings, youth groups are more egalitarian than adult groups, and unmarried girls have more mobility than women.

However, gender issues are seldom considered in national health policies for youth. Except in terms of sex education, youth appear to have no gender. According to a WHO (1989b) report, health statistics and studies have often excluded adolescents and youth as a specific category and qualitative data on gender issues for youth are hard to find. Age together with gender discrimination accounts for the special problems of youth. For example,

+ Consider the gender bias in the label "unwed teenage mother." How does this stigma affect her willingness to seek prenatal care? What about the responsibility of the unwed teenage father?

+ The blame for infertility falls mainly on girls who can be abandoned even after marriage if they do not produce sons, even though infertility is often the result of her poor health.

+ Child prostitution is growing with the AIDS epidemic as clients look for AIDS-free partners; these children are powerless to avoid infection.

+ Girls work as electronic and textile workers, in service industries and in small sweatshops, but sexual harassment, sexual exploitation by management, and wage discrimination are the rule; most factory girls fear being fired if they report even illnesses.

In addressing these issues, the strategy should include promoting youth leadership within the women's health movement and at international forums. Existing youth programs should be strengthened to include gender. UNICEF, UNFPA, and WHO's Adolescent Health Program and MCH–FP projects have raised self-esteem among youth, particularly girls, so that they are better prepared to assert themselves, rather than yield to peer pressures.

Learning from previous successes

Collaboration among the UN, governments, NGOs, and social movements has an important outcome. Looking at leadership role models for both men and women and sharing success stories of women's leadership and participation across many sectors will slowly dissipate the image of women as "victims" in the health system.

Educating women as a means to improve child health and reduce population growth rates is an example of a successful national policy intervention. This approach, which is supported by WHO, UNFPA, and UNICEF, appears to be one of the most successful intersectoral interventions with a health impact. Although the reasons for the correlation between women's education and health are still debated, data suggest a close cause and effect. Countries where almost all women are literate have significantly lower infant mortality rates, independent of income (WHO 1992).

The Expert Group Meeting on Population and Women in Gabarone, 1992, emphasized that women are not only users, but they are also providers of health services (WHO 1992). Many role models and success stories within the health-care delivery system can be found among the "heroines" of medicine: the midwives, volunteer health workers, nurses, and women doctors. In Bangladesh, for example, female workers spent more time with family-planning clients, were more likely to recommend a range of methods, and less likely to urge women to choose sterilization. In Matlab, when midwives working at the community level were empowered to refer complex cases or treat complications in the home, the result was a 68% reduction in maternal mortality in only 3 years (Thapa 1992).

With the assistance of the Carnegie Corporation, the Sierra Leone Midwives Association and Home Economics Association carried out a health-systems research project aimed at introducing appropriate technologies in rural areas. After gathering information on women's perceptions and practices, traditional technologies, and constraints, the project team identified the technology gaps. They noted the suitability and acceptability of a scale to weigh newborns and support technologies such as pregnancy-risk cards, delivery-record cards, and birth cards. TBAs were trained and evaluations indicated that they were capable of providing the care needed to reduce maternal deaths. Replicability and feedback to national health planning was ensured as the government and NGOs were collaborators in designing and evaluating the project.

The Kenya Water and Health Organization was an experiment in close government collaboration with NGOs and community water management groups. In 1983, the project was developed to solve the water shortage and sanitation problems in two districts by testing 12 kinds of handpumps. It was soon recognized that local input would be needed to establish a maintenance system. Five years later, the project was on its way toward national coverage. In 1988, all local water-management committees included women. Nearly 70% had opened bank accounts with savings, which were used to buy spare parts and correct pump breakdowns. Success was a result of the recognition of the central role of women and communities. Women reported saving time and effort as they did not have to carry water long distances. Most important, the project had found a way to be responsible for its own technology development and keep the pumps working.

Most success stories are relatively small scale, but they represent significant "social mutations" because they succeed even when overall development trends are in a downward spiral. In India, for example, a women's group called CHETNA is making a difference in women's health through innovative means. Using puppets, plays, and women's networks, CHETNA is a major source of nutrition information for poor urban and rural women. A women's NGO in Bangladesh is changing the concept of "health" services. In a single clinic, a woman can get information on family planning, agricultural technologies (such as seed selection), banking and credit, and also get a medical check-up. Women's groups in the Pacific islands and the Caribbean have joined international NGOs, such as WorldWIDE, in global networks to share information about environmental issues and advocate national policies.

Information, education, and communications

IEC is another important entry point in addressing gender equality in health. Visual media are rarely used in a systematic manner to create awareness of major health issues (WHO 1991b). Neither are there sufficient communication skills among peripheral health workers to make person-to-person education effective. Participants at the interregional workshop on Leadership and Participation of Women in MCH–FP recommended that country teams implement mass-media campaigns to make women aware of their rights and empower them through training.

To make these good intentions a reality, the medical profession must leave its ivory tower of documents and go into the streets with leaflets. IEC materials are only useful if they are the tools of a social movement, appropriate in terms of local language and images, and developed with the participation of the target audience. Slide shows, audiocassettes, videos, television, radio, and multimedia forms of IEC should provide research results in ways people can understand and remember.

Health knowledge is increasingly becoming an important health "technology." It is one of the most effective tools for prevention, as well as cure, because changing patterns of diseases like AIDS require changes in behaviour to prevent epidemics. Knowledge about the appropriate use of medical technologies will also be a key factor in determining their potential. Antibiotics sold "over the counter" in many developing countries are often used inappropriately; Korean women reported taking antibiotics to "warm up their wombs" and improve their chances of conception. Meanwhile, the problem of drug-resistant strains of pathogens is exacerbated. Judicious use of such medications will ultimately depend on buyers' knowledge.

Sound medical knowledge empowers women to be more assertive patients and make better use of health services and drugs. Typically, uneducated women believe that a well-equipped local hospital with qualified staff will solve all of the health problems, even when these could be better handled through improved nutrition and better hygiene.

Some governments attempt to reform medical-technology development to complement a national PHC policy. However, unless consumers are convinced, informed, and use the technology, public hospitals will soon be empty. Instead, a private sector is likely to do a booming business meeting the demands of a high-technology hungry clientele. As one report from the Philippines noted, private physicians have become major importers and users of medical technologies to improve their competitive status in a growing medical business.

Revising school and nonformal education materials to remove gender bias is another important part of an IEC strategy. However, this has often been recommended and is seldom carried out. Governments can take a bold step toward gender equality in education by finding cost-effective, feasible means to eliminate gender bias in medical education materials. For example, typically in water and sanitation education, the traditional division of labour is perpetuated by examples of mothers and girls carrying water instead of having the man with the bicycle help them. In family-planning posters and portrayals of good nutrition for pregnant women, there are few images of fathers or husbands encouraging them to eat well. Invariably, MCH information is aimed at women. Where is the father in the chapter about low-birthweight children?

Specific subgroups for education are medical and nursing students, pharmacists, and medical researchers and scientists. Gender training for both female and male medical students sounds like a social issue, which usually gets a cold shoulder compared with hard sciences subjects. At times, women, health, and development training has rebounded to produce an even more hostile student body. Attention to extracurricular forms of presentation, such as movies and videos, as well as inclusion of gender issues (rather than "women's issues") at professional meetings may be effective in making inroads into student programs.

As a leading UN technical agency in health, WHO should set guidelines for research, development, testing, and pilot studies of IEC materials for students and medical education. Training is also needed within WHO and its agencies. However, gender sensitivity training should not be forced, but should focus on how including a gender perspective will make programs work better. Workshops might include project planning exercises during which participants are given evidence and data illustrating how gender issues have an effect on their particular program areas.

A comprehensive IEC approach would make the existing plethora of health information and data more comprehensible and accessible to women and media groups. This would require collaboration with women's education, training, communications, and media centres in developing countries or international ones such as the IWTC and Third World Women's Media. Computer networks and database systems are potential purveyors of information. Currently, medical references "on line" allow a health consumer to get information on side effects of pharmaceuticals and cautions. There is also a database on emergency first aid. A woman can gain access to medical networks used by health professionals, often at reasonable costs. However, there is little information on women's health in developing countries. Such material could be provided at low cost immediately, and made available internationally through the Internet.

Research priorities

It may appear that considerable research has been conducted on gender and health issues. However, both more and better quality data are needed. As *Women's Health: Across Age and Frontier* (WHO 1992) points out, much current information is based on limited case studies, and national statistics are often inaccurate: maternal mortality and morbidity figures are often grossly underestimated due to underreporting and lack of standardization in registration; data on women's mental health and cases of violence against women are lacking in most developing countries. Although mapping out the best available information on women's health, the WHO document also highlights important research questions in a number of areas from neglect of the girl child to tropical diseases and aging.

NGOs, health groups, WHO documents, and other reports on women and health reflect a deep malaise within the women's movement about the ethical premises of current biomedical and health-technology research. Concerning reproductive technologies, activists have demanded a place on national ethics review committees so that women's welfare will be considered in choices affecting safety, efficacy, affordability, and acceptability of reproductive technologies (WHO 1991a). They also want health researchers and policymakers to look beyond narrow medical research paradigms and incorporate the social, cultural, economic, and personal realities of women. The following research approaches and priorities might facilitate the application of ethics to health research. They are also examples of major gaps in basic knowledge required to reorient health policies and planning toward a gender perspective.

Social, cultural, economic, and political data on etiology, epidemiology, and health behaviour: The research and database on which current health services are based are largely inadequate and even misleading. For example, health statistics may be gathered in such a way that the female population cannot be divided into social and economic risk groups. Employment and marital status are often omitted from survey information.

Although data disaggregated by sex and age are a fundamental requirement for health planning, they are still uncommon in most industrializing countries. Improving the quality of information, testing the results of case studies, and ensuring that these results are used in delivery of health care is a starting point. However, a gender and health paradigm that is useful to health development will also have to include better social, cultural, economic, and political data.

Safe womanhood: A second issue is looking at "safe womanhood" instead of simple "safe motherhood." "While the global campaign for safe motherhood has been vital in improving the health status of the world's women, the focus on women's health needs to be expanded to include the determinants of health and health risks during a woman's entire life cycle" (Lewis et al. 1994). Interventions during the reproductive years alone have generally been limited because many health problems have developed before those years.

As common sense as this may seem, adequate longitudinal studies in gender and health are rare. Few studies have tracked cohorts of women over time. How does early socialization into gender roles affect self-esteem and female health behaviour at different ages? What are the linkages to psychological disorders? What are the long-term consequences of environmental degradation and occupational health hazards on women and their children? Do these change the genetic base of the population? How can health services better cope with "environmentally caused" health problems?

Other areas for research: In addition to these two broad research approaches, the following more specific research topics would contribute significantly to gender and health:

+ Integration of modern technologies into traditional medical systems: determining the impact of allopathic medical S&T on women's health regarding etiology, epidemiology, and quality of services, in the context of their complex interaction with traditional medical cultures, self-care, and traditional medicine.

+ Women's health and the environment: testing indicators using women's health as a quantifiable, sensitive indicator of sustainable development; longitudinal studies of the impact of ecological degradation and poverty on the health of poor women and children; considering occupational and reproductive health.

+ Women as scientists and health-care providers: studying gender discrimination within the health-care delivery system as it affects female health scientists, health-care workers, and professionals in developing countries, particularly young, single women, focusing on issues of work mobility, sexual harassment, and upper-level management training.

In addition, the following are research priorities in the area of reproductive technologies:

+ Abortion: women's decision-making processes about the safety and appropriateness of traditional methods and new ones for menstrual "regulation" and abortion, such as RU486, compared with surgical or vacuum-aspiration abortion.

+ Barrier methods: affordable barrier methods, such as the female condom, which is also woman-controlled, combined with microbicide to prevent HIV infections; socioeconomic research to ensure acceptability and low cost; other possibilities include male barrier methods, female diaphragms, vaginal sponges, and spermicide or viricide.

✦ Sexually transmitted diseases (STDs): Basic research on user perspectives related to sexuality, treatment-seeking behaviour, and use of health services for the treatment of STDs and AIDS by men and women at different ages; research on the effects of psychosocial, cultural, and economic factors on health behaviours such as prevention, risk behaviour, and use of services.

Conclusion

What would the world be like if women could achieve health as a "state of complete well-being?" In the draft *NGO Platform for Action for the 1995 Beijing World Women's Conference*, the answer lies in this statement:

> Freedom from violence and coercions, whether physical, intellectual, or cultural, freedom from hunger, freedom of expression and reproductive choice are basic human rights of all human beings which should be exercised and enjoyed on an equal basis.

Women's right to health is a fundamental human right. However, looking at health through women's eyes, you do not see a vision just for women. Rather, it is one that transforms society for men and children as well.

Considerable effort and success on the part of women and health activists has resulted in better access to the health system for women. Concerning the impact of S&T on women's health, much more research is required, particularly in the complex interactions between demographic transitions, environmental degradation, and the impact of modern medicine on indigenous medicine. The development of health technologies is a newer issue for gender and health activists, but there is some indication of progress, notably in reproductive health technologies.

At the global level, such institutions as WHO and conferences as the Social Summit, the Population Conference, and the World Women's Conference, are important steps toward providing international support for national efforts. Among these is the recently formed Gender Working Group of the UN Commission on Science and Technology, which has the broad mandate to advise governments and the UN system on gender and S&T policies. Although WHO's efforts are noteworthy, considerably more attention must be paid to gender training within the organization and on stronger linkages between NGOs and WHO.

Even these efforts cannot be effective at the national level unless there is greater coherence in the overall direction of S&T. A national S&T policy and advisory body would help ensure that policies are mutually supportive. Good gender and health policies cannot be effective if development, as a whole, is moving in the wrong direction. Policies in economics, communications, alternative medicine, and information technologies all affect women's health. Therefore, health S&T policies and institutions, such as medical research councils, must be closely linked to national S&T mechanisms.

S&T development alone cannot create gender equality or solve women's health problems. Indeed, the abuse of amniocentesis and the many problems associated with contraceptive research show that advanced medical technologies can be used to infringe on women's human rights.

Health is a "women's sector" in the sense that most traditional health caretakers, lower-level professionals, and family decision-makers are women. However, these greater numbers have not necessarily meant that women have been able to change how decisions about S&T are applied to health. Major changes are thus needed in the systems of decision-making, management, and monitoring of the health system for this to take place.

Strategic actions and entry points for implementing policies are feasible at this stage, but the social, economic, and political contexts of S&T must be looked at more closely and partnerships must be broadened to make S&T work. Youth, people in the mass media, and researchers, as well as the women's movements, are important groups to bring together to reexamine how to evaluate the broad effect of government S&T policies on health.

The UN and governments must also find room for women to take their place, not as victims, but as citizens in a new civil society based on participatory democracy. As the UN takes greater cognizance of gender issues in a wide range of technical fields, it invites greater interaction with the international women's movement. If the UN is to evolve and change, it must increasingly open its doors to NGOs, social movements, and individuals who challenge it to be accountable to the people it represents.

Through the work of the UN Commission on Science and Technology, the gender and health issue may become more firmly rooted within the S&T debate. However, this also requires an ethical stance in which women as providers and users of health technologies have the right to equal access and evaluation of the impact of health S&T. This "human right" must be safeguarded as the fundamental value basis of the gender perspective on health S&T.

Chapter 7

Doing the right thing, not just doing things right

A framework for decisions about technology

Arminée Kazanjian

Interest in technological choices and their effects on health has accelerated in recent years; it is manifested by the global trend to bring about health reform. Marked decline in overall economic growth and the consequent increased pressure on public budgets has been cited by public policymakers as the reason for a desire for more appropriate and effective delivery of health care. Because of the globalization of world economies, all countries have simultaneously experienced this phenomenon, albeit to different degrees.

However, health reform is variously perceived (and implemented) by countries, states, and other jurisdictional levels. Governments have sought to deal with pressures on health-care budgets in different ways, often undertaking (or contracting) evaluative studies and technology assessment to provide them with direction in reducing the cost of publicly funded services. In contrast, changing public expectations and the proliferation of medical technology, two important "external" pressures frequently cited by health policymakers, are rarely examined in the broader context of technological development and diffusion. A critical approach and feminist analysis, as expounded in this paper, provide a different frame of reference.

New health technologies (drugs, devices, and procedures) are becoming available at an increasing rate. Unfortunately, the development and diffusion of technology is associated neither with its inherent attributes nor with the prevalence of disease. Furthermore, not much is known about the diffusion of health technology — new or old. Technology does not dictate its own range of applications, nor its price; societal reaction to the technology is a key determinant of its use. For example, electronic fetal monitoring was adopted in the absence of any evidence as to its effectiveness and substantial evidence of harm to pregnant women. Subsequent epidemiologic research confirmed that the device was of no specific value in improving fetal outcome, but doubled the rate of caesarean sections (Bassett 1993). The technique remains firmly established in obstetric practice. This example also illustrates the vulnerability of all women in the health sector as nurses, midwives, and technologists continue to use it, as well as birthing mothers, who expect it to be part of the obstetric routine.

The role of national governments in the development and diffusion of health technology is an influential one, and numerous opportunities exist for adopting a theoretical framework to guide technology decisions. In the absence of a national technology policy, decisions regarding health technology are often contradictory. How much technology and for whom? These decisions are usually made intuitively, without systematic consideration of possible alternatives and consequences of various options. A framework that puts technology into a social context and provides a critical analysis of the broad range of potential issues and interests would make the decision-making process more transparent and equitable.

Decision-support models are used to make explicit the process of thinking about alternatives and to make transparent to the decision-maker available choices and consequences of such choices. Because the human mind is limited in attention, memory, and calculation, and imperfect in perception, we tend to simplify, use limited viewpoints, highlight some aspects; unless the decision-making process is an explicit, stepwise activity, limited rationality will prevail. Policymakers respond to situations as they interpret them, not as they exist in some objective reality; the same problem in a different frame can elicit a very different response. As well, decision-making often involves difficult trade-offs, and most people adopt a simple rule that does not require trading-off incommensurables. Finally, the policymakers rarely find out the broad consequences of their decision or whether the decision was considered "good" or "bad" (Carroll and Johnson 1990).

The conceptual framework proposed here focuses on how alternative choices may have diverse consequences that stretch beyond immediate outcomes and seeks to identify desirable or preferable futures. Because it relates the technology under consideration to human needs in the broadest sense, the framework provides a synthesis of the social dynamics of each situation; it presents a critical perspective that delineates issues of power and dominance, as well as technological impact. Policy researchers erroneously assume that decision-making always occurs in a series of fairly well-defined stages (that could also repeat and backtrack):

- ✦ Recognition of a problem;
- ✦ Formulation of possible interventions;
- ✦ Generation of alternatives;
- ✦ Information search;
- ✦ Judgement or choice;
- ✦ Action; and
- ✦ Feedback.

However, most often decision-making comprises only information search and choice (Payne et al. 1978; Svenson 1979). A broader "problem-solving" approach is adopted for the proposed framework to ensure a comprehensive understanding of the specific problem or deficit as well as a thorough examination of the consequences of alternative courses of action. The framework can be used during policy formulation as a proactive analytic tool that explicitly considers possible alternative courses of action and their respective consequences. This application also facilitates public consultation as well as solicitation of expert opinion. Alternatively, the framework can be used to analyze and aid understanding of how a past (or current) situation has occurred, especially in the case of a "wrong" technology, delineating the reasons for the negative consequences of the technology.

Society seems to be unable to manage technological change in a way that respects and serves the broad range of human interests and needs. On a global level, historic and continuing efforts to include women's needs and concerns in the way science and technology (S&T) are developed and evaluated have not yielded discernible results. Over the last two decades, many official documents containing long lists of recommendations have been produced. In *The Vienna Programme of Action on Science and Technology for Development*, it was recognized that "modern technological developments do not automatically benefit all groups of society equally ... and may have a negative impact on the condition of women and their bases for economic, social and cultural contributions to the development process" (UN 1979b). An appeal was made to strengthen support of national government efforts to promote full participation of women in the application of S&T for development.

Some years later, the *Report of the Ad Hoc Panel* of the Advisory Committee on Science and Technology for Development, postulated that the absence of women from the highest policy and decision-making ranks in S&T "affects the process, quality, and outcomes" of the latter (UN 1984). The panel concluded that, although it is not clear how this would take shape, women should be given access to the process. Furthermore, "inadequacies of existing indicators of the impact of technological change on women" were noted and the need for better measurement of relevant concepts was identified.

Yet, S&T policy, at national and international levels, remains unresponsive to women and their needs, although there is recognition in these documents and in others that assessment, monitoring, and measurement of the effect of S&T on development is desirable. At present, any change in this regard can only occur as part of an intentional prescriptive process where goals are clearly defined at various levels and decisions are aimed at reaching those goals. The framework developed in this paper stimulates the articulation of goals, enabling the systematic monitoring and broad assessment of technological change.

Although most decisions do not follow the explicit stage-by-stage process, implicit rules of decision-making are, nevertheless, operant. Published material on decision research indicates that, in making important decisions, general, formal, or complex rules are usually desirable. Furthermore, a combination and mix of general and specific, simple and complex rules give the best results in terms of better decisions (Gustafson et al. 1992). The proposed framework meets these criteria. Consistent dimensions, identified as policy concerns, are developed for application to all technology decisions. Clearly defined, accurately measured indices of each dimension may be combined with less specific ones, or qualitative measures, to develop composite measures for each of the dimensions. The proposed model comprises several components or dimensions and provides a comprehensive approach to decision-making. However, it is designed with ease of application in mind and should not be too onerous to use.

Building on two previous studies on this subject (Kazanjian and Cardiff 1993; Kazanjian and Friesen 1993), the framework (Table 1) for technology decisions in health care was developed incorporating five key dimensions. The first four — population at risk, population impact, economic concerns, and broad social context (including ethical, legal, and political concerns) — are descriptive elements of the health problem in question and the social, environmental context within which the problem is defined. The fifth component — technology assessment — is the scientific evidence about the health problem and the technologies used to alleviate the problem. It provides information on the strength and quality of the evidence on a technology or health program.

Table 1. Framework for health technology decisions.

Dimension	Indicators	Target/goal (examples)
Population at risk[a] ♦ Epidemiological orientation ♦ Health systems research orientation	♦ Mortality: death rates, cause-specific death rates, proportionate mortality ratio, case-fatality ratio ♦ Potential years of life lost (PYLL) ♦ Morbidity: incidence rates, prevalence rates ♦ Use of health services ♦ Access to services and geographic indicators ♦ Impact of violence on health ♦ Lifestyle-related health indicators	♦ Reduced health deficits of the population ♦ Increased accessibility to services ♦ Healthier lifestyle
Population impact[a] ♦ Epidemiological orientation ♦ Health systems research orientation	♦ Disability: functional or physiological (quality of well-being); for example, functional assessment inventory, sickness impact profile, Nottingham health profile, quality of well-being scale, social relationship scale ♦ Potential impact: "etiological fraction" ♦ Quality of life	♦ Improved quality of life and well-being ♦ Reduced burden of illness
Economic concerns ♦ Compares the inputs of an intervention with some combinations of the outputs	♦ Cost-effectiveness analysis ♦ Cost-benefit analysis ♦ Cost-utility analysis ♦ Opportunity costs	♦ Optimization of total social returns by weighing estimated costs and perceived benefits ♦ Recognition of allocative efficiency
Social context[b] ♦ Individuals (by gender) ♦ Communities ♦ Organizations and groups ♦ Institutions and systems	♦ Social context ♦ Ethical acceptance ♦ Political will ♦ Legal framework ♦ Power and dominance issues	♦ Balanced gender participation in decision-making ♦ Fostering gender autonomy ♦ Gauging political will ♦ Development of legal perspective
Technology-assessment activity ♦ Role of scientific evidence ♦ Quality of scientific evidence	♦ Comprehensiveness of scientific evidence ♦ Source of scientific evidence ♦ Convergence of scientific evidence	♦ Increased understanding of conflicting interests ♦ Improved relevance of evaluative research

[a] Of problem, disease, or health issue. All indicators should be by gender, age, and cultural group.
[b] Including ethical, legal, and political concerns.

To show clearly how the framework can be applied to a health technology decision, a hypothetical situation requiring a policy decision is presented and examined: the use of ultrasound during pregnancy. The use of this procedure is common in developed countries and is rapidly increasing in developing countries, where its cost is moderate. The hypothetical decision is whether the procedure should be publicly funded and under what circumstances. Ultrasonography is the imaging technique that permits "seeing with sound" (Yoxen 1987). Its use during pregnancy is a major (albeit not exclusive) application of the technology. Sound waves sent through amniotic fluid bounce off structures to produce a two-dimensional, cross-sectional picture of the woman and the fetus on a video display screen (Gold 1984). It is used to assess the duration of pregnancy and position of the fetus in the womb.

The first two dimensions of the framework, population at risk and population impact, represent the epidemiologic orientation of health research. Epidemiology is the study of the distribution and determinants of diseases and injuries in human populations. It is concerned with the *extent* and types of illnesses and injuries in *groups* of people and with the *factors* that influence their distribution (Steiner et al. 1989). Epidemiology is concerned primarily with three major variables: person, place, and time.

+ *Person* characteristics include gender, age, race, marital status, and socioeconomic status, among others.

+ The *place* or geographic distribution of a health-related outcome of interest can also be important in understanding causal relations or planning health services to meet the needs of a particular community. Geographic differences can suggest a role for factors such as climate or cultural practices, including diet, method of food preparation and food storage, in the incidence and prevalence of a particular disease. Alternatively, geographic differences may be due to differential access to health services.

+ Variations in the *time* of occurrence of a particular disease can also indicate causal relations along with the other factors that can account for the changes in disease distribution over time.

The variables of person, place, and time are important in understanding the nature of person–environment fit, a key construct in assessing the risk and protective factors that determine health status in groups of people.

Identifying the population at risk

Population at risk takes into account the magnitude of the problem. In health research, this population is usually defined in epidemiologic terms, such as the number of new cases of the disease or problem (incidence) or the number of existing cases (prevalence), which are known as morbidity rates (Mausner and Bahn 1974). These rates are usually known in varying degrees of precision in developed countries and may be more crudely estimated in developing countries; statistics may be compiled at national or local levels. Population at risk can also be defined in different terms such as general death rates or cause-specific death rates, known as mortality statistics. A comprehensive consideration of the population at risk includes relevant measures such as age, sex, socioeconomic status, access to health programs (that is, individual characteristics), as well as natural history of the disease or health problem and relevant social indicators, such as measures of income disparity or illiteracy rates (that is, collective characteristics).

The first step is to identify the population of interest vis-à-vis the technology under consideration. It is important to be inclusive at this stage to determine the magnitude of the phenomenon under examination. For ultrasound, all women of childbearing age (say, 15–45 years) would comprise the population of interest; however, those who are pregnant are the more likely population at risk.

To determine the size of this group, simple empirical evidence can be sought, such as the proportion of women in the age-groups of interest and fertility rates. More elaborate estimates of the potential population of interest could also be obtained by factoring in average family size, number of multiparous women, and so forth, with assistance from demographers. The important point is to determine the level of empirical precision required for the particular decision under consideration, then seek this evidence with or without assistance from empiricists in the field. Although accuracy and precision of data are desirable objectives, variations in availability and accuracy should not become a major deterrent to this approach. For example, it would be important to ascertain the geographic or ethnic distribution of the population of interest only if services are delivered in a decentralized fashion, or if cultural factors are known to contribute to risk factors. Otherwise, aggregate statistics expressed as actual counts or estimated rates would suffice.

Other statistical indicators may be of interest depending on the intended use of the technology, that is, whether ultrasound will be made available as a screening tool to all pregnant women (the current practice in developed countries) or whether (to contain costs) it will be used only as a diagnostic tool, available to women identified by primary-care providers as high-risk pregnancies.

In summary, the decision-maker would raise two basic questions as a first step: who is the population at risk (that is, those who need this technology) and what qualitative and quantitative empirical evidence is available to describe that population in epidemiologic terms? The extent to which answers to these questions can be provided will indicate the clarity with which the magnitude of the problem at hand is defined and the degree to which an empirical appreciation of the problem exists. Furthermore, a statistical profile of current service use and, if possible, the demand for such services completes the picture. All along, the decision-maker may consult with researchers to establish the relative quality of the empirical evidence and with interested parties for assistance with broad or specific definitions of the population at risk.

Estimating population impact

Population impact takes into account the known, expected consequences of the intervention. The impact on population health is often measured by examining both functional ability (physical and social) and psychological status (quality of well-being). Measures of functional status and well-being can be either generic or system-specific (see Table 1). A wide range of narrowly defined health-status measures has been described, and discussion generally includes information about the purpose, reliability, and validity of the measurement instrument (McDowell and Newell 1987). However, these particular measures are not usually gender specific, and there is no feminist critique of them. Special effort would be required to address this obvious research gap.

In addition to population impact, other useful measures of impact include quality of life and "potential" impact. Measures of potential impact reflect the *expected effect* of changing the distribution of one or more risk factors in a particular population. Although the utility of this measure may be somewhat limited, it has important value in decision-making related to public-health issues. For example, this measure would be valuable for proactive assessment of public-health programs aimed at eliminating risk factors in a population.

The purpose of this step is to examine and understand the burden of illness. If ultrasound is being used as a screening tool, then what are the expected consequences of this screening? Once again, it is more important to raise the appropriate question and attempt to obtain some quantifiable measure for its answer than to seek to be particularly precise in that answer. If, for example, reliable statistics exist on maternal and infant morbidity, then the decision-maker will be better informed. The next question to consider is: how much of the burden of illness may be reduced by using ultrasound technology? Often, expert clinical opinion or consensus statements may be the only available information; in this case, good epidemiologic information is available (Anderson 1994).

Another important point related to screening or diagnostic interventions is the availability of therapy or cure. Once problems have been identified by ultrasound, are there health-care or other measures to attenuate the burden of illness? Does ultrasonography provide the type of diagnostic information that, if acted upon (treatment), would make a difference to women's and babies' health and quality of life? As direct intervention to treat the fetus in utero is unusual, identification of abnormalities may not be of great value except to offer abortion.

Finally, questions regarding the potential health risk of the technology and whether it is offset by potential benefits should be raised. This is similar to risk assessment. For example, there are no known major medical or health risks associated with the use of ultrasound imaging itself, but problems of false diagnosis (due to machine or human error, or both) and subsequent investigation and treatment cannot be overlooked.

It is also important to note that the choice of statistical indicators and quantitative measures to depict the epidemiologic dimension can affect the way a situation is portrayed. For example, maternal mortality rates are expressed as maternal deaths per 100 000 (or 10 000) live births. Rates of 100 to 200 are considered very high, but pale when compared with a different expression of the same situation: years of life lost (YLL). The YLL statistic would take into account age at death and the average life expectancy of women of that age and present the cumulative figure for the 200 women at, roughly, 7 000–8 000 YLL.

Economic concerns

The economic component of the decision framework considers what society can reasonably afford. How society arrives at decisions about what it can afford is an important but opaque question. How a government agency decides appears to be based on finite financial resources. Those who plan, deliver, and pay for health services are constantly faced with the fact that the supply of professionals, hospitals and other facilities, and technologies cannot meet the demands or needs of all patients (Sackett et al. 1985). Decision-makers must decide how to apply limited resources where they will do the most good. The solution involves both costs and consequences and, because it implies a choice between alternative courses of action, it constitutes an economic evaluation. Money may be the unit of measurement, but the real or "opportunity" cost of any health program or technology is the sum of effects or benefits foregone by committing resources to this program rather than to another one.

The economic dimension of the decision framework compares the inputs to a health-care program with some combination of the outputs. The inputs usually include:

✦ Direct costs to the health-care sector and to patients and their families — in aggregate, they correspond to the portion of gross national product spent on health care;

✦ Indirect costs expressed in terms of production losses because of morbidity, mortality, and use of health care; and

✦ Intangible costs — pain, suffering, grief, and so on, that is, any nonfinancial outcomes of disease and medical care.

The outputs of a health technology can be summarized in three categories.

✦ *Conventional clinical outcomes*, such as number of cases treated or number of life years saved. When compared with inputs, this type of analysis is referred to as cost-effectiveness analysis (CEA). It considers the possibility of improved outcomes in exchange for the use of resources. It cannot be used to choose between technologies with different outcomes or to determine what weights should be put on human life, but gives an indication about the quantity of life of a person with a given health condition (Eisenberg 1989; Bowie 1991; Feeny and Torrance 1992).

✦ *Monetary value of different health effects.* Comparing technology costs with its effects defined in monetary terms is referred to as cost–benefit analysis (CBA). CBA is an attempt to link cost information with medical evidence on the outcomes of treatment, but forces an explicit decision about whether the costs are worth the benefits by measuring both in the same unit of currency (Drummond and Stoddart 1984; Sisk 1987).

✦ Outcome is measured not only in terms of quantity of life, but also in terms of *quality of life* using such indices as quality adjusted life-years (QALYs) and disability adjusted life-years (DALYs). Cost–utility analysis is yet another method of weighting for quality of life variations (Drummond 1987).

The choice of measure depends on the health outcome of interest. A *cost-effectiveness ratio* would be used when there is only one health outcome of interest; for example, comparing two technologies in terms of their cost per life-years gained, such as in an immunization program. A *cost–benefit ratio* would be applied when there are multiple health outcomes of interest, such as degree of hypertension and level of cholesterol. Monetary values are given to outcomes to allow comparison of the merits of each intervention. Finally, a *cost–utility ratio* would be used when the interest is on quality of health outcome, not just quantity.

Several problems arise in economic analysis, related to both theory and measurement. The theoretical basis of CBA lies in new welfare economics and is designed to identify the economic conditions that will maximize the social welfare under various resource restrictions. Changes in social welfare are not easy to evaluate. CBA cannot determine whether the objective is worth achieving; it just examines the much narrower question of payoff resulting from the use of a technology. Similarly, social costs are usually omitted from consideration because of measurement problems. As CBA for a single technology can be undertaken from the different perspectives of each interested party (or constituency), the decision-maker will possibly be able to identify potential opposition but will not have an understanding of the reasons. Cost-effectiveness is not grounded in theory and does not assist in the identification of policy direction. It does provide a comparison of cost for a selected outcome or desired effect. Thus, neither CEA nor CBA are advisable as primary tools for decision-making.

However, efficiencies in health and health care are particularly important during times of economic restraint. To apply limited resources where at least some good will result, the decision-maker has to raise the question of cost-effectiveness. Despite the difficulties cited above, a number of fundamental cost-and-benefit questions should be raised and empirical measures examined carefully.

To begin a fiscal analysis, costs beyond that of capital or acquisition costs should be ascertained, that is, operating costs for various levels of throughput (productivity). For example, once ultrasound equipment is purchased, what is the cost of providing services in hospitals (public or private), in community clinics, in urban centres only, or across the country to reach remote areas? What are the costs for service provision during regular business hours, for additional hours of service, and for multiple shifts? The higher the acquisition cost, the higher the level of productivity required to off-set such costs. In addition, costs associated with human-resource requirements should also be carefully considered. For example, pay-ment of technologists and specialist physicians are important expen-ditures. However, additional costs to the system may include those for credentialing professionals, the academic research interests of clinicians, and continuing education for staff.

Once costs for a single imaging unit are ascertained, esti-mates of total cost can be computed for the entire population at risk and for subpopulations. This information, coupled with nonpriced (human) cost information on population impact, can begin to provide the decision-maker with a sketch of the economic dimension of options. In some situations, full-scale cost-effectiveness or cost-utility evidence might be available, including costs for alternative and com-plementary interventions and health outcomes.

Opportunity costs should also be examined. For equivalent expenditures, what other services can be purchased or are being for-gone. Such costs can be articulated either in terms of other services to the population of interest or to another population. For example, what level of services can be purchased and what results can be obtained if the same amount of money were allocated to nutrition or to infection control for pregnant women? The effectiveness of prena-tal care with a focus on nutrition is indisputable. Or, what would an investment similar in amount to that for ultrasound yield toward devices to assist handicapped women?

Finally, decision-makers should at least strive to establish a value-for-resources-expended ratio to women, service agencies, and to the health-care system for a specified quantity of fetal ultrasonog-raphy services. Value may be expressed in other than monetary or health-outcome measures, and pertinent socioeconomic factors may also be appropriate indices for such analysis.

Social context

As the health-care system is a subsector of the larger social system, the diffusion of a technology in health care should be analyzed in that context. The development or diffusion of a single health technology has implications for consumers, health professionals, taxpayers, ser-vice agencies, educational institutions, and industry, as well as social institutions such as the family, the community, and the economy (to name a few). The reason and direction of these relations have not been well investigated in health assessment.

Social-impact analysis is a way to understand, explain, and predict the potential effects of technology on social systems. Social indicators, the quantitative measures of interest, can be expressed at the level of the individual, family unit, community, organization, or system. However, the boundaries between social and ethical, ethical and legal, or legal and political aspects are not always clear and inter-active effects occur (Duncan 1984). For example, the use of health technology could result in a demographic change that might interact with an altered economic base in a region to change the power of the regional political institutions. Conversely, understanding the relations between social structure or values and health technology is equally important in the assessment of that technology. For example, why is the electronic fetal monitor firmly established in obstetrical practice despite the evidence of harm to pregnant women? Legal implications are often cited; but does litigation influence medical practice or vice versa? The value of a "perfect" child from every birth is a socially determined phenomenon; technology that is perceived to promote such "perfection" is wholeheartedly adopted. Ethical implications are focal points in all reproductive technologies, as questions are often raised about the "commodification" of women and babies. In addition, ethical implications of genetic testing and the enormous powers vested in that type of knowledge are of ultimate importance from a social policy perspective as well as from a health-care delivery perspective.

An increasingly important component of health-care evaluation concerns the expected effects of new technologies, or technology transfers, within the spheres of medical ethics and social justice. Appropriate indicators within each of these dimensions can be compiled from published research and ranked according to relative importance by panels of experts, then taken to the community (or interested parties) for consultation. In the framework proposed here, social values and technical expertise are considered to be complementary in a process that strives for justice and fairness (Garland 1992).

Specifically, constituencies and interested parties should be consulted regarding their views of the relative importance of the four major tenets of medical ethics; autonomy, beneficence, nonmalfeasance, and justice (Beauchamp and Childress 1989). *Autonomy* refers to the extent to which patients and their families are able to remain in meaningful control of their care, including decisions about which interventions to undergo (or to refrain from undergoing) as part of their care plan. *Beneficence* relates to the extent to which technologies provide true health benefits in the areas most favoured by patients, such as enhanced quality of life and prevention of disease. *Nonmalfeasance* refers to the potential for certain technologies to produce a net harmful effect on patients. Certain painful or risky procedures of dubious or minimal benefit may fall into this category. Finally, considerations of *justice* are increasingly important in the area of health-care technology assessment because of the growing tension in some countries between a tradition of egalitarianism in health-care delivery (universal public coverage) and the shrinking pool of resources available to pay for all effective services. This consideration is of particular importance when new technologies are expected to be very expensive and of potential benefit to small numbers of patients or specific subpopulations.

Although several distinct dimensions are subsumed under this one category of social context, the framework is not intended to simplify these complex phenomena. For the sake of parsimony, and because all provide the context within which public-policy decisions ought to be examined, these dimensions are presented collectively. Depending on the situation, some permutation of them may be relevant. More likely, all these concerns may be of relevance in varying degrees.

In the case of fetal ultrasonography, the social as well as the ethical dimensions may be more important than the legal and political. To ground the technology in its social context, ask: Is this a socially acceptable technology? Finding an answer requires both empirical (objective) and subjective information. For example, social scientific research on whether ultrasound technology is congruent with the social values of the country pertaining to the care and welfare of pregnant women may be available. By providing visual access to the fetus, ultrasonography conforms with a growing trend in obstetrics to give the fetus patient status, somehow separate from its mother (Mattingly 1992). This may or may not be an acceptable change in social values. Ultrasound can also be used to make a "media spectacle" of pregnancy (Petchesky 1987) and has contributed to a change in women's and men's experience of pregnancy and expectant motherhood and fatherhood (Sandelowski 1994). Are these congruent with local social norms? The impact of technological change on social relations can vary greatly from one group to another, requiring different degrees of social change. On the other hand, the inverse may be the case; different types of social change can culminate in different levels of technological development. Critical feminist analysis has provided pertinent information on issues of power, control, and dominance (Wajcman 1991; Lindenbaum and Lock 1993).

In addition to examining empirical evidence, the decision-maker should consult women or women's groups to obtain their assessment of the issues and their particular perspective on the subject of ultrasound. Again, using the framework facilitates this process of consultation because the decision-maker can approach the interested parties with a set of criteria (the previously discussed dimensions) already elaborated. Those being consulted can follow the decision-maker's process of thought through the material presented and can take issue with any or all of the foregoing logical arguments, if they wish. Without an explicit decision framework, communication between policymaker and others can be a guessing (and outguessing) game.

Another important aspect of the social context is equity: would all those who could benefit from the technology have equal access to it? In the case of fetal ultrasonography, two questions can be raised. First, would this technology be available to all pregnant women? If so, particular attention should be given to designing a service-delivery structure that will reach all pregnant women and allow equal access. Second, if this publicly funded technology is to be made available only for certain medical indications, for example, previously defined high-risk pregnancy, the question of equal access becomes even more important, especially for rural or isolated areas or disadvantaged groups, because a "gatekeeper" to the technology has to be consulted first, requiring perhaps initial travel or forgone earnings, and further displacement for the subsequent services of interest.

Two of the major tenets of medical ethics are particularly relevant to the decision on ultrasound: autonomy and beneficence. The use of this technology often promotes the "commodification" of the fetus and pregnant woman (Sandelowski 1994), while maximizing the male role and expectant fatherhood. Seeing and getting a picture of the fetus becomes as significant as carrying the fetus, thus reducing a woman's control over the situation. This is a hindrance to the pregnant woman's autonomy, as defined by medical ethics.

The extent to which ultrasonography provides true health benefits to the pregnant woman and her fetus has been seriously challenged (Oakley 1986a,b). Ultrasound use becomes even more problematic if it is consistently and routinely misused or abused. The use of ultrasound for sex selection (undertaken routinely in some countries) has now been documented (Royal Commission on New Reproductive Technologies 1993; Wertz and Fletcher 1993; Global Child Health Society 1994). The ensuing abortion of female fetuses raises serious questions regarding beneficence as well as morality. The availability of a technology that is potentially exploitative of women and contributes further to their subjugation should be curtailed immediately until further policy action to stop such undesirable practice is fully implemented. If there is evidence of potential and possible abuse by the health-care provider, or the consumer of the services, regulatory mechanisms to remedy this situation should be concurrently developed and legal implications fully explored and documented.

General and specific questions regarding government regulation of facilities and service organizations, as well as the professionals who provide these services are often desirable and always necessary steps in the decision-making process. Speaking at the opening of the 19th session of the Program Committee of World Health Organization's (WHO's) executive board, Director-General Dr Nakjima stated that "in the field of health, technology cannot be left to govern ethics on an empirical basis. Decisions must be made consciously by us all" (Global Child Health Society 1994).

Political concerns may vary widely among health-care systems and countries. However, in a rational stepwise approach to decision-making, political implications of technological development and change should be raised and considered. If the political imperative will, ultimately, be the only factor driving the decision, at least the decision-maker should be fully aware of the consequences of the decision along all the other dimensions. Finally, it may be desirable to weight each dimension, rather than attributing equal importance to all of them.

Technology assessment

In a narrow sense, health-technology assessment (HTA) involves the evaluation or testing of a technology for safety and benefits when used under ideal conditions (efficacy). In a broader sense, it is the process for policy research that examines the short- and long-term consequences of the technology in question. Health technology has been defined to include the drugs, devices, and medical and surgical procedures used in health care and the organizational or administrative and support systems within which health care is delivered (Institute of Medicine 1985).

The assessment of a technology sometimes combines concerns from the clinical, epidemiologic,. economic, and sociolegal perspectives. These aspects are usually specific to the technology in question. The assessment would consider:

+ The safety of the technology — a judgement of the acceptability of risk in a specified situation, which may include comment on the quality of provider or type of facility within which the technology is used;

✦ The benefit of using a technology or procedure for a particular clinical problem under ideal conditions (efficacy), such as within a study environment in a laboratory or at a teaching hospital;

✦ The benefit of using a technology or procedure for a particular clinical problem under general or routine conditions (effectiveness), such as in a field situation or within a rural or nonteaching hospital;

✦ Considerations of costs, volume of services, and benefits in terms of cost savings and other factors such as lives saved or serious illness prevented; and

✦ The implications of using the technology in the context of societal norms, cultural values, and social institutions and relations.

Some, and on rare occasions all, of these concerns form part of the analytic frame that is used to approach the technology-assessment activity.

Assessments usually incorporate one or more methods. The first step is a thorough search of published information through library databases, as well as all fugitive information, which does not appear in peer-reviewed publications. The information is examined for strength and quality. Research that has been conducted using rigorous methods is generally given more weight than research using weaker methods of study. For example, evidence obtained from at least one properly designed, randomized, controlled trial is viewed as stronger than evidence from nonrandomized or descriptive studies. An assessment will be more powerful when it is based on meta-analysis, for example, or reports of expert committees. Systematic evaluation of a technology can draw on research using any assessment method, but, currently, most technology assessments use primarily synthesis of the literature, expert opinion, and cost analysis.

Most health technology falls into one of six categories of application: prevention, screening, diagnosis, treatment, rehabilitation, and palliation. The application of the technology is particularly important as the assessment usually focuses on this aspect. Clear criteria exist for evaluating technologies or health programs for screening, diagnosis, and treatment. Technologies may be assessed at different stages of diffusion — the process by which a technology enters and becomes part of the health-care system (OTA 1976). These stages include: emerging, new to practice, established, almost obsolete, and outmoded.

Under ideal conditions, a technology should be assessed *before* diffusion into the social system. However, in the real world, most health technology is adopted before it is examined for efficacy or effectiveness (for example, diethylstilbestrol (DES), thalidomide, and birth-control pills). The costs to the system and society are sometimes enormous, as was the case when thalidomide was used to treat nausea in pregnancy.

HTA attempts to make sense of the available information regardless of its source. Evaluation is based on analysis of the evidence and the strength of the findings. Logical and defensible conclusions about the technology are formulated in reports usually prepared for the decision-makers. Generally, assessment is undertaken to examine only the effectiveness of health care and to provide information in a timely manner for more informed decision-making by policymakers, industry, health professionals, and consumers. It is also undertaken to reexamine technology critically at various stages of diffusion. Technology assessment may be used to slow the adoption of emerging or new technologies but, most often, it is to help decision-makers allocate resources among established technologies.

The technology-assessment dimension incorporates a different type of factor into the decision process: the weight of scientific evidence specific to the health technology. Methodologic rigour and the application of rules of evidence to what is known about the technology under consideration provides arguably the most reasoned of decisions. However, complete scientific evidence is rarely available, or even possible to obtain concurrent with the decision-making effort. Health technology diffuses much faster than the time-frame required to undertake good, scientific research. The inclusion of this dimension in the framework yields new information about the interplay between research, scientific evidence, and health-technology diffusion.

The importance of this dimension in the framework depends on the weight subjectively assigned to it by the decision-maker. As a final step in the rational process, the decision-maker should consider the availability and quality of scientific evidence regarding the technology under consideration, in this case, ultrasonography. Although there is appreciable research on the efficacy of this medical imaging technology in prenatal care, information on its effectiveness and cost-effectiveness is scant and may be much less conclusive.

All the dimensions of the framework depend on reliable indicators (empirical measures) that define and accurately describe the specific policy issues of importance to the decision-maker. The potential contribution of research to policymaking in the health sector is made more evident through the use of the framework and its explicit deliberation of each policy dimension separately, as well as of overall, integral consequences from a societal perspective. The availability and quality of the scientific evidence are, therefore, important factors; however, the lack of accurate data should not lead to the abandonment of the conceptual framework, because raising appropriate questions about the broader context of health and human needs is itself a desirable objective.

Making choices without taking chances

The dominant institutions that structure technological options in health have historically been controlled by the church, the state, the medical profession, research bodies and funding agencies, and drug companies. These technologies develop within a science culture that defines women by their biological function — child bearers — and their social function — child rearers — and research priorities are identified by male scientists. For example, research on contraceptive technologies has examined only clinical efficacy and effectiveness; the question of why particular contraceptive technologies have been developed in preference to others remains unanswered. Also, we know little about the influence of social institutions on the development of reproductive and other health technologies. Decisions about who will get how much of what in health care are made daily, mostly in an ad-hoc fashion that tends to be biased in favour of those in power; women are absent from these circles. Policy mechanisms pertaining to health technology and its diffusion are neither coordinated between local, regional, national, and international levels, nor applied consistently to ensure allocative efficiency (that is, doing "the right thing") in addition to technical efficiency ("doing things right"). Women's concerns and needs would be better met if technological choices were more informed choices.

The framework provides guidelines within which the appropriate information is sought and examined. This is achieved through raising questions for which there may or may not be answers at the time. Because of the framework's explicit and stepwise approach, it can expose the ideologic and social power of those who make decisions during the development and diffusion of technology. Focusing on analysis of the dynamics of the social context reveals women's technological concerns as well as their absence from decision-making roles. This can be corrected.

Where there is evidence of the possibility of harm to women's health and well-being, analysis using the framework exposes conflicting interests that may attempt to mask that situation. In addition, even where the technology of concern is not directly related to women's health, the framework's consultative capacity invites the participation of women in the decision process.

That process, in the hypothetical example of ultrasound imaging for pregnant women, can be rapidly demystified. Policy-makers will become aware of the bias in the language of clinical practice, where ultrasound measurements during pregnancy are known as "fetal" measurements, not "pregnant women" measurements, showing a male medical bias. Epidemiologic evidence indicates that screening of all pregnant women through ultrasound imaging, on balance, does more harm than good. Although it is desirable and necessary to reduce maternal and infant morbidity and mortality rates, such evidence is not forthcoming in developed countries where there is widespread use of this technology. The evidence indicates that programs of prenatal care, such as nutrition education and food distribution, are effective in reducing slow development and other problems of pregnancy. As for economic concerns, the adoption of inappropriate technology at *any* cost is unacceptable.

Within the social context, evidence points to altered social relations, not just between mother and child or father and child, but also among members of larger groups: health-care providers, facilities, and communities. The autonomy of the expectant mother is appreciably reduced by the use of this technology, which ignores a major tenet of medical ethics. Finally, the overt misuse of the technology for sex selection is regarded as immoral and would incur political costs to the present authorities. The right decision for the policymaker (most probably in a developing country where this technology is beginning to be adopted) would clearly be not to purchase ultrasound technology.

In summary, the framework is proposed, not as a substitute for HTA, but in conjunction with it. Others have discussed the methods and limitations of HTA (Banta and Luce 1993; Morgall 1993); they observed that there is almost unanimous agreement on the need for technology assessment in general. However, little mainstream HTA is context-oriented and gender-specific; technology is rarely viewed in a social context of conflicting human interests; and an attempt to make HTA more directly relevant to policymaking is very recent (Battista 1992). The proposed theoretical framework addresses these important issues.

The framework draws on a number of disciplinary perspectives, incorporating theories of epidemiology, sociology, economics, and systems science, and combines a critical feminist approach with that of health-services research. Application of the framework generates a package of information that includes social values. It identifies possible choices by providing an evaluation of the relative sociomedical merits of technological alternatives under consideration; the decision-maker still makes the choice, cognisant of its many consequences.

Future research needs

The recognition that empirical evidence can contribute enormously to health policy and planning has not been uniformly espoused and promoted across time and countries. Funding available for health-systems research has been low relative to that spent on health services, and has not been forthcoming in a predictable, stable pattern. Through a detailed discussion of health-policy issues, this paper emphasises the many areas where there is a lack of knowledge and lack of understanding of population health needs in general, and women's health issues in particular. This information deficit can be appreciably reduced through special, targeted funding of priority areas and continued, stable funding of all areas.

Three areas or types of research can be delineated.

+ *Epidemiologic research* that expounds on the distribution and types of illnesses and injuries in human populations and the factors that influence their distributions. Particularly lacking are studies on women's health.

+ *Health-systems and population-health research* which are multidisciplinary fields that recognize that health is more than medicine. For health-systems research, the focus is on system organisation and delivery of care recognizing that these are at least as important as the content of care. Research on the social indicators of health and illness constitute the major focus for population-health research. Both would contribute enormously to understanding women's health issues.

+ *Health-policy development and analysis research* that expounds specifically on how health decisions are made, who makes decisions, and how best to incorporate empirical evidence into health-policy decisions, given a better understanding of the process and the people. Research on decision-support models or frameworks that facilitate a rational and integrated approach to health policy is a relatively new field. A rational, explicit approach to health policy would, at least in the long term, be useful by bringing women's experiences into the policymaking arena.

Some official international efforts promote the use of research evidence in the health sector. In 1993, at an international consultation convened by WHO in Geneva, studies identified as "health futures" research were presented and discussed. This area is being promoted and supported by WHO because it is perceived to be essential to evolve and develop new approaches that will assist in formulating public health action aimed at accelerating progress toward health for all. The importance of futures research in this context was recognized by the World Health Assembly in 1990 (Taket 1993).

Although the "health futures" label is comparatively recent, the studies identified as such by WHO are concerned with the future of health or health services using methods more broadly defined as epidemiology, systems research, strategic planning, or modelling. The International Health Futures Network is undertaking some projects on modeling futures; however, these are generally described as projection or simulation models either based on the status quo or using hypothetical scenarios for the future. A rational, prescriptive, prospective model, such as the framework proposed herein, has not existed previously, but is particularly supported by the related "health futures" research as a possible and desirable tool.

Chapter 8
Schooling for what?

Education and career opportunities for women in science, technology, and engineering

Eva M. Rathgeber[1]

By 1990, on a global level, 36% of people employed in the formal sector were female. However, in most countries, women continue to be concentrated in lower level and less well-paid types of employment (ILO 1993). Almost universally, female participation in modern science- and technology-based occupations has been remarkably limited despite the important roles traditionally played by women in the development and management of tools and implements in households and in family autarkies. Although they have always been users and often developers of technology, women have rarely been recognized as central actors in science and technology (S&T).

Although historians of science have provided evidence of female scientific activity — as physicians in the Middle Ages, mathematicians in early modern Italy, and natural scientists in the 19th century (Mozans 1991) — female participation in S&T was discouraged during most of modern European history. Britain's Royal Society, established in 1662, did not admit women until 1945; even today only 2.9% of its Fellows are female: only seven women (3.5% of new Fellows) were elected in 1989–93. Britain's Royal Academy of Engineering has elected three women out of 901 Fellows. The American National Academy of Sciences has 1 750 living members, only 70 of them female (Holloway 1993). Where women have been involved in science, their contributions have often been minimized or overlooked. For example, Rosalind Franklin, the British X-ray crystallographer, provided critical information on the structure of DNA that enabled James Watson and Franklin Crick to undertake research on the double helix for which they later won a Nobel Prize. By the early

[1] I am indebted to Patricia Stamp of York University, Patricia Connelly of St Mary's University, and Eglal Rached, IDRC Cairo, for helpful comments on earlier versions of this paper.

1990s, only nine women had been awarded a Nobel Prize in science subjects, compared with more than 300 men.

Feminist theorists have emphasized the biased nature of science, pointing out that it is a human activity heavily influenced by prevailing social, political, and economic factors (Rosser 1988). Some have argued that a feminist science would differ from "masculine" science because of fundamental differences in female perspectives and female approaches to problem solving. Science, as commonly practiced, espouses an essentially male world view, and women scientists who wish to succeed must of necessity work within this view or perspective. One object of continuing debate is the preeminence of scientific method with its emphasis on "rational" thought processes. Definitions of rationality should be expanded to include at least some aspects of other cognitive styles and other "ways of knowing" (Brush 1991). For example, greater emphasis might be placed on evidence from other sources, including various types of intuition. To date, there has been little empirical exploration of whether female scientists really do work differently from male scientists or whether they bring different qualities or emphases to the scientific task (Sorensen 1992).

During the past decade, growing feminist concern with the exclusion of women from S&T has led to determined efforts to correct gender imbalances. However, attempts in North America to increase the numbers of female students in science and engineering programs have had mixed results. Indeed, in the late 1980s, the interest of all American freshman college students in science and engineering subjects declined by one-third during the previous two decades (Task Force on Women, Minorities, and the Handicapped in Science and Technology 1988). An increasingly large number of places in American science-training programs were being filled by foreign students.

Despite this decline in overall interest in science among American students, some critics have maintained that S&T will take women's concerns into account only when more women become scientists and technologists. However, the current model of S&T has been internalized by those (including both women and men) who have gone through and succeeded in the system. The mere fact of increasing the *numbers* of women scientists will not necessarily effect fundamental change in the *conception and practice* of science. If the current practice of S&T is to be reformed, then it will be necessary not only for more women to be represented, but also for a critical assessment to be undertaken of the underlying assumptions that guide the creation of S&T knowledge.

International efforts to integrate women into S&T

During the past 15 years, there has been increasing international concern about the more effective integration of women into S&T. Numerous international conferences have touched on the issue of gender and S&T and many governments have publicly acknowledged that effective development depends on the full utilization of all existing human resources. As such, there is a need to ensure that women's capabilities and strengths are recognized and put to full use. In this context, a number of United Nations (UN) conferences have emphasized the need for better integration of women into global economies.

The Vienna Programme of Action on Science and Technology for Development (UN 1979b) stressed the need for all types of training and education for women. Five years later, the report of the panel of the Advisory Committee on Science and Technology for Development (UN 1984) made a more specific set of recommendations including the participation of women in technical training; the establishment of special apprenticeship programs for women; and the support of women entrants into nontraditional areas such as engineering. The report also suggested a review of school curricula and textbooks; the encouragement of female participation in science clubs; and the development of science teaching materials that incorporate women's needs and perspectives.

The Nairobi Forward-Looking Strategies for the Advancement of Women (UN 1985b) made similar recommendations: the promotion of literacy among women; the promotion of equal opportunity at all levels of education and careers; the elimination of gender stereotyping in education; and the introduction of programs to enable men to share responsibility for child-rearing and household maintenance. Such recommendations were aimed at creating an enabling environment for women to participate fully in S&T (as well as in other aspects of social, economic, and political life). More recently, the UN Conference on Environment and Development (UNCED) in Rio de Janeiro in 1992 emphasized once again the key role of women in environmental preservation and stressed the need for measures to increase education and training opportunities in S&T, especially at the postsecondary level.

All of these recommendations emerging from major international gatherings have reinforced the centrality of women's contribution to economic, social, and political development. There especially has been overwhelming support for the provision of equal educational opportunities to enable women to acquire appropriate knowledge, skills, and training to participate in the practice (and formulation) of S&T.

Concurrently, since the 1970s, a growing number of networks and organizations have emerged, aimed at increasing women's participation in S&T. For example, the Association for Women in Science (AWIS) in the United States was founded in 1971 to promote equal opportunities for women to enter scientific professions and achieve their career goals. Some of AWIS's activities include the promotion of networking among female scientists, recognition and promotion of the achievements of women scientists, and the support of programs and laws intended to eradicate inequities encountered by women studying and working in the sciences. A similar role is played by the Third World Organization of Women in Science and Technology (TWOWS). Founded in the mid-1980s, TWOWS aims to survey and analyze the status and prospects of women in S&T in the Third World; improve access to education and training opportunities; increase the scientific productivity of women scientists in the Third World; and promote collaboration and communication among women scientists and technologists in the Third World and with the international scientific community as a whole. TWOWS was an active partner in organizing a conference on women in S&T, held in Cairo in 1993.

The International Women's Tribune Center (IWTC) in New York has also been an active proponent of women's participation in S&T, particularly in making it more easily comprehensible to less-educated and nonelite women. IWTC has put special emphasis on demystifying and popularizing S&T for and among women globally through the production of simplified texts that combine striking artwork with scientific information written in clear and concise language.

The Gender and Science and Technology Association is a global network that holds regular symposia on the role of women in S&T. It encourages research into all aspects of gender differentiation in science, technology, and employment and fosters gender equality and women's entry into science professions. Recruitment and retention of girls and women in science, engineering, and technology and the development of feminist perspectives on the practice of S&T have been particular areas of concern.

In March 1994, an international panel convened by the US National Research Council's Board on Science and Technology for International Development (BOSTID) in Washington identified five key areas for urgent corrective action. These included communication and dissemination of information; integration of local development and traditional S&T; education and training; facilitating opportunities for women in research; and access.

These represent just a sample of the many networks, organizations, and initiatives that are under way. The integration of women into S&T is a vital area of concern not only for scholars and policymakers but also for activists and development practitioners worldwide. Nonetheless, in virtually all regions of the world, the participation of women in S&T comes nowhere near reflecting their representation in the population.

The following recommendations, among others, have emerged from expert meetings, UN conferences, and various other international forums during the past 15 years. They have accurately diagnosed key weaknesses that have impeded the participation of women and girls in S&T.

+ The social interactions within the family, in schools and churches, and in society at large through which girls and boys acquire a sense of their own role and place in society are potent factors in creating certain assumptions about the respective roles and responsibilities of women and men. Efforts must be made to ensure widespread gender sensitization to ensure that opportunities for girls are not abolished before they have even had a chance to discover their own potential.

+ Curriculum materials must be redesigned to ensure that they are equally relevant for girls and boys. At the same time, science teachers must be sensitized to treat girls and boys the same way in the classroom. They must avoid assuming that girls will be less interested or less competent in science subjects, and they must provide opportunity for girls to find their own solutions to problems rather than giving them answers.

+ Efforts must be made to recruit representative numbers of female science teachers at all levels, including at the tertiary level and in engineering faculties. The importance of role models both by including the achievements of female scientists and technologists in educational materials and as teachers and S&T professionals is critical in "normalizing" the concept of female opportunity and potential success in S&T. Similarly, role models and mentors can help young people develop self-esteem and a sense of capability. Efforts should be made not only to ensure that girls have opportunities to meet and interact with female S&T professionals, but also that male professionals exhibit positive attitudes toward the idea of women in science.

◆ Special efforts should be made to involve girls and young women in science-related events such as science fairs or school science clubs. Girls should also receive information about S&T opportunities through school counselling, interaction with professional societies, and so forth.

◆ Efforts should be made to ensure that women are encouraged to participate in nontraditional careers, such as auto mechanics, construction trades, and so on. Girls who show an aptitude for or interest in such areas should be given opportunities to obtain appropriate training in technical colleges or as apprentices in the workplace. Similarly, women should be included, together with men, in industrial retraining exercises, when new technical skills are being taught.

However, progress in implementing these recommendation has, at best, been mixed. In some countries, efforts have been made to revise existing school systems and create opportunities for girls and women, but in others, the issue has received little or no attention. In many cases, prevailing cultural norms and practices have posed strong deterrents to reform.

Statistical evidence of the participation of women in S&T

Participation rates for women in science are relatively low in most countries. In Sweden, which has a long history of promoting equality between the sexes, women accounted for only 11% of employed nonacademic scientists and engineers in 1985. In Japan, by 1992, fewer than 8% of scientists and engineers were female, most of them employed in less-prestigious scientific institutions.

In the United States, by 1992, the figures were considerably higher, although still not representative of women's numbers in the general population. About 22% of nonacademic scientists and engineers were female; but although women constituted 36% of employed nonacademic scientists, they constituted only 8% of employed nonacademic engineers. In the United Kingdom, the numbers of women studying science and engineering were sufficiently low to warrant concentrated efforts to increase them in the late 1980s when science and mathematics became compulsory core subjects for all children aged 5 to 16 years. However, there has been only a slow increase in the proportion of girls choosing to study sciences to A level. As in the United States, girls who do choose to study sciences tend to concentrate in the biological sciences rather than in natural or physical sciences and engineering. In 1991–92, women in the United Kingdom constituted only 27% of full-time science postgraduate students and 10–25% of postgraduates in engineering, mathematics, and the physical sciences (Committee on Women in Science, Engineering and Technology 1993). Less is known about the numbers of women scientists in developing countries, but evidence suggests that trends parallel those in the industrialized countries, with a tendency toward even greater exclusion (Table 1).

In all countries, the number of women enrolled in medical and health-related fields is substantially higher than in engineering. However, the "medical and health-related" category used by the UN Educational, Scientific and Cultural Organisation (Unesco) does not differentiate between physicians and other types of health workers — such as nurses, physiotherapists, and social workers — making it difficult to assess the extent to which women are enrolled in the most prestigious and potentially well-remunerated area of health studies, that is, medicine. Unlike engineering, medical and health-related careers carry connotations of nurturing and social service. Even at an early age, girls tend to express a preference for careers with a strong element of social service.

Table 1. Proportion (%) of women enrolled in tertiary-level engineering, medical, and health-related courses in various countries, 1985.

Country	Engineering	Medical and health-related
Africa		
Côte d'Ivoire	3.6	32.2
Kenya	1.6	24.7
Senegal	14.0	34.6
Tunisia	9.6	52.2
Zambia	—	31.1
Caribbean and Latin America		
Jamaica	—	41.3
Chile	20.6	56.3
Colombia	26.5	56.6
Nicaragua	25.8	68.3
Asia		
Indonesia	16.4	32.0
Malaysia	14.0	47.0
Philippines	14.5	77.2
Sri Lanka	19.8	45.8

Source: Compiled from Unesco (1987).

It is worthy of note that the largest proportion of women engineers occurs in Central and Latin America, and the number of women of that region enrolled in the medical and health-related fields is also relatively high (Table 1). However, although relatively many women *study* engineering and medical and health-related subjects, they will not necessarily *work* in those areas after graduation. For Latin American women in particular, the linkage between higher education and productive employment needs further examination. With respect to Nicaragua, the participation of women in higher education was at an all-time high during the Contra war in the mid-1980s.

Based on Table 1, African women seem to have the lowest participation levels in science programs. This may be due to continuing deficiencies and inadequacies in the teaching of science to girls in many African countries.

In an analysis of 41 developing countries in Asia, Latin America and Africa, Gail Kelly (1991) presents some surprising statistics about enrolment of women in natural sciences and medical and health-related fields. For example, in eight countries (Afghanistan, Argentina, Cuba, El Salvador, Nicaragua, Panama, Philippines, and Singapore), 50% or more of the students enrolled in natural science subjects were women. The proportion of women in medical and health-related fields was even greater; in 13 countries, it exceeded 50% (Argentina, Barbados, Brazil, Cuba, Jordan, Laos, Lesotho, Madagascar, Malawi, Mozambique, Nicaragua, Panama, and the Philippines). However, in no country did female enrolment in engineering exceed 50%: Cuba has the highest proportion at 32%. As already noted, this low participation rate for women in engineering holds true in industrialized countries. For example, in the United States, there are fewer women in engineering than in any other science-based profession, and the feminist movement has had limited effect in encouraging male members of the profession to reexamine their assumptions and biases (Hynes 1992).

Education and cultural factors

Educational disparities between girls and boys at all levels are a primary cause of female underrepresentation in the sciences. In many parts of the world, female enrolment is substantially lower, especially at the secondary level and even where they are proportionately represented, girls' secondary education often differs from that of boys. There appears to be a stronger correlation between parental income and social status and school enrolment for girls than for boys (Kelly

1984); during the 1980s, girls were disproportionately affected by the imposition of structural adjustment policies and education user fees in various countries. Where poor parents have had to choose between educating sons and daughters, the preference usually has been for male education. Data from Kenya's Central Bureau of Statistics reveal that, by 1989, there was already a slight drop in the proportion of girls attending secondary school. In Tanzania, during the 1980s with the imposition of structural adjustment policies, there was a dual effect of lower school enrolments and higher drop-out rates (Meena 1991).

There is considerable evidence that girls receive less-intensive training in science and mathematics at the primary and secondary levels. Studies in Canada, the United Kingdom, and the United States have revealed that girls routinely get less attention from teachers and that teachers often give answers directly to girls but provide boys with further information to enable them to solve problems for themselves. Male attitudes, particularly among peers, can have a negative effect on girls' aspirations in science. In a study of secondary school students in Swaziland, Smith (1988) found that gender biases with respect to "appropriate" male and female occupations were held much more strongly by boys than by girls.

Although girls' science achievement levels frequently equal or exceed those of boys in early primary school, they commonly drop in secondary school. To understand this trend, sociologists of education have studied classroom interactions between girls and boys and students and teachers. In Britain, adolescent boys consistently undermined girls' efforts to participate in science classes by making disparaging remarks and indicating that they considered science to be a male domain (Kelly 1985). There is evidence, however, that girls' performance in science is more likely to remain stable in single-sex schools where, in the absence of male students, girls face less pressure to conform to predetermined "feminine" roles. Science teaching in such schools can have a positive impact. In Nigeria, for example, girls enrolled in science programs at university were more likely to have attended single-sex secondary schools (Erinosho 1993).

In Kenya, the number of girls attending secondary schools increased in the 1980s, but they were more likely to be at unaided *harambee* schools with inadequate teachers and facilities, especially for science (Kinyanjui 1993). Even relatively prosperous girls' secondary schools often do not offer science courses, sometimes because of difficulty in finding qualified female staff to teach sciences (Eshiwani 1989). Analysis of the Kenya Certificate of Education Examination results for 1985 and 1986 showed that girls chose subjects that were less cost-intensive to teach. Moreover, curricular changes in the mid-1980s reduced the amount of compulsory time spent on sciences from 17 to 12 class-periods per week, creating greater pressure on students to be self-motivated and to work independently outside the classroom. More than 75% of the girls who sat for mathematics exams in 1985 and 1986 failed (Kinyanjui 1993).

Girls tend to be more attracted to science if they see it as socially relevant. A British study showed that girls were less interested in science that involved defense-funded work or animal experimentation (Wellcome Trust 1994); a Nigerian study revealed that "usefulness" was one of the three most important factors (together with personal interest and ability) influencing female university students' choice of a career in science (Erinosho 1993). In Swaziland, male secondary-school students were much more likely than girls to think that success in science would lead to a good job (Smith 1988). Finally, girls tend to perceive science as a male-dominated area with very long working hours (Wellcome Trust 1994). All of these studies suggest significant attitudinal differences between male and female students at secondary and tertiary levels. In general, girls have a stronger interest in people and social issues, whereas boys often show interest in tinkering and understanding the mechanical foundations of technology (Kelly 1985). However, science curricula tend to be structured to appeal primarily to boys. If more girls are to be attracted into science, then school science courses must appeal to the interests and tastes of both boys and girls. In most countries, these differences have not been taken into account in science-curriculum design.

Research has shown the significance of cultural and socioeconomic factors in steering women toward science careers. In the United States, foreign graduate students from Africa and Asia cited strong family pressure to enrol in science programs (Bellisari 1991). Similar pressure existed for African-American and Asian-American students, but not for students of European background. African and Asian foreign students also regarded national development goals as an incentive to pursue science-based careers. The close linkages between science, technology, and development have been emphasized for several decades and the message apparently has been internalized by many young people. However, in Africa, girls specializing in natural sciences tend to come from more affluent socioeconomic backgrounds and to have better educated parents with less strongly held notions of sex-role stereotypes (Erinosho 1993). If this is the case, then it would seem that it is mostly girls coming from social elites who even have the option to contribute to national development through pursuit of careers in S&T.

Most girls have few role models of successful female scientists. Sex role stereotyping in school textbooks continues to be significant, and girls are rarely depicted as active participants in science textbook illustrations (Kelly 1985). More commonly they are shown as participant observers or as amazed onlookers. With the exception of Madame Marie Curie, few if any female scientists are identified for students. In Africa, where women are key subsistence food farmers, texts rarely even portray them as farmers. In some cases, curricular expectations differ for men and women. For example, at a Kenyan technical institute training junior-level agricultural officers, women were required to take practicals in home economics whereas men took agricultural engineering (Bahemuka et al. 1992). Prevailing stereotypes of "appropriate" roles for girls and boys, men and women continue to inform the design of education programs at all levels, especially in countries where the influence of feminist thinking on curricular reform is still at an early stage. Even in the United States, in 1985, women constituted only 13% of science faculty and 2% of engineering faculty (Task Force on Women, Minorities, and the Handicapped in Science and Technology 1988). Women have a much higher drop-out rate from science and engineering graduate programs than their male counterparts. One reason may be a lack of female role models.

Finally, in developing countries, girls are faced with a variety of factors that conspire to reduce their participation in higher education and in S&T. These include higher opportunity costs for girls to stay in school in the loss of their labour both in the productive sector and in the household. Teenage pregnancy and a range of socioeconomic, religious, and cultural influences all affect parental decisions to educate daughters. In some countries, legal constraints also make it difficult for women to work in certain industries or under certain kinds of conditions. For example, until quite recently, in many African countries women, were prohibited from working between the hours of 6 p.m. and 6 a.m. In other countries, Islamic law prohibits the employment of women in situations where they will have to interact with men. Such obstacles create a further set of structural barriers to full participation of women in economic development and S&T.

The following factors all influence the success of girls in S&T programs:

- ✦ Poor science teaching in schools and differential treatment from teachers;

- ✦ Strong social pressure against excellence in science because it is seen as "unfeminine";

- ✦ Science curricula designed to relate to the interests of boys rather than girls;

- ◆ Socioeconomic and family background;
- ◆ Lack of female role models; and
- ◆ Cultural expectations.

Most of these issues were identified as deterrents to the participation of women in S&T by the ad hoc panel of experts organized by the UN Advisory Committee on Science and Technology for Development and the American Association for the Advancement of Science. The panel made recommendations directly aimed at ameliorating the situation (UN 1984). However, most were implemented only partially or not at all. If such recommendations are to have an effect, they must be accompanied by a strong political will.

Women in S&T careers

Women's experiences as scientists in the workplace usually differ from those of men. In the United States, female scientists are more likely to be unemployed or underemployed, and their salaries are lower than those of equally qualified males (White 1992). By 1990, women constituted only 4% of employed engineers and 30% of employed scientists, although by 1986 women had earned 30% of all first degrees in science and engineering. Moreover, employed female scientists and engineers tended to be young; in 1990, 39% of employed PhDs in science and engineering were under the age of 40, compared with 25% of their male counterparts (White 1992).

In Britain, the trend is similar. The proportion of women scientists decreases at higher levels in industry, the civil service, and academia (Committee on Women in Science, Engineering and Technology 1993). The only scientific occupation in which women outnumber men is that of laboratory technician. Moreover, between 1980 and 1990, the proportion of women employed in engineering actually fell. In the civil service, women scientists are also underrepresented; in 1992, they constituted only 9% of "senior scientific officers." In British universities in 1991, of 24 000 full-time academic staff, women accounted for only 15.5% in the biological and physical sciences, chemistry, mathematics, computing, engineering, technology, and subjects allied to medicine.

Less information is available about employment opportunities for women scientists in developing countries. Moreover, it is difficult to ascertain whether women are underrepresented because they are few in number or because employers discriminate against them, or perhaps both. For example, Ghana's Council for Scientific and Industrial Research employs 171 scientists, only 17 of them female and 9 of those in food research (Beoku-Betts and Logan 1993), but given the fact that the pool of female science graduates is low to begin with, this may be an accurate reflection of the proportion of female science graduates.

Women in academic science careers in the United States are less likely to be promoted to high rank and, in general, their professional advancement is much slower than that of men (see Brush 1991). In 1990–91, only 17% of female full-time faculty at US universities were full professors, compared with 44% of the men. In developing countries, the situation is similar. For example, only 10% of Côte d'Ivoire's full professors in 1987–88 were female (Beoku-Betts and Logan 1993). In the Chinese Academia Sinica, there are 286 female directors or deputy directors of research laboratories, accounting for 11.9% of the total (Guan Tao 1992). During the past decade, there has been a steady, if modest, increase in the numbers of women scientists engaged in all sectors of research and industrial production. In China as elsewhere, however, women scientists are most likely to be concentrated in the biological sciences. For example in 1992, 47.3% of the Chinese Academy of Medical Sciences's research projects were led by women. Moreover, there is some evidence that, as provisions for maternity leave and other benefits become enshrined in Chinese law, there is a growing tendency for employers to prefer to hire men. A Colombian study on research funding for social scientists found that over a 7-year period in the 1980s, three male investigators were funded for each female investigator, even though the numbers of male and female investigators and the quality of their research was equal (BOSTID 1994).

A similar situation is emerging in some of the countries of Eastern Europe in face of growing unemployment. In Romania in 1994, 60% of the unemployed are women, and those who continue to be employed have sometimes kept their jobs only because they accepted lower salaries. In times of economic stress, women are often the first to be released from the workforce under the (often wrong) assumption that they will be supported by working husbands. Moreover, women are likely to receive fewer benefits such as for housing or tax allowances, as it is assumed that they will live with and be supported by husbands (BOSTID 1994).

In all countries, employment prospects for female scientists are negatively affected by their need to combine professional and home responsibilities. Employers often assume that women's commitment to science will be less sustained than that of male colleagues, particularly if they are married and have families. This can have an effect not only on their decision to hire women scientists but also on the type of work to which women are assigned. Women's employment and promotion opportunities are frequently curtailed or hampered when they take time out for childbearing and rearing. Sweden has made an attempt to equalize the situation for men and women with historic legislation in 1994 that fathers must take compulsory leave after the birth of a child. Another positive advancement during the past decade has been the increasing acceptance of family-planning policies in many developing countries.

Finally, the interruptions of daily domestic life that are a reality for most working wives and mothers, are highly disruptive to the pursuit of science, especially scientific research (Arianrhod 1992). Periods of uninterrupted laboratory time are difficult to reconcile with the daily demands of domestic life. Are women expected to make greater sacrifices than their male colleagues to succeed in science? Marriage and motherhood create pressures, expectations, and obligations that are sometimes at odds with total dedication to scientific research. Although there are many examples of women who manage to reconcile domestic and professional lives, it requires considerable organizational skill. This gives further credibility to the argument that neither the practice nor content of science is neutral and reinforces the feminist appeal for a rethinking of the fundamental assumptions of science.

Women scientists are often at a disadvantage in the workplace. They have a more difficult time finding employment; they receive lower salaries and slower promotions; and they must reconcile their private and public lives in an unobtrusive way. However, to a considerable extent these problems lend themselves to legislation. In fact, as noted above, Sweden has already made some progress in this direction.

Learning S&T on the job

Although the main focus of this work is on the integration of women into S&T careers through access to and participation in formal science training, it is important to consider some of the other media through which S&T skills are transmitted. During the past decade, efforts have been made in many countries to integrate women into nontraditional, S&T-based careers. One successful example is that of the Jamaican Women's Construction Collective, which has provided poor Jamaican women with carpentry, masonry, and other construction skills. Graduates of the program have been able to apply for higher paying jobs in the construction industry, although they have faced some discrimination in the workplace because many Jamaican employers are skeptical about hiring women for work traditionally defined as men's. Again, this is an area where legislation could be helpful.

Another example comes from the Sarvodaya Movement in Sri Lanka, which has conducted workshops in water-pump maintenance for young women, teaching them plumbing and welding. The objectives of such initiatives have been to create new sources of employment for poor women, break down existing sex-role stereotypes, and ensure that women share with men the everyday skills essential to the maintenance of communities. The Sri Lankan project came about when it became apparent that men did not place high priority on the repair of water pumps because they viewed water as a female responsibility in most households. Because women's interests were more immediately involved, it was logical that they acquire the skills needed to repair pumps themselves. Groups of young women learned theory and machine-shop work, as well as pump assembly, installation, monitoring, and repair. Women handpump technicians then became educators, change agents, and role models in their own communities.

Despite such success stories, it is relatively rare for women to be given technical training outside formal education systems. Although women are often employed in industries undergoing technical change, they rarely benefit from corporate-sponsored programs to retrain workers and upgrade their skills. For example, some aspects of Japanese JIT (just-in-time) technology were introduced into two small- and medium-sized Argentinean factories (Roldan 1993). The JIT system requires multiskilled labourers who can rotate between jobs and carry out different functions. In both factories, women were kept in the same positions or even phased out while men were given training to enable them to rotate between jobs and become multiskilled. Women were excluded because it was assumed that they did not have the basic technical competence to learn many skills. The firms considered it cheaper to invest in training men, even those with low bases of technical knowledge. In an electronic plant with an all-female labour force, although the (male) production manager was aware of Japanese techniques, he did not plan to adopt them because it would be too costly to provide technical training for women (Roldan 1993). Thus he was willing to forgo the potential benefits of the technologies to avoid having to invest in technical training for women. In Argentina, the introduction of new production technologies seems to be weakening the position of women in the labour force and leading toward a masculinization of factory labour.

The computer explosion of the past decade provides another example. Although facility with desktop computers is based on a mastery of typing, a skill that has been strongly associated with women throughout most of the 20th century, computers have become another area of male dominance. In the United States, although boys and girls show equal interest in computers in early primary school, girls' interest tends to decline after age 10 or 11 while that of boys continues to grow. Not surprisingly, the computer games industry is aimed primarily at boys, with great emphasis on games of violence and destruction.

To a significant extent, the exclusion of girls and women from participation at higher levels in the computer industry reflects general sex-role stereotyping and the assumption that women are "not technical." It is often assumed that women will not even desire such training because it is "unfeminine" and "too difficult." Various strategies have been employed to break down such stereotypes and to encourage an interest among girls in the computer industry — which is projected to be a significant employer into the 21st century. In Australia, week-long computer holidays are organized annually for groups of young girls. In Australian secondary schools, educational videos showing women successfully at work in the computer industry and questioning traditional stereotypes about women computer professionals have been shown to girls with positive results. In the United States, some schools have experimented with the establishment of individual mentor programs; others have set up girls-only hours in computer labs.

On-the-job technical training is frequently acquired through formal apprenticeship or informal mentoring, whereby an older worker teaches a younger one. In most countries, both systems are heavily dominated by men. Apprenticeship programs, which grew out of the medieval trade guilds, have always been male-oriented and, although there are examples of efforts in many countries to provide opportunities for young women, these are difficult to legislate or enforce in the private sector, where most apprenticeship opportunities arise. With respect to mentoring, given the separation of the sexes that occurs as part of childhood socialization processes in most societies, it is not surprising that older men prefer to train young men rather than young women. However, this means that an important potential source of technical learning is less accessible to women. Again, it is difficult to legislate on this matter because mentoring is commonly an unstructured and voluntary undertaking.

Finally, the profusion of new information technologies provides a rich source of instructional media for the transfer of S&T knowledge and skills. These include computer-aided learning systems, transmission of training courses into factories by satellite, interactive video, and various other methods. If women are given equal opportunity to benefit from such courses, they should be able to acquire new technical skills and knowledge to enable them to compete effectively for better-paid positions in the industrial workplace. At the same time, however, older technologies including radio should be used systematically in developing countries to demystify aspects of S&T for rural women. There is also much scope for the use of popular education materials and popular theatre, songs, and dance to impart S&T information. For example, a Ugandan dance company currently is teaching soil conservation techniques to rural men and women through expressive dance performances.

Areas for further research

Would S&T indeed be different if women had a greater voice? It seems evident that the problem goes beyond a mere increase in the numbers of female scientists and technologists. There is need for a complete reconceptualization and reorganization of the culture of S&T. This must encompass the provision of space for alternative viewpoints and perspectives and the humanization of an area that traditionally has considered itself to be "neutral" and beyond the reach of immediate social, cultural, political, and economic manipulation. There is abundant historical evidence that science has never really been neutral, but the challenge lies in persuading its practitioners to accept this and to work from that basis rather than assuming its neutrality.

There is also a need for science and scientists to move beyond the conceptual boundaries imposed by formal training and to recognize the significant contributions that have always been made (and continue to be made) by grassroots practitioners — many of them women. Science tends to be organized in an inherently hierarchical and elitist fashion. In developing countries, extension of technology (in agriculture, health, or other areas) is almost exclusively one way. Scientists or technologists rarely examine existing agricultural or health practices with the thought that they can provide valuable insights or understanding about human-survival strategies. Instead there is always an assumption that knowledge held by the scientist or technologist is of a higher order than that held by the practitioner. This assumption is the foundation stone upon which most extension services have been built.

It might be argued that S&T facts are often presented in deliberately arcane language aimed at creating "insiders" who have the training and expertise to understand and "outsiders" who do not. Women are frequently relegated to the latter status and, although they may have much to gain from understanding the mechanical details of a particular technology, for example, it is rare that efforts are made to explain these in such a way as to be nonthreatening and comprehensible. Instead, women's lack of understanding is once again seen as an example of their intrinsically "nontechnical" nature. We need to demystify and democratize scientific knowledge and involve women as agents of change.

Although, there is already a substantial amount of published information on women and S&T, there continue to be key areas and issues about which relatively little hard evidence is available. Such questions must be examined, both generally and specifically, in the context of existing social and cultural conditions in different countries. Some of the research questions worthy of further study follow.

✦ Do women scientists have different perspectives and work patterns than their male colleagues? Is there a female world view or perspective that would change the way "science" is currently done?

✦ What happens to female S&T graduates? Do they get the same types of jobs as their male colleagues? Do they necessarily work in S&T at all? Do they advance at the same rates?

✦ How can science curricula be designed to account for the interests of both girls and boys?

✦ Do girls in developing countries and in industrialized countries study S&T for different reasons? What are the key motivating factors?

✦ Is it more expensive to train women than men on-the-job? Do women actually bring an inferior basis of technical knowledge to such training?

✦ What have been the experiences of girls and women in technical apprenticeship programs? Are women adequately served by existing programs or should such programs be organized differently?

✦ Do women benefit from on-the-job mentoring? How can such mentoring be effectively encouraged and nurtured?

✦ How can the everyday experiences of women in household management, agriculture, and informal-sector employment be validated as work that requires a level of S&T expertise?

Recommendations

As discussed above, lack of political will remains a compelling reason for the exclusion or underrepresentation of women and girls in S&T. Although many recommendations have been aimed at amelioration of this situation, there has been relatively little effective implementation, especially in developing countries. Many governments have emphasized the importance of S&T policy without recognizing the inherent gender biases in their own systems. For example, although attention has been given to the development of more effective science teaching, it has rarely been accompanied by gender analysis. Consequently, there remains a necessity for science education curricula to be reorganized at the primary, secondary, and tertiary levels. Although girls often perform as well as boys in science and mathematics in the early years, their interest declines as they become older. There also seems to be a strong correlation between girls' interest in S&T and the extent to which they see these issues as related to social and community concerns. Thus, there is a strong argument for the redesign of science education materials to focus on the role of S&T in societal development and more specifically on the *usefulness* and *relevance* of S&T in everyday life rather than on the capacity of *man* to *master machine*.

In its efforts to improve the current situation, the UN Commission on Science and Technology should consider the following suggestions.

◆ All governments should make an explicit commitment to ensure that women and girls are given equal opportunities to participate in S&T programs. Specific targets should be established for enrolment of girls in science programs at secondary and tertiary levels and for the employment of women in government S&T establishments.

◆ To improve the level of comparative international statistics, all governments should collect systematic data about the number of girls enrolled in science education programs and the number of women employed in the S&T sector.

◆ Agencies throughout the UN system should ensure that they employ representative numbers of women in S&T positions and that women are given equal opportunity for promotion into management positions. Women's childbearing and rearing responsibilities should not be used as the basis of discrimination against them. Daycare centres should be provided where possible and special efforts should be made to accommodate women's dual responsibilities through the institution of part-time work, job-sharing, flexible hours, or other creative possibilities.

✦ UN agencies that provide research grants, scholarships, or professional development grants (including conference participation grants) should systematically ensure that at least half of the grants go to female applicants. If necessary, special efforts should be made to attract such applicants. Also, where necessary, agencies should be flexible in setting the terms of the grants to accommodate women's dual responsibilities.

✦ The technical work done by women both in the household and in the productive sector should be recognized by the UN system as having an S&T base and be valued accordingly. For example, women farmers should be seen as decision-makers who make science-based choices, taking into account local soil, water, and weather conditions, availability of inputs, availability of labour-saving technologies, and so forth. Similarly, work done by women in the household should be seen as based on knowledge of nutrition, health, child survival, and so on, rather than as work devoid of expertise.

Chapter 9
Literacy for all

Educating and empowering women

Pamela Fraser-Abder and Jayshree A. Mehta

All over the world, education is regarded as the key factor in overcoming the barriers that women face and the basic tool for empowering women and bringing them into the main path of development. The rapid pace of development of science and technology (S&T) and their effect on all walks of life is apparent. No society can keep half its population from basic understanding of S&T developments. Education must play a vital role in establishing equality and empowering women. What type of education will allow women to meet the challenges of the year 2000 and beyond? In a fast-changing economy and global market trends, women's struggle for survival has become increasingly difficult as they encounter social and religious prejudices and economic disadvantages.

Studies, particularly in developing countries, have revealed that there are wide disparities and inequalities between men and women in all areas, including access to education, health care, food, energy, income, and employment. Technological modernization has led to a concentration of women in domestic and labour-intensive activities. Women are being displaced from remunerative and skill-related employment as a result of the introduction of new technology in many regions of the world. The need to shift the focus from women as a target of welfare policies to women as a group for development has been felt by all development agencies, and S&T literacy must be used as a major tool.

Women — the traditional educators and health providers in the family — have benefited least from technological developments. They are the last to receive training, and their unrecorded and unpaid work in all fields, from domestic work to agriculture, has provided them with the fewest assets. Research shows that female literacy plays an important role in raising productivity levels and in reducing child mortality rates and population growth. Women must be exposed to various technologies (from simple to complex) and use them in their daily lives. Technology must be made woman-friendly and women must learn to be comfortable with technology.

The global perspective

Currently, the majority of the world's out-of-school youth are female. In most regions, girls are underrepresented at every level of formal education. Keeping girls in school, even at the primary level, and their performance depend largely upon socioeconomic factors and upon the attitudes of teachers.

When daily survival involves overcoming problems of pollution, malnutrition, and lack of basic health care, spending on women's education is a social investment. Research has shown a direct link between women's education and child-mortality rates, fertility rates, and income-generation activities. Environmental degradation has affected women most by interfering with their daily quest for fodder, fuel, and water for their families. In most countries, women have been the primary environmental caretakers for generations, and they are often the custodians of indigenous knowledge about herbal medicines, agricultural practices, and food preservation. Yet policymakers continue to ignore the importance of women's interests and needs. Women's participation in the management of resources and in decision-making processes at every level will bring a new perspective to the system.

However, worldwide, one out of three women is illiterate compared with one out of five men. The discrepancy is even greater in developing countries where one in four men and one in two women are illiterate. More than 60% of illiterate people in the world are women (about 600 million). Over 100 million children of school age (mainly girls) do not attend school; most are in developing countries. How do we reach these groups?

- ✦ There is a great need to develop S&T courses with several entry and exit points.

- ✦ Materials and courses must be developed in local languages and must be easy to understand.

- ✦ Female leadership at the local and national levels must be encouraged.

- ✦ Programs related to skills development to help women choose a career and work must be developed.

✦ Groups of educated, dedicated women must be formed to communicate aspects of science to local and rural women's groups.

Who has access to S&T education?

Several recommendations resulting from United Nations (UN) forums have addressed the need to improve the quality of education females receive, remove obstacles to female access, ensure equity in access to S&T, provide adequate resources, and make S&T mandatory in the school system (UN 1979b, 1984, 1985b, 1990, 1992a; Unesco 1993).

Research indicates that there are no physical or intellectual barriers to women's full participation in S&T. However, in some countries, formidable legal, cultural, or socioeconomic barriers result in the continuing underutilization, devaluation, and disregard of the knowledge women can contribute to the male-dominated S&T fields. Harding (1992) presents a noteworthy argument for including women in S&T.

> Since women are as potentially able as men to contribute to S&T, then national development, which depends on applications of S&T, will be limited if women are barred, and there will be a loss of talent to the nation. Lack of access to S&T prevents women from operating within S&T, where appropriate qualifications lead to financial rewards and interesting work. Barriers lead to alienation and transmission of that alienation to their children, particularly their daughters. Leaving women out results in a loss to science. Men and women bring different specific strengths and limitations to S&T. This is reflected in the type of thinking and problem solving associated with S&T.

Nevertheless, equity of access continues to be a major problem. In principle, nations have declared a commitment to equity in access to S&T and to provision of resources to achieve this objective. Unfortunately many economic and social constraints affect their ability to put these policies into practice. In many cultures, schooling is still seen as a necessity for males, but an expensive and useless experience for females; among the developing nations in Africa, Asia, and Latin America, 38% of school age girls never enrol in school. Even in countries where enrolment rates of females are high, the data do not always accurately reflect the actual situation. These rates often

disguise the problems of absenteeism and dropout that occur predominantly in the female population because of the conflicting work
and cultural demands on girls' time. For example, in India and Africa,
girls are often withdrawn from school because of early marriage.

Even when girls do attend school, the generally poorer quality of girls' education contributes to lower S&T competence of girls.
Because basic education is a requirement for access to S&T, those
(mainly females) who are denied access at the basic levels tend to fall
farther and farther behind, thus increasing gender inequities. Girls
who do have access to basic education must still overcome immense
problems as they strive for equity in access to S&T. Most schools still
consider science to be a subject for boys, and girls are subsequently
shunted into home economics and other "more appropriate" subjects.
This practice is often fully supported and reinforced by teachers,
guidance counsellors, family, and peers.

If girls do enrol in S&T programs, they are faced with teachers who do not use gender-sensitive pedagogy, but employ teaching
strategies that "shortchange" girls. At the secondary and tertiary
level, a hostile and unaccommodating climate is also the norm.
Those who survive these challenges move into a corporate climate
that fosters inequity; to achieve success, females must be part of the
"old boys' network." Given cultural norms, this is often not possible
and women eventually reach a ceiling that prevents them from entering the upper echelons of science.

In 1980, the UN Educational, Scientific and Cultural Organisation (Unesco) initiated case studies of the access of women to S&T
training and associated careers in Czechoslovakia, France, Malaysia,
Senegal, and Venezuela, which resulted in training workshops,
regional seminars, and fellowships. This initiative has led to some
improvement in the quality of education for females in the participating countries.

Policy recommendations

Assist governments to formulate economic policy and training programs to ensure equitable access to S&T by women and girls. Governments should be encouraged to adopt the following action
strategies:

- ◆ Allocate resources to increase female literacy and their
  involvement in S&T;

- ◆ Develop and implement gender sensitivity and awareness
  training for educators and policymakers;

+ Develop and implement strategies to increase access to general literacy programs for females;

+ Include science in general literacy programs;

+ Evaluate the effect of female involvement in S&T on cultural values and norms. Is it in the interests of society to change these values? Do these societies want to see changes? Can the society adjust to the differing life-styles associated with exposing women to S&T? and

+ Design systems of accountability to ensure that policies are being implemented.

The successful enactment of this policy requires commitment from national leaders, top administrators, and funders, in principle and in practice; fundamental changes in ethical, cultural, and societal norms; and the involvement of women in the process of change. Economic and training programs should be facilitated by Unesco, governmental agencies, nongovernmental agencies (NGOs), policymakers, educators, and others concerned. They should be informed by what is happening in other countries that are striving toward equity in access to S&T. Networks should be established to publish and disseminate successful models (with details of populations and strategies) to facilitate replication.

What S&T curriculum is taught?

Over the past decade most UN recommendations on the teaching of S&T point to the need to develop "female friendly" science by reorganizing science curricula and textbooks to address women's needs and to create and sustain interest among female students (UN 1984, 1985b; NABST 1988; Aghenta 1989). They also suggest that throughout the education system, from preschool to university level, both girls and boys should be exposed to the same curriculum and types of experience in the areas of science, technology, and technical skills, and children should be encouraged to develop an interest in science and become involved in activities that are considered "more proper" for the other sex.

Curriculum developers must integrate indigenous S&T into the frameworks they prepare for national or global curricula. Currently, the material included in curricula is often borrowed from highly industrialized sectors of society and holds little relevance for the people being introduced to S&T literacy. Irrelevance is a major cause of the massive dropout rate in science. Children and adult members of society need to hear and understand the impact of S&T on their lives; for example, why they should stop polluting streams. Appropriate curricula transmit such information, and giving this information to more women increases the chance of the ideas becoming inculcated into our societies.

Education must be relevant to people's lives. Curricular reform can address gender roles either by being designed to fit existing roles, or by attempting to alter traditional roles and provide new opportunities for both boys and girls to meet the challenges and needs of a technologically driven society. Local policymakers need to determine which of these directions is appropriate, and curriculum developers need to produce appropriate S&T curricula that will foster progress in that direction and facilitate gender equity.

Most nations have been involved in S&T curriculum revision, and some have included components on gender issues. However, because of the lack of coordination between teacher educators and curriculum developers, issues addressed during the S&T curriculum-revision process often are not included in teacher-training programs. Teachers are not taught adequate gender sensitivity and the awareness necessary to implement the revised classroom curricula.

Consequently, few nations have made a concerted attempt to provide girls and boys with the same kinds of experiences. For example, it was not until the publication of the report, *How Schools Shortchange Girls* (AAUW 1992), that many US science teachers became sensitized to their classroom behaviour which discriminated against girls in a variety of ways.

Policy recommendations

+ Identify in each culture the knowledge, skills, values, and attitudes needed by citizens to function productively in a technological society.

+ Identify in each culture whether S&T education should conform with existing gender roles or should provide opportunities for both boys and girls to meet the challenges of technologically driven society.

+ Provide resources to develop a relevant S&T curriculum that includes elements of "Western" and indigenous S&T and is designed to foster interest and participation of both girls and boys, to create a scientifically and technologically literate population.

The following action strategies should be adopted:

✦ Determine the relevance of S&T education for the country.

✦ Identify issues that influence the country's ability to incorporate S&T into its educational programs.

✦ Establish whether traditional gender roles should continue to define girls' educational needs.

✦ Educate parents about the appropriateness of science for girls.

✦ Develop plans to educate girls for roles in an S&T-literate society congruent with parental perceptions of relevance and their aspirations for their daughters.

✦ Develop S&T curricula and textbooks that are "female friendly" and capable of encouraging girls' participation and interest in S&T.

✦ Where appropriate, incorporate in curricula elements of S&T that are traditionally deemed more suitable for the other sex.

What do teachers of S&T need?

Policy recommendations in this area have generally addressed teacher educators' need to be sensitive to the issues of gender and the importance of these issues to the outcomes of all education and training programs (Aghenta 1989; UN 1990, 1992a). Because of the ever-changing and expanding world of S&T, administrators must ensure and support appropriate preservice and continuing-service provisions for those responsible for all forms of S&T education by formulating guidelines for the preparation and continuous professional development of S&T educators. They must also provide leadership, coupled with assistance, to countries implementing them. Nations must recognize the central role of teachers in achieving S&T literacy for everyone and enhance the status of careers in S&T education at all levels.

Achievement in and attitudes toward science are significantly influenced by teachers. Particularly at the elementary level, teachers often demonstrate a negative attitude toward science, which is transmitted to students (Fraser-Abder 1992). The "Pygmalion syndrome" — differential treatment based on expectations affects achievement — plays a significant role in female science achievement (Rosenthal and Jacobson 1968). If teachers expect males to be good at math and females to be good at reading then the students will live up to these expectations (Brophy and Evertson 1974). Teachers interact differently with the sexes and for varying amounts of time: during reading lessons, females receive greater attention; during math and science classes, teachers interact more with males and give them more encouragement (Sadker and Sadker 1986; Jones 1990).

Again, coordination between curriculum developers and teacher trainers is lacking, gender issues addressed in revised S&T curricula are not adequately addressed in the implemented curricula. Teachers must be aware of contemporary research findings on gender and S&T. Part of their training must include exposure to research findings on teacher–student interactions and the teacher's attitudes and expectations in the S&T classroom. This is an area in which most teacher educators also need training.

Teacher-education programs are slowly beginning to introduce modules on gender sensitization and development of strategies to ensure equity in the classroom, largely because of the inclusion of equity issues on the agenda of the annual conferences of many S&T education associations. Workshop manuals on sex stereotyping developed by Unesco have also been useful to some countries.

Policy recommendations

Develop strategies to ensure gender sensitization and gender equity in the S&T classroom and in all S&T training programs.

In addition, the following action should be taken: educate policymakers, teacher trainers, and researchers on key S&T gender issues.

Pedagogical and contextual frameworks in which S&T is taught

Pedagogical considerations

Previous recommendations have pointed to the need to provide positive and appropriate learning experiences and environments for females (UN 1985b; Unesco 1993). Educators have been called upon to provide a positive and appropriate learning experience so that young women can develop self-esteem. Governments, industry, public- and private-sector interests, and education and other authorities in all countries have been asked to review existing provisions for S&T

education at all levels and in all settings, giving attention to development and maintenance of learning programs responsive to the needs of individuals and communities, and to establish teaching and learning milieus that are conducive to achieving S&T literacy for all. In addition, effective communication, assessment, and evaluation strategies must be developed.

Inappropriate pedagogy is the major factor influencing girls' negative attitude toward S&T and their decision to drop out of science and math courses at the elementary and junior high-school levels. Research indicates that girls' attitudes toward science, their achievement, and experiences in science decline considerably during high school (Mullis and Jenkins 1988).

At the college level, most problems shared by female students are structural or cultural, notably poor teaching, faculty who are unapproachable, the fast pace of curricula, work overload, insufficient faculty help through periods of academic difficulty, inadequate preparation in high school, and financial difficulties (Seymour 1992). Language encourages and strengthens societal norms and mores (Hellinger 1984), but the language used in science and mathematics often reflects a male bias inadvertently directing females away from the field (Damarin 1992). Females are more likely to experience "math and science anxiety" than males. They believe that these subjects become more difficult as they progress through school, causing their anxiety to increase (Brush 1985). Coupled with inadequate pedagogy, this creates a downhill spiral to S&T illiteracy.

Implementing the recommendations mentioned above depends on the ability of teachers to use appropriate methods. For example, at Lehigh University, Pennsylvania, bilingual students involved in a hands-on, nontextbook science program run by graduate students learned the required content and began to regard science as fun.

Stereotyping

Previous recommendations have highlighted the need to eliminate gender stereotyping and suggest the development and implementation of strategies and programs as early as the preschool stage to counteract it (UN 1984, 1985b; NABST 1988). All curricula and teaching–learning materials should be free from stereotypical images of males and females. Guidelines designed to eliminate gender biases and discriminatory practices should be developed on a regional basis and made available to those involved in the administration of educational services in every territory.

A concerted effort is required to eliminate gender biases and stereotyping and promote S&T as avenues for all. Many teachers still identify a scientist as white, male, bald, boring, and unattractive. This inaccurate image is partly due to their lack of interaction with scientists. The traditional image of a mathematician, engineer, scientist, or medical doctor has been a white man, although this image is evolving to include Asians of either sex (Halleck 1993).

Textbooks and many classroom instructional materials continue to reinforce the invisibility of women in science (AAUW 1992) and girls continue to perceive science as a masculine domain (Linn and Hyde 1989). Stereotypes, including media images that show only men as users of science, influence parents' expectations for their children and students' expectations for themselves (Reyes and Padilla 1985). These attitudes may cause females to consider more stereotypical female disciplines and be less motivated in science and math (Stage et al. 1985). They also believe that the time needed to pursue careers in science will usurp time they need to engage in their traditional roles as wife and mother. The traditional gender-role beliefs of household responsibilities and child-rearing practices keep many women away from S&T.

In 1981, Unesco's section on Equality of Educational Opportunity for Girls and Women launched a program aimed at promoting better awareness and understanding of the problem of sex stereotyping in educational materials; stimulating and encouraging action to eliminate such stereotyping; and developing positive attitudes with regard to equality and mutual respect between men and women. This program included eight national studies and three regional guides for North America and Western Europe, the Arab World, and Asia and the Pacific (see Sundal-Hansen and Schultz 1984; Whyte 1984; Bisaria 1985; Jaarsma 1987). The guides present an excellent rationale for eliminating sex stereotyping, with evidence of problems created by stereotyping and workshop interventions for eliminating stereotyping. They could be used successfully in S&T teacher-training programs. A recently published book on female scientists in Indonesia has begun to make inroads in showing girls that women can indeed be scientists.

Participatory factors

In the formal education system, girls often avoid science courses because they lack confidence in their ability to pursue science careers and they do not wish to go against the expectations of teachers, peers, and parents (Sherman and Fennema 1977). Girls' interest in science decreases as they move from elementary through high school. Accompanying this decrease is a perception of the irrelevance of science to their lives (Linn and Hyde 1989).

Males exhibit greater confidence in their mathematics and science abilities; they view themselves as math learners and have higher expectations of future math courses (Linn and Hyde 1989). Science is perceived as a masculine realm. Consequently, males are more inclined to offer assistance to less able peers and, in the process, learn more science themselves (Linn and Hyde 1989). Females, even when they perform equally or better than males, believe that science is better understood by males. As a result, girls take the minimum number of science and mathematics classes for graduation from high school (Oakes and Rand 1990) and, subsequently, will probably not meet the science requirements of most 4-year college courses.

Research emanating from the Center for Research on Women (Rayman and Brett 1993) highlights four factors that keep undergraduate women in science:

- ✦ Encouragement from parents, with mothers' encouragement being as important as fathers';

- ✦ Consistent encouragement from mentors and overall interest in the experiences of the student;

- ✦ Opportunities to do hands-on research, which is critical to the choice of specialization as well as to whether women stay in science after college; and

- ✦ Comprehensive career advice about a range of science-related jobs.

Providing adequate pedagogy, curricula, facilities, equipment, and supplies for teaching girls is an excellent first step toward increasing their participation, but the situation requires continuous monitoring.

Policy recommendations

- ✦ Develop guidelines to eliminate gender bias and discriminatory practices in S&T education.

- ✦ Provide infrastructure and funding to develop networking of female scientists, educators, and students.

- ✦ Provide infrastructure and funding for international interaction and teacher training to increase the involvement of girls in S&T.

✦ Develop monitoring systems to ensure progress toward sustained effectiveness of gender equity in S&T teaching and learning.

The following action strategies must be adopted.

✦ Identify and adapt teaching content, methods, and student activities to provide a positive experience for girls and women in classroom settings, especially through the use of techniques that are proven to be effective for females.

✦ Promote and replicate a broader range of gender-fair methods for testing and assessing S&T.

✦ Design S&T lessons that show males and females in nontraditional roles and depict successful women in S&T.

✦ Encourage formation of and participation in both regional and international forums to exchange information and data on successful implementations.

✦ Design data-collection systems that are always disaggregated by gender.

✦ Examine the effect of S&T education policies and programs on females and males.

Nonformal S&T education

An appreciation of nonformal education for S&T literacy is a concept that has developed only in the last two decades, and the various nonformal and formal methods and techniques used in different regions of the world still require careful study and analysis. A diversity of programs and a variety of media have emerged in different societies and one must be careful in using or adapting the ones that are suitable to the social and cultural fabric of the society.

Advantages of a nonformal approach

Educators have felt the limitations of the formal education system in a rapidly changing society that is experiencing a population explosion. Because of its rigid structure and limited resources, the formal system is constrained in some areas. S&T literacy, for example, can be attained through out-of-school learning or through learning in informal situations. Decentralization of the development process, action at a local level, and participation by communities are important in creating scientific awareness. The strength of the non-formal system lies in its diversity, its vitality, and its ability to respond quickly and creatively to local needs. Materials that provide enjoyment and flexibility have also been missing in the formal system, but can be carefully woven into a nonformal science education and popularization program.

Institutions for informal S&T

Science centres and museums all over the world have a positive role to play in creating scientific literacy. In the last three decades, such institutions have adopted innovative approaches, such as the shift from "touch me not" exhibits to participatory, "hands on" experiences. Science centres operate on the principle that exploration of science is a joyful activity. They emphasize learning by doing, rather than the type of teaching that takes place in schools.

Planning new science and interpretive centres now requires a basic line of thought or parameters, not simple imitation of what developed countries have done. This philosophy is critical in developing countries, where the real needs and aspirations of common people in the various socioeconomic groups are quite different. A cultural backdrop must be woven into the process. A common characteristic of all visitors to science centres is their curiosity, interest, and desire to learn something. Science centres in developing countries have a greater responsibility, because more than half of the children there have never been to school or have left school before completing primary level.

Background experience plays an important role in learning science. The preexisting, sometimes mistaken or naive theories of people visiting science centres must be accounted for in any exhibit design or development strategy. Understanding these preconceptions is indispensable in developing strategies to enhance the effectiveness of informal science experiences; extensive research is required in this area. Few science centres in the world have developed effective programs for women. Science centres should steer away from science "gimmicks," presenting science as something mysterious, and exhibits that do not reveal the way they work.

An important illustration of the way in which science can be related to society took place in one of the poorest areas of Rio de Janeiro. Science events — centred around a total solar eclipse, for example — were conducted in public plazas to develop science awareness before going on to establish a community science centre. "Living science" or practicing science is a good example of informal science teaching in developing countries. Another approach is the use of indigenous crafts, such as weaving and basketwork, and games to communicate mathematical principles. Such activities are extremely effective, as they relate to people's daily lives.

Folk formats and science theatre have been attempted by several groups in Asia, Europe, and the United States. Science theatre can be an effective way to communicate certain aspects of science. Puppetry and folk farms are extensively used by popular science groups in India.

Intuitive mathematics

For many cultures, the current method of learning science is alien, but their use of mathematics is deeply ingrained. An illiterate woman vegetable vendor or a fruit seller who has never attended formal school can do arithmetic calculations with great speed and accuracy. Women in Gujarat make the most intricate geometric designs on clothes in their traditional art and crafts and create new ones. Where does their knowledge come from?

The language used in mathematics textbooks is complex and abstract. Children often fail to read or comprehend such textbooks. Are we repeating the same mistake in nonformal education? The language or symbols used must be easy to understand or decipher by ordinary people. Few mathematics programs for radio and television at the popular level require analysis. Even science centres and museums have not developed many exhibits or programs in mathematics for the masses. The "equals" program at the Lawrence Hall of Science in California aims at involving girls in learning mathematics and tries to break down their resistance to mathematics learning, because they think it is difficult.

The relation of formal and informal education

Does communicating science require an institution or can it be accomplished by hundreds of science workers and communicators visiting one village after another on a bicycle and talking directly to people, demonstrating simple things, taking examples from the local environment? In the Gender and Science and Technology program, examining water from the village pond on a slide under a low-cost microscope, then talking about the necessity of clean drinking water and methods of purifying water evoked an enormous response. Seeing was believing. Science must be connected to society.

Active science workers seldom write, and writing without sufficient first-hand experience becomes theoretical and bookish.

Women write very little. Most science centres in developing countries are headed or managed by men who decide on programs and policies; education programmers in major science centres of developed countries are women. Does this make any difference in the way the programs evolve or are given importance? Do women educators, curators, program planners, and designers bring new perspectives to informal or nonformal communication of science?

Conclusion

Analysis of the recommendations that have been made over the past two decades reveals a need for better communication, collaboration, and cooperation among agents of change. This need is reinforced by the recommendation of participants at Unesco's international forum (Unesco 1993) that Unesco make provision, in its medium-term plan (1996–2001) in the field of education for an international program, to develop cooperation among all countries and, in particular, to focus on regional and subregional cooperation in the area of S&T literacy for all.

There is also an overwhelming need to record and disseminate available data. Lack of communication mechanisms means that colleagues at the same campus may not be aware of research being conducted by fellow faculty. The results of local research and international studies should be published and disseminated in nonacademic language and made available to formal education institutes, NGOs, and individuals involved in S&T training. This material should include directories of women who have successful careers in fields related to S&T and technical trades and who can act as role models.

Although researchers have tried to account for the underrepresentation of females in science, there is no quick and easy way to redress the imbalance; the causes and solutions are complex. Educators and policymakers must be aware of research findings and realize that the value and costs of S&T courses and careers as perceived by females are influenced by their present intrinsic values, anticipated future values, gender-role issues, and competition with current activities. Success or failure in S&T is determined by self-perceived abilities, attribution processes, stereotypes, and expectations of others. School policies and classroom practices that deal with role models, teachers' expectations, interactions, instructional materials, teaching and learning methods, number and quality of required science and math courses, mechanisms for placement in these courses, and career guidance all play a major part in encouraging, recruiting, and retaining girls in S&T.

As a community strives to address the issue of S&T for development, it must address the following questions:

✦ What are S&T?

✦ Who should participate in S&T?

✦ Who will be affected by this S&T?

✦ What is S&T literacy?

✦ Should we aspire to global S&T literacy? Is local S&T sufficient?

✦ Should we be preparing a young girl in the middle of Africa or India to be S&T literate at the global level?

At the global level, we need to ask the following questions:

✦ What barriers exist to female participation in S&T?

✦ How do these barriers differ from country to country?

✦ What do S&T mean in a developing country?

✦ What do S&T mean in a developed country?

✦ What are the expected end products of S&T education?

✦ Do these products differ from country to country?

✦ Are there global end products of S&T education?

✦ How should we be preparing global citizens for life in a technologically driven environment?

Without collaboration and cooperation we will continue to see billions of dollars wasted as a result of inappropriate replication and lack of communication. It is time for governments, NGOs, the UN, and other intergovernmental agencies to work together to achieve economic development through universal S&T literacy. UN agencies and other intergovernmental organizations should initiate and support programs that allow countries and populations to shape their own future and NGOs active in S&T education should enter into partnership and make their knowledge and experience known to the UN and other intergovernmental bodies and participate in national, regional, and international programs to achieve the goal of S&T literacy for all (Unesco 1993). Successful access to high-quality education that includes S&T requires action by governments, NGOs, and the UN.

Action by governments

- ✦ Make the necessary expenditure so that all girls can be enrolled in and complete primary education, including S&T, on the same basis as boys.

- ✦ Reform curricula to ensure that education is gender-neutral and that gender awareness is integrated into all aspects of teacher-training programs.

- ✦ Make basic and functional literacy programs available to all women and girls.

- ✦ Promote women's interest in S&T education and encourage women to enter nontraditional fields.

Action by NGOs

- ✦ Monitor the extent to which S&T educational reforms favouring gender equity are implemented.

- ✦ Provide community-based informal training in S&T.

Action by the United Nations

- ✦ Provide gender-awareness programs for all officers engaged in designing and implementing S&T education and training.

Increasing S&T literacy among women will contribute to higher levels of productivity, a lower rate of child mortality, and stable population growth. It will add female dimensions to biological, agricultural, information, communications, military, and industrial technologies and result in overall economic development for nations that are willing to make the necessary policy recommendations and strategic planning to achieve S&T literacy for all.

With communication, collaboration, and cooperation, we can ensure that both men and women are S&T literate.

Chapter 10
Who benefits?

Measuring the differential impact of new technologies

Swasti Mitter

Technology is becoming pervasive in the lives of working women, even in the poorest countries. Udogini, a nongovernmental organization (NGO) in New Delhi, assists and trains small-scale vendors and self-employed manufacturers — mostly women — in business skills and marketing. In their intense struggle for survival, these women now make use of computer-assisted financial accounting, through the efforts of Udogini. The organization is by no means at the cutting edge of technological change. Inexpensive, older models of computers and systems, bought and maintained with funds from donor agencies, are enough for its present needs. However, the activity highlights the way in which the efforts of NGOs, donor agencies, middle-class organizers, and women themselves make it possible for women who are usually excluded from the benefits of information technology (IT) to use them in a cost-effective way to improve their economic position. None of the members of Udogini had either the resources or the expertise to use the accounting system individually, but together they were able to take advantage of it to improve the efficiency of their organization and its membership.

In the context of the ever-expanding role of new technologies in the lives of women and men in poorer countries, this paper aims:

+ To highlight the relevance of new technologies in improving the quality and quantity of women's employment in the modern sector;

+ To identify the differential effects of these technologies on women and men;

+ To explore the reasons, social and economic, that lead to such differential impacts; and

✦ To help national and international policymakers locate effective points of intervention for redressing gender imbalances in the structure of paid employment, in collaboration with the corporate sector and women workers' organizations.

Relevance and definition of new technologies

The term "new technologies" refers to recent developments in computer-aided systems and some types of biotechnologies. In the broad spectrum of technological developments, new technologies encompass mainly areas where mode of production depends on storing, retrieving, and applying knowledge and information. Whereas some modern technologies are labour-intensive and some capital-intensive, new technologies are primarily knowledge-intensive. In many ways, their effects are similar to those experienced in the wake of previous innovations in production. However, unlike other technologies, they assume and demand certain cognitive skills among workers. Women's exclusion from scientific, technical, and business training thus limits their opportunities to participate in paid productive activities in all societies, including the poorer ones, where the spread of these technologies has been or is likely to be wide.

Do women, especially women from developing countries, need to bother about the possible effects of new technologies or, for that matter, of all modern Western technologies that support and are supported by Western capital and patriarchy, which exploit nature, women, and the poor (Shiva 1989, pp. xiv-xx)? Ecofeminists, postmodernists, and advocates of indigenous knowledge systems, among others, are understandably skeptical about modern technologies that are male oriented, Eurocentric, and antipoor. Given the havoc modern technologies have played in the developing and developed world, many concerned people plead for consideration and appreciation of indigenous technologies, which are embedded in a country's cultural traditions and, as a result, are more appropriate to the needs of women and the poor.

The focus on the effects of new technologies in this paper does not imply total endorsement of these innovations. However, I am against an uncritical rejection of knowledge systems that could, with vision and tenacity, be made compatible with the values and needs of different interest groups in human societies (Mitter 1994). Only increased cross-fertilization between indigenous knowledge systems and formal science will produce a paradigm of science and technology (S&T) that is geared to the needs of men and women alike.

It would be unwise to deny that modern S&T have benefited women immensely, even those in developing countries. They have opened up new career paths for women, lowered the mortality rates of children and adults, and allowed women to control (albeit to an imperfect extent) their own fertility. On the other hand, advancement in formal technologies has also made women's traditional skills redundant in the workplace and brought unforeseen health hazards into the productive and reproductive spheres of their lives. Faced with such complex and contradictory effects on women's lives, it is not easy to formulate strategies that are universal or ahistoric. However, one can safely predict that only women's increased autonomy and choice — in the workplace as in the domestic sphere — will be likely to redress male bias in the current technological trajectories. The employment implications of new technologies assume a special importance in the context of augmenting women's autonomy and choice. Women's limited access to paid employment and corporate networks explains the current gender bias in the adoption of technology.

It would be rather unwise to promote a universal utopian feminine vision of S&T. Women, even in a single given society, do not form a homogeneous category. The needs and experiences of different groups of women require serious study, especially in relation to policymaking. In their dual role as mothers and workers, however, most women do face certain common difficulties. The reproductive role of women, to a large extent, explains differential effects of technological changes on women and men.

Trade flows and technology transfer

The adoption and diffusion of technology depend primarily on decisions at the firm level, but macroeconomic policies often define the environment in which firms make those choices. In the context of new technologies, the most important policies, by far, are those determining the flow of trade, particularly between developed and developing countries. Almost all research and development (R&D) is carried out in the developed world, and technology is transferred through trade, which encompasses buying and selling machinery and knowledge through licensing, patents, direct foreign investment, and the sale of "turnkey" projects, in which software is embedded in the equipment bought.

The linkage effects of technology transfer are complex and depend on the quality of workers and the infrastructure in the countries concerned. In some countries, particulary in east Asia, the driving force behind the adoption and adaptation of new technologies was, at least in the initial stage, to move up the learning curve through "reverse engineering" or "unpackaging the black box." Given the complexity of new technologies, the prospect of moving up the learning curve may not be so easy for countries that have only very recently embraced knowledge-intensive modes of production.

Trade in technology also depends on the national and international legal framework that determines the pattern and volume of exports and imports. In some countries, restrictions on importing foreign hardware, partly to protect the domestic industrial base, have affected the rate at which new technologies are adopted in the process of modernization. The pattern of industrialization, and of women's employment in the urban industrial sector, changes when an economy opens its doors to international competition. The international legal framework related to trade, incorporating such issues as intellectual property rights, determines the extent to which developing countries may be able to adopt the technological breakthroughs experienced and implemented in the more affluent parts of the world.

In this externally constrained environment, technological diffusion, through trade, alters both the comparative advantage of countries and the gender structure of employment. In the short term, the major effect on developing countries is expected to result from agricultural biotechnology. Tropical export crops can be genetically engineered to allow them to be grown in temperate climates; or genetic engineering could produce lower-cost substitutes. For example, oil palm exports may be threatened by the development of canola. There may also be shifts of comparative advantage within developing countries, as those with more advanced capabilities in agricultural biotechnology improve their speciality or commodity crops faster than others, or displace imports from other countries. For example, genetic engineering may be used to shift coffee production from Africa to Southeast Asia; virus-free clones of cardamom are likely to have a significant effect on the relative competitiveness of the leading producers, India and Guatemala.

Examining the differential impact of trade flows with respect to gender and region will be necessary to ensure equitable distribution of the costs and benefits of technological changes. A methodological framework for such an evaluation should be part of the future research agenda. Such an evaluation will be pertinent also in making a case for "managed trade" — trade that is not quite "free," but subject to careful planning — on the grounds of distributive justice, in all spheres including employment (Beneria 1993).

Impact of technological changes

Advanced technologies alter the position of women in the world of paid work through: replacement of direct labour, changing skill requirements, and innovative work organization. It is useful to assess the impact of biotechnologies and computer-aided technologies in relation to these three areas.

Biotechnology: friend or enemy of women?

Although often described as a recent scientific breakthrough, biotechnology has a long history. It refers essentially to a set of processes that involve the use of biological organisms. First-generation biotechnology generally refers to such processes as fermentation. Second-generation biotechnology emerged around the 1930s with the advent of petrochemicals and later antibiotics. Third-generation biotechnology, which I deal with here, is based on the systematic manipulation of material at the level of the genetic code. This biotechnology is expected not only to have wide applications covering a variety of industrial sectors and markets — pharmaceuticals, plant and animal agriculture, speciality chemicals and food additives, environmental applications, commodity chemicals and energy production, and bio-electronics — and to open up a range of new (and currently unforeseen) possibilities in the future. Changes in the first three of these areas will have the greatest effect on the structure of women's employment, in developed as well as in developing countries.

Studies of the employment implications of agricultural biotechnology have often focused on the differential effects on small farms and large-scale plantations. Potential or actual effects on men and women have generally not been discussed despite the current economic importance and potential vulnerability of women in biotechnology-related industries (Ahmed 1992). Even radical feminist literature has yet to systematically examine the gender implications of biotechnology (Mies and Shiva 1993). However, this type of research is critical to inform policymaking in developing countries. The pharmaceutical and food-processing sectors may be the most appropriate initial foci because technological and market developments are the most advanced in these sectors and, therefore, effects are likely to be apparent soonest; and their effects will particularly affect women, who form a large proportion of the workforce in these sectors in developing countries. Although women's use of new techniques of biotechnology has so far been insignificant, the technology is relatively cheap and is already spreading.

Improved methods of agricultural and industrial production in industrialized countries will adversely affect the level of employment in developing countries by displacing more traditional products from the world market. In the sugar industry, for example, fructose from maize grown in industrialized countries is emerging as an economically feasible and widely used substitute for cane sugar. This has spelled disaster for cane sugar-exporting countries, as they can no longer control the price of exports or compete in quality. They are losing an export crop and the workforce involved in sugar-processing industries faces redundancy.

The rapid commercialization and worldwide distribution of the genetically engineered herbicide-resistant plant varieties will lead to the increasing use of chemical herbicides in place of the manual weeding performed by the female waged labour force. The use of tissue culture has distinct advantages over the traditional technique of extracting chemicals from plants. Artificially grown tissues yield products that are more easily purified and both quality and quantity are predictable. As a result, these techniques will probably be used more frequently, even in some developing countries. This shift from field to laboratory, however, will be accompanied by reduction in the workforce. Tissue culture factories are unlikely to generate significant employment, as they are highly automated.

It is too early to assess fully the implications of the introduction of biotechnology on the structure of industrial employment; yet emerging evidence indicates that new jobs will be ones that require a high level of technical skill and managerial competence. Consequently, women's prospects for retaining their share of employment in industries, such as food processing or chemicals, will depend on the following factors:

+ The ability of developing countries to create an institutional and educational infrastructure to teach the necessary skills;

+ The success of developing countries in resisting recent moves to impose intellectual property laws on the fruits of the research undertaken in developed countries; and

+ The willingness and support of national governments and intergovernmental organizations in extending opportunities to acquire relevant skills to women as well as men.

Displacement of female labour from paid work is likely to be accompanied by the increased use of unpaid female family labour.

Scale-neutral biotechnology, unlike Green Revolution technology, will be much more accessible to small farms, which depend on the unpaid services of family members.

Biotechnology opens up fresh challenges for the generation of technology as much as for its application. Women currently are far more visible in the field of biotechnology than in other "high-tech" sectors. Although, on average, women are underrepresented in tertiary education, their proportions are highest in the biological sciences. Women dominate the micropropagation laboratories in Mexico and the Philippines; women constitute 74%, 80%, and 85% of the membership in the Philippine societies for Cell/Molecular Biology, Microbiology, and Biotechnology, respectively (Halos 1992). One reason for this concentration of women scientists is that jobs in biological sciences have been considered low-paying, concerned with basic science and with limited links to industry (hence shunned by male scientists). Work in tissue-culture laboratories is also generally tedious, requiring patience and perseverance. However, the picture may alter quite drastically. If the rapid commercialization of patented biotechnologies brings large profits to the corporate sector, it may lead to better remuneration of poorly paid women scientists, although the higher salaries may then attract male scientists.

New biotechnology firms tend to be small and knowledge-intensive. Thus, they offer the potential of upward mobility to women in smaller-scale enterprises. However, there are also constraints, both to developing countries and to women. Although the production of knowledge as well as of goods can be undertaken in small firms in a cost-effective way, the marketing of products, an essential condition of success in business, is not so easy. Access to venture capital or to bank loans determines the viability of small companies; women's exclusion from such access, especially in developing countries, limits their opportunities. To remedy this, S&T education should go beyond purely technical training. An understanding of marketing, finance, and quality control will ultimately determine women's roles as entrepreneurs in the biotechnology business.

Retaining and expanding the roles of women in this area will increase a nation's endogenous capacity-building. It may also lead to a change in the direction of scientific research and its application to biotechnology. Scientific capacity in this field is currently being channelled toward the needs of the commercial world, and it may not be a coincidence that the most vocal arguments against commercially profitable, but socially and environmentally irresponsible, uses of genetic engineering come from natural and social scientists who are women.

Computer-aided technology

Although the use of biotechnology is still at the early stages in developing countries, computer-aided technologies have already affected the structure of employment. Combined with telecommunications and satellites, these technologies have changed the skill requirements, and the nature and number of jobs available to women employees.

Automated manufacturing

Computer technology has eroded the comparative advantages of developing countries. As computer-controlled machines take over work that was formerly labour-intensive, multinational companies are no longer locating plants in developing countries to take advantage of cheap labour. Currently, the flow of direct foreign investment is toward countries that provide cheap but *skilled* labour. Countries of the Association of South East Asian Nations (ASEAN) have been significant recipients of such investments: there, women have a relatively better chance of acquiring the requisite training and skills.

Domestic companies are also demanding new kinds of expertise in the wake of new technologies. Even in countries where there is a surplus of labour, manufacturing companies are adopting automated methods to achieve speed, flexibility, and quality control. As a result, even with the diverse patterns and directions of manufacturing jobs in all parts of the world,

- ✦ The cost of capital is rising;

- ✦ The input of labour is falling;

- ✦ Demand for multiskilled operators is increasing;

- ✦ New skills requiring hardware and software development are becoming important;

- ✦ Expertise in material resources planning and total quality management is proving crucial;

- ✦ Marketing skills are gaining in importance; and

- ✦ Skills in management of organizations as well as technologies are becoming essential.

Changing skill requirements often mean displacement of women workers, even in an expanding industry. In Malaysia, for example, the introduction of modern management systems in the semiconductor sector increased the demand for expertise in material control systems. Because of new management techniques, most firms in Penang have reduced machine set-up time, idle time, and manufacturing lead time. Increased overall productivity, however, has meant a reduction in the proportion of women employed in the electronics industry of Malaysia. Whereas up to 80% of the workers were women in the industry's first development phases, by 1986 the proportion had fallen to 67% and it continues to fall today.

Computer technologies have affected the quality of women's employment as well. By decreasing the number of highly repetitive manual operations, computer-aided technologies have reduced the physical strain of assembly-line work. Yet, the increasing productivity rates achieved through technological progress have also reduced employees' opportunities to regulate their work rhythm (Mitter 1992). Frequently, workers have to work within ever narrower limits set by faster machines.

Assembly workers' tasks are becoming more versatile and changing qualitatively, from working on a manual assembly line to servicing and maintaining machinery and quality control. Thus, in the pioneer days of Thailand's electronics industry, employers needed the nimble fingers of women workers to connect tiny wires to a semiconductor. The same task is now being done automatically, with as many as 10 machines in the charge of just one woman. Labour content is decreasing, but the quality of labour demanded of electronics workers is rising (Financial Times 1990).

Changes in the organization of work
The nature and conditions of women's employment have also been influenced by changes in the organization of work at the enterprise level. Innovations in work organization have been prompted precisely by the need for continuous work flow to make the expensive technologies cost effective. At the corporate level, the trend has been toward "lean," quality-conscious management, based on the just-in-time (JIT) management philosophy developed in Japan, which stresses the benefit of reducing inventories and waste, both of materials and of final goods and services. Companies that have embraced the JIT philosophy follow a two-pronged policy: eliminate inefficiency and waste, in terms of defective work and waiting time, by streamlining the organization of work and diversifying employees' skills (internal); and establish an effective network of subcontractors ensuring fail-safe delivery of quality goods, services, or materials at all times (external).

Crucial to JIT policy is total quality control, including "zero" defects, after-care servicing, and guaranteed standards for products, aspects that are of key concern to the customers and thereby to the competitiveness of the companies. This philosophy is often referred to as total quality management (TQM) to emphasize the significance of an integrated approach to quality in management policy (Roldan 1993).

TQM, or internal JIT management, presents contradictory possibilities to women employees. At the organizational level, the approach entails a transition from the traditional division of labour between different sections and categories of employment, toward integration of functions, skills, and experiences within a company. The key to success is viewed in terms of "interfunctionality" between different sections of the company, so that efficient communications among employees will improve the quality and timing of products and service deliveries. This paradigm shift in management practices demands of employees: complex and multiple business and technical skills; professionalism; high levels of education; and the ability to change.

As women are generally in the lower employment echelons and have limited access to relevant education and training, the introduction of TQM is likely to lead to their displacement in core enterprises. At least in principle, however, TQM holds promise as well. The move away from "Fordist" division of labour implies new flexibility in existing bureaucracies. The democratic approach requires employee involvement. TQM companies believe that the alienation of employees can be reduced by providing opportunities and training for self-development through resource centres, discussion groups, and action learning. These activities may give women confidence and polyvalent skills.

The impact of TQM and JIT on women at the "shop floor" level has not been sufficiently explored. The paucity of knowledge is even more marked in the context of developing countries. In some cases, the universal, undifferentiated application of TQM simply intensifies work and, thereby, health hazards for women employees. The increased expectations of employers often lead to physical and emotional stress. Under TQM, employees working in "quality circle groups" are expected continually to think of ways to improve the product. Although this forum allows women to contribute innovative, challenging ideas and to feel important or involved, there is fear that management gains from the experience of blue-collar women workers without any compensation for the added responsibility. In Argentina, when temporary technology groups were formed, they gave rise to stomach ulcers and nervous ailments among women (Roldan 1993). While juggling the demands of family and working life, women find it more difficult than men to cope with the expectations attached to the TQM approach. Thus, the JIT and TQM philosophy leads to a reduction in the number of women's jobs in the core enterprises and the external goal exacerbates this trend by transferring some of the feminized jobs to smaller subcontracting units.

Information technology in the service industries
While robotic technologies, combined with new management practices, are posing threats of redundancy for blue-collar women workers on the assembly line, telecommunications and computer technology are opening up new avenues of employment for women in service industries. Stereotyped views of women's abilities have made them the preferred employees for all kinds of office work. Typing skills are valuable in many information-processing jobs. The entry of women into banking, insurance, and telecommunication industries has been impressive in both rich and poorer parts of the world. In some of the major foreign banks in India, for example, women make up 70% of the workforce (Gothoskar 1995); in the 1970s, the figure was only 5%. A similar increase in the proportion of women's jobs in the telecommunications sector has also been reported in Malaysia (Ng 1995).

In the printing and publishing industry, the proportion of female employment increased in both the United States and Denmark (ILO 1990b) with the introduction of microelectronics; in the United States, the increase was 56% in absolute terms. This gain by women was accompanied by a fall in male employment, as traditionally male jobs, such as linotype setting, now required the office-type skills of women, such as inputting text on phototypesetting visual display units. Even in poorer countries like Tanzania, women have made strides in the printing, publishing, and media industries, with effective use of computer technology (Haddon and Silverstone 1993; Alloo 1995).

However, there is a dire need for aggressive training programs for women in these new occupations in poorer countries. The shortage of people with computer-related skills is now being felt acutely in transitional economies, such as those of Romania and Vietnam, that have only recently embraced computer-aided technologies. African countries are facing similar problems. In one financial firm in Kenya, for example, nearly a third of the openings in the data-processing department remained unfilled (Mureithi and Ndiritu 1991).

It is not enough to give women workers one-time access to computer training. In this rapidly changing field, skills must be upgraded continually. Women's entry into new occupations has so far been mainly as clerks and typists. These are precisely the jobs that are likely to be automated in the next phase of technology development.

Women in these new occupations in the information and services sectors are generally from a different background than the blue-
collar workers in manufacturing. Moreover, they are younger; the
redundant female workforce in manufacturing is generally over 35.
In formulating appropriate policies, it becomes important to note this
polarization among women themselves on the basis of class background and age group. The field of software programming has
opened up new opportunities, but for women from relatively privi-
leged backgrounds. The proportion of women in this field is quite significant in some developing countries, such as Brazil (25%) and India
(15%) (Gaio 1995). However, the proportion remains low because
women often do not accept a challenging career because they see it
as lowering their overall quality of their life. To entice educated
women into these emerging fields, policymakers must encourage corporate bodies to experiment with flexible hours and work organization. The cognitive skills of women will be crucial both at the
enterprise and national levels. Strategies to encourage women in the
new technological fields would increase the competitiveness of countries in the international economy.

The telecommunication revolution and distant working

Modularization and miniaturization of products have made it possible
for a large portion of manufacturing to be moved away from core
enterprises to smaller companies. However, externalization of parts
or all of the production process is not limited to manufacturing. Innovations in computers and office equipment, changes in telecommunications technology, and in regulation of telecommunications
services have affected volume and structure of work. The increased
flexibility offered by the new hybrid technologies has enabled major
users of information processing to decentralize parts of their work.
Large companies are able to separate the physical location of labour
and space-intensive operations — such as invoicing, payroll accounting, stock control, sales records, market analysis, and routine
accounting procedures — away from the headquarters of the company to a location where the cost of appropriate labour and office
accommodation is considerably lower. The decentralization of office
work has taken a variety of forms, referred to as "teleworking,"
"telecommuting," and "distant working."

A teleworker is usually defined as one who regularly works
from home, using some form of telecommunications link to the outside world. However, such a narrow definition excludes a number of
other interesting new forms of work organization, such as tele-
cottages (neighbourhood work centres where a small group of

self-employed or employees share an office space), satellite offices, and teleservice centres. It is difficult to gauge accurately the extent of different forms of telework in advanced countries, and it is almost impossible to give any quantitative estimate of such work in poorer parts of the world. Scant information in this area confirms the view that the spread of electronic "homework" has been rather limited in the developing countries. There, even homes of white-collar workers are not often suitable for installing the equipment necessary for working electronically at home. Nonetheless, the prevalence and spread of such work has already been identified in South Korea, Malaysia, the Philippines, and Singapore (Kelkar and Nathan 1992).

In developing countries, decentralization of white-collar work is likely to result in satellite offices and in telecentres. The trend is already discernible and the implications of such work patterns are particularly significant for women. The experience of women in the more affluent parts of the world in this respect is fruitful for women of the developing world, where distant working in information-processing jobs is rather a new phenomenon.

It is difficult not to recognize a gender dimension in analyzing the social implications of telework (Wajcman 1988; Huws 1991; Haddon and Silverstone 1993). Technology that allows women to combine child care and homemaking with a reasonable career is, of course, a welcome possibility. In addition to spatial flexibility, teleworking, at least potentially, also offers the prospect of flexibility in working hours. In practice, evidence gathered so far suggests that women's gains in this direction, contrary to the dream of many futurologists such as Alvin Toffler, has not been substantial. In employer-led teleworking schemes, it is usually the employer who has control and the power to define how the employee should fit into a new set of flexible impositions (Huws 1991). Employees often end up working at unsocial times and for longer hours. Telework, especially if conducted from home, reinforces the traditional gender division of labour rather than being liberating (Haddon and Silverstone 1993). The freedom from domestic duties that often comes when women go out to work is lost. The duties and the tools of work conflict with the demands and the design of the home, causing stress both within work and the family domain. Men work "from" home; women work "at" home. In evaluating the impact of teleworking, one should bear this in mind.

Some of these problems become less relevant when work is done in small-scale satellite offices or neighbourhood centres. The problem of isolation is also less acute in this form of distant work. Yet, there are warning signs, especially when the skills content of these jobs is low and workers have little bargaining power. In Brazil, workers employed at a decentralized (branch) office of a large public-administration agency found, for example, that lack of contact with the head office meant they had no input into determining skills and training needed and job content, in spite of the flexibility required from them in carrying out their tasks. Their work and performance was subjected to increased control, both by supervisors and by electronic surveillance. There was little scope for communication among workers, as a result of the physical fragmentation of the workplace into individual workstations. Data-entry clerks were forbidden to talk during working hours; they were allowed only short rest periods; and group solidarity was discouraged by a payment-by-results system, which encouraged an individual rather than a collective work ethic.

A survey carried out in Japan on the effect of working with computer terminals in banking and other sectors tends to confirm the pessimism generated by the Brazilian study. The Japanese office workers were convinced that their working conditions had deteriorated as a result of computerization. They complained of intensive electronic surveillance; restrictions on their physical mobility; high levels of exhaustion; and dissatisfaction with the monotonous and repetitive nature of the work (Pearson and Mitter 1993).

Bargaining power determines women's capacity to enjoy the advantages of flexibility that the telecommunications revolution has made attainable. In the absence of such power, telework becomes an extension of traditional part-time or piece-rate work — with similar insecurity and a marked absence of career progression. It is hardly surprising to find that the occupational distribution of telework is not very different from that found in traditional jobs. In Britain, a 1992 survey (Huws 1993) revealed that:

> Women make up nearly nine out of ten teleworking secretarial and administrative workers, three-quarters of writers and journalists and nearly two-thirds of training and education staff. They make up over half the home-based managers and sales and marketing staff, and half the researchers, but otherwise they are in a minority. In the case of engineers, this is quite a large minority, at 48%, but in other cases it is very small. Only 16% of home-based consultants are, on average, female, while women make up a mere 14% of home-based computer professionals. Among accountants and financial services workers the male majority is even more overwhelming, at 96%.

Even for professional women and men, telework often poses problems in terms of employment contracts. It is often difficult to establish whether a teleworker is a freelance consultant or distant employee of an established business organization. The security and the benefits that an average employee derives from employment often elude the teleworker, who in many cases is reclassified as a freelance worker by employers.

Relocation of data-entry jobs

The creation of distant work is also related to the internationalization of the market and of information processing. There has been marked differentiation in the quantity and quality of relocated information-intensive jobs by region as well as by gender (Mitter and Pearson 1992). Despite a dramatic increase in the subcontracting of software programming work to a number of poorer countries, their overall share in the production of software has been small. Women's role in this sector has been minuscule. In contrast, women in developing countries have gained a major share of semiskilled data-entry jobs — especially when they have been relocated from high-wage countries.

Offshore data entry or data processing is the term applied to such relocation of new technology clerical work to low-wage countries. Pearson and Mitter (1993) give a comprehensive picture of the working conditions of women in these jobs. The major location of such activities has been the Caribbean, principally Barbados and Jamaica, and more recently the Dominican Republic, with a handful of facilities in Nevis, St Christopher, St Lucia, and St Vincent. Other facilities are known to operate in China, India, Ireland, the Philippines, and Singapore. Most of the foreign-owned subsidiaries in the Caribbean region and elsewhere are located in Free Trade Zones, in which governments provide incentives to foreign investors parallel to those offered to offshore manufacturing. Incentives available to foreign-owned data-entry firms in Jamaica's Montego Bay Free Zone include low-cost space, tax benefits, and full repatriation of profits and dividends to the home countries.

There are similarities in the working conditions of offshore data workers and teleworkers in industrialized countries, especially in terms of the insecurity of their contractual situation and earnings. In Jamaica, workers are frequently hired only after a lengthy period of selection and training, during which they are paid no more than a training allowance, although they are already processing data for commercial contracts.

Despite the precariousness of employment contracts and low basic-wage rates, total remuneration for offshore data-entry clerks often compares favourably with earnings in other local employment. A US-owned data-processing company in the Philippines advertised to potential clients that wages were pegged to the US dollar and adjusted to compensate for any devaluation of the local currency. The minimum wage rates cited were comparable with those of local white-collar workers and professionals. However, in the early 1980s, such wages were 6 to 12 times higher in the United States than in Third World offshore locations (Pearson and Mitter 1993).

Employment in Free Trade Zones often precludes the right to organize. In Jamaica, no unionization was allowed among data-entry workers; in both Jamaica and Barbados, keyboard operators were encouraged to think of themselves as white-collar employees to preempt development of the militant characteristics of organized industrial workers. Management styles were often based on notions of responsibility for the employees' welfare, highlighting caring rather than conflictual relations between workers and management. In the Philippines, managers stressed the benefits granted to their employees, including bonuses, medical care, and profit-sharing plans, while confirming these employees' nonunion status.

Women's net benefits from the new jobs and novel work practices must be carefully evaluated. Most research in the field of technology has so far been geared to manufacturing and has lacked an appropriate focus on gender. A limited amount of research, undertaken by committed women academics, provides some basis for undertaking a more ambitious evaluation of the advantages and disadvantages of flexible service work.

Women in the decision-making process

Even in sectors where women have gained in terms of number of jobs, they have remained invisible in the decision-making process. Women are virtually absent from top management positions in both the developing and the developed world. Women's under- or nonrepresentation in the decision-making process is particularly striking in the new IT industries, which are relatively free of the historic gender-based division of labour and, therefore, where one expects women to fare better. In the large telecommunications companies of Europe, however, the gender structure is similar to that in traditional sectors. Women are predominant at the lower levels of the occupational pyramid, where jobs require less skill, little formal training, and are repetitive and tedious; they are less visible near the apex (Shapiro et al. 1995).

The reasons for this are complex. Women's invisibility in management positions cannot be ascribed only to their relative exclusion from formal technical and managerial education. An in-depth analysis of career progress of women managers in two large IT-based companies in the United Kingdom revealed little difference in the formal qualifications of men and women junior and middle managers (Shapiro et al. 1995). The differential rate of progression may be a result of women's poorer understanding and grasp of informal pro-motion procedures in predominantly male-oriented organizations. Until a critical number of women reach senior-management posi-tions, it will be difficult to change organizational culture.

The difficulty of reconciling family and working lives also poses a problem for women candidates for senior management posts. A demanding management job puts strain on family life; thus, women in all societies often choose family over promotion. By allow-ing flexibility of location and time of work, new technologies might be instrumental in reconciling the family and working lives of women. However, because of their underrepresentation at planning levels, women fail to negotiate such flexibility on their own terms.

Emerging management philosophies in the era of new tech-nologies may create patterns and practices of work that will entice trained women to enter and progress in senior technical and man-agement jobs. Qualities that have been considered feminine are now highly prized in IT-based companies, as they move away from assembly-line activities to group technology and teamwork. In some IT-based companies, management explicitly stresses the need for a feminine style of leadership to ensure TQM in processes and prod-ucts. I am skeptical of such essentialism, but an open acknowledge-ment of women's potential contributions to management style may bring about a "woman-friendly" orientation in the pattern of work.

New technologies and small- and medium-sized enterprises

The introduction of information- and knowledge-intensive industries has contributed to the importance and growth of small- and medium-sized enterprises (SMEs) in all parts of the world. Small firms have often taken the lead in generating knowledge and marketing prod-ucts; their role has been acknowledged in the field of biotechnology as well as computer-aided technology in general.

Knowledge-intensive small firms are most commonly found in affluent areas of the world. Even there, however, SMEs may find it difficult to enter, or maintain a share of, markets that are dominated by larger companies, who have greater access to capital and knowledge of the preferences of buyers. As a result, the knowledge-intensive small firms frequently act as subcontractors, supplying goods and services not directly, but to large companies that dominate the market. Alternatively, they carve out a niche for themselves in a market where flexibility is of paramount importance. For example, microelectronic components, such as integrated circuits, are supplied by large-scale multinational corporations operating in global markets. In some areas, where barriers to entry are low, this globalization has allowed both large and small producers in developing countries, particularly in east Asia, to act as subcontractors of the multinationals. Production of electronic modules (peripheral equipment and consumer electronics) is a niche for SMEs in both developed and developing countries.

There are also opportunities for SMEs in certain segments of the high-tech service sector. Software development is the prime example. Generally, software is divided into three categories: systems software, applications software, and tailored software. Although systems software and, to a certain extent, applications software tend to be proprietary, barriers to production of tailored software are relatively low, making this area potentially attractive to small- and medium-sized firms.

The extent of women's role in these SMEs has not yet been documented. Currently, entrepreneurs in this area come from an elite educational background; women with such a background may be able to overcome some of the obstacles that poorer women generally face regarding access to knowledge, credit, and networks. A study of these women would likely reveal the kind of obstacles women face in occupations that are free of traditional expectations in terms of the gender division of labour. It may require a reevaluation of the nature and organization of a formal education that excludes women from vocation-specific technical and business training at all levels.

For poorer women in the developing world, the field of knowledge-intensive industry remains closed. However, they also face changes in the structure of businesses and production. Decentralization of production and the use of telecommunications technology in management opens up possibilities of entrepreneurship among women even in traditional sectors such as clothing, consumer electronics, and publishing. Challenges that women face in achieving a sustainable existence in these fields are not necessarily in the sphere of production. Their chief problem lies in their inability to respond to market demands. Even in richer parts of the world, the survival of SMEs depends as much on their "tangible" assets, such as technologically suitable equipment, as on their "intangible" investments in expertise to obtain technological and commercial information (OECD 1993b). Innovation and flexibility are also crucial. Women in any society, especially in the developing world, have trouble acquiring such expertise and skills. An intervention by government and donor agencies to give women access to commercial knowledge and business skills would augment their opportunities in the SME sector.

The role of national and international policymakers assumes a special importance at this time, when in most countries substantial numbers of female workers are losing jobs in the formal sectors, because of world recession, technological changes, and lean management policies. Rising rates of unemployment in the formal sector are correlated with growth of self-employment in the SME sector. In Portugal, for example, between 1986 and 1990, during the peak period of recession, female entrepreneurship rose by a massive 48%. Self-employment, in many cases, is an alternative to unemployment — especially in societies where the cushioning of social assistance is absent.

In formerly socialist countries, the transition to a market economy is causing women to lose jobs at a much higher rate than men. This differential effect on men and women of a new economic orientation is visible in all regions: it is as pronounced in present-day Romania (Alatescu 1993; Sandor 1994), as it is in a socialist country such as Vietnam. In these countries, as elsewhere, women generally haver fewer qualifications and less training than they need to obtain technical positions. In the economic climate of shrinking state sectors, maternity leave and higher absenteeism among women make them a less-preferred workforce than men in the corporate sector. In this climate, basic computer knowledge and managerial competence would, to a certain extent, help women to sustain a career in SMEs in countries where the female literacy rate is reasonably high.

Labour standards and new technologies

In the context of new technology, the question of labour standards assumes an important dimension. Health and safety issues relating to the electronics industry have received some attention among both the workers and the policymakers (Chee Heng Leng 1992). Not only in the manufacturing sector, but also in the services sector, health hazards related to the use of video display units (VDUs) assume special urgency. These hazards particularly affect those working at the lower end of the office hierarchy: typists, telephone operators, and data-entry specialists.

Pearson (1995) has drawn attention to the way women academics have raised the issue of health hazards of VDUs with policymakers. A conference organized by the Women's Development Collective in Malaysia in 1993 provides a model of NGOs' effectiveness in giving these issues a high profile. By involving the Minister of Social Development and Unity, the conference paved the way for including health issues in the national policy dialogue on technology. The conference, attended mainly by workers, also included academics from Australia, Germany, India, Sweden, and the United States. The conference proceedings are aimed at disseminating this information to other non-European countries (Ng and Munro-Kua 1994).

In countries where the dissemination of new technology is not carefully monitored by government agencies, difficulties arise. For example, increases in foreign investment have opened up employment opportunities for many millions of women in South China; however, it has also led to much publicized safety hazards, such as fire leading to the death of young female factory workers. The increased incidence of fire has alerted national policymakers, women's organizations, and trade unions to the need to devise and monitor safety legislation for firms in the private sector.

Training in new skills for corporate jobs

The quality of women's employment and the number of jobs open to them depends on their ability to acquire relevant skills. Some skills are learned on-the-job, some through in-house training, and some in formal training institutes. However, in developed and developing countries, women are finding it difficult to enrol in formal training institutes (Acero 1995). The hours of training, the costs involved, and the structure of the courses conspire against them.

For young school leavers, the cost of training, especially in computer courses is the greatest deterrent (Banerjee 1995). Although an average family views the education of sons as an investment for the future, it perceives expenditure on daughters' education as a luxury. In most parts of the world, state subsidies are being withdrawn from postprimary schools. Thus, it is becoming extremely difficult for young women to continue expensive vocation-specific education. In certain countries, such as South Korea, daughters are expected to give their parents a certain amount of money before they get married. In fulfilling this traditional obligation, they enter the job market precisely at the stage when their brothers are getting vocational training.

There is a negative correlation between skill requirements for an occupation and the proportion of women in it. Since 1965, export-oriented *maquiladoras* on the United States–Mexico border have been employing mainly women who, with primary schooling, were suited for repetitive, unskilled jobs in the apparel and electronics industries. In the 1980s, however, changing conditions led to the need for more technical workers and engineers, and there was a concomitant fall in the proportion of women employed: from 77% to less than 60%. The downward trend continues (Hualde, personal communication, 1994).[1]

Women's relative exclusion from skilled technical work is a common occurrence. The difficulties of reconciling the demands of such jobs, which require continuous upgrading of skills, with women's commitment to running a home are often insurmountable. Studies of interconnections between the productive and reproductive spheres of women workers' lives, in their specific cultural context, would allow policymakers to identify appropriate points of intervention for ensuring women's access to tomorrow's jobs.

It is not easy to locate a model for training in the public sector, particularly in developing countries. However, there are some good examples of programs in the European private sector for retraining women workers facing the threat of technological redundancy (European Commission 1994). Policymakers in developing countries should examine, for relevance and efficacy, the range of programs now being collated by the Equal Opportunities Unit of the European Commission at the Directorate General of Employment, Education and Training.

Research agenda to guide policy

To ensure that women receive adequate employment protection and training in necessary skills, some areas of research must receive urgent priority. The mode of research should be participative, involving governments, NGOs, and federations of employers. Projects should be driven by demand and respond to the needs of both women and employers. No positive action will be sustainable unless it proves to be profitable.

---

[1] A. Hualde, "Trade flows, gender, and training in the maquiladora," El Colegio de la Frontera Norte, personal communication, 1994.

To this end, policymakers must ensure that:

✦ Technical training and retraining programs for women take note of the cultural and ideological constraints within their societies;

✦ The health and safety hazards facing women in new technology jobs are included in programs for national human-resource development;

✦ Women have access to knowledge and training that are relevant for small- and medium-scale new technology enterprises;

✦ They identify the cultural and organizational barriers that women face in entering managerial and technical occupations in high-tech industries; and

✦ Accumulated knowledge of the effects of technological changes on women's employment receives priority in worldwide dissemination.

Role and concerns of UN agencies

For nearly a decade and a half, the United Nations (UN) has been alerting national policymakers to these issues. In various reports, the UN has drawn attention to two disturbing dimensions in the current paradigm of technology:

✦ It fails to elicit and appreciate what women could contribute to modern S&T; and

✦ It overlooks women's specific needs and, thereby, affects women's opportunities and career progression adversely.

Even as early as 1979, the UN emphasized the importance of human-resource development for endogenous capacity building in developing countries. It encouraged policymakers to "facilitate constant training, development and upgrading of their labour force so that they may be better able to assimilate and benefit from the swift changes characteristic of the modern world" (UN 1979b, para. 34).

Later UN documents have consistently acknowledged the need to evaluate the differential impact of technological changes in the North and the South as well as on women and men. The report of the 1980 world conference of women, for example, advocated a worldwide "collaborative effort towards making science and technology a tool to eliminate rather than to amplify inequalities between women and men" (UN 1980, chapter 1, section A). In addition, the report stressed the need to recognize women as an important component of a country's human resources and a source of technological innovation. *The Nairobi Forward-Looking Strategies* likewise made a case for women in the context of human-resource development plans (UN 1985b, para. 191):

> Their technological and managerial skills should be enhanced in order to increase self reliance in industrial production, and to promote innovations in productive design, product adaptation and production techniques.

Including women-specific issues in the policy dialogue was an acknowledgement of women's role as agents of change. Governments were urged to include women workers' organizations in policy discussion and to pledge their commitment to disseminating information regarding technological changes to workers to improve their negotiating power (UN 1984, para. 96).

> Concerned women scientists should establish linkages with women's groups to monitor and publicize the impact of new and emerging technologies on women's lives.

These reports have enhanced the awareness of UN agencies of the importance of the gender dimension in research and action related to S&T. The results have been impressive in some areas, but not in the field of new technologies. The International Labour Organisation (ILO) and the UN Industrial Development Organization (UNIDO) are most concerned with the role of women in technological change and industrialization. ILO has been more concerned with the context of new technologies rather than gender analysis. It has emphasized occupational safety and health hazards, and the implications of flexible employment for women, as epitomized by telework, in developed countries (ILO 1989b, 1990a,b, 1991c).

UNIDO has not yet focused specifically on the needs and potential of women in new technology industries; its most important contribution has been in stressing the need to take seriously the role of new technologies in women's future employment (UN 1989). In addition, UNIDO's (1993) study of the textile and clothing industry in Asian developing countries exemplifies the way gender awareness could enrich the analysis of industrial restructuring in response to computer-aided technologies.

A new research initiative

To redress the current gaps in research and analysis in this field, we have initiated a number of projects at United Nations University, Institute for New Technologies (INTECH). Between 1991 and 1993, the Gender and Technology Group at INTECH collected preliminary data and sketched a conceptual framework for analysis of the employment implications of new technologies in collaboration with 14 researchers from different regions of the world (Mitter and Rowbotham 1995). The latest phase of this work, focuses not only on collecting more information but also on adopting a novel mode of research, bringing together researchers and representatives of NGOs and governmental bodies to facilitate a policy dialogue centred on endogenous capacity building.

The primary goal of the project is to improve the advocacy skills of women workers' organizations, by giving them access to key knowledge. The project, which is partly funded by the UN Development Fund for Women (UNIFEM), is focused on Asia and is guided by the conviction that women who bear the consequences of technological and industrial policies should have an adequate voice in the formulation, implementation, diffusion, and evaluation of those policies. Its goal is to contribute toward ensuring that the countries, and women in them, benefit from the potential of new technologies.

Chapter 11
The "double bind"

Women in small- and medium-sized enterprises

Gillian M. Marcelle and Merle Jacob

Since the 1960s, technology has been an important element in development. During the 1970s, experience in developing countries and critiques of development efforts (Baran 1959; Frank 1967) converged on the fact that industrialization and modernization policies were not producing the expected social and economic improvements. Far from allowing Third World countries to leapfrog their way to development, existing policies had widened the gap between industrialized and developing countries, particularly with respect to:

+ The ability of developing countries to absorb and apply technological innovations developed in the socioeconomic contexts of industrialized nations — the technology gap; and

+ The integration of women into the process of development — the gender gap (Benería and Sen 1981; Sen and Grown 1987).

As a consequence, the theory and praxis of development began to shift toward analysis of the problems associated with the gender and technology gaps. This shift was reflected in the program of action adopted at the 1979 Conference on Science and Technology for Development (UN 1979b). Participants at the meeting noted that there was a connection between the gender and technology gaps; changes that accompanied the transfer of Western technologies often eroded women's status. In an effort to redress this imbalance, they recommended that "all members of society be given real and equal access to and influence upon the choice of technology" (UN 1979b, para. 5).

Unfortunately, concerns over debt, macroeconomic adjustment, trade liberalization, and, more recently, sustainable development relegated technology and gender issues to the background in the policy and theory debates of the 1980s. Ironically, the shift toward short-term policies exacerbated existing contradictions in the development process and produced a series of effects that propelled technology- and gender-related issues back to the top of the development-policy agenda. It became obvious that growth-oriented strategies alone could not meet the needs of the poorest sectors of society, particularly women (Mackenzie 1993; Cornia 1987). Restructuring the production process in developing countries under structural adjustment programs led to the substitution of contract labour and small-scale enterprises in the informal sector for the regular labour force and a renewed "feminization" of labour activity. As a result, examining technology and gender issues related to small- and medium-sized enterprises (SMEs) in developing countries is necessary if policy changes at the national and international levels are to keep pace with socioeconomic reality.

Despite the well-recognized linkage between the gender and technology gaps (UN 1979b; Bourque and Warren 1987), the corresponding research and policy-making communities remain institutionally and conceptually separate. Research, policy formulation, and analysis occur at separate sites, and those involved make strategic alliances with different groups in the political arena. Separation is also conceptual in that different methods are used in technology and gender research. Whereas research on technology and development has, for the most part, relied on the analytical devices of the traditional disciplines, gender research has had to develop new techniques because many of the existing conceptual categories were unable to describe or explain the issues. The separation has contributed to a situation in which researchers in these fields focus on different aspects of the same problem.

A lacuna exists at the intersection of science and technology (S&T), gender, and development. Thus, an important prerequisite to understanding technology and gender issues in the context of SMEs is integrating existing information. In this paper, we pursue that objective and distil from published reports the policy recommendations that would assist women in the SME sector with technology development.

Defining small- and medium-sized enterprises

Many people have offered definitions and labels of the SME sector and the "informal economy" (for a survey of definitions, see Lubell 1991). None of the descriptions is completely satisfactory, particularly when applied to women's activities.

In this paper, we focus almost exclusively on SMEs in urban areas, partly because much income and employment generation in rural areas is agriculturally based and issues relevant to that sector are covered in "Can Science and Technology Contribute to Food Security?" (Muntemba and Chimedza, this volume). However, particularly with respect to policy, there is significant overlap among urban and rural SMEs. For example, policies aimed at stimulating agricultural productivity in rural areas have indirect effects on the viability of urban-based food-processing enterprises.

In describing women's activities in urban enterprises, we have tried to be as inclusive as possible. We have included activities that, in traditional statistical classifications, are separated under headings of manufacturing, trade, and services. Such an approach differs from that used by developed nations, which can rely on reasonably reliable data to classify firms according to annual turnover and employee base (OECD 1993a). The gender dimension also further complicates matters and makes otherwise useful classifications, such as the World Bank's SME scheme, less interesting. It differentiates SMEs according to stage of development: subsistence enterprises; new microenterprises; growth-oriented microenterprises; and small-scale industries. However, the significant differences between men and women's economic activities preclude application of this classification, because it would most likely relegate all women's activities to the "subsistence" category.

Classification of SMEs in developing countries is difficult because enterprises are small in terms of turnover and employee base; often use temporary facilities as a base of operations; operate seasonally; and may use domestic premises and furniture for business purposes. These problems have meant that few studies use quantitative data in their analyses.

Definitions such as those provided by Lubell (1991) and Chen (1994) adequately describe the enterprises and activities we are attempting to reach in our policy interventions; they also defend the need to be creative and critical when discussing women's activities in terms of existing definitions. According to Lubell (1991):

> Most working women in the cities of the Third World work in the informal sector occupations such as petty retail traders, as market women, as prepared food sellers or as family workers in household-based enterprises.... The majority are on the border-line of survival, supplementing family income if they are part of a married household and providing family income when they are unmarried, divorced or widowed heads of household.

And, according to Chen (1994):

> In many classifications of small and micro-scale enterprises, the bulk of women's work or economic activity is classified as *survival activities* or *subsistence activities* and considered non-productive and pre-entrepreneurial.... The impact of this classification is quite clear: many women workers are excluded from not only mainstream economic policies but also from micro-enterprise programs.

These authors convey a sense of the heterogeneity of the informal sector and the extent of women's involvement in this diverse set of economic activities. In particular, Chen (1994) warns against policy approaches that continue to ignore the marginalized activities of women; she provides examples of SMEs that are viable and have been transformed into sustainable enterprises capable of generating income for human development. Her classification of women's enterprises, which focuses on the working mode of the enterprise, is useful. She identifies two main categories: contract labour, that is, women employed on a piece-rate, time-rate, or subcontract basis; and self-employment, either singly or as part of a family business. These enterprises can be found in manufacturing, trade, services, or hybrid categories. However, despite this diversity, four characteristics define women's enterprises: *invisible*, in that the contributions are not recognized, counted, or valued; *small-scale*, insofar as women are most likely to be self-employed in family concerns or as piece workers in larger enterprises; *informal*, in the sense that the enterprises are unorganized, unprotected, and operate without benefits or privileges; and *subject to legal and institutional barriers* that, in turn, limit productivity and economic returns (Chen 1994).

In terms of technological needs, Jeans et al. (1990) argue that microenterprises in developing countries are characterized by limited and inadequate resources for innovation, adaptation, and dissemination of technology; poor communication systems and lack of information on a range of technologies and sources of technological inputs; a nonsupportive policy environment and uncertain markets for their outputs. These characteristics highlight the "double bind" gripping women in SMEs in developing countries: inadequate support for income-generating activities and inability to obtain and use one of the most important resources for economic enhancement, that is, technology.

For small open economies, such as those of the English-speaking Caribbean, the small- and medium-sized sector accounts for the vast majority of production outside the transnational or mineral sector (Girvan 1994). Therefore, technology policy for the SME sector, in regions with similar characteristics, is central to economic survival and competitiveness rather than an add-on to policy for other sectors.

Key issues

We have chosen to focus on the main sites of intervention where gender equity in technology policy for SMEs can be achieved. The starting point is the near invisibility and lack of priority given to the two central issues: women in SMEs and technology needs of SMEs. In considering policy options, we pay attention to the configuration of existing structures of policy formation and delivery and identify necessary changes. What kind of socioeconomic and political environment would favour achievement of our objective? Which policy mechanisms and institutional arrangements have been successful? What factors contribute to this success? What changes are required in terms of institutional reform on the part of policy-formulating and policy-delivery agents?

Our recommendations are all aimed at improving S&T policies in the SME sector and promoting gender equality in SMEs in developing countries. They build on the existing policy frameworks contained in the series of documents and declarations from the United Nations (UN) that addressed women and S&T. Because past approaches have not lived up to expectations in terms of making improvements or presenting fresh approaches, we also consider the constraints to implementation (the UN agreements are summarized in Appendix B).

Past work of international organizations

The United Nations

Since its establishment in the aftermath of World War II, the UN has been a major proponent of gender equality at the international level. The UN Commission on the Status of Women (1947), International Women's Year, the world conferences in Mexico City (1975) and Copenhagen (1980), and the UN's 4th Conference on Women are important landmarks on the unfolding route toward global gender equality. The significance of these events stems from the fact that they linked gender equality with the more traditional objectives of development and contributed to the process of eliminating obstacles to the improvement of the status of women. The UN's more recent emphasis on gender in the context of technology and development generally, and SMEs specifically, is thus a logical extension of its previous activity.

The Vienna Programme of Action on Science and Technology for Development (UN 1979b): This program was, for the most part, preoccupied with the problems of North–South technology transfer and the issue of fostering endogenous technological development. It did note, however, that special problems arose as a result of the differential impact of technology on men and women: "modern technological developments ... may have a negative impact on the conditions of women and their bases for economic, social and cultural contributions to the development process" (UN 1979b, para. 5).

Participants at the meeting recommended

+ Strengthening S&T capacities of developing countries with the inclusion of women (para. 23e,g);

+ Removing discriminatory conditions affecting the training of personnel in developing countries (para. 59e);

+ Encouraging the transfer of technology from developed to developing countries by SMEs (para. 67a); and

+ Supporting national efforts to promote the participation of women in S&T and development (para. 99g).

The emphasis on the subject of endogenous technological capability at the Vienna meeting was a reflection of the prevailing consensus among some analysts of development that Western technologies were for the most part inappropriate in Third World contexts. This view was also reflected in grassroots campaigns for appropriate and intermediate technologies to be made widely available. Surprisingly, however, the *Programme of Action* did not address this aspect of the political debate.

Advisory Committee on Science and Technology for Development (UN 1984): The role of women in S&T was the main theme of the background papers and discussion of this committee's report to the UN General Assembly. Although the resulting document did not focus on women in S&T in the context of SMEs specifically, it did provide a number of relevant recommendations. Noting that women were often among the groups negatively affected by S&T, it recommended:

+ Securing rural women's access to land, capital, technology, know-how, and other productive resources through legislation and institutional arrangements (para. 182);

✦ Integrating women into modern technology programs;

✦ Giving high priority to research and development (R&D) that serves women's needs; and

✦ Adopting policies to promote R&D on technologies that aim at relieving women from time- and energy-consuming work (para. 34).

The Nairobi Forward Looking Strategies for the Advancement of Women (UN 1985b): The meeting in Nairobi was convened to evaluate the achievements of the International Decade of Women. The resulting UN declaration is the only one that provides extensive recommendations for women and technology in the context of SMEs. Conference participants took the view that the problems related to the industrial development of developing countries were a reflection of the dependent nature of their economies; thus, promoting transformation industries based on domestic agricultural production was a fundamental issue of development (UN 1985b, para. 189). Given the symbiotic relation between the informal sector and agriculture that often exists in the rural areas of developing countries, this recommendation is particularly important in the context of SMEs. Because of the prevailing emphasis on structural adjustment, governments were cautioned to be sensitive to the potential impact of short-term economic adjustment policies on women in commerce. Other more direct recommendations for S&T and gender in the SME context include:

✦ Governments should expand women's employment opportunities in the modern, traditional, and self-employed sectors of both the rural and urban economy and prevent exploitation of female labour (para. 193);

✦ Governments should recognize the importance of the informal sector to national industrial development and the role of women in this sector (para. 195);

✦ Support structures identified as particularly important to this sector include credit, marketing opportunities, technological guidance, encouragement of women to establish, manage, and own small enterprises (para. 195, 197, and 198); and

✦ With respect to credit, positive measures such as legislative and administrative reform are needed to ensure equal access of women to credit, technical advice, and marketing and development services (para. 197).

Agenda 21 (UN 1992a): *Agenda 21* primarily addresses the question of sustainable development. However, the recommendations in its chapter 24 are of direct relevance to SMEs. Among them are:

✦ Countries should collect data and analyses on the impact of structural adjustment programs on women (para. 24.8c); and programs to create rural and urban training research and resource centres to disseminate environmentally sound technologies (para. 24.8g); and

✦ Governments should promote and strengthen the role of women as full partners in S&T disciplines (para. 31.4).

Although *Agenda 21* is clearly concerned with empowering women, its language sometimes suggests doubts as to how far this goal can be achieved. For example, although it acknowledges that women possess knowledge and experience in conservation that should be recorded in a database (para 24.8a), it is assumed that such knowledge is not technological nor can women translate it into that form by themselves (para. 24.8g). Thus women's information should be *collected*, then environmentally sound technologies will be *disseminated* to them. Women are viewed as the objects of development processes, even when there is specific mention of their role as agents.

Two trends can be seen in the UN's position on women, technology, and SMEs. The first is the shift of focus from women as beneficiaries of development and technology transfer (UN 1979b) to women as agents (UN 1985b). This shift closely reflects the simultaneous movement in development theory toward a notion of people as subjects rather than objects of development and the push for integration of gender issues into the analysis of technology transfer (Carr 1981; Ahmed 1985; Bourque and Warren 1987). Second, a significant problem related to UN policy is that its translation into legislation and policy at the state and other levels in individual countries is entirely dependent on the political will of national governments. This means that there is either a significant lag between global policy and national praxis or no implementation at the national level.

For example, although the UN has been advocating equal access to education since 1947, unequal access remains the biggest obstacle to gender equity in developing countries. Factors such as the poverty of Third World countries and the need to respect the sovereignty of member states are significant obstacles to the UN's taking a more aggressive position on the question of implementation. However, the lack of progress in implementing critical UN decisions suggests that it would be prudent to invest some UN resources in finding alternative mechanisms to stimulate nation state compliance.

Specialized UN agencies

Within the UN system, the UN Development Fund for Women (UNIFEM), the Consultative Group on International Agricultural Research, the International Labor Organisation, the UN Industrial Development Organization, the UN Conference on Trade and Development, the Inter-American Development Bank, and the World Bank have policies and programs that directly affect the productivity of women in the SME sector in both urban and rural settings. We chose to look at the World Bank's enterprise development activities as an example of the work of a UN agency in this area.

The World Bank does not seem to have a formal mechanism for promoting gender-specific goals within its projects, although policy has increasingly focused on enhancing women's participation in economic development in borrower countries. In the last decade or so, the Bank has also been increasingly involved in the promotion of SMEs and, in this capacity, has found it necessary to address issues directly related to gender equity.

A survey of information gleaned from seminar and technical papers prepared by Bank staff about their experience revealed a concentration in Asia, where increasing women's productivity and earning potential is seen as a means of promoting sustainable growth. The objectives of the Bank's projects include increasing women's access to technology, and this is frequently cited as a priority, second only to income generation. Income-generating and enterprise-development schemes include attention to strategic gender needs as defined by Moser (1993) and others; credit programs must include mandatory savings schemes with accounts held in women's names only. These enterprise promotion programs focus on reinvestment of surpluses into the business, primarily because the Bank is interested in seeing enterprises move along a path of evolution from subsistence to small, formal enterprises (Bennet and Goldberg 1993). Significant Bank efforts include the Women's Enterprise Management Training Outreach Program and two pilot projects now under way in India and the Philippines (Edgerton and Viswanath 1992).

Our survey of Bank reports revealed the following policy recommendations, many of which converge on recommendations from more traditional sites of gender research. However, they reveal insufficient emphasis on S&T policy issues:

✦ Removing regulatory barriers that discourage ancillary relations between small and large firms and inhibit expansion of successful firms in the informal and small-scale sectors (Bennet 1992);

✦ Reserving products and subsidizing credit to assist the small-scale sector; such schemes often act as incentives for businesses to remain small and invest in capital-intensive production technologies — the latter, of course, reduces the employment-creation effect (Bennet 1992);

✦ Stimulating the employment potential of firms of all sizes;

✦ Because SMEs are hard to reach by direct-support programs, shifting focus from support to SMEs themselves to capacity building of intermediaries, such as NGOs, and to upgrading the latter (Dessing 1990);

✦ Preceding programs to support SMEs by investigations of local conditions (Dessing 1990); and

✦ Urging governments to pay attention to long-standing policy goals, such as equal access to education and training for women.

International agencies outside the UN system

The Commonwealth Secretariat's triennial meeting of ministers responsible for women's affairs is the main arena in which policies regarding women and development are considered. In addition to deliberations by government representatives, the meetings are supported by background research papers and the participation of observer organizations, including the World Bank and NGOs. In addition to recommendations on the general economic and political environment, reports of the meetings include specific policies relevant to women in SMEs (Commonwealth Secretariat 1990, 1993). Training programs of the Secretariat include entrepreneurship programs for girls and women (Commonwealth Secretariat 1992a).

The triennial meetings have also resulted in specific recommendations that have been taken up at the Commonwealth heads of government meetings and given support at the highest levels of national governments. *The Ottawa Declaration on Women and Structural Adjustment* is one important example. It called on governments to use their structural adjustment policy interventions to improve the lives of women and committed governments to "invest in enhancing women's productive activities, especially in key areas such as enterprise development ... appropriate technologies ... and training" (Commonwealth Secretariat 1992a, para. 7).

Unfortunately, an evaluation revealed only limited progress in implementing the recommendations of this declaration (Commonwealth Secretariat 1993). It recognized that, because governments often lack the political will to make changes, the agenda could only advance by devoting as much effort to sensitizing and training planners and decision-makers as to encouraging the implementation of existing recommendations.

The *Plan of Action for Women*, which is produced by the Commonwealth Secretariat, forms an important part of that organization's policy. When the Commonwealth heads of government meeting in Harare in 1991 produced its Declaration to Equality of Women, the *Plan of Action* was revived and strengthened. More emphasis was placed on implementation, and the Secretariat has been urged to play a major role in providing resources on a multilateral basis through its Commonwealth Fund for Technical Cooperation. Revisions called for inclusion of women and technology and strengthening and enhancing the role of community-based organisations and NGOs. An Expert Group is revising this new *Plan of Action*, and its recommendations will be presented at the Beijing Conference in 1995.

Examining current needs

S&T and development

The technological needs of microenterprises, microproducers, and the informal sector have been examined by Jeans et al. (1990), Gamser and Almond (1989), and Maldonado and Sethuran (1992), respectively. These studies provide a useful catalogue of the deficiencies of the SME sector in terms of technological capability and the problems faced by this sector in overcoming these deficiencies. Although many of their recommendations deal with technology capability in general, the focus on SMEs produces some surprising and original recommendations. We have adopted many of these recommendations, although these authors did not consider gender as an independent variable.

The work of Carr (1984) and Appleton (1994) in appropriate technology and gender issues is much more specific; it presents policies relevant to technology utilization and is sensitive to gender differences. However, the appropriate technology literature has been criticized for not taking account of the international and systemic nature of technological change and for failing to account for shifts in technological paradigms, such as that thought to be associated with information and communication technologies (Bourque and Warren 1987; Stamp 1989).

Tadesse (1982), Ahmed (1985), Bryceson (1985), and Bhaskar (1987) treat gender as an independent variable in the discussion of technological capability building and demonstrate the effects of gendered technological development. The main findings of the early studies were that technological development could, and usually did, have detrimental effects on women. The noninclusion of women in decisions about technology policy has been cited as the main cause of this disadvantage (Pfafflin 1982; Kanno 1987). Later studies also question the direction of technological development itself. Women's knowledge and local knowledge systems are offered as a curative for the debilitating effects of technological change based on wholesale importation of technologies with Western and masculine biases (Shiva 1989).

In Appleton (1994), the role of women's knowledge and local knowledge systems available for technical innovation in microenterprises is the main focus. Appleton (1994, p. 6) defines innovation as:

> Any change, however small, in the skills, techniques, processes, equipment, type of organisation of production that enables people to cope better or take advantage of particular circumstances.

She draws examples from the International Technology Development Group's (ITDG's) "Do It Herself Project" of technical innovation by women in such diverse areas as lighting systems, food cultivation and processing, and organization of production including raw material supply (IWTC n.d.). Using a social-system view of innovation and drawing on evidence from case studies, Appleton claims that technological improvements and innovations can result from improvements in skills and organizational systems, for example, and, more interestingly, from attitude changes on the part of the agents of change. The recommendations in that paper are broad and specifically account for the need to recognize and remove constraints on women who are well outside the technological sphere.

In a report to UNIFEM, Brayman and Weiss (n.d.) take a more conventional approach in discussing the usefulness of technology to women's enterprises. The definition of technology used in their report, although encompassing the various components (hardware and software elements), does not explicitly emphasize the need to include local knowledge in the technological system. The major recommendations of the report echo other nongender-specific studies of technology and microenterprises. The authors suggest rereading familiar case studies to distil the technology implications as a research strategy and advocate promotion of technological developments and change in all women's activities including group projects.

They also recommend more effective involvement of private-sector suppliers of low technology inputs. Citing case-study material (Carr 1984; Downing 1990), they carefully analyze the barriers facing women in SMEs and the biases in industrial policies that favour the formal sector through direct support and other microeconomic policy interventions.

Gender and development

In India (Bennet 1992), Latin America (Standing 1989; Hertel 1990; Wilson 1993), and Africa (Buvinic 1993), women's participation in a wide range of economic activities as wage workers, on a self-employed basis and as piece-rate workers has been described. Increasing female participation in paid and unpaid employment has been accelerated by large-scale restructuring of production in services and manufacturing, which has led to a rapid growth of a system whereby large- and medium-scale formal-sector enterprises contract out parts of the production process on a piece-rate basis. Although this restructuring has had some positive effects in that it integrates women into the productive sector, it has a number of questionable characteristics in terms of sustainability of income, transferral of skills, and its ability to improve the status of women in the long term. Mitter (this volume) discusses the role of information and communication technologies in this restructuring. Pearson and Mitter (1993) and Pearson (1993) provide analyses of these changes in the information-processing sector and suggest that the outcome of this restructuring is not necessarily negative.

Women in the SME sector generally earn low wages or contract salaries; enjoy only limited protection by labour regulations; are isolated from production and informal information exchange; and face insecure employment or marketing contracts. These negative aspects are coupled with advantages, such as flexibility and the freedom to combine income-earning activity with domestic responsibilities.

Researchers provide a great deal of insight and evidence to support the claim that development-planning practices ought to take into account a wide range of social and political needs and rights of women if more narrowly defined economic goals are to be achieved. They define new concepts for planning and policymaking by explicitly considering gender equality (Lycklama à Nijeholt 1992; Østergaard 1992; Buvinic 1993; Holcomb and Rothenburg 1993; Moser 1993). If we treat S&T development or planning as a special issue within development planning, these lessons about the importance of including contextual variables and redefining concepts are also relevant.

Promotion of small- and medium-enterprises

Rhyne and Holt (1993) provide a useful starting point for discussing gender and enterprise promotion strategies, that is, a description of the nature of women's entrepreneurship in developing countries outside the agricultural sector. They make use of empirical research material such as Downing (1990) and Downing and Daniels (1992) to provide a comprehensive survey of female entrepreneurship patterns in Africa, Latin America, and Asia. Their detailed findings on female owned and run enterprises include the following.

✦ The number of female owned and run enterprises is far greater than indicated in earlier studies. The percentage of small businesses (firms with 50 or fewer employees) owned by women ranged from a high of 84% in Swaziland to 20% of newly created small private firms in Poland.

✦ These firms are clustered in a small number of sectors: commerce, services, and light manufacturing such as garment construction, food processing, and assembly. Many manufacturing businesses are located in the home and form part of the informal sector.

✦ Women's enterprises equal male firms in terms of longevity, but show slower rates of growth.

✦ The income earned by women in productive enterprises is often spent on household maintenance rather than reinvested in the business.

✦ On average, women's firms are smaller than firms owned and run by men. In southern Africa, the difference was threefold. Interestingly, in Lesotho, Swaziland, and Zimbabwe, there was no significant variation in firm size between rural and urban areas.

The study offers some explanation of the difference in performance and nature of women's enterprises and identifies significant social, technical, and legal barriers facing women in SMEs. Barriers to access to technological resources were clearly identified as a significant problem.

In Thailand, low rates of technological innovation in the systems used by women played an important role in limiting markets by restricting output to the low-priced, domestic market rather than higher value-added segments (Haggblade and Ritchie 1992). Women working in the Thai silk industry using traditional weaving equipment could not produce goods of sufficient quality for export, but were able to upgrade their techniques by introducing new reeling equipment and hybrid mulberry propagation and, thus, increase their incomes. This was a good example of how specific technological intervention can support women's economic activities. In interventions of this kind, technological training is needed to ensure that the women who will use the new techniques fully understand them. A full range of technical and vocational training as well as basic literacy, basic numeracy, and entrepreneurship training were suggested.

The recommendations of the Rhyne and Holt (1993) study are aimed at the full range of constraints and restrictive factors facing women in SMEs. They call for:

- ✦ Strategies to raise women's social and intrahousehold status;
- ✦ Stable macroeconomic conditions and poverty-alleviation programs; and
- ✦ Strategies to increase access to financial and enterprise development services.

Nonfinancial services discussed in this paper are aimed at providing poor entrepreneurs with access to skills upgrading and markets. Poor women (and men) need access to "social intermediation services" to enable them to bridge the gap separating them from the formal-sector organizations with which they need to interact. Social intermediation services include training to change values and attitudes; networking and information sharing; and confidence building through participation in group activities. We recommend this approach to policy formulation and commend the analysis of Rhyne and Holt which locates SME promotion in a specific political and economic context. The study also details a number of institutional changes required of multilateral organizations, NGOs, and other SME training and development organizations.

Development project evaluation

Cultural, ethnic, and regional variations in the gender division of labour and the experience of gender roles in societies must be specifically considered in project evaluation (Downing 1991). In female entrepreneurship, there are as many differences as commonalities. Specific SME programs must be based on needs identification at the local level and aimed at a defined group (Male, personal communication, 1994).[1] *Changing Perceptions* (Wallace and March 1991) summarizes the attempt of a large international development NGO to review its progress in considering women's views at the project level. It supports our contention that it is necessary to make historically and culturally specific recommendations in any policy intervention and to identify policy alternatives in a fully participatory mode.

Evaluation studies, produced by international agencies, by research scholars, and by staff members of NGOs and development agencies also provide "soft" data useful in examining the relations and effectiveness of many types of development organizations. These nonspecific evaluations can be used to assess the claims made by formal organizations.

Not surprisingly, technology issues have been secondary to other concerns and not well specified or integrated. Budinic (1993) corroborates our assessment that technology is often treated as a subordinate issue. However, although descriptions and case studies seldom explicitly and systematically examine technological change, they are a rich source of information about the context for technological intervention.

Success stories

No one project completely integrates gender, S&T policies, and microenterprise support. However, programs aimed at supporting nontraditional technological development, such as the "Do It Herself Project," contain many commendable elements, although the range of technologies included in these projects are fairly specific to rural communities.

NGOs such as the Self Employed Women's Association, the Bangladesh Rural Advancement Committee, the Grameen Bank, and Acción International have achieved well-documented levels of success in enterprise promotion and support. However, their programs have not emphasized technological development; perhaps fusion of their best practices in credit and financial support with the approach taken in nontraditional technological projects can yield results.

International NGOs such as CARE, Technoserve, Appropriate Technology International, and ITDG are good deliverers of technological training. The United States Agency for International Development has a good record of including technical concerns in its

---

[1] C. Male, interview on SME project evaluation, London, UK, May 1994.

SME promotion programs. The World Bank has made considerable progress in providing appropriate business and attitudinal training in its SME development programs. However, donor coordination must be improved. Mainstream organizations such as the World Bank are identifying strategic gender needs of women in their microenterprise project objectives. Despite the varied sites of success, SME programs with an integrated approach to the inclusion of technology as an important element are unfortunately still not the accepted practice.

Agenda for future research

Alsop (1993, p. 368) summarized the problem with the current situation succinctly when she contended that:

> At the policy level there continues to be a noticeable discrepancy between policy documents which stress gender as an issue and project documents which offer workable mechanisms for addressing this concern.

Although interest in gender issues by researchers and policymakers has been growing, particularly in the last decade, a gap exists between policy and practice. On the subject of gender and technology policy specifically, the gap to which Alsop refers is even wider. Over the last decade, gender research has produced rich and insightful theoretical and empirical surveys of the relation between gender and technology. These studies as well as the contemporary environmentalist critique of development show that Western science and technology is hierarchical and incorporates unequal gender relations at its inception and throughout its processes of development (Harding 1991; Noble 1992).

Surprisingly, however, policies on gender and S&T still assume a largely uncritical stance on the thesis that technology is a liberating force for women of the Third World. Therefore, research is needed, within development studies, to investigate the findings of gender research. Care will need to be taken to solve the problems of what we have termed conceptual and institutional separation and what Stamp (1989) defines as the "boundary problem." At the intersection of these issues with the SME sector much remains to be learned.

Regarding gender and S&T in the context of SMEs, several types of inquiry need attention. We concur with the recommendation in *Agenda 21* (UN 1992a, para. 24.8) that individual countries (or international organizations) "should develop gender-sensitive databases, information systems and participatory action-oriented research and policy analyses with the collaboration of academic institutions and local women researchers." Critical areas are:

+ Comparative studies on the effects of SME-support programs including their indirect effects and qualitative social dimensions;

+ Indigenous informal mechanisms for technology development and the potential for linking these with formal structures and systems;

+ Programs to create rural and urban training, research, and resource centres to help women develop and gain access to environmentally sound technologies (UN 1992a, para. 24.8g); and

+ Methods for giving equal priority to stimulating innovation in indigenous technologies as well as developing the capability to apply and produce Western technologies.

On a conceptual note, research methods employed in the studies suggested above must consider the interdependence of household and market activities and the triple role of women. Doing that would better equip researchers to understand problems related to science, gender, and SMEs in developing countries. In addition, the objectives of development projects should be reinterpreted in terms of the distinction between practical and strategic gender needs and interests.

Many of the recommendations presented in this paper call for institutional reform at the international and national levels. Many similar suggestions in the past have been ignored despite their well reasoned and researched supporting evidence. Moser (1993) and others have suggested that research is needed to develop tools to support the implementation of these recommendations. However, research has also pointed to the importance of political context; in light of this, research is required to build the capabilities of the organizations and individuals who may influence these political contexts in directions that benefit women in developing countries. Many NGOs and other developmental agencies require advice on strategies that would be more successful in influencing decision-makers and improving the political climate in which S&T policies are devised (Moser 1993; Harcourt 1994). Scientific research on influencing strategies is needed.

Research is needed on appropriate management structures and styles within women's SMEs that incorporate economic objectives, empowerment of women, and other strategic gender interests.

Little, if any, gender disaggregation of data is carried out in research on S&T and development, SME promotion, and development-project evaluation. Without this basic analysis, terms such as technological capability, technological choice, entrepreneurship, empowerment, and participation will continue to be less meaningful to women. Development-project evaluations, in particular, contain many rich and varied analyses that can be reexamined in terms of gender roles and relations. Stamp (1989) presents a similar proposal in her research agenda when she suggests that technical literature on pieces of equipment (mills, presses, and so forth) can be mined for data on gender and technology assessment.

Policy recommendations

Any effort to outline policies to promote gender equity must begin with the fact that gender relations differ across regions and individual societies. Failure to consider the importance of cultural context has compromised the effectiveness of development programs, in economic terms and in terms of the objective of empowering women.

To understand the needs of women in SMEs, one must be familiar with the specific activities within the enterprises and understand the effects of macropolicies on individual SMEs. To further complicate matters, strategic gender considerations must be included, and these change over time.

Currently, technology and women's lives and interests do not match. In research reports, women have been presented either as rejectors of technology or as willing acceptors once some minimal conditions of appropriateness have been met. Neither of these situations is satisfactory. We believe that women in developing countries are capable of holistic technological assessment.

Our task as researchers and policymakers is to design technological systems and policy interventions that make sense in the context of women's lives, free them from drudgery, allow their creative and innovative potential to be demonstrated, fit into the fabric of their lives, and perhaps change their material and nonmaterial conditions. Lessons from on-going projects suggest that it is possible to use technological inputs effectively in women's SMEs. The best practices from these individual cases should be identified and applied.

Recommendations requiring legislative reform

+ Ratify the *Convention on the Elimination of All Forms of Discrimination against Women* (UN 1979a), *Agenda 21* (UN 1992a), the legal and administrative reforms suggested in the

1989 World Survey on the Role of Women in Development (UN 1989), and the proposals in the *1995 Platform for Action*.

✦ Introduce legislation and administrative reform needed to remove barriers to women's physical presence in the workplace.

✦ Extend labour regulations to include the informal sector.

✦ Make employer-sponsored medical insurance plans mandatory for all sectors.

✦ Streamline procedures and regulations governing SMEs and simplify eligibility criteria for licenses, credit, and technical assistance.

✦ Repeal laws that bar specific ethnic groups from participating in business activities as this affects large numbers of women.

In making these recommendations, we recognize that countries have been slow to implement recommendations from previous UN agreements dating as far back as 1947; therefore, we urge that consideration of these recommendations take into account the need to create alternative mechanisms to ensure compliance with UN resolutions and agreements within existing international law and within the on-going reorganization of the UN. Although these recommendations are general, their implementation will provide a favourable climate for addressing the more specific concerns of technology policy for SMEs. More specific recommendations can only succeed in a permissive environment.

Recommendations requiring government support, but not legislative reform

✦ Provide technical education to girls and women.

✦ Give women equal access to all education and training.

✦ Recognize indigenous S&T systems and integrate their development with formal S&T training and development programs.

✦ Require development-financing agencies to adopt and exercise gender equality in their lending practices, particularly for the SME sector.

♦ Improve access to financial capital for the purchase of tools, equipment, and related technical information and know-how.

♦ Strengthen the S&T policy and implementation delivery agencies in developing countries, and reorient their channels for providing technical information and support so that they include SMEs in their client base and are able to communicate effectively with these SMEs.

♦ Recognize that the most effective mechanism for reaching SMEs is through small, flexible, responsive organizations with sufficient autonomy to make ad-hoc decisions yet with adequate coordination at the national level (Dessing 1990; Olivares 1989).

♦ Provide financial and technical support to NGOs, cooperatives, and women's groups in their promotion of SMEs.

♦ Introduce an institutional mechanism with a two-tier structure for designing and implementing policies for SMEs (Dessing 1990) — minimize bureaucratic procedures to create flexible, highly responsive, simple structures: one possible model is the Entrepreneurship Development Program in India (Patel 1985).

♦ Improve cooperation between the NGO sector and governments in a manner that maintains the advantages and neutrality of NGOs, but minimizes their resource constraints.

♦ Encourage coordination among donors who support SME development.

♦ Develop a registry of independent experts who agree to provide services to NGOs and SMEs on demand, below market rates, in return for nonmonetary incentives.

To achieve maximum success, countries will have to adopt a perspective that is broad and deep enough to allow the fundamental issue of women's status in society to emerge as a common factor linking a number of sector-specific manifestations of poverty. An overall commitment to gender equity and women's empowerment and emancipation is required, as well as consideration of specific implementation issues. For example, the recommendation concerning workplace health may have to be preceded by significant reform of extant health-care delivery systems and introduction of occupational health-care schemes.

Recommendations aimed at the nongovernmental organization sector

+ Promote economic objectives and income generation in women's SMEs in addition to welfare objectives.

+ Encourage the inclusion of nontraditional skills training in SME development programs aimed at women.

+ Make S&T training and use a priority in women's SME development programs.

+ Encourage outside and internal appraisal of NGO programs by urging governments and international organizations to provide funding and technical assistance for periodic, systematic evaluations. One possible source of revenue is the creation of a fund that would accumulate a small proportion (surcharge) of all incoming donor and project funds.

Governments have been enthusiastic about NGO involvement in implementation and service delivery, but less committed to partnership in program design. Both parties must make efforts to ensure that there is genuine partnership, and the NGO sector must adopt a strategic and realistic approach to these joint undertakings.

Recommendations aimed at women and men in small- and medium-sized enterprises

+ Join cooperative associations and other group ventures that would provide access to information; improve negotiating position with technology suppliers; and reduce the costs associated with acquiring upgraded tools, equipment, and related technical skills.

+ Encourage girls and young women to enter nontraditional fields and support these efforts with apprenticeship schemes.

+ Participate actively in training programs provided by groups or individuals, particularly those committed to furthering the strategic objectives of gender equality.

We realize that some difficulty remains in striking a balance between the gains made in programs that have taken an empowerment approach to women in SMEs and those that emphasize commercialization and growth of SMEs in traditional business terms. Bridging this gap in approaches to SME development has not been accomplished, and finding a solution to this problem will directly influence the policy and management approaches and training strategies used with women in SMEs.

We have identified many types of development organizations that deliver services, provide information, and implement policies that shape the lives of women in SMEs. They include NGOs, government agencies, development agencies, technical research centres, small business promotion agencies, standards organizations, and industry licensing bodies. A major recommendation is for institutional reform of these delivery and policy organizations. Changes in the content and coverage of the services provided to the SME sector are also needed. In terms of research, policymaking, and action, technology is still not well integrated in SME promotion and development programs; this situation must be changed.

We recommend that the suggestions made in the *1989 World Survey* (UN 1989) and in past UN agreements be implemented, noting that the spirit of these agreements reflects the importance of technology as an integral factor in development, but practice has lagged far behind. The calls for revisions to the Commonwealth Secretariat's *Plan of Action on Women* to include consideration of technology support our view of the importance of such support.

Women's needs vary in the many countries of the developing world. Their interests, needs, and everyday situations have to be reflected in technology programs if these are to succeed. We recommend that learning from empowerment and emancipation, which explicitly seeks to redress historic and systemic gender inequality, be incorporated in policy formulation efforts in S&T policy for women in the SME sector. In this way, support for SMEs will empower women while promoting balanced growth to bridge the gender and technology gaps.

The double bind created by male-biased technological systems and the gendered nature of economic systems, which relegates the majority of women in SMEs to vulnerable, uneconomical activities, may yet be unlocked.

Chapter 12

Information as a transformative tool

The gender dimension

IDRC Gender and Information Working Group[1]

Acquiring knowledge is the first step toward change, whether this change be technological, social, economic, cultural, legal, or political. Information is the catalyst, fuel, and product of this process of transformation. Inevitably, information systems — both formal and informal — play a central role in our lives. The flow of information and the associated information and communication technologies (ICTs) constitute a fundamental component of science and technology (S&T). Advances in ICTs are having an increasingly profound effect on the landscape of human activity.

"We are in the midst of a fundamental economic and social transformation whose extent and implications we only partially grasp" (Rosell 1992). This transformation is being driven by an interplay of social and technological dynamics, in particular: developments in information management and telecommunications and the increasing number of links between those technologies; the expanding role and reach of the media; higher degrees of specialization in a more knowledge-based economy and consequent changes in the structure of work; rapid global interaction among organizations; and a vast increase in the availability of information. The product of this transformation has been labelled "the information society."

There is every reason to expect this current trend to continue, but not everyone has shared equally in the benefits. Despite the potential ability of information to modify attitudes and behaviour and empower disadvantaged groups and despite the massive investments in information and communication technologies in the North, there are still two major gaps. First, most of the positive outcomes of

---

[1] The IDRC Gender and Information Working Group comprises Martha B. Stone, Guy Bessette, David Balson, Bev Chataway, Atsuko Cooke, Paul McConnell, Martha Melesse, Tavinder Nijhawan, and Pat Thompson.

the "information revolution" have bypassed women; the information society has remained largely silent on gender issues (Jansen 1989). Second, little readily available research has specifically addressed the circumstances of women and information in developing countries.

In considering the link between gender and S&T in developing countries, it is important to remember that "technology" includes not only physical innovations but also social and cultural artifacts that result from historic experiences (Stamp 1989). In addition, the significant role already played by women in many areas of scientific activity (for example, agriculture and health) has been underestimated. Although relatively little attention has been focused specifically on the intersection of information, gender, development, and S&T, the field of information and communication

+ Influences the content and mechanisms whereby women (and men) in developing countries learn about S&T;

+ Constitutes an increasingly significant component of S&T — ICTs have the potential to enhance the ability of women (and men) to learn, interact, and participate; and

+ Has profound implications for women (and men) in terms of employment, education, training, and other aspects of productive life.

Consequently, there is considerable potential for research, policy formulation, and action on the implications and opportunities for women, particularly in developing countries, of information services, systems, and associated technological innovations.

In the following sections, we identify several research issues of practical and strategic concern to women as providers and users of information. As providers, their contribution ranges from sharing traditional practices within the community through to formal membership in the information and communication professions. As users, regardless of their location, they have needs that could be met through access to information, the most abundant reusable resource in the world. However, these two roles are not being played to their fullest potential. Is due recognition given to the value of indigenous knowledge? Do women enjoy equal professional opportunities in the information sector? Do women have ready access to the information they need? Are they being well-served by the mass media? Are they ready to take full advantage of the new technologies? Evidence suggests that the answer to all these questions is "no." The assumptions governing information interactions are increasingly suspect. A new orientation is required so that women around the world can become full and equal members of the information society.

Inevitably, when attempting to define the scope of such a cross-cutting field as information and communication, some aspects will overlap other disciplines. This is particularly the case in matters of employment, education, and training. Consequently, we emphasize the issues of access, use, and control of information and of ICTs. Even with this qualification, the scope of coverage is potentially immense, encompassing development communication, alternative media, broadcasting, village information centres, libraries, computer-based networking, the Internet, as well as their combinations and interactions.

Policies and action in the information and communication domain must address a basic set of interrelated topics: user needs, content, format, access, system control, utilization, and impact. Each must be explored in a participatory way involving the various stakeholders in the information system. Specific research issues and their policy implications can be grouped into two basic categories:

- ✦ *The information environment — the message:* What information is needed? Does everyone have access to it? Are gender differences accommodated? and

- ✦ *Enabling technologies — the medium:* Are electronic networks, microcomputers, multimedia systems, and television available? Are they adaptable and easy to use? What is their effect? Are employment, education and training, technology policymaking processes, and so forth open to women?

The information environment

Defining information needs and requirements

To determine what constitutes information, or more precisely valid information, one must closely examine "the rules of right" as defined by the power relations within a society. What is considered valid information in a particular society is often "produced and transmitted under the control, dominant if not exclusive, of a few great political and economic apparatuses" (Foucault 1980).

The content and format of information made available to women is usually determined without their advice or consent. In low-income countries, for example, women are caught in a web of political and economic dependency on the men in their lives: their father when they are children, their husbands when they are married, and their brothers if they are widowed. Relative to men, they have little power at the local, national, and international levels of society, and let others decide what is important for them to know, particularly when it comes to S&T (Stamp 1989, pp. 46–47). In developing and industrial counties alike, the male voice has assumed dominance for some time and women do not usually have choices about what information they need. Is the information that women are receiving appropriate? Often, it is irrelevant to their needs and aspirations.

Women and men have different information requirements based on their life experiences. These differences are often reflected in language (Anand 1993).

> Men and women may speak in different languages that they assume are the same, using similar words to encode disparate experiences of self and social relationships. Because these languages share an overlapping moral vocabulary, they contain a propensity for systematic mistranslation, creating misunderstandings which impede communication and limit the potential for cooperation and care in relationships.

Women's information needs can only be understood and adequately met if women are actively involved in the identification and definition of those needs and in the selection of mechanisms that are best suited to deliver such information. Only when women receive information relevant to their needs are they equipped to carry out activities that will benefit them, their families, and their communities. Women must acquire a voice, and they also must be heard.

Empowerment through access to information

Access to information is empowering. It allows people to monitor policy, lobby, learn, collaborate, campaign, and react to draft legislation. It is also one of the most powerful mechanisms through which social and economic progress can be achieved.

Democratization of society and elimination of poverty can only occur if men and women have equal access to the services and resources they need to perform their productive tasks. Democracy means being aware of choices and making decisions; the extent to which this is possible depends, in large measure, on how much information is available to the people and how accessible it is. To date, a combination of factors has prevented women from gaining equitable access to the information they need and, thus, has limited their ability to participate more actively in the transformation of society.

As in the determination of information requirements, language can also be a constraint to women's access to information. The whole focus of women's alternative communication efforts is viewing life from women's perspective. Until this perspective has been given equal time and opportunity for expression, language cannot be assumed to be objective. The desire to be heard, to speak in their own words, will also affect what women want to hear or learn.

Relevant technologies have a great potential to transform the lives of women in a positive manner. Yet women, particularly those in rural areas, have relatively little access to information about these technologies. They have fewer channels than men to information; even when they have equal access, many are illiterate and cannot benefit from printed material. It *is* possible to communicate with these women, however, as information on family planning, health, and nutrition has reached a considerable number of women in rural areas (IWTC and UNIFEM 1990).

To encourage greater control of and access to information services for women, the International Women's Tribune Center (IWTC) has identified several questions (IWTC 1990):

- ✦ How can we ensure the sustained and timely delivery of information?

- ✦ What institution can best respond to such a challenge?

- ✦ Do we have any basis for determining what kind of information a woman needs to make a decision about a technology so that useful information can be provided?

- ✦ How and who can begin the process of repackaging information? and

- ✦ What institutional linkages must be forged to ensure that the ongoing flow and transformation of information will actually reach rural women?

The information formats and delivery mechanisms most appropriate for women depend on the local context. The active participation of women in the design and implementation of dissemination efforts is critical for the success of the overall communication process.

The relation between women and the media has been the subject of much study, yet this channel has been underused as a means for disseminating relevant S&T information. Again, it is essential that the socioeconomic position of the women being addressed be taken into account when determining the most effective media to use.

In most low-income countries, the information disseminated through the media has enormous reach and power. Mass media include radio, television, and newspapers. Radio transmission tends to have the greatest effect because radios are affordable and the message is clear even to those who may be illiterate. Moreover, this medium involves low production and transmission costs and it can reach relatively remote areas. It can be used as a tool for providing informal education, distance education, and information about technical innovations and other development-related activities.

The effect of television is somewhat limited at present, as it is less affordable and its geographic coverage is less extensive than radio, and its transmission is concentrated in urban areas. Use of television also involves access to electricity, which for many is impossible. However, the reach of this medium is expanding, and it can have an exceptionally powerful influence on its audience. Its use in developing countries is growing rapidly and has great scope for timely research and action. Film and video, too, can be positive media but are used less often than others. Video is a valuable medium for women to record their positive experiences and share their development concerns with other women. Sound–slide packages are less expensive and are still more suitable in some developing-country contexts. As a teaching tool, they are relatively low in cost and easily adaptable to specific situations.

For women who are literate, the greatest effect is achieved by print media, particularly reports that are focused on women's issues. A wealth of magazines, newsletters, pamphlets, and other materials is available, much of it in local languages and contexts.

Some concern has been expressed over the tendency of mainstream media and communication formats to dominate, ignore, stereotype, or misrepresent women and their concerns. Much of this has to do with the nature of mainstream media — who controls it, defines it, and sets its goals. The major media have the power, through newsprint, radio, and television, to transform people's opinions overnight. They also have the power to legitimize the small, the insignificant, and the most noteworthy.

In many developing countries, "alternative media" represent the most effective way to reach women. They include street plays, puppet shows, dance, and music programs. The real difference between the two forms — mainstream and alternative — lies more in treatment, style, and content of the message than in the distinctive format of the medium.

Women's input into science and technology

In the "cultured construction of genderedness, women are largely absent from the realm of what counts as technology" (van Zoonen 1992), that is, what women do is usually defined as something other than technology. Furthermore, although women are active agents of development, their knowledge is often ignored or diminished because their role in production does not fit neatly into existing economic models. Along with the invisibility of women's knowledge is the assumption that women are essentially users as opposed to producers of information. As a result, technological development is often approached without the input of women, even though they may be involved with its use or may be affected by it. When it comes to women and technological development, the term "appropriate technology" is a familiar slogan but technology is often inappropriate when gender concerns are recognized and taken into account: "Who decides what technology is *appropriate* and whose interest does it serve?" (Stamp 1989, p. 50).

Women need information about new technologies, but they also require an increased capacity to share the information they already possess. To ensure this, one must examine the cultural rubric of a particular society that defines S&T, particularly if one is to achieve effective strategies for meaningful change. Values attached to technological practices are often seen as masculine. This raises questions such as the following: How is the meaning of gender expressed in technology? What effect does technology have on gender relations? What effect does the value system underlying technologies have on society and gender relations?

One issue of current concern that is very relevant to the issue of women's knowledge is "indigenous knowledge." Foucault (1980) refers to the "insurrection of subjugated knowledges." This involves historic knowledge that has been buried, disguised, disqualified as inadequate, or insufficiently elaborated, that is, naive knowledge, located low in the hierarchy of knowledge beneath the required cognitive or scientific level. Current debate recognizes the value of what has been described as local, discontinuous, disqualified, illegitimate knowledge, now popularly called indigenous knowledge. In most societies, the holders of this knowledge are mainly women.

Education, training, and sensitization

Identifying appropriate information and ensuring access to it have enormous implications in terms of education in the area of information and gender. The most immediate need is for education and sensitization of women and men about the current norms and constraints that militate against women's equal partnership in society. Strategies for providing such training must be developed at all levels of society. In addition, educating women in information management, technologies, and policy development would promote their understanding of the issues involved in these areas and permit the capture, organization, and sharing of information by and for women. Women should also be encouraged to pursue education and professional careers in broadcasting, journalism, communications, and similar fields.

How can women be assured of an effective and equitable role in the area of information and communications? *Women* must define what information they need and identify appropriate delivery mechanisms. Women simply need the same resources and support that men have received, but in ways that complement their lives. At the same time, more is involved than simply gaining technological equity; once women have acquired a voice, they must also ensure that they are being heard. As part of this, men must raise their awareness and comprehension. There is a need to examine how information about women is disseminated to men. Often, men in positions of influence and with decision-making power know very little about the women who will be affected by their policies. If women are truly to establish equity in the area of information and communications, dissemination efforts about women and by women must be delivered to men as well.

Enabling technologies

The information and communication technology environment

Several recommendations of *The Nairobi Forward-Looking Strategies for the Advancement of Women* (UN 1985b) addressed information and related technologies. However, almost 10 years later, it is now widely recognized that this document, while comprehensive in its coverage, was too grand, too vague, and, therefore, not effective enough. The search for innovative ways to strengthen the role of women as both participants and beneficiaries of development is still being pursued. New ICTs have great potential to support such a goal. Although women's involvement with these technologies has increased over the last 10 years and their use for communication and information sharing has expanded, much is left to be done.

In general, the percentage of women involved in information technologies, in terms of both employment and education, is low. This situation is apparent in both the North and South. At a global level, women's employment in telecommunications, or information technologies more generally, is almost invisible. In addition, the proportion of women employed in telecommunications tends to decrease at higher levels of the hierarchy.

Of significant concern is computerized automation, which is leading to unemployment of women. Labour-intensive assembly tasks traditionally performed by women, particularly in low-income countries, are being automated; the use of new software and training skills are being taught primarily to men; and, in second-generation newly industrialized countries, computer-based programming jobs are dominated by men and women's access to these jobs is limited.

Of equal concern is the devaluing of clerical work. Computer and technological skills tend to be gender-labelled. Women tend to use computers only in low-paying categories of employment; positions requiring highly skilled use of computers and other technology are most often held by men. While women are moving down in the employment hierarchy, men seem to be moving up in this field.

Research on gender and ICT in the public realm confirms that women tend to use computers in low-paying, less-prestigious jobs, and the technology tends not to address women's practices (Frissen 1992, pp. 37–38). Because information technology has such great influence, women's relative exclusion could contribute to their further marginalization. In addition, ICT is creating new types of low-paying jobs for women (for example, electronics assembly or telephone answering services) that will intensify the traditional gender-based division of labour (Frissen 1992).

Constraints and barriers

Microelectronic or computer-based technologies are being introduced around the world into environments where gender equity has not been attained or even encouraged. Technological practices, including the new information technologies, are often perceived as masculine, and women have been discouraged from their use (Frissen 1992, pp. 31–32). Studies have documented women's low use of computers, for example, among girls in mathematics and science classes and in university computer labs (Light 1994, p. 1).

Computer training seldom focuses on topics and approaches of direct concern to women. However, there is some cause for optimism. In 1984, a survey conducted on the first day of an introductory computer class designed for business students revealed a gender-based attitudinal gap; women expressed significantly more apprehension than men about learning to use computers. However, in 1993, there were no statistically significant differences in the responses of men and women; indeed, men were beginning to report more concern than women (Callan 1994). Although this study was undertaken in the North, it tends to challenge certain assumptions about the attitudes of women to ICT. Evidently, the constraints and barriers are not insurmountable.

Control, access, and rights to new information technologies

To date, women have been far less involved than men with new ICTs. However, the question of their control, access, and rights to these new technologies cannot be answered through an assessment of the extent to which they use them. Many interrelated factors must be considered. Many of the obstacles arise from long-standing expectations about stereotyped gender roles and behaviours.

There is some evidence that women's control, access, and rights to new information technology are gradually increasing. The "gender identity" of a technology can be modified by the modes of interaction users develop; for example, the telephone was originally intended as a business instrument, but has been substantially transformed into a means of communication by isolated women. Computerized telecommunications share this empowering potential for "adapter reinvention" to aid women's networking (Light 1994, p. 4).

However, even for women who have moved through the process of adapter reinvention, a number of more concrete factors determine access to and control of new ICTs.

✦ Consideration must be given to whether a network is public or based on subscriber fees, whether there are public terminals and instructional sessions, and whether a group moderates its use and establishes policies. For example, the National Women's Agenda Satellite Project was stalled by the National Aeronautics and Space Administration's (NASA's) control of the topics that could or could not be discussed.

✦ Potential users may lack the necessary infrastructure, such as access to a computer or telephone line, encouragement from parent organizations, knowledge, and resources.

✦ Language can be another barrier to access. For a worldwide women's network, translation and mediating regional language differences may be expensive but vital.

✦ Broad-based networks such as the Internet are currently expensive for developing countries; consequently, discussion groups devoted to gender issues are usually centred in Northern academic institutions and are biased in favour of academic interests. Indeed, there is real concern that access to networks might make information more expensive and increase the gap between those who can afford to be connected and those who cannot. Technology transfer and donor assistance will be necessary to keep the gap between the information rich and the information poor from growing.

Electronic mail (E-mail) is a technology that women can approach in a practical way. E-mail is important because it is more "horizontal" in nature than some of the other "hierarchical" communication formats. For many, E-mail is a great communication tool because it is relatively inexpensive and much faster than other modes of communication. Such efficiency is valuable when an idea can be shared and feedback received within a relatively short timeframe, regardless of physical location. Computer-mediated communications have capacities that offer women the potential for community control in three ways (Light 1994, pp. 5–6):

+ They facilitate interaction and group decision-making;

+ They emphasize message content rather than unrelated details about the author; and

+ They reduce time and spatial constraints to organizing for political purposes.

Women's networking groups report that isolation can be reduced and empowerment enhanced in a liberating way. Within communities, networks facilitate the voicing of opinions. Unfortunately, for some, this way of communicating can lead to "information overload." Furthermore, relatively few women in low-income countries are in a position to take advantage of such technologies, because they lack the necessary resources and infrastructural support.

However, over the last 5 years, the accessibility of the new communications technologies has been improving. Some women's nongovernmental organizations (NGOs), including some in developing countries, are participating more effectively in networks. One of the most significant implications of this is the ability of grassroots organizations in the South to provide meaningful, ongoing input into national and international debates for the first time. Computer networking can facilitate women's access and input to decision-making and the power structures essential for participation. This was demonstrated by the NGO electronic networking initiative (NGONet) leading up to and during the UN Conference on the Environment and Development in Rio de Janeiro in 1992. The Association for Progressive Communications, an international network dedicated to serving the information and communication needs of NGOs around the world, was a key player in the NGONet project and will be active in preparations for the sixth world conference on women. Lessons must be learned from these initial successes so that women's groups can take full advantage of the benefits made available through this technology.

Education and training

One of the biggest factors impeding women's ability to work in the area of telecommunications relates to their underrepresentation in technical education. These education opportunities tend to be geared toward the needs and aspirations of men. Although entry may be gender neutral, the incentive to enter and the incentive to remain reveal a significant degree of gender bias.

Relatively few women study computer science at higher levels of education. In this day and age, information technologies have the power to change the world through their effect on economic growth and production. Women have much to offer, and their absence in this field must be investigated and given greater attention.

Women have fewer opportunities to pursue computer training than men. Even though access to computers and computer training has expanded substantially, women are more likely to seek training to survive in a transformed workplace than to advance their interests.

To improve women's ability to work with computers in a positive way, one approach might be to break away from formal training and develop programs that focus on issues of concern to women. Currently, the computer programs and training are seldom relevant or practical for women. There should also be more women trainers, especially for women who are learning how to use computers.

Three modes of training are required by women: the use of computers, that is, aspects of the keyboard and typing, basic concepts, operating systems, and software; computer networking, in terms of how to use e-mail and bulletin boards; and computer-assisted training, which is provided by software that allows a student to work through a lesson or presentation on a monitor and to respond as outlined by program instructions. No matter which mode of training women are interested in, they need appropriate support to overcome negative stereotypes associated with computer technology. Training must be extensive, on-going, and gender-sensitive.

More generally, outreach programs, help desks, on-screen help menus, and user-friendly software are vital if women are to make use of the new information technologies. In poorer countries particularly, the technology may be seen as "foreign" and not as malleable to local needs. Nevertheless, "once the technology is understood by some and used by many in the developing world, it becomes domesticated, familiar, non-threatening, and therefore capable of being harnessed to meet one's own needs" (Munasinghe 1989). The effects of ICT on women and on gender equity must be examined on a case-by-case basis with attention not only to intended purpose but also to the practical services it offers, its marketing and promotion, media attention, training opportunities, infrastructure available, and costs.

Policy issues and recommendations

International discussion about policy for the gender-and-information dimension of S&T for development is conspicuous by its absence. The report of the International Commission for the Study of Communication Problems, the McBride report (Unesco 1980), included a specific recommendation on equal rights for women. It concluded:

> The world cannot afford to waste the great resources
> represented by the abilities and talents of women. This
> is the thought that should be constantly in the minds of
> those responsible for decisions in communication.

Since then, although work on national policies for information and the associated technologies has been extensive (ITU 1984; Westely-Tanaskovic 1985; Hill 1989; OECD 1989; Bender et al. 1991), few have made explicit reference to gender considerations. Clearly, there is scope for action.

Policy recommendations should account for the following factors:

+ *The policy vacuum:* Existing policy frameworks and policy-making processes should be examined and used as a basis for introducing change rapidly.

+ *Gender equity:* Policymakers should not assume that women are simply lagging behind and need to catch up in their perceptions, use, and the value they place on information systems as defined by men. Instead, policies should account for the information needs of both men and women and foster an understanding of the mutual benefits to be gained by society.

+ *Time frame:* Policies should account for short-term and long-term needs, that is, both the present condition and the long-term strategic interests of women.

+ *Participatory approach:* The policy formulation process should encourage full participation of women and of the community in the design and management of all development information and communication initiatives.

✦ *Build on success:* Positive experiences of policy development in this field should be identified, shared, and examined for their broader relevance.

Many of the following policy recommendations can be applied equally at various levels, for example, local institution, national government, and international organization.

The information environment

✦ Include gender-and-information issues routinely, as an integral component of all international development forums and action plans.

✦ Identify, document, and promote successful women's information and communication activities, including their effects on women.

✦ Identify, document, and promote successful information and communication policies that have incorporated gender considerations.

✦ Examine and update all existing information and communication policies to ensure that they incorporate gender equity.

✦ Ensure that all development strategies and action plans routinely incorporate a development communication component that is sensitive to gender considerations.

Information needs

✦ Promote effective participation of women throughout the process of developing information services, that is, from determination of needs, through system design, access, management, and control.

Access and delivery

✦ Encourage discussion at all levels on the right of access to information.

✦ Formulate communication policies and standards that address the quality and quantity of media coverage of gender equity and issues of concern to women.

- Support innovative approaches in the media to enhance gender equity, to respond more effectively to the needs and interests of women, and to improve women's access to relevant S&T and other information.

- Support communication efforts that recognize the need for information to be presented and disseminated in appropriate channels and formats that are meaningful to women.

- Promote measures to increase information flows and networking relating to women and technology for development, especially South–South cooperation, including women's information resource centres to facilitate training and information-access appropriate to local needs.

Women's knowledge

- Encourage development policies that acknowledge and build on the true productive role and expertise of women.

- Recognize the value of women's local knowledge and promote its use by documenting it and disseminating it among community groups, and from the grassroots level to policy-makers.

Education, training, and sensitization

- Promote sensitization to gender issues through more effective provision of information on gender equity and the relative circumstances of women and men.

- Develop and expand appropriate education and training services for women and girls in the information and communication fields, and ensure that they have effective access.

- Increase women's awareness of the availability of various media and the ways they can be used and adapted for their own purposes.

Employment

- Ensure equitable opportunities for employment and advancement within national and international organizations involved in the information–communication field.

Enabling technologies

- Incorporate analysis of the economic and social implications for women as an essential step in the development, acquisition, and use of these technologies.

- ✦ Ensure equitable access by women to ICTs, to their development and adaptation, and to the benefits that can be derived from them.

- ✦ Identify, document, and promote successful experiences of women in using ICTs.

- ✦ Identify, document, and promote successful policies and strategies for addressing ICT gender issues.

- ✦ Increase the involvement of the donor community and development agencies in issues relating to gender and information technology.

- ✦ Ensure that ICT policies consider gender issues and that women play an active role in their development.

- ✦ Acknowledge that the relative absence of women from the field of information technology is to the detriment of all society and must be addressed in development strategies.

- ✦ Ensure that research and development (R&D) of ICT have considered gender issues, and give priority to R&D responding to the needs of women.

Information and communication technology needs
- ✦ Establish collaboratively the needs, priorities, and corresponding research in the field of gender and ICTs.

Access and delivery
- ✦ Implement government policies that promote equitable access to ICT. Ensure that acquisition of ICT among the more prominent sectors of society is not carried out at the expense of disadvantaged women and other less-visible groups.

- ✦ Expand support for community-based ICT centres, public-access electronic networks (freenets), and other measures to promote women's access and collaboration, especially South–South links.

- ✦ Ensure that ICT adoption proceeds in a constructive way and does not widen the gap between the information rich and the information poor.

Education, training, and sensitization
- ✦ Identify and strengthen local capacity and mechanisms for adapting ICT to women's needs.

- ✦ Build awareness of the connection between the need for women to acquire computer and information skills and the need to enhance women's participation in politics and leadership, and to encourage proactive policies among political parties, international and national NGOs, and other institutions.

✦ Support national research in the fields of science and education to develop a more contextually relevant computer science that will be more applicable to women.

✦ Review education and training policies, programs, and curricula to eliminate gender bias and to ensure that women and girls are better equipped to work with the new technologies.

✦ Develop programs for retraining and upgrading the skills of women in computer-based technologies to improve their employment options.

✦ Promote awareness of gender inequity currently evident in the design and management of ICT activities and take positive measures to increase the participation of women.

✦ Review gender sensitivity in S&T education to improve equity in enrolment and course material.

Employment

✦ Support enterprises that develop women-oriented software, hardware, training, and applications, together with gender-related ICT research.

✦ Identify and address the constraints that limit women's employment in high-technology fields; ensure equity in employment opportunities associated with ICT and, where new jobs arise, ensure that women are not confined to assembly or clerical tasks.

✦ Design and implement human-resource development policies that are gender-sensitive and include studies to identify and correct gender imbalances and programs to allow equitable opportunities for staff development.

International research agenda

Most available research on gender, information, and S&T has been carried out in the North; research in the South is not as visible and is less accessible through the usual channels. Furthermore, much of the research has focused on two areas: the implications of ICT for education and employment. One such analysis concluded, "There is no evidence to suggest that women are benefiting from the widespread diffusion of the new technologies through increased access to the *new technology jobs*" (Henwood 1987). This observation could well apply across the information–communication field, in all areas from mass media to software design. If this is the view from the North, the picture from the South is hardly likely to be less bleak. A new international research agenda is needed to focus on the many neglected areas of practical and strategic concern to women.

Such an agenda should take into account the following four factors:

✦ *Collaborative approach:* The scope of the research agenda is vast and potentially overwhelming. The most effective way to ensure rapid progress in key areas is to encourage coordination of effort through national and international research networks, fuelled by effective exchange of information.

✦ *Practical focus:* Research programs must be linked to policy change and development action. The use of case studies will provide a particularly valuable source of practical lessons learned.

✦ *Capacity-building:* The research agenda should be structured to ensure that it strengthens the local research capacity and accounts for existing local knowledge and expertise.

✦ *Sharing knowledge:* Successful research is of little value if the findings are not shared within the concerned community and converted into action. Priority must be given to capturing new knowledge systematically and to finding appropriate ways of bringing it to the broader audience.

Research entry points are numerous and can be found throughout the information–communication spectrum, for example, identifying needs, providing access to information in various channels and formats, promoting use, networking, technological innovations, managing the information system, and measuring effects on the target group.

The information environment

✦ How effective are information activities, including S&T information, in bringing about change for women? How can the effect be measured?

✦ How can linkages be strengthened between researchers in this field and NGOs and other groups working on implementation at the community level?

✦ What financial, marketing, and long-term sustainability issues of information communication services should be addressed, and what lessons have been learned to date?

✦ What gender issues and biases influence control, access, and rights associated with information systems in different settings?

✦ What are the research policies and programs of the donor community and development agencies in the field of gender and information, and how can the available resources be applied most effectively?

Information needs

✦ How are information and ICT needs defined within societies, and what is the extent of gender bias?

✦ What information on S&T is currently being disseminated to women? Is it relevant to their needs as defined by them?

Access and delivery

✦ What role do national and international institutions currently play in reinforcing or overcoming gender-biased information diffusion?

✦ Which information formats and delivery mechanisms are most appropriate for women, accounting for cultural and other considerations, and how can their use be expanded and improved?

✦ What are the positive and negative effects of transborder information flows on gender issues and the status of women?

✦ How should "information clearinghouses" be established to serve women's needs and allow them to share successful experiences of women and technology?

✦ How can the structures and informal communication networks that exist at the local level be used to improve women's access to information?

✦ What institutional linkages must be forged to ensure the ongoing flow and transformation of information that will actually reach rural women?

Women's knowledge

+ Can the addition of women's traditional knowledge redefine what has previously been defined as S&T?

+ Are important technologies being overlooked because they are associated with women's work, and because women's knowledge is not generally considered scientific and valuable?

+ How can the traditional, indigenous knowledge on technologies (held mostly by women) be captured, shared, and used more effectively? How can its value be communicated to policymakers so that they recognize and build on it?

Education, training, and sensitization

+ What changes to the existing education and training efforts are needed to enable women to participate more effectively in the evolving information sector?

+ What are the most effective processes for sensitizing men and women about gender equity issues? How is information about women best disseminated to men?

Employment

+ What are the effects of technological change on employment of women in information activities?

Enabling technologies

+ What would be the feasibility and design of an international research network on ICT, gender, and the related policy implications?

+ What are the effects (positive and negative) of ICT on empowerment, decision-making, development action, and change with respect to both women and men? What are the different implications, South and North?

+ What are the constraints, technical and other, to more effective and equitable use of ICT by women in developing countries? What are the gender issues concerning control, access, and rights associated with these technologies?

+ What lessons have been learned so far about electronic conferencing and how can this knowledge be shared with women's groups and other potential users?

✦ What role can ICT play in ensuring more effective participation by women in the decisions that concern them — locally, nationally, and internationally?

✦ To what extent are national governments and development agencies aware of gender-related ICT issues and incorporating relevant responses in their policymaking processes?

✦ What financial issues are associated with adopting and using these technologies, and what are the related policies and activities of the donor community and development agencies?

Information and communication technology needs

✦ To what extent can women adapt ICT to local needs? Beyond adaptation of existing models lies the ultimate objective of redesign. What can be done to write computer interfaces, programs, applications, and languages that better suit women's needs?

✦ How do ICT developments relate to women's needs at present, and what mechanisms will ensure women's participation in developing research priorities?

Access and delivery

✦ What research is feasible to develop translation software, beyond the major world languages, to help ensure that women have access to local languages and that information gaps are not increased?

✦ What strategies have been, or might be, used to reduce start-up and access costs for women's groups adopting ICT?

Education, training, and sensitization

✦ What education and training opportunities will ensure that women can use ICT and participate in their further development? What are their implications, particularly in developing countries?

✦ What gender-related issues underlie these technologies (for example, vocabulary, location, and interaction with the technology)?

✦ What gender bias is evident in skill labels (such as technical versus nontechnical work), and the designation and allocation of the qualities that merit training and promotion in the wake of technological upgrading?

Employment

- ✦ To what extent will differences in access to ICT between men and women contribute to inequities in performance, productivity, and competitiveness?

- ✦ What are the effects of ICTs on employment of women and men — in the past, present, and future — both within the information technology sector and in other sectors directly affected by it?

- ✦ How do gender biases act as a ceiling for women faced with new technologies in the workplace?

- ✦ What will be the long-term effect of the diffusion of computer technology on skills and employment of men and women, and how can adverse effects on women be avoided?

Past UN and NGO activities

Innumerable NGOs are actively concerned with gender and information issues; many are also involved in development: the IWTC, Women's Environment and Development Organization, the Intermediate Technology Development Group (ITDG), the Inter Press Service International Cooperative, ISIS International, Women's Feature Service, Kali for Women, and the Association for Progressive Communications. An extensive catalogue could be produced of the valuable information and communication activities of these and other NGOs, ranging from video production to compilation of databases on women and development. However, there has been a relative lack of activity at the intersection of the four dimensions with which we are concerned: gender, development, information, and S&T.

IWTC and the UN Development Fund for Women (UNIFEM) have been active in this field through workshops, training sessions, and publications. For example, they organized a "brainstorming" session in 1990 on *Reaching Rural Women with Information on Technology* (IWTC and UNIFEM 1990). Its goal was to explore "ways in which innovative communication techniques can be used in identification of rural women's needs and technology dissemination." Participants were drawn from various sectors — women's groups, media, technology institutions, communications, and United Nations (UN) agencies — and the initial meeting in New York was followed by regional workshops in Africa, Asia, and Latin America. This process generated a considerable amount of practical information that can be used in designing communication strategies to account for the social and cultural environment of rural women; their particular information needs related to food production, small businesses, and trading, for example; their existing sources and channels of information; the participatory process for identifying local needs and priorities; the preferred formats for receiving information; and cost considerations.

Another approach, supported by ITDG and UNIFEM, has been the "Do It Herself Program" on women and technological innovation (IWTC n.d.). Its aim is to stimulate policymakers into recognizing women's existing technical knowledge and account for this capacity when designing technology-development strategies. The program is based on research carried out in Africa and Asia on women's local technological knowledge and their role in technological adaptation and change. Among the conclusions (IWTC n.d., pp. 1–2) were the following:

- ✦ Technology is more than just hardware. It is also skills, expertise, organization, techniques, and knowledge, all of which are connected to production processes.

- ✦ Women's knowledge of production processes is scientific in nature, but is not recognized as such, and is often invisible altogether.

- ✦ Although women's knowledge and skills are central to household survival and food security, they are of low status. When their knowledge *is* recognized as crucial, they tend to lose ownership of it.

- ✦ Women's informal communication systems, are crucial to the survival of their technological knowledge and yet they often remain unrecognized.

Two seminars were held to discuss these points, in Bangladesh and Zimbabwe, bringing together 160 people from universities, NGOs, women's groups, the private sector, credit institutions, international agencies, and government offices. Some of the research and policy issues they identified (IWTC n.d., p. 2) were the following:

- ✦ Women's local technological knowledge must be documented and disseminated broadly at all levels.

- ✦ Technology development must account for and be based on existing local knowledge and skills, ensuring local capacity to innovate and decrease dependence on external intervention.

- ✦ Policies should encourage and protect those involved in small-scale production, and should recognize that women tend to be the experts on local production, processing, and marketing.

UNIFEM is one of the most prominent UN agencies in this field and has participated in both of the activities mentioned above. However, all UN agencies can make a significant contribution in this field, whether through major program support via the UN Development Programme, UN Educational, Scientific and Cultural Organisation (Unesco), the World Health Organization, the International Labour Organisation, or others, or through specific research activities of specialized institutions such as the International Research and Training Institute for the Advancement of Women (INSTRAW) and the United Nations University, including its Institute for New Technologies at Maastricht.

The *international donor community* has manifested little interest in this field to date. Despite the ramifications of the expanding information society, few donors and development agencies have yet to accord priority to the information sector per se (or to gender issues for the most part). However, to obtain some estimate of the volume of activity, an analysis was undertaken of entries in the database of the International Network for Development Exchange. In 1993, this database contained 88 000 records of development initiatives supported by 60 donors and other organizations (Coordinating Unit, International Network for Development Information Exchange, International Development Research Centre [IDRC], Ottawa, Canada). The United States Agency for International Development was sponsoring the largest number of activities (80) related to the gender–information–development theme, followed by IDRC, the Canadian International Development Agency, and the Swedish Agency for Research Cooperation with Developing Countries. These four organizations accounted for some 160 activities — an extremely modest share of all development efforts. The following examples of successful activities might stimulate more concerted efforts in this field.

Examples of "success stories"

Relatively little experience has been documented on the central issues of this paper, located at the convergence of gender, S&T, development, and information, although much has been recorded on combinations of two or three of these dimensions. The two areas of experience, which sometimes overlap, are:

+ Information-sharing to allow women to gain access to S&T for development; and

✦ ICT as a major component of S&T that can have a significant effect on women's empowerment and development.

To illustrate the first category, in 1993, a useful model of a gender-based development communication strategy was produced jointly by UNIFEM, the Instituto Interamericano de Cooperación para la Agricultura, and the International Fund for Agricultural Development (IFAD et al. 1993). It is targeted primarily at governments, NGOs, and other agencies implementing programs that are intended to enhance the ability of women in Latin America and the Caribbean to contribute to the rural economy and agricultural production. The communication strategy is particularly appropriate for overcoming the drawbacks of traditional extension services.

Another type of "communication action plan" that relates to both categories identified above was developed at the International Conference on Women Empowering Communication (WACC 1994). The 40 working groups at the conference identified issues and resolutions that together constitute a comprehensive plan of action. Specific reference to S&T issues was limited, but the framework lends itself to addressing this field. Illustrative of the coverage are sections on satellite television, women in mass media, alternative media strategies, women's publishing houses, women's radio stations and programs, documentation and resource centres, networking, and new communication technologies for women in development.

Several women's media and information services have proven their viability. ISIS International, Women's Feature Service, and Women Ink all have an international profile, and there are many others at the local level. Again, their present coverage of S&T issues is somewhat limited, but the potential exists.

Within the category of the impact of ICT on women, the role of computer-based electronic networking is becoming increasingly apparent. NGONet was established before the Earth Summit to provide an innovative information-sharing process for women, Southern groups, indigenous peoples, and grassroots organizations. It is an effective mechanism for participating in preparatory discussions, monitoring progress, and lobbying for action, even in forums from which the NGO community has previously been excluded. NGONet has contributed to the formulation of the Women's Networking Support Program of the Association for Progressive Communication, which is now taking on a similar networking role during preparations for the world conference in Beijing.

In 1991, IWTC organized a workshop with several women's organizations from around the world to develop skills associated with desk-top publishing and computer networking. Nine groups attended, all but two of which used computers already. They had the technical capacity but not the expertise required to communicate effectively. The workshop focused on how to improve the efficiency and effectiveness of their work and generated much interest and enthusiasm. With the new tools they acquired, these women gained control over production. Previously, they would have sent their work out for typesetting; now they can do it themselves. Their work can be more reflective of who they are and how they think. They can use their own graphics, as opposed to "clip art" which is often based on negative, stereotyped images of women. The enthusiasm generated in this workshop was so great that a publication, *Computer Newsnote*, with a circulation of 7 000, was started as a result.

In the world of film, television, and radio, there are numerous success stories involving women and development. The emphasis is more on the broad range of women's interests, issues, and concerns, rather than any specific focus on S&T. A recent development in television has been the emergence of WETV, the Global Access Television Service. As an alternative to the mainstream channels, WETV seeks to promote social and cultural self-expression through the dominant medium of our time. WETV will "explore new, educative, and entertaining forms of programming, produced by women, for women. Independent women producers will be encouraged and supported to create programs depicting the reality of their lives. Through the support of women producers, WETV will create an entirely difference mix of programming reflecting different life experiences, values, ideas, and perspectives" (WETV 1994). WETV will be launched in September 1995 at the 4th UN World Conference on Women in Beijing, demonstrating its firm commitment to women's expression.

Conclusion

Gender considerations have not played a significant role in shaping the design and use of information services for development, nor the application of ICTs. The consequences of this for women have been limited access to information and to the new information technologies, negative effects on employment and education opportunities, and constraints on the benefits to be gained through active participation in the evolving information society. The constraints have been particularly evident in developing countries.

The current situation can be changed through research, policy development, sensitization, and action. Furthermore, progress on gender issues in such a cross-cutting, multidisciplinary field as "information" could serve as a catalyst for action in other sectors. In any event, given its potential for improving the well-being and status of women, the present lack of research, the numerous research entry points, and the policy implications, clearly the information sector warrants more concerted attention.

Chapter 13
Just add women and stir?

Sandra Harding

There is widespread recognition that, for the last 40 years, development projects have fallen far short of their goals. Why is this so? One major reason is slowly becoming apparent: because women have been disempowered by the major development actors, development has either not reached them or, worse, has "dedeveloped" them. Conventional androcentric assumptions have not yet been critically examined in scientific and technological (S&T) culture; in the international, national, and local mediating agencies that deliver S&T development; or in the communities that are the recipients of development. However, because women are primary deliverers of community welfare on a daily basis to children, the sick and elderly, their households, and the larger social networks that maintain communities, the failure of development projects with respect to women is automatically felt by the social groups who depend on their labour and social services.

These failures increase public skepticism in both the North and the South about the ability of development projects to increase or even maintain democratic social relations. They also threaten public perceptions of the legitimacy of the large social investments that modern S&T require. Yearning for democratic social relations is increasing and becoming more apparent in virtually every part of the world. People don't want to be impoverished, exploited, and even exterminated for the benefit of others. Because the world is shrinking, such processes are much more visible now in the Amazon, in India, in Southern Africa, and elsewhere than they were even a decade or two ago. Moreover, modern S&T have always justified their high costs in terms of the social benefits they can deliver, and development projects have been conceptualized in terms of just such deliveries. If this promise cannot be fulfilled, skepticism can only increase about the legitimacy of the large social investments that modern S&T require. These considerations, too, make rethinking the relation between gender and sustainable human development an increasingly urgent task if modern S&T and the development projects that draw on them are to retain any moral or political legitimacy in the eyes of their donors or recipients. Everyone has interests in this task.

Until recently, few would have imagined that gender, on the one hand, and S&T, on the other hand, could have anything significant to do with each other. Gender differences were thought to be more or less caused by biological differences and the term "gender" was usually taken to refer to "women's problems" that were assumed somehow or other to be an effect of women's biology. Science was assumed to refer to value-neutral knowledge claims and technology to value-neutral artifacts, neither of which could possibly have anything to do with "women's problems." However, these conventional views are no longer held by anyone in the new disciplines that have been studying gender and S&T in action, in the real world, during the last three decades. Now, it is understood that "gender" names the social dimension of women's and men's situations, not their biological causes. It is local cultural arrangements that assign different access to social and natural resources to women and men. Moreover S&T are not value neutral or outside culture; they are fully embedded in their local social relations even as they are also constrained by the natural world. Indeed, it turns out that this must be so if they are to advance the growth of knowledge continually (Van Fraassen and Sigman 1993). S&T are social as well as natural products. They are not exceptions to the general rule that all human products bear the fingerprints of the processes that generated them; they simply bear their social markings in ways pertinent to how they work.

Limits of the "add women and stir" strategy

One major approach to dealing with women's concerns has been to try to "add women" to S&T educational programs and workplaces and, sometimes, as beneficiaries of S&T products in such areas as health maintenance and domestic work. Such efforts are extremely valuable and far too scarce. Principles of social justice require that women, as well as men, gain access to the benefits of S&T development. Moreover, because women tend to be more alert to the distinctive needs and aspirations of women and their dependents in every generation, they try to get these addressed whenever they have the opportunity. Thus, women educate men as individuals and in their roles as community leaders, policymakers, and administrators about those parts of human needs and aspirations that appear primarily in women's worlds. Furthermore, access to S&T work can often bring women together in public settings in ways that enlarge women's consciousness of their role in social relations and empower them as community representatives (Collins 1991). For these reasons, even greater efforts should be made to increase the participation of women.

However, it was clear from the beginning that such additive projects made unrealistic predictions about the likelihood of gaining equality for women, or even of achieving significant improvements in women's situations, through such strategies alone. "Adding women" to S&T development has all too often meant adding a few elite women to the high-prestige areas of S&T — a Nobel Prize here, a university appointment there — and otherwise recruiting women's labour for low-skilled and low-paying jobs to benefit their families, their employers, local governments, consumers in the North, and multinational corporations, but not women themselves. It quickly became apparent that merely "adding women" to existing S&T development projects would not advance either women's situations or sustainable human development. The S&T sites that women entered remained structured by the understandings and interests of men, for women had been excluded from their design and management.

Critics pointed out that the conceptual schemes favoured in S&T institutions, like those in the mediating agencies and surrounding culture, were largely dissociated from women, women's concerns, and anything conceptualized as feminine. Women are assigned responsibility for the household, children's welfare, everyone's daily subsistence, local social networks, and "emotional work" in the household and at work; "manly" S&T policy has distanced itself from these "womanly" areas of human life. Thus, the concepts and theoretical frameworks, within which questions about S&T change are posed, have made it difficult to grasp how development policy does and should affect women's lives. Consequently, development has often meant only incorporating women into work that benefits others but not themselves; that destroys the environment upon which their daily subsistence often depends; that leaves them with no time or resources to provide for their children and others who are dependent upon them. It has resulted in women's "dedevelopment" or maldevelopment and, consequently, in the maldevelopment of the communities that depend so heavily on women's services. Whatever forms of local prestige and status women already had were undermined by powerful "foreign" androcentric forces of modern S&T cultures and of national and international political economies (see Mies 1986; Shiva 1988; Enloe 1989; Seager 1993; and essays in this volume).

What is gender?

In some languages it is difficult to distinguish sex differences from gender differences. Indeed, until three decades ago, in most cultures observable differences between men and women — their physical appearance, emotional and mental tendencies, and their social conditions — were usually thought of as a direct consequence of biological differences. However, 30 years of research on the historically and culturally shifting social constraints on womanliness and manliness have succeeded in identifying many ways in which social relations, not nature, are primarily responsible for shaping gender differences. For example, no matter how distinguished some women's objective achievements in mathematics, science, and engineering, these are still thought of as masculine activities. In Northern cultures, people say that women "can't do math and science," that they are illogical or irrational and unsuited to learning technical skills. These beliefs then justify excluding most girls and women from mathematical, scientific, and technological training and careers, thus making girls and women unable to demonstrate their competence at such activities.

"Gender" is now used to refer to the differences between women and men that cultures create, and "sex" to the biological differences related to our way of reproducing. Dogs, birds, and ants also have sex-differences, but none of these or any other nonhuman species has the gender differences created throughout history by cultures. Many writers now prefer to reserve the terms "male" and "female" for sex differences, using "man" and "woman," "masculine" and "feminine" for the gender differences organized only by human cultures. (In English, at least, biologists speak of male and female dogs, birds, and ants, but do not refer to them as "men" or "women," "masculine" or "feminine.")

Six distinctive features of gender differences are beyond the limitations of earlier biological reductionist understandings. First, gender is fundamentally a relationship and an oppositional one, not an independently specifiable thing or property; in this respect it is like class. Studying only poor people reveals little about how class and race relations are organized, and organized so differently in different cultures. Similarly, studying only women explains little about how gender relations are organized, and why they are so differently organized in different societies. Thus, patterns in women's or men's lives cannot accurately be described or explained apart from the oppositional relation between them.

For example, women who work for wages usually do a double day of work, because they are also responsible for child care and domestic work. This is usually justified by insisting that child care and domestic work are women's natural talent and inclination and are not men's. This double workday affects women's health and earning capacity, and leaves them little time for increasing their S&T literacy, organizing for better working conditions, or participating in S&T policy decisions. If women are to have time, health, and energy for these projects, men will have to share more of the world's workload. Such examples show that it is important to avoid sliding from honorific references to gender relations to discussions of only women's situations. Of course, far too little attention has been paid to women's situations. However, their lives, like men's, are not understandable unless situated within the gender relations they have with their fathers, brothers, sons, husbands, employers, and — regardless of whether they ever interact face to face with them — national and international administrators, policymakers, and the beneficiaries of such administration and policy who are located far from women's daily lives.

Second, gender is not just a characteristic of relations between individuals. The more revealing gender relations are those characteristic of social structures and symbolic systems. Gender is created through a society's assignment of some activities to women and others to men. For example, in the United States, most occupations are gender specific and the vast majority of women work in only three: as secretaries or clerical workers, lower-level teachers, and nurses. Of course, some men do these jobs also, and women also work as administrators, managers, university professors, and doctors. However, the vast majority of workers in the latter fields are men. The extent to which activities are assigned by gender determines how "gendered" a society is; some societies have less gender than others and, thereby, can draw more effectively on the rich and diverse talents potentially offered by all of their members rather than limiting their resources by narrowly restricting what women and men are permitted to do. Rigidity of gender structure limits the flexibility of a society in addressing changing needs and aspirations and in responding to crises created by natural and social changes.

Finally, as a symbolic system, gender relations give meaning to activities otherwise remote from sex differences, and construct stereotypes of womanliness and manliness that are used to limit the human opportunities of both sexes. For example, certain restricted forms of objectivity and rationality are associated with manliness in cultures where modern scientific thinking is highly valued. A woman who achieves these forms of objectivity and rationality is often thought of as less womanly. No matter how the meanings of objectivity and rationality change historically, they always appear to be defined against "the feminine" (Lloyd 1984). Moreover, these associations of restricted notions of objectivity and rationality with manliness lead to systematic ignorance, and to S&T projects that endanger the survival of human societies and the environments upon which they depend (Harding 1986, 1991, 1992; Sardar 1988; Shiva 1988; Nandy 1990).

Third, gender differences are also always hierarchical, although to different degrees and in different ways in different cultures. Gender complementarity does not exclude gender hierarchy. Men usually have more control over the distribution of social benefits and costs, that is, over the gender structure of a society and gender meanings. They are able to hold more positions of social power than women. Moreover, manliness is usually taken to designate whatever counts as the distinctively or ideally human in a culture, while the characteristics associated with women signify only the womanly and not also the distinctively or admirably human. Most distressingly, men often think that the mark of a real man is the extent to which he has been able to define himself precisely against whatever his culture thinks of as womanly: he is a warrior, not a mother (heroically, actively, choosing to risk death versus "naturally," passively, delivering life); through his talents and skills, he provides family income, not mere unskilled child care and domestic labour; or he is rigorously objective and dispassionate, not subjective and emotional. Hierarchically organized values are assigned to the meanings of manliness and womanliness.

Fourth, gender is interlocked with class, race, ethnicity, and whatever other hierarchical social relations organize a society's institutions and practices. That is, masculinity and femininity as individual variable, structural location, and systematic symbolic relations appear only in class, race, and ethnic forms. Gender, class, and so forth are mutually constructing and maintaining. They form a social matrix in which each of us has a determinate location (individual, structural, and symbolic) at the juncture of gender or class social relations (Collins 1991). Class, ethnic relations, or policies are also always gender relations or policies and vice versa. Thus, for example, structural adjustments are having different effects on women in different classes and on men in different classes, as well as on women and men in any given class. The already least-advantaged women are bearing the greatest cost of structural adjustments as literacy, health maintenance, sustainable food supports, and other social welfare services are discontinued to service debts to the North, leaving the already worst off with the fewest other resources to maintain daily subsistence. Projects to eliminate each kind of inequality cannot succeed unless they also eliminate the others.

Fifth, some people think that once we understand that gender is a social construct and not an effect of biology, then gender becomes, somehow, less real and gender inequalities will somehow disappear by themselves as soon as people realize that they have no biological basis. This kind of idealism benefits only the powerful as it relieves them of any obligation to change oppressive gendered social structures and gender meanings, and it justifies, they think, belittling attempts to improve women's situation as merely misguided, special interest politics. However, the fact that gender is socially constructed does not make it any less real. Gender relations are both social and material; they have just as powerful effects on bodies, minds, and social relations as if they were entirely a product of nature. We "live in" gender relations that are social products. Gender relations shape our bodies and the material world with which we interact daily as well as their social meanings.

Sixth, gender relations are dynamic, historically changing, ways of obtaining and distributing scarce social resources. They are sites of political contestation during every kind of social change, including S&T changes (Mies 1986; Wajcman 1991). These dynamic political histories often tend to be subsequently buried, forgotten and, where possible, naturalized. Thus, much of what is referred to today as customary or traditional is the result of vigorously contested social changes that occurred not too long ago. For example, Western expansionism has frequently strengthened colonized men's control of women in exchange for their loss of community governance, which was shifted to the imperial powers (Mies 1986; Enloe 1989; Parker et al. 1992). At other times, such as in slavery in the United States and the French occupation of Algeria, colonized men's role in their families was weakened so that the colonizers might disrupt networks of resistance to their colonization projects (Caulfield 1978). To cite another example, children are often said to be the responsibility of their mothers because of women's natural motherly disposition, although it was only with the passing of laws against child labour in the United States (turning children from economic assets into liabilities) that custody was shifted from fathers to mothers and then said to naturally belong to them (Brown 1975).

Thus, extensive research and scholarship has demonstrated the existence of gender relations as a partially independent force in history, interacting in complex ways with other hierarchically organized social relations such as class or ethnicity. S&T changes become sites for political struggles over who is to direct such changes, who is to benefit from them, and who will pay their costs. Included in such struggles are those between women and men, and between different groups of men over who will control women's labour and the gendered meanings of social change (Wajcman 1991). Transforming gender relations in S&T development should be the focus of concern, rather than only "adding women." To appreciate more completely what is involved in such a task, however, we must briefly review ways that S&T, also, are socially shaped. How can gender relations have a significant effect on them if they are value free, as the older, conventional, assumptions held?

What is science?

Conventional notions of science view modern physics as not just one science among many, but the model that all others, present and future, should strive to emulate. Moreover, they restrict "science" to its supposedly distinctive method (although it has proven impossible to specify uncontroversially just what this method is) or its formal claims, such as Newton's laws or mathematical statements of Einstein's relativity theory. However, a less partial and distorted understanding is gained by viewing sciences as diverse in their "logics" of research and explanation, and as including their entire cultures and practices — their origins, purposes, institutions, traditions, individual and collective practices, knowledge claims, meanings, technologies, applications, languages, interests, and values (Pickering 1992).

Such a concept has enabled historians, sociologists, and philosophers, as well as scientists, to detect many ways that political values and interests (sexist and androcentric ones as well as democracy-advancing ones) enter the cognitive core of scientific methods, descriptions, and explanations of nature and social relations. Observations are theory laden; in principle, our common sense and scientific beliefs are not immune from revision. The current widespread understandings have emerged from more than 30 years of research and scholarship by thinkers who were not at all interested in gender or development issues or political economy (see, for example, Quine 1953; Hesse 1966; Kuhn 1970; Feyerabend 1975; Latour and Woolgar 1979; Pickering 1984; Shapin and Schaffer 1985).

Recently, this leeway in scientific belief-sorting has been recognized, not as a defect, but as a resource for the growth of scientific knowledge. It permits more than one theory to fit any set of observations, more than one interpretation of any theory to be reasonable, and, consequently, the growth of science in ever new directions. Scientists have the opportunity to "see" nature in ever more comprehensive ways, only because nature can be observed through the lens of other than the currently favoured values and interests (Van Fraassen and Sigman 1993). For example, the facts about women's biology have been explained by theories that justify discriminating against women in education, employment, and other areas, and by other theories that do not (see Harding and O'Barr 1987; Hubbard 1990; Schiebinger 1993; Fausto Sterling 1994). Moreover, evolutionary theory, like all other scientific theories, has more than one reasonable interpretation; even antisexist biologists differ about whether evolutionary theory should be interpreted as a form of functionalism. If so, then it makes sense to look more closely at the animal kingdom to develop antisexist forms of sociobiology (Haraway 1991).

Frequently people assume that the technologies and applications of science may carry social or political values, but not its cognitive core. This view has been widely criticized, but one argument is particularly telling: namely that modern science is precisely distinguished by its dependence on technologies for producing its knowledge claims. According to Rose and Rose (1976):

> Modern science and technology are indivisible. The particular character of modern science ushered in with the Galilean revolution is precisely that it is directed towards experiment, use, technology itself; it is this which sets modern science apart from that of classical Greece, Babylon or India. The contemporary production of scientific knowledge is predominantly through the method of experiment, inherently committed to acting on the natural world, in order to understand and control it. At the level of consciousness of individual scientists, a quite contrary view was commonly expressed from the 19th through to the mid-20th century. This emphasized the disinterested and non-utilitarian nature of the work of the "man of science"…. Their belief that they were pursuing knowledge for knowledge's sake savours more of the social functions of pre-modern science, where science is on a par with other intellectual and aesthetic activities such as music or poetry, than those of contemporary science.

Thus scientific methods themselves direct the development of subsequent technologies and applications of the results of research. In other words, the information that sciences gain about how to manipulate nature and social relations is precisely and only what their particular research methods permit.

In one sense, this is so familiar and obvious that it is not even worth stating. In another sense, it radically undermines common sense notions that sciences are separate from their technologies and applications, that in a world where the technologies and applications of science can obviously be "politics by other means," the scientific knowledge that made them possible can be pure. This understanding of how social values and interests shape scientific discovery and information gathering implies that the cognitive cores of sciences are fully permeated by, constructed by, the values and interests that shape their discovery and information-gathering technologies. This is not to say that information gained through politically unattractive methods can never be valuable for sustainable human development, but only that a certain range of kinds of interventions in nature are made visible and attractive through the selection of some scientific methods over others. For example, even though the most powerful causes of cancer are known to come from the environment, the interests of medical research establishments, cigarette companies, and, more indirectly, military and industrial polluters have shaped the way cancer research is preoccupied with biological causes located inside individuals. Will gene manipulation or restriction on industrial and military polluting be favoured as the way to prevent cancer? That depends upon whether the new environmental sciences and their related social movements can gain the political clout to overcome powerful commercial interests and the mystique about the purity and (paradoxically) value of medical sciences that work against them.

More than two decades of criticism of sexist and androcentric results of research in the natural and social sciences has identified many other ways in which the questions sciences ask in the first place shape, in culturally distinctive ways, the images of nature and social relations that emerge in the results of research (Merchant 1980; Harding and Hintikka 1983; Keller 1985; Harding 1986, 1987, 1991, 1992; Harding and O'Barr 1987; Rose 1987; Smith 1987; Shiva 1988; Hubbard 1990; Haraway 1991; Schiebinger 1993; Seager 1993; Fausto Sterling 1994).

What is technology?

Technologies, too, have politics, including gender politics. One might not think this is so if one thinks of technologies only as hardware. However, a particular arrangement of pieces of metal, plastic, wire, rubber, and oils becomes a technology — a washing machine, plow, computer, or car — only when someone knows how to design and construct it, how to use it, and how to repair it. Moreover, such techniques are always embedded in cultural practices that give them and the hardware culturally differing meanings and uses (Winner 1986; Wajcman 1991).

Will attempts to lower birth rates focus on distributing contraceptive devices imposed as a condition of aid by international agencies, levying extra taxes or other costs on families with "excessive" births, or increasing women's education and social welfare? The answer depends upon how contraceptive devices and their techniques are inserted into local cultural practices as these are shaped by negotiations between engineers, manufacturers, advertisers, educators, international and national agencies, religious groups, health providers, and other interested parties. Are representatives of women — the diverse groups of women that exist in any culture — invited to be significant participants in such negotiations? Without their participation, the first two strategies have been favoured; yet increasing women's education and welfare is widely recognized as the most effective way to lower birth rates.

This kind of social shaping contrasts with the view that technologies are free of social values and interests. It also contrasts with various forms of technological determinism that present technological change as either utopian or dystopian — promising unmitigated benefits or disasters. Instead, the effects of technological changes depend upon the outcome of political struggles over who will bear their costs and reap their benefits. The social shaping account also contrasts with accounts that assume that we should hold policymakers accountable only for those meanings and consequences of their policies that they intended; not all unintended consequences are foreseeable, but many more are than policymakers have been willing to take responsibility for.

S&T at their best, not just at their worst, are fully open to shaping by social structures and cultural meanings; or, rather, both new S&T and new forms of social relations become available at moments of social change (see Harding 1992, 1993). Which social values and interests the new sciences, technologies, and social relations will favour depends upon the outcome of struggles between groups with investments in the direction social change will take. Although the gender critiques have focused on the bad consequences for women and gender relations of recent and past S&T changes, their social character also offers reason for hope. We can learn better how to identify which social values and interests advance the growth of S&T and democratic social relations, and which tend to retard them. The social shaping accounts of S&T can be joined to the new understanding of gender as a social dimension to offer valuable new resources for more effectively moving toward sustainable human development.

Designing sustainable human development from the perspective of women's lives

S&T changes that are designed only from the perspective of men's lives cannot produce an overall improvement in women's conditions nor, consequently, can they generate sustainable human development for men or the communities that both constitute. This is the lesson of the past, and we can now understand why this is so. The gender dimensions of S&T cultures and practices, of social relations in local communities, and of the mediating institutions and agencies that deliver S&T change to local communities all conjoin to block development for women and, through them, the communities within which their labour and services are so crucial.

In theory, the solution to this problem is obvious: S&T changes must be designed from the perspective of women's lives — not "women" as an abstract category, but the particular groups of local women who will otherwise bear the bad consequences of such changes. Ironically, such "standpoint" approaches, as they are called, use existing inequalities of social location (gendered social structures and meanings) as resources for gaining the most accurate accounts of both women's and men's lives (Harding 1986, 1991; Rose 1987; Smith 1987; Shiva 1988; Collins 1991; Wajcman 1991). In social relations organized by power inequalities, no "view from nowhere" is possible, as everyone has interests in the outcomes of knowledge and policy projects. Such standpoint approaches show how to use social inequality as a resource for knowledge about "how the world is" and, thus, how to overcome the perpetuation of inequality — here in the form of the failure of development projects.

Does "starting from women's lives" doom a project to subjectivism or relativism? Not in any scientifically or epistemologically objectionable way. Such approaches, in fact, call for, and generate the resources for, a "strong objectivity" — a far stronger one than can be produced by notions of maximizing objectivity that require maximizing neutrality, for the latter block critical examination of the accepted conceptual frameworks within which S&T problems are identified, hypotheses for their solution are formulated, and research designs are selected. To challenge these widely accepted conceptual frameworks is always perceived to be "introducing politics" into S&T. For example, attempts to identify the gender dimension of S&T conceptual frameworks has often been labelled as only "politics." Yet gender analyses do not introduce politics into S&T; instead they identify the ways S&T cultures and practices are already constituted within an androcentric gender dimension.

The kind of strong objectivity identified here demands that knowledge producers be more accountable for nature and social relations; to their critics inside and external to scientific communities; to those likely to be disadvantaged or marginalized by the dominant conceptual frameworks whether they are in a position to bring their disadvantage to the attention of distant policymakers or not; and to S&T practitioners' strong commitment to avoid "might makes right" in the domain of knowledge production. It also demands that policymakers be accountable in their goal of moving toward sustainable human development, even when it leads them to challenge "might makes right" (see Harding 1992).

A form of the democratic ethic clearly states the moral grounds for such a solution: those who bear the consequences of a decision should have a proportionate share in making it. Of course, enacting such a democratic principle is a far more complex and conflicted matter. The social institutions and practices that people will find most effective and culturally appropriate for organizing this kind of democratic participation, obviously, will differ from culture to culture and context to context even within a culture. Democratic decision-making can flourish in small, face-to-face communities with different kinds of institutions and practices than are required in national or international contexts. Moreover, decisions about which institutions and practices to establish so that gender and other inequalities in S&T policymaking can be eliminated will have to be worked out at local levels through attempts at achieving the very kinds of democratic decision-making that are supposed to be the end product of such institutions and practices! There is nowhere to start but "in the middle" when it comes to achieving more democratic social relations, for any antidemocratic process of establishing democratic institutions undermines the legitimacy and, consequently, effectiveness of the latter. In this case, at least, the means does determine the outcome.

The Gender Working Group

of the United Nations Commission on Science and Technology for Development

Mandate

1. The Gender Working Group is to assist the United Nations Commission on Science and Technology for Development in providing guidelines and recommendations on science and technology policy to UN member states — in particular, developing countries — concerning the gender implications of science and technology, to ensure sustainable development.

2. The Gender Working Group is to provide recommendations on ways to improve the effectiveness of the UN system in dealing with issues pertaining to gender, science, and technology.

3. The Gender Working Group is to provide expert advice to other organizations on policies in the domain of gender, science, and technology.

Members of the Gender Working Group[1]

Commissioners

Burundi	Stanislas Ruzenza
Costa Rica	Orlando M. Morales (to June 1994)
	Jaunita Carabuigaz (substitute)
	Eugenia Flores Vindas (from July 1994)
Netherlands	George Waardenburg

---

[1] Listed by country of representation.

People's Republic of China	Wang Shaoqi
	Xuan Zenpei (substitute)
	Fan Lijun (substitute)
Romania	Georges Matache
Saudi Arabia	Mansour Almalik
Tanzania	Titus Mteleka
United Kingdom	Geoffrey Oldham (Chair)

Advisors

Brazil	Sonia Corrêa
Egypt	Farkhonda Hassan
Netherlands	Joske Bunders-Aelen
People's Republic of China	Dong Guilan
Peru	Maria E. Fernandez
Romania	Monica Aurite (to December 1994)
	Marina Ranga (from January 1995)
Uganda	Winnie Byanyima
United States of America	Shirley Malcolm

Contributors and Consultants[2]

Canada	Catherine L.M. Hill
	Bonnie Kettel
	Eva M. Rathgeber
	Martha B. Stone
	Roger Young
Democratic People's Republic of Korea	Soon-Young Yoon
Egypt	Arminée Kazanjian
India	Jayshree A. Mehta
	Swasti Mitter

[2] Listed by country of origin.

Kenya	Shimwaayi Muntemba
	Judi Wangalwa Wakhungu
Peru	Maria E. Fernandez
Sri Lanka	Priyanthi Fernando
Trinidad and Tobago	Pamela Fraser-Abder
	Merle Jacob
	Gillian M. Marcelle
United Kingdom	Helen Appleton
	Marilyn Carr
United States of America	Sandra Harding
	Elizabeth Cecelski
Venezuela	Consuelo Quiroz
Zimbabwe	Ruvimbo Chimedza

Gender Working Group Secretariat

Director of Studies	Elizabeth McGregor
UNCSTD Secretariat	Zeljka Kozul-Wright
Administrative Assistant	Johanne Hamelin-O'Connor
Research Assistants	Fabiola Bazo
	Catherine L.M. Hill
	Perpetua Kalala
	Angela Pasceri
	Ioanna Sahas
	Jeea Saraswati

Previous recommendations

Building on two decades of research[1]

Reviewing the recommendations of previous UN conferences helps to consolidate gains achieved, shed light on events that have brought us to where we are today, and illuminate the path forward. For the first time, this appendix assembles in one place the policy advances dealing with gender that have been achieved at major global conferences over the course of the last two decades in the science and technology sector. The list is classified by the nine sectors selected as themes of the Gender Working Group: environment and natural resources, energy, microenterprises, education, information and communication, health, technology transfer and trade, food security, and indigenous knowledge.

Environment and natural resources

The Vienna Programme of Action on Science and Technology for Development, UN 1979

Para. 21 (b): Assess "availability of national resources and S&T potential."

Para. 26 (b,ii): "Ensure optimal utilization of all inputs through an integrated use of natural, human, and other national resources...protect and develop resources of the biosphere."

Para. 36 (a): Formulate S&T policy framework for effective use of national resources.

Para. 38 (a): "Undertake joint initiatives relating to the exploration and utilization of...natural and other resources."

Para. 77 (f): "Promote S&T projects among developing countries with similarities in natural and social factor endowments."

---

[1] This appendix was assembled by members of the Gender Working Group Secretariat, including Elizabeth McGregor, Perpetua Kalala, Fabiola Bazo, Catherine L.M. Hill, Angela Pasceri, Jeea Saraswati, and Ioanna Sahas.

Advisory Committee on Science and Technology
for Development, UN 1984

Rec. 77: Improve "access to adequate water supplies for household use...design and develop relevant technologies. Women should also be involved in planning for and maintaining water supplies."

The Nairobi Forward-Looking Strategies for
the Advancement of Women, UN 1985

Para. 151: Provide access to water and sanitary facilities; involve and consult women in water and sanitation projects and use of technologies.

Para. 188: Include women in policy planning, implementation, and administration of water supply projects; train women to manage and maintain hydraulic infrastructure.

Para. 222: Initiate innovative programs, such as farm woodlot development with the involvement of both women and men.

Para. 224: Ensure opportunities for women in wage-earning environmental programs.

Para. 225: "Improve sanitary conditions...[including] improvements in the home and the work environment...with the participation of women."

Para. 226: Enhance awareness by women of environmental issues, and the capacity of women and men to manage their environment and sustain productive resources. Disseminate information on environmental sustainability, and recognize women as "active and equal participants" in ecosystem management and the control of environmental degradation.

Para. 227: Assess "the environmental impact of policies, programmes and projects on women's health and activities...and [eliminate] negative effects."

World Survey on the Role of Women in Development, UN 1986

p. 204: Provide training projects such as fuel-wood plantations, forest rejuvenation, and new cooking technology.

p. 222: Provide wells, piped water, electricity, energy, etc., to improve rural women's working conditions.

World Survey on the Role of Women in Development, UN 1989

p. 75: Recognize impact of sustainable agricultural projects on rural women re: modernization of technology, use of high-yielding varieties, fertilizers, etc., and of women's economic role in agriculture and rural development and food production.

p. 77: Integrate women into mainstream agridevelopment; gender-disaggregated data on women's roles, responsibilities in the agroecological environment, farming systems, etc. Attention to role of women in sustainable development (i.e., land, water conservation, use of resources.)

p. 89: Resolve issues of lack of access to land titles, production inputs by women.

p. 97: Recognize effects on women of environmental degradation re: health, livelihood.

pp. 98–99: Support role of women in water management and agroforestry.

p. 100: Pay attention to links between population and water resources use and conservation.

p. 103: Incorporate women in fisheries and forestry projects, programs, and training.

World Women's Congress for a Healthy Planet, WEDO 1991

p. 17: Adopt an international code of environmental conduct to encourage consideration of "the effect on women when planning activities that may affect the Earth." Implement full cost accounting of environmental and social costs, and assign full value to women's labour.

pp. 18–22: Recognize links between women, militarism, and environment; poverty, land rights, food security; biodiversity and biotechnology; sustainable technology transfer; role of women as consumers in sustainable development.

p. 23: Create gender-balanced UN Commission on Environment and Development; support the United Nations Environment Programme, gender-balanced policymaking, provision of information and funding for women in environmental management.

Agenda 21, UN 1992

10.11 (c): Provide information on land use and management and on combatting deforestation [11].

Promote participation of women in forest-related activities [11.3 (b)], forest maintenance [11.13], improved land use, agroforestry systems, combatting land degradation [12.14 (a)], desertification [12.56 (d)], water management [18.59 (f)], and recycling [21.25 (d)].

Provide education and training for women in forestry industries [11.3 (f)], drought and desertification [12.14 (b)], sustainable development of mountain ecosystems [13.11 (c)], and alternative nonchemical pest control in agriculture [14.81 (b)].

13.17 (b): Take full account of women's role in data on alternative livelihoods (tree crops, livestock, etc.).

14.14, 14.18: Ensure women's legal access to resources: water, forest, land, etc.

20.26 (b): Conduct research on effects of hazardous wastes on women's health.

24.3 (d): Promote (government) environmentally sound technology designed and developed consulting women.

24.7: Involve women in decision-making and sustainable development activities

24.8 (c): Develop research and policy analysis on impact of environmental degradation on women, i.e., drought, toxic chemicals, etc.

Draft Platform for Action, Beijing 1995

Art. 29: Improve women's access to and control over land and other means of production.

Art. 51: Recognize daily reality of women's management of natural resources, obtaining fuel and water, managing household consumption.

Art. 53: Include women in decision-making re: environment.

Art. 54: Include women and their perspectives in environmental policies; recognize effects of environmental degradation on women.

Art. 55: Involve women in environmental management, protection, and conservation programs.

Other documents

UN Conference on Settlements (HABITAT) Global Strategy for Shelter to the Year 2000.

1994 Draft of *Gender, S&T: An Environmental Perspective* [to UNCSTD] recommended applying gender and environments analysis to development interventions; inclusion of women, their views and interests in use, management, policy planning re: natural resources and environment; policy and research to consider links between poverty, environmental degradation, women's health, literacy, and employment.

Energy

Advisory Committee on Science and Technology for Development, UN 1984

Rec. 74: Emphasize "R&D on ways and means of exploiting locally available alternative forms of energy."

Rec. 75: Transfer and develop technologies "to enable women to utilize effectively agricultural wastes...for fuels, animal feed and construction materials."

Rec. 76: "Undertake major afforestation programmes and...introduce technologies for more efficient use of firewood."

The Nairobi Forward-Looking Strategies for the Advancement of Women, UN 1985

Para. 191: Apply industrial technologies to women's needs to free them from time- and energy-consuming tasks.

Para. 218: "Rationalize energy consumption...improve energy systems...increase technical training...with a view to women as producers, users and managers of energy sources."

Para. 219: Assess new energy sources and reduce drudgery of women's work.

Para. 220: "Support grass-roots participation of women in energy needs assessment, technology and energy conservation, management and maintenance."

Para. 221: Introduce improved on new energy sources to reduce drudgery, muscle use in women's work.

Para. 222: Develop fuelwood plantations, diffusion of fast-growing varieties of trees and technologies; promote use of solar energy and biogas with regard to use and management by women.

Para. 223: Involve women "at all levels of decision-making and implementation of energy-related decisions," provide information, educate, and train women in energy-related areas.

World Survey on the Role of Women in Development, UN 1986

pp. 201–202: Attention to drudgery of women's work in energy policies, equity constraints in design and access; data disaggregated by gender to reflect use, development, and conservation of energy by women, re: training and employment of women in energy-related fields.

pp. 202–203: Plan methods to include women in energy decision-making; integrate women's concerns re: procedures, energy development, use, conservation, technologies, strategies, supply and demand, compatibility of fuel substitutions; ensure equitable distribution of benefits of new energy development; provide training in skills needed for women to contribute to energy decisions and technology.

p. 210: Enlist participation of women in design, planning, testing, management, maintenance, conservation of new and traditional energy technology.

p. 227: Encourage role of women in rational and proper use of renewable energy sources; consider multiple role of women in energy development and use at all stages of energy projects.

World Survey on the Role of Women in Development, UN 1989

pp. 97–98: Address effects on women of deforestation, desertification, i.e., re: access to energy, fuelwood, fodder for livestock, income-earning activities; detrimental effects of alternative (i.e., use of agricultural wastes for energy deprives soil of fertilizer).

p. 99: Integrate women's roles and needs in energy resource planning; disseminate information on household energy conservation.

World Women's Congress for a Healthy Planet, WEDO 1991

p. 18: Recognize impact of nuclear energy and nuclear R&D on women's health; advocate halt to all nuclear R&D and replacement with alternative fuels.

p. 19: Provide women with access to water, fuel supplies; develop alternative energy sources.

pp. 21–23: Use self-renewing sources as alternative to nuclear power, fossil fuels; promote mass transportation systems; develop more energy-efficient motor vehicles; encourage initiatives to reduce fossil fuel and energy use, waste, overconsumption.

Agenda 21, UN 1992

11.3: Provide education and vocational training for women on forestry technology and industry.

24.8 (b): Assess impact of structural adjustment policies on women, i.e., in terms of removal of subsidies on food and fuel.

34.3: Consider gender-relevant aspects of technology transfer.

Draft Platform for Action, Beijing 1995

Art. 29: Women's access to and control over technology and other means of production.

Other documents

UN 1981 meeting on New and Renewable Sources of Energy led to the report of the UN Solar Energy Group, *Solar Energy: A Strategy in Support of Environment and Development*.

Committee on the Development and Utilization of Nairobi Programme of Action for the Development and Utilization of New and Renewable Sources of Energy, 5th session, examined draft proposal, *The Role of Women in New and Renewable Source of Energy*, which recommended that governments follow role of INSTRAW in R&D and training efforts.

1994 draft of *Gender, S&T: Probing the Question of Energy and Development* [to UNCSTD] recommended including women's views and interests in S&T, and energy research, education, policy and decision-making institutions and processes.

Microenterprises

The Nairobi Forward-Looking Strategies for the Advancement of Women, UN 1985

Para. 195: "Governments should recognize the importance of improving the conditions and structure of the informal sector for national industrial development and the role of women within it.... Small industrial efforts of women should be supported with credits, training facilities, marketing opportunities and technological guidance.... Women should be encouraged to establish, manage and own small enterprises."

Para. 294: Recognition that women who are supporters of families "are among the poorest people concentrated in urban informal labour markets."

World Survey on the Role of Women in Development, UN 1986

p. 18: Improve women's role in the informal sector of manufacturing, in particular through appropriate technology, which remains a problem.

p. 81: Recognize women as entrepreneurs in the small-scale sector, as less-heavy workers with fewer technical skills. Choice of technology is extremely important to women workers who are the more vulnerable partners of development.

p. 113: Train women in simple accounting procedures and other aspects of managing small ventures. Provide information on market conditions and demand trends, credit facilities, technological guidance at the national, regional, and international level of action for development assistance.

Part 6: Study done of women as traders, but no study of women and technology within microenterprises.

p. 170: Acknowledge the informal sector as major employer and a major contributor to national incomes in the developing world.

World Survey on the Role of Women in Development, UN 1989

p. 129: Recognize that women contribute as invisible, hidden, or unregistered workers in the informal production sector. Women provide vital labour for international as well as national markets, and they number more than men.

p. 151: Recognize the wage differential between men and women. Women receive little protection and few benefits as wage earners, either as outworkers or as employees in small units.

p. 169: Acknowledge the need for human resource development that focuses on women in the informal sector with a different approach and strategies than directed toward the formal sector.

p. 171: Entrepreneurship has not been part of previous informal sector programs. Instead, programs have been directed at income-generating activities, lower-level training. As a result, women remain isolated from technical and professional expertise. Recommendation: "A training programme for female entrepreneurship should include technical assistance, identification of new marketing outlets, participation in trade exhibitions and conferences, and access to credit and business information." Efforts in changing the current direction: the Indian Council of Women Entrepreneurs and the Women's Chamber of Industry and Commerce in Sri Lanka.

p. 188: Recognize the need to study the links between the formal and informal manufacturing sector, especially regarding women's participation in the industrial sector. Furthermore, it is necessary to understand and use these studies when human resource programs are designed. The number of women working in the informal industrial sector and the tasks they perform need to be identified. "The opportunities that the informal sector offers for paid employment should [also] be examined.... Additionally, the practice of large firms in the formal sector sub-contracting to small/home-based units in the informal sector needs monitoring as this practice offers opportunities for women as small-scale entrepreneurs." Measures are required at enterprise level and in society to alter gender stereotyping of occupations and workers.

p. 189: The role of international organizations should be to ensure that protective legislation is extended to the informal sector as far as possible, and to develop gender-specific databases re: participation of women in formal and informal industrial sectors.

p. 191: NGOs and donors should provide a package of services that will help low-income women in the informal sector, including: access to capital, credit, technological and industry-related vocational training, and assistance in areas such as quality control, market knowhow, and entrepreneurship. "A coherent programme for achieving quantitative and qualitative improvements in women's employment in manufacturing and in other fields will require the direct participation of women themselves at all levels...[it] will be prerequisite for enhancing women's opportunities in the industrial sector."

p. 239: Policy design: "training of women employed in [the informal] sector to augment their productivity and efficiency, with a resultant increase in income...; developing policies and programmes for technologies improvement, directed towards improving ways of organizing production and production techniques; these are of particular importance for women engaged in handicrafts."

World Women's Congress for a Healthy Planet, WEDO 1991

p. 12 [M. Carr, "Appropriate technologies and technology transfer"]: Encourage women's control over technology, e.g., Gameen Bank of Bangladesh.

p. 19: "We call on multilateral and bilateral development funds and programs and NGOs to promote women's access to credit. They should increase their support for micro-enterprise lending through women-run financial institutions as well as central banks in developing countries."

p. 22: "Benign technology transfer should include public transportation and computer technology and training, with guarantees that computer data and other information technologies not be used to violate rights to privacy and security.... UN, governments, and NGOs urged to create rural and urban training centres of excellence, North and South...to disseminate environment-friendly technologies to women."

Agenda 21, UN 1992

3.8 (o): "Consider making available lines of credit and other facilities for the informal sector. In many instances special considerations for women are required."

7.16 (b,i): "Support of economic activities in the informal sector, such as repairs, recycling, services, small commerce."

24.3 (f): "Programmes to support and strengthen equal employment opportunities and equitable remuneration for women in the formal and informal sectors with adequate economic, political and social support systems and services, including child care, particularly day-care facilities and parental leave, and equal access to credit, land and other natural resources."

30.17: "Small and medium-sized entrepreneurs, in particular play a very important role in the social and economic development of a country. Often, they are the major means for rural development, increasing off-farm employment and providing the transitional means for improving the livelihoods of women. Responsible entrepreneurship can play a major role in improving the efficiency of resource use, reducing risks and hazards, minimizing wastes and safeguarding environmental qualities."

30.24: "Business and industry should establish national councils for sustainable development and help promote entrepreneurship in the formal and informal sectors. The inclusion of women entrepreneurs should be facilitated."

34.14 (C): "Facilitate the maintenance and promotion of environmentally sound indigenous technologies...taking into account the complementary roles of men and women."

Compendium of Excerpts on Science and Technology Related Issues and Recommendations, UN 1992

9: "Promote the research, development, transfer and use of the improved energy-efficient technologies and practices in all relevant sectors."

30.29: "International organizations should increase support for research and development on improving the technological and managerial requirements for sustainable development, in particular for small and medium sized enterprises in developing countries."

Draft Platform for Action, Beijing 1995

Report of the Secretary General, promoting women's economic self-reliance, including access to and control over economic resources — land, capital, and technology: Para. 63: Equal opportunities for working women and men, to promote safer working conditions, child care in the formal and informal sectors; Para. 64: Action by NGOs, private sector, and trade unions in support of women choosing nontraditional professions; Para. 65: "Further efforts to build gender factors into development assistance, including lending, technology transfer and technical cooperation."

Annex: Orientation Arising from the Examination of the First Draft of the Platform for Action. Secure Economic Rights for Women: Para. 20: "Governments and private sector institutions should eliminate all laws and regulations that discriminate against women in economic activities, especially those that discriminate against rural women, those in the informal sector and self-employed in their access to economic resources."

Women, Science and Technology: Towards 1995 and Beyond — a proposal presented by the Once and Future consortium of agencies involved in promoting women's role in science and technology (Sept. 1993, New York): "The growth in the number of major gender, science and technology agencies/networks since 1985" (p. 3); Agencies: IFIAS, TWOWS, APPROTECH Asia, Consultative Group on International Agricultural Research (CGIAR) "are planning to build databases on women in science and technology" (p. 5); "At the informal level, the role of *ordinary* women in science and technology is being recorded and given recognition by agencies such as the International Federation of Inventors Association (which has produced several books on women inventors), and WEDNET and ITDG (which have documented many cases of grassroots women's indigenous technical knowledge" (p. 5).

Education

The Vienna Programme of Action on Science and Technology for Development, UN 1979

Para. 59 (e): Developed countries should "remove any discriminatory conditions affecting the training of personnel from developing countries."

Para. 99 (g): The organs, organizations, and bodies of the United Nations system should "strengthen support for national efforts to promote the full participation of women in the mobilization of all groups for the application of science and technology for development."

Advisory Committee on Science and Technology for Development, UN 1984

Rec. 36–53: Adopt measures to increase female literacy and ensure participation in existing technical training; special programs for women's apprenticeships; support women moving into engineering; review school curricula and textbooks; admission policies to break gender stereotyping; encourage girls in science clubs; education materials language, format for women's needs; ensure employers in S&T incorporate women fairly; family responsibilities or marital status no deterrent.

Rec. 36–44: Governments to increase S&T training facilities supportive networks, scholarships and incentives for women.

The Nairobi Forward-Looking Strategies for the Advancement of Women, UN 1985

Para. 163–173: Educate women to fulfil their role as full members of society; promote functional literacy among women; provide equal opportunity at all levels of education and career; eliminate gender stereotyping in education; promote women's studies; introduce programs at all levels to enable men to assume responsibility for child upbringing and household maintenance.

Para. 169, 171, 203, 223: Support incentives for females to study S&T at all levels.

World Survey on the Role of Women in Development, UN 1986

p. 148: Make technology more meaningful to women by linking it to their everyday experience; increase participation of women in S&T, especially R&D; increase their participation in S&T education; remove barriers to higher education; provide role models; scientific institutes and conference centres to provide daycare and flexible working hours.

World Survey on the Role of Women in Development, UN 1989

Chapter VII (C): Women's education in the areas of S&T are discussed: important that people recognize value in S&T skills, especially women's. Women should participate in planning and implementing policies so that their interests are represented. Problems with access to technology information and funds and lack of participatory opportunities have meant that not much has improved in the last 5 years.

Chapter VII (D): Initiate special measures to ensure that rural women have equal access with men to education, technology, training, and other resources [p. 271]. Measures concerning training require modernization, diversification, and reorientation of women's training institutions and programs; training and education programs particularly for upgrading women's skills; grass-roots action and participation in development of training schemes to include representation of women; special programs for women of marginalized groups [p. 272]. "Promote such education as will encourage the sharing of family responsibilities between men and women" [p. 274].

World Women's Congress for a Healthy Planet, WEDO 1991

p. 22: "We call for more education and training of women and girls in sciences and technology worldwide and emphasize the need for training women in the developing countries at college and university levels."

p. 23: "We recommend that all countries offer environmental education at the primary and secondary levels, including ecology and consumer education." "We will promote environmental ethics education in our schools and in informal learning settings."

Agenda 21, UN 1992

24.2 (e): Implement curricula and other educational material to promote "the dissemination to both men and women of gender-relevant knowledge and valuation of women's roles through formal and non-formal education...[and] training institutions."

24.2 (f): "Implement clear governmental policies...for...promotion of women's literacy, education, training...."

24.3 (c): "Measures...to increase educational and training opportunities for women and girls in S&T."

24.3 (i): Implement programs "to eliminate persistent negative images, stereotypes, attitudes and prejudices against women through changes in socialization patterns, the media, advertising, and formal and non-formal education."

24.8 (g): "Programmes to create rural and urban training, research and resource centres...to disseminate environmentally sound technologies to women."

36.5 (m): "Foster opportunities for women in non-traditional fields and eliminate gender stereotyping in curricula."

36.13 (a): "Establish or strengthen vocational training programmes that meet the needs of environment and development with ensured access to training opportunities regardless of...gender."

Draft Platform for Action, Beijing 1995

Para. 70: Governments should ensure that girls are given the same education as boys; gender-neutral curricula for young students and teacher training programs; promote women's interests in S&T education.

Para. 71: NGOs should monitor the effectiveness of educational reforms and participate in informal education.

Para. 72: Nonformal education conducted by intergovernmental organizations should include component on gender awareness, especially rural extension programs.

Report of Participation of Women in Science and Technology Committee, Canada 1988

Rec. 1.4.1 (a–f): Provide information and raise awareness among women, i.e., high school programs emphasizing the importance of mathematics and sciences; information on jobs and working conditions; role models; encourage media to publicize female scientists and technicians; financial assistance to groups that organize events to make sciences more appealing to girls; scholarships.

Rec. 1.4.2: Provide incentives (i.e., funding) to agencies and departments to guide female students into the S&T fields.

Rec. 1.4.3: Reorganize curricula to create and sustain interest among female students; facilitate access to S&T occupations for women; raise societal awareness of the need for greater sharing of family responsibilities; daycare; work schedules compatible with family responsibilities; equal opportunity programs in government labs and crown corporations.

Women's Vocational Education and Training, European Perspectives Conference, Scotland 1988

Rec. 1–3 on vocational educational guidance: Career development should be free and an integral part of all training; it should include assessment and feedback; it should be gender sensitive and available in various languages.

Rec. 1–3 on reorientation courses: Specific long-term financing should be provided both in each country and at the level of the European Community for the professional development and education of women and

provide specific courses for underprivileged women and women returning to work after an interruption.

Rec. 1–3 on introductory courses in new technology: European Bureau of
Adult Education should be a stronger lobby force for a European centre
for new technology for women; it should be obligatory for all industries
and services to promote the education and training of all women in their
field.

Rec. 1 (a–c), 2 (a,b), and 3 (a–f) on career development: Include a component on gender in teacher training courses and courses taught; trade
unions and professional associations should negotiate reentry and "keeping in touch" schemes; employees should be profiled so that positions
held by women are known. Advisory services set up to inform education
providers and employers on the needs of women reentering employment. Also curricula, teaching methods, and entry requirements should
be reviewed to make entry routes for women possible. Each member
country should have a return to work directory.

Rec. 1–3 on support services: Coordination between union, local government, training, and local employment initiatives should be improved to
remove institutional barriers. Training allowances and flexible childcare
should be provided to women returning or entering employment. Methods and content of training should enhance women's capacity to control
their own lives.

World Conference on Education for All, Thailand 1990

Art. 1 (6): Women and girls often inhibited for cultural reasons.

Art. 3 (3): Ensure and improve quality of education for girls and women;
remove obstacles; remove gender stereotyping.

Measures Increasing Participation of Girls and Women in Technical and Vocational Education and Training: A Caribbean Study, 1990

Rec. 1, 4, 5, 7, 8: Government, NGOs, and relevant agencies coordinate
and formulate a clear national policy for introduction of gender-sensitive
vocational education and training at all levels of the education system.
Responsibilities of the various actors should be clearly designated and
subject to review.

Rec. 9, 10, 13, 16–18: Beginning at preschool level, eliminate sex stereotyping from the curricula and teaching–learning materials. Provide public awareness programs and make vocational guidance and career
counseling an integral part of the school system.

Rec. 11, 12, 19: Training of teachers and others involved in the delivery of
education should be mandatory. Training programs should include a
component that sensitizes trainees to gender issues. Guidelines designed
to eliminate gender biases should be developed on a regional basis and
made available to every territory.

Rec. 20, 23, 25: Incentives such as scholarships and awards should be available to encourage more women to enter nontraditional training programs.

Rec. 21: Research findings should be published in nonacademic language and made available to all.

Rec. 22: A directory should be compiled of Caribbean women in successful careers related to S&T.

Rec. 26–31: National governments could create campaigns to encourage employers to accept and employ more women in nontraditional areas; provide funds or loans to women who have completed their training and want to start their own business; organize career showcases to promote women in nontraditional fields; set up national industrial and complaints boards, and mechanisms to implement existing antidiscriminatory laws; make extensive use of the media for publicity.

More than Just Numbers, Canada 1992

Rec. 1: Active role of women in engineering should be made visible so that parents and the public will encourage women to enter the field.

Rec. 2: Educators should provide a positive and appropriate learning experience so that young women can develop self-esteem.

Rec. 3: Education curricula should include components on gender issues and concerns.

Rec. 4: Enhance mathematics, science, and technical learning experiences of girls in elementary and secondary schools so that they develop interest in these areas.

Rec. 5: Career information in engineering and related fields should be free of gender bias.

Rec. 6: Educators should introduce girls and young women to role models in the fields of mathematics, engineering, and S&T.

Rec. 7: Innovative extracurricular programs should be geared toward developing self-confidence in girls and young women in the areas of mathematics, engineering, and S&T.

Rec. 8–17: Universities should be committed to recruiting and retaining women faculty and students.

Rec. 18–22: All employers of engineers should develop and implement strategies for hiring, promoting, and career development of women professionals.

Rec. 23–28: Associations of professional engineers should ensure full acceptance of women engineers and eradicate discrimination, i.e., through public awareness; raise an interest in engineering in young girls at elementary and secondary schools; volunteer career advisory programs; work closely with faculties of engineering to make associations' expectations of fairness and equity known.

Rec. 29: Associations of professional engineers should make employers aware of the different perspectives and qualities women bring to engineering work.

Winning with Women in Trades, Technology, Science and Engineering, Canada 1993

Rec. 1, 6, 24, 25, 29: Change the image of women in S&T through media and role models.

Rec. 3, 5, 7: Include gender issues in teacher training; provide career information and guidance free of gender bias; develop extracurricular activities to encourage girls in S&T and maths.

Rec. 2, 3, 5, 7, 16, 17, 24, 26, 27: Increase women's self-esteem, knowledge, work experience, and skills base.

Rec. 8, 9, 12, 28: Academic excellence at women-friendly technical institutions, colleges, and universities.

Rec. 8, 11, 13, 17, 24: Increase the number of women in trades, engineering, and S&T.

Rec. 8, 13, 14, 15, 24: More women faculty should be promoted and tenured in engineering and S&T.

Rec. 4, 5, 7, 16: Revise curricula to include women's perspectives.

Rec. 18, 22, 24: Women-friendly workplaces to allow women to be hired and promoted, i.e., daycare, management training, mentor and career-development programs.

Why May Women Science Undergraduates and Graduates not be Seeking to Take Up Careers as Scientists? United Kingdom 1994

A.1-2: Science research funding bodies to facilitate part-time working and career breaks for women scientists.

A.3: Devise ways of fulfilling professional development needs of personnel (i.e., training for women in management, assertiveness, and teaching skills).

A.4: Funding bodies to cooperate with universities and industry to find ways of solving the "problem of the following partner."

B.5: Universities to "gender audit" courses.

B.6: Universities to review their approaches to teaching techniques, course design, and content to ensure equal opportunity.

B.7: Universities that have special study programs or project options for students in their final year should give thought to how these programs and options are advertised, negotiated, and agreed upon.

The RisingTide: A report on women in Science, Engineering and Technology, United Kingdom 1993

1.11: Create a development unit under the auspicies of the Office of S&T for an initial 3-year period to implement recommendations.

1.12 (i): Ensure initial and in-service training of teachers on gender issues.

1.12 (iii): Equal opportunity policies to become part of an establishment's employment strategy, which should be monitored and reported in annual reports.

1.12 (v): Personal development plans for women employees, i.e., "keeping in touch" for those on career breaks, home computer terminals.

1.12 (vi): Child-care costs to be tax deductible and government to increase number of publicly funded child-care services.

1.12 (vii, viii): Funding bodies make research funding arrangements for principal investigators and research fellows more flexible to allow family responsibilities and successful returners schemes for women in S&T.

1.12 (x): Employers and professional institutions should set up databases and networks of women scientists and engineers qualified for appointment to their boards and committees or for nomination to public appointments. A central catalogue of databases should be held by the Office of S&T and updated annually.

1.12 (xi): Government departments and other employers to set goals for all public appointments and senior positions in S&T to be 25% qualified women by no later than the year 2000.

1.12 (xii): The office of S&T should promote public awareness and maintain media contacts encouraging coverage of women's contribution to S&T.

Project 2000 and Forum Unesco, 1993

Rec. 4 (a–j): Call on government, industry, public and private sectors, and providers of educational services to review critically existing provisions for S&T education at all levels; give priority to the development and introduction of programs leading to S&T literacy; ensure equal access for everyone to S&T education; develop appropriate in-school opportunities, programs, curricula, and assessment procedures for S&T education; encourage and support education in both formal and nonformal sectors; enhance the status of careers in S&T education at all levels; ensure adequate resources are available to achieve these aims.

Rec. 6: NGOs to make their knowledge and experience in S&T education known to UN agencies and other intergovernmental bodies.

Rec. 7: Unesco to provide, within its medium-term plan (1996–2001), in the field of education for an international program to develop cooperation between all countries, in particular, focus on regional and subregional cooperation in the area of S&T literacy for all.

Rec. 8: By year 2001, there should be structures and activities in place to foster S&T literacy for all.

Information and communication

Advisory Committee on Science and Technology for Development, UN 1984

Rec. 30: "Governments should appoint or nominate...women to participate in international, regional and national bodies that deal with S&T for development."

Rec. 33: Ensure women's "active participation and involvement in [development] projects from the beginning."

Rec. 35: Strengthen existing S&T cooperation among developing countries, "paying particular attention to issues involving women."

Rec. 45: Ensure that communication on technological innovation is not restricted to literate populations.

Rec. 46: Develop education materials appropriate for people with little or no literacy skills, "with special attention given to the integration of technical information relevant to women's needs into functional literacy programs."

Rec. 47: "Ensure that women scientists and engineers are provided with equal access to all installations...and placements...to enable them to study and participate in S&T to the fullest extent possible."

Rec. 53: "Provide leaders of women's organizations with timely and appropriate S&T information to assist them in participating in decisions affecting their community."

The Nairobi Forward-Looking Strategies for the Advancement of Women, UN 1985

Para. 200: "Governments should reassess their technological capabilities and monitor current processes of change so as to anticipate and ameliorate any adverse impact on women, particularly...upon the quality of job."

Para. 206: Ensure "participation of women at all levels of communications policy and decision-making and in programme design, implementation and monitoring.... [Ensure that women] have an equal say in the determination of the content of all public information efforts."

Para. 207: Increase enrolment of women in public mass communication networks.

Para. 208: Assist organizations that promote the role of women in development as contributors and beneficiaries to establish effective communications and information networks.

Para. 367: Eliminate or reduce sex stereotyping in the mass media.

Para. 368: "Disseminate information on the role of women in achieving equality, development, and peace through the mass media."

Para. 369: Ensure that women receive training in the use of audiovisual forms of information dissemination.

World Survey on the Role of Women in Development, UN 1986

Para. 35: Strengthen S&T cooperation and exchange of information and expertise among developing, paying particular attention to issues regarding women.

Para. 53: Provide leaders of women's organizations with S&T information to assist them in participating in decisions affecting their community.

Para. 55: "Encourage the active involvement of women in decisions and discussions related to the design, development, selection, introduction, and use of technologies in their communities."

Para. 59: Use existing national grassroots women's organizations and groups to introduce and popularize new technologies among women.

Para. 60: Increase contact between women scientists and women's organizations to promote the "demystification" of S&T.

Para. 61: "Disseminate S&T information through all existing channels of communication that have proven effective in reaching women...[using] these channels for a two-way exchange of information."

Para. 62: Use multidisciplinary approaches "in the selection, design, development, adaptation, and dissemination of technologies for use by women."

Para. 63: "Provide information on the potential negative [and] positive effects of new technologies, including their potential impact on women and women's activities."

Para. 72: "Ensure that women have access to information, knowledge, training and retraining, and employment associated with [new] technologies."

Para. 88: Provide opportunities for women scientists, particularly those from developing countries, to publish in journals.

Para. 100: Collect data regularly to determine the progress for women in S&T.

World Survey on the Role of Women in Development, UN 1989

p. 185: Implications of new information and computer technology must be taken into account when designing programs to train women in new skills.

p. 281: Information technologies have increasingly affected the parts of the labour force in which women are highly represented. Ensure that low-paid, low-skill tasks not seen as an extension of traditional women's skills of patience and manual dexterity.

p. 283: Address problems of access to information by women.

World Women's Congress for a Healthy Planet, WEDO 1991

p. 22: Provide women with immediate access to appropriate technologies, including computer technology and training. Support and promote communications strategies for disseminating information on appropriate and inappropriate technologies to women; the flow of information should be South–South, North–South, and South–North.

Agenda 21, UN 1992

3.8 (j): "Implement...measures to ensure that women and men have the same...access to...information."

10.11 (c): "Provide the appropriate technical information necessary for informed decision-making on land use and management in an accessible form to all sectors of the population, especially to local communities and women."

12.14 (b): "Promote the involvement of the local population, particularly women and youth, in the collection and utilization of environmental information through education and awareness-building."

12.58 (a): "Review, develop and disseminate gender disaggregated information."

24.8: "Develop gender-sensitive databases [and] information systems.

Draft Platform for Action, Beijing 1995

Art. 48: "Enhance the role of the traditional and modern communications media effectively to promote awareness of equality between women and men."

Art. 49: "Guarantee the access of women to information and participation in the media."

Art. 50: "Eliminate gender stereotyping in the media." May use communications technology to link women nationally and internationally.

Health

Advisory Committee on Science and Technology for Development, UN 1984

Rec. 34: Give high priority to R&D serving women's "health and nutritional needs and promoting their general well-being."

Rec. 65: Structure mechanisms to monitor the impact of new technologies on women's health.

Rec. 71: Criteria for selection of technologies for use by women should include improved hygiene.

The Nairobi Forward-Looking Strategies for the Advancement of Women, UN 1985

Para. 151: "Provide immediate access to water and sanitary facilities for women...; [consult women] with regard to technologies used in water and sanitation projects."

Para. 155: Conduct general screening of women's diseases and cancer; provide services in harmony with timing and patterns of women's work, needs, and perspectives; ensure women have same access as men to affordable, curative, preventive, and rehabilitative treatment.

Para. 162: Enhance occupational health and safety for men and women; address health impact of new technologies and the harmonization of work and family responsibilities.

World Survey on the Role of Women in Development, UN 1986

p. 97: Inadequacies and deficiencies in protective work legislation for women.

World Survey on the Role of Women in Development, UN 1989

p. 281: "The application of biotechnology in health and pharmaceutical could contribute to the improvement of health for all...thus relieving some of women's burdens."

p. 282: "Any assessment of reproductive technology must also take into account the rights of parents and...women's rights to health and education."

World Women's Congress for a Healthy Planet, WEDO 1991

p. 20: "We condemn any attempt to deprive women of reproductive freedom or knowledge...we demand women-centred, women-managed comprehensive reproductive health care and family planning;...research and remedial action should also focus on the effects on health of toxic chemicals, nuclear wastes, radiation, pesticides and fertilizers."

p. 21: "We are concerned about genetic engineering...and oppose the release of genetically manipulated organisms into the environment; we call for immediate and direct regulation of R&D in biotechnology; we urge that [nuclear technology] be stopped."

Agenda 21, UN 1992

3.8(j), 5.51: Governments to strengthen preventive and curative health facilities, ensuring they are women-centred and women-managed.

6.27 (c.i): "Involve women's groups in decision-making at the national and community levels to identify health risks and incorporate health issues in national action programmes on women and development."

6.29: Technical support to women's organizations in the health sector.

16.13 (c): Screening of medical technology, especially that relating to reproductive health.

Draft Platform for Action, Beijing 1995

Annex Art. 33: "Traditional health knowledge should be used and respected."

Annex Art. 35: Support "research on prevention, treatment, and health care systems for diseases and conditions that affect women and girls differently, including drugs and medical technology."

Art. 74: "Action by NGOs might include nonformal health education and advisory services for women...giving particular emphasis to women's traditional health knowledge."

Other documents

Report of the Technical Discussions on Women, Health, and Development: Established Global Commission on Women's Health (1992). Commission's action agenda includes increasing awareness of women's health issues; promoting women's health through all mass media; providing forum for consultation.

International Conference on Population and Development (WHO-UNICEF 1994): Topics pertaining to women's health identified at the preparatory conference — Rec. 8: safe abortion; Rec. 11: access to family planning; Rec. 12: STD protection; Rec. 24: prevent women's exposure to harmful material; Rec. 27: contraceptive R&D.

WHO Project 2000 + : 38 appropriate health technology assessment mechanisms to be in place by 1990.

Technology transfer and trade

The Vienna Programme of Action on Science and Technology for Development, UN 1979

Para. 23 (g): Ensure full participation of women in S&T development process.

Para. 27: Formulate a policy on transfer and acquisition of technology as an integral part of country's national policy for S&T development.

Para. 99 (g): "Promote the full participation of women in...all groups for the application of S&T for development."

Advisory Committee on Science and Technology for Development, UN 1984

Rec. 54–59: Encourage the active involvement of women in decisions and discussion related to the design, development, selection, introduction, and use of technologies in their communities.

Rec. 63–68: Advisory committees to monitor and assess positive and negative effects of new technologies, impact on women and women's activities, and legal status of technologies in country of origin.

Rec. 71: Criteria for selection of technologies for use by women to include time-saving, increased output, productivity, improved hygiene, energy-efficiency, income generation, employment, etc.

The Nairobi Forward-Looking Strategies for the Advancement of Women, UN 1985

Para. 191, 192: Enhance women's S&T skills; adapt technology to women's needs; introduction of new technology to allow women to enter nontraditional sectors.

Para. 198: Training opportunities in processing technology should be provided to women traders.

Para. 204: Assess impact of technology development on women's income, health, and status.

World Survey on the Role of Women in Development, UN 1986

p. 23: Women must participate in the planning, designing, manufacturing, managing, and use of new technologies.

World Survey on the Role of Women in Development, UN 1989

p. 278: Technological modernization should be appropriate to women's needs.

p. 279: "A participatory approach to involve both men and women is crucial to successful adaptation of new technologies." Promote the concept of blending new and traditional technologies.

pp. 280–281: Mechanization, automation, and modernization of technology in industry may impact negatively on women's participation in the formal and informal sectors.

World Women's Congress for a Healthy Planet, WEDO 1991

p. 22: We demand that all technology transfer be appropriate and sustainable, with special attention paid to long-term costs and benefits for people and the environment. We support communications strategies to disseminate appropriate technology and information to women.

Agenda 21, UN 1992

24.8 (g): Rural and urban training centres to disseminate environmentally sound technologies to women.

34.3: HRD and local capacity building aspects of technology choices, and gender-relevant aspects to be addressed in discussions of technology transfer.

34.14 (c): Facilitate maintenance and promotion of environmentally sound indigenous technology, with attention to needs and role of women.

Draft Platform for Action, Beijing 1995

Art. 47: New technologies to increase interaction among people; can be used either for social progress or to reinforce stereotypes.

Art. 65: Further efforts to build gender factors into technology transfer.

Food security

Advisory Committee on Science and Technology for Development, UN 1984

Rec. 77: Give high priority to improving access to adequate water supplies; involve women integrally in planning and maintaining water supplies.

The Nairobi Forward-Looking Strategies for the Advancement of Women, UN 1985

Para. 62: Agrarian reforms to "guarantee women's constitutional and legal rights in terms of access to land and other means of production."

Para. 174–178: Development strategies in food and agriculture to integrate women at all levels of planning and implementation; women to be fully integrated and involved in agricultural research; governments to implement equitable and stable investment and growth policies for rural development; establish multisectoral programs to promote productive capacity of rural women in food and animal production; provide women with food technology training; resources and investment to go to women's programmes re: food security; rural extension to women.

World Survey on the Role of Women in Development, UN 1986

p. 19: Access for women to official support services (extension services, credit, inputs, fertilizers, and new technologies).

p. 44: Introduction of modern agricultural technology primarily aimed at male tasks and used almost elusively by men, whereas women tend to be left out.

p. 46: Women farmers are responsive to innovation and willing adopters of profitable technologies, but are usually "relegated to subsistence agriculture using traditional technologies and obtaining low yields."

p. 47: To prevent negative consequences for food production, agricultural modernization efforts should not exclude women.

World Survey on the Role of Women in Development, UN 1989

p. 84: Need for "comprehensive, reliable and unbiased statistics on the nature and role of women's contributions to food and agricultural production."

p. 89: Ensure access of women to capital resources and credit. Labour-saving technologies should be made available simultaneously through structural adjustment packages to allow women to switch from food crops to higher value crops.

p. 90: Adjustment policies should favour production of food crops for consumption and export rather than of nonfood export crops so as to avoid malnutrition problems which arise from the shift to cash crops from food crops by women farmers.

World Women's Congress for a Healthy Planet, WEDO 1991

p. 15: Ensure that women participate in and benefit from rural development; provide women with access to credit loans.

p. 19: Ensure women's access to food, land inheritance, tenure and ownership; basic human rights; increase food security resources; limit discriminatory land practices; encourage use of indigenous foods and preparation methods; women to have greater access to food processing technology; no patenting of life forms, including nongenerating seeds; agricultural sustainability; ban bovine growth hormone and others; oppose genetic manipulation and release of such products into environment.

Agenda 21, UN 1992

7.30 (f): Ensure appropriate land tenure for women.

11.3 (f): Provide forest education and training for youth and women.

11.13 (i): Forest-related programs to improve opportunities for women.

14.27 (a): Develop integrated farm management technologies (i.e., crop rotation, organic manuring, etc. to farming households) noting women's role.

14.81 (b): Train women and extension workers in crop health and alternative nonchemical pest control.

Draft Platform for Action, Beijing 1995

Art. 29–32: Inequality in women's access to and control over land, capital, technology and other means of production; women the primary producers of food; women infrequently part of decision-making processes.

Other documents

WCARRD 1979 Program of Action IV: Integration of women in rural development. Government to take action to ensure equality of legal status in land ownership, economic transactions and voting rights, women's access to rural services including training, promotion of women's organization and participation, similar quality and content in education, equal pay/equal value work, reduce negative effects of agricultural technology transfer.

General Assembly of Economic and Social Council (1993): Overall recommendations on women in rural areas

Report of the Economic and Social Council (1990): Achievements of the International Drinking Water Supply and Sanitation Decade 1981–90; note women's involvement critical to safe water supply. Task Force on Women and the International Drinking Water Supply and Sanitation Decade established 1982; supported by PROWWESS and INSTRAW; changed orientation toward women's involvement from sector approach to overall approach permeating all project components, leading to development of planning and evaluation framework (PEGASUS).

Indigenous knowledge

The Vienna Programme of Action on Science and Technology for Development, UN 1979

Para. 21 (g): "[Stimulate] demand for indigenous research, technology and other S&T services in general."

Advisory Committee on Science and Technology for Development, UN 1984

Rec. 24: The concerns and priorities of women and the impact of endogenous R&D on women must be considered in efforts to promote R&D in a country or region.

Rec. 54, 55: Potential users should participate in all stages of technology development or adaptation, including upgrading of traditional technologies; encourage active involvement of women.

The Nairobi Forward-Looking Strategies for the Advancement of Women, UN 1985

Para. 179: Improve traditional knowledge and introduce modern technology through research and experimentation.

Para. 303–304: Governments to promote human rights and full participation in societal change of indigenous women and populations; fundamental human rights guaranteed also to women in minority groups and indigenous populations; ensure that women have access to services in their own language; set up Indigenous Peoples Year emphasizing role of women.

World Survey on the Role of Women in Development, UN 1986

Para 32 (Part V Annex): National governments to build endogenous R&D capabilities by adopting a policy of total human resource development that would give women full participation.

p. 231: Acknowledge that "women are a pool of technological knowledge in farming, livestock-raising, gardening, preparation of foods, indigenous medicine, some aspects of education, small-industry production, and many other fields" and that "the technological knowledge that they possess has often been well adapted to both ecological and local societal environments."

World Survey on the Role of Women in Development, UN 1989

p. 279: Promote blending of new and traditional technologies to minimize negative impacts of introducing new technologies in agriculture or industry. Upgrade rather than replace traditional technologies. Involvement of women to ensure the relevance of application of new technologies to societal needs in upgrading traditional methods.

World Women's Congress for a Healthy Planet, WEDO 1991

p. 14: "States should recognize the right of indigenous people to take part in decisions relating to the development and use of their traditional lands."

p. 21: "Aboriginal and indigenous peoples, and specifically women, must be recognized as providing vital wisdom and leadership in [sustainable development]."

Agenda 21, UN 1992

7.76: Take account of traditional cultural practices of indigenous people and their relationship to the environment.

12.56 (d): "Support local communities in their own efforts in combatting desertification, and draw on the knowledge and experience of the populations concerned, ensuring the full participation of women.

15.4 (g): "Recognize and foster the traditional methods and the knowledge of indigenous people and their communities, emphasizing the particular role of women, relevant to the conservation [and sustainable use of biodiversity]."

15.5 (e,f): Take action to respect, record, protect, and promote the wider application of the knowledge, innovations, and practices of indigenous and local communities, including women; long-term biodiversity research to include indigenous people and women.

17.94: Maintain and exchange traditional marine knowledge.

26.5: "UN organizations and other international development and finance organizations should...incorporate [indigenous people's] values, views and knowledge, including the unique contribution of indigenous women in resource management and other policies."

26.5 (c.ii): Increase efficiency of indigenous people's knowledge and management systems by promoting the adaption and dissemination of suitable technological innovations.

34.14(c): Facilitate maintenance and promotion of environmentally sound indigenous technology, with attention to needs and role of women.

Draft Platform for Action, Beijing 1995

Art. 74: Particular emphasis to women's traditional health knowledge.

Other documents

WCIP Declaration of Working Group of 11th Session "solemnly proclaims the following UN Declaration of the Rights of Indigenous Peoples": Art. 22: right to special measures for effective improvement of economic and social conditions, including in the areas of vocational training, special attention to women, etc.; Art. 29: full ownership of intellectual property and special measures to control their sciences, technologies, medicines, and knowledge; Art. 43: all the rights and freedoms are equally guaranteed to male and female indigenous individuals.

Acronyms and abbreviations

AICRPDA	All-India Coordinated Research Project on Dryland Agriculture
AIDS	acquired immune deficiency syndrome
ASEAN	Association of South East Asian Nations
AWIS	Association for Women in Science
BOSTID	Board on Science and Technology for International Development
CBA	cost–benefit analysis
CEA	cost-effectiveness analysis
CGIAR	Consultative Group on International Agricultural Research
CIDA	Canadian International Development Agency
CIKARD	Center for Indigenous Knowledge for Agriculture and Rural Development
CIRAN	Centre for International Research and Advisory Networks
DALYs	disability adjusted life-years
DANIDA	Danish International Development Agency
DES	diethylstilbestrol
EDI	Economic Development Institute
e-mail	electronic mail
ESCAP	Economic and Social Commission for Asia and the Pacific
FAO	Food and Agriculture Organization of the United Nations
GIS	geographic information systems
HIV	human immunodeficiency virus
HRP	Human Reproduction Program
HTA	health-technology assessment
IAEA	International Atomic Energy Agency
ICCBD	Intergovernmental Committee on the Convention on Biological Diversity
ICRAF	International Center for Research in Agroforestry

ICT	information and communication technology
IDB	Inter-American Development Bank
IDRC	International Development Research Centre
IEC	information, education, and communication
IFAD	International Fund for Agricultural Development
IFIAS	International Federation of Institutes for Advanced Study
IK	indigenous knowledge
ILO	International Labour Office
INSTRAW	International Research and Training Institute for the Advancement of Women
INTECH	Institute for New Technologies
IPBN	Indigenous Peoples' Biodiversity Network
IPR	intellectual property rights
IT	information technology
ITC	International Trade Centre (UNCTAD)
ITDG	International Technology Development Group
IUCN	International Union for the Conservation of Nature
IUD	intrauterine device
IWTC	International Women's Tribune Center
JIT	just-in-time
LEAD	Leiden Ethnosystems and Development Programme
MCH	maternal and child health
MCH–FP	maternal and child health–family planning
NGO	nongovernmental organization
NGONet	NGO electronic networking initiative
OFSP	On-Farm Seed Project
PAHO	Pan American Health Organization
PAIGC	Africa Party for the Independence of Guinea and Cape Verde
PEDO	People's Environment and Development Organization
PHC	primary health care
PRA	participatory rural appraisal
QALYs	quality adjusted life-years
R&D	research and development
S&T	science and technology
SEI	Stockholm Environment Institute
SIDA	Swedish International Development Authority
SME	small- and medium-sized enterprise

STD	sexually transmitted disease
SWAG	Senior Women's Advisory Group on Sustainable Development

TBA	traditional birth attendant
TCC	Technical Consultancy Centre
TQM	total quality management
TWOWS	Third World Organisation of Women in Science and Technology

UN	United Nations
UNCED	UN Conference on Environment and Development
UNCTAD	UN Conference on Trade and Development
UNDP	UN Development Programme
UNEP	UN Environment Programme
Unesco	UN Educational, Scientific and Cultural Organisation
UNFPA	UN Fund for Population Activities
UNICEF	UN Children's Fund
UNIDO	UN Industrial Development Organization
UNIFEM	UN Development Fund for Women
UNRISD	UN Research Institute for Social Development
UNV	UN Volunteer

VDU	video display unit
VITA	Volunteers in Technical Assistance

WCED	World Commission on Environment and Development
WCIP	World Council of Indigenous Peoples
WEDNET	Women, Environment and Development Network
WFP	World Food Program
WHO	World Health Organization
WIPO	World Intellectual Property Organization
WWF	World Wide Fund for Nature
WWF	Working Women's Forum

YLL	years of life lost

Bibliography

AAAS (American Association for the Advancement of Science). 1993. Science in Africa: women leading from strength. Sub-Sahara Africa Program, AAAS, Washington, DC, USA.

AAUW (American Association of University Women). 1992. How schools shortchange girls: a study of major findings on girls and education. AAUW Educational Foundation and National Education Association, Washington, DC, USA.

Acero, L. 1995. Conflicting demands of new technology and household: women's employment in the Brazilian and Argentinian textiles industry. In Mitter, S.; Rowbotham, S., ed., Women encounter information technology: perspectives of the Third World. Routledge, London, UK.

Advisory Panel on Food Security, Agriculture, Forestry and Environment. 1987. Food 2000: global policies for sustainable agriculture. Zed Books, London, UK.

AFCZ (Agricultural Finance Corporation of Zimbabwe). 1991. Annual report, 1990. AFCZ, Harare, Zimbabwe.

Agarwal, B. 1992a. The gender and environment debate: lessons from India. Feminist Studies, 18(1), 119–158.

———— 1992b. Gender relations and food security: coping with seasonality, drought and famine in South Asia. In Beneria, L.; Feldman, S., ed., Economic crises, persistent poverty and women's work. Westview Press, Boulder, CO, USA.

Aghenta, J.A. 1989. Access by women to scientific studies and technological training. UN Educational, Scientific and Cultural Organisation, Paris, France.

Ahmed, I., ed. 1985. Technology and rural women: conceptual and empirical issues. George, Allen Unwin, London, UK.

———— ed. 1992. Biotechnology: a hope or a threat? Macmillan, London, UK.

Ahooja-Patel, K. 1992. Linking women with sustainable development. Commonwealth of Learning, Vancouver, BC, Canada.

Akhtar, R. 1987. Introduction. In Akhtar, R., ed., Health and diseases in tropical Africa. Harwood, Chur, Switzerland.

Aklilu, D. 1991. Gender training: experiences, lessons and future directions. UN Development Fund for Women, New York, NY, USA. Review paper.

Alatescu, I.M. 1993. Human rights — ideals, realities, perspectives. Andre Publishing House, Bucharest, Romania.

Alloo, F. 1995. Media as a mobilising force: Tanzania Media Women's Association. In Mitter, S.; Rowbotham, S., ed., Women encounter information technology: perspectives of the Third World. Routledge, London, UK.

Alsop, R. 1993. Whose interests? problems in planning for women's practical needs. World Development, 21(3), 367–377.

Anand, A. 1993. Changing women, changing communication. Development, 3, 52.

Anderson, G.M. 1994. Use of prenatal ultrasound examiniation in Ontario and British Columbia in the 1980s. Journal SOGC, 1994(February), 1329–1338.

Appleton, H. 1993a. Gender, technology, and innovation. Appropriate Technology, 20(2), 6–8.

——— 1993b. Women, science, and technology: looking ahead. Appropriate Technology, 20(2), 9–10.

——— 1994. Technical innovation by women: the implications for small enterprises. Small Enterprise Development, 5(1), 4–13.

APPROTECH Asia. 1992. Mainstream women in science and technology. Report of the International symposium on women in science and technology, development and transfer, 13–17 July 1992, Bangkok, Thailand. APPROTECH Asia, Bangkok, Thailand.

Arianrhod, R. 1992. Physics and mathematics, reality and language: dilemmas for feminists. In Kramarae, C.; Spender, D., ed., The knowledge explosion: generations of feminist scholarship. Teachers College Press, New York, NY, USA.

Azad, N. 1985. Improving working conditions for rural women through creation of alternative employment options: cases of the Working Women's Forum in Dindugal dairy women's project and Adiaram Pattinam women's project. In Muntemba, S., ed., Rural development and women: lessons from the field (vol. 2). International Labour Organisation, Geneva, Switzerland. pp. 9–24.

Bahemuka, J.; Mbula, C.; Nzioka, B.K.; Mbatia, P.N. 1992. Women professionals in the agricultural sector: Kenya case study. Winrock International, Morrilton, AR, USA. Development Studies Series.

Banerjee, N. 1995. Something old, something new, something borrowed: microelectronics in Calcutta. In Mitter, S.; Rowbotham, S., ed., Women encounter information technology: perspectives of the Third World. Routledge, London, UK.

Banta, H.D.; Luce, B.R. 1993. Health care technology and its assessment: an international perspective. Oxford University Press, Oxford, UK.

Baran, P. 1959. The political economy of growth. Monthly Review Press, New York, NY, USA.

Bassett, K.L. 1993. Taming chance and taking chances: the electronic fetal monitor in a rural Canadian hospital. McGill University, Montreal, PQ, Canada. PhD dissertation.

Baringa, M. 1994. Surprises across the cultural divide. Science, 263(5152), 1468–1472.

Bates, D.; Conant, F. 1981. Livestock and livelihood: a handbook for the 1980s. In Galaty, J.; Aronson, D.; Salzman, P.C., ed., The future of pastoral peoples: research priorities for the 1980s — proceedings of a conference held in Nairobi, Kenya, 4–8 August 1980. International Development Research Centre, Ottawa, ON, Canada. pp. 80–100.

Battista, R. 1992. Healthcare technology assessment: linking science and policy making. Canadian Medical Association Journal, 146(4), 461–462.

Beauchamp, T.; Childress, J.F. 1989. Principles of biomedical ethics (3rd ed.). Oxford University Press, New York, NY, USA.

Bellisari, A. 1991 Cultural influences on the science career choices of women. Ohio Journal of Science, 91(3), 129–133.

Bender, D.R.; Kadec, S.T.; Morton, S.I. 1991. National information policies: strategies for the future. Special Libraries Association, Washington, DC, USA.

Benería, L. 1993. Trade, technology transfer and gender. Paper presented at the Gender, Science and Technology Conference, 16 December 1993. Gender Working Group, UN Commission on Science and Technology for Development, New York, NY, USA.

Benería, L.; Sen, G. 1981. Accumulation, reproduction and women's role in economic development: Boserup revisited. Signs, 7, 279–299.

Bennet, L. 1992. Women, poverty, and productivity in India. World Bank, Washington, DC, USA. Economic Development Institute Seminar Paper 43.

Bennet, L.; Goldberg, M. 1993. Providing enterprise development and financial services to women: a decade of Bank experience in Asia. World Bank, Washington, DC, USA. Technical Paper 236.

Beoku-Betts, J.; Logan, B.I. 1993. Developing science and technology in sub-Saharan Africa: gender disparities in the education and employment process. In Science in Africa: women leading from strength. American Association for the Advancement of Science, Washington, DC, USA.

Bhaskar, B.N. 1987. Technological innovation and rural women. In Ng, C., ed., Technology and gender: women's work in Asia. Women's Studies Unit and Department of Extension Education, Universiti Pertanian Malaysia and Malaysian Social Science Association, Kuala Lumpur, Malaysia.

Biggs, S. 1989. Resource-poor farmer participation in research: a synthesis of experiences from nine national agricultural research systems. International Service for National Argricultural Research, The Hague, Netherlands. On-Farm Client-Oriented Research Paper 3.

Bisaria, S. 1985. Identification and elimination of sex stereotypes in and from education programs and school textbooks: some suggestions for action in Asia and the Pacific. UN Educational, Scientific and Cultural Organisation, Paris, France.

Bleir, R. 1984. Science and gender: a critique of biology and its theories on women. Teachers' College Press, New York, NY, USA. Athene Series.

Bonair, A.; Rosenfield, P.; Tengvald, K. 1989. Medical technologies in developing countries: issues of technology development, transfer, diffusion and use. Social Science and Medicine, 23, 769–781.

BOSTID (Board on Science and Technology for International Development). 1994. Workshop on barriers faced by developing country women entering professions in science and technology (final report). BOSTID, National Research Council, Washington, DC, USA.

Bourque, S.; Warren, K. 1987. Technology, gender, and development: incorporating gender in the study of development. Daedalus, 116, 173–197.

Bowie, R. 1991. Health economics: a framework for health services decision-making. New Zealand Medical Journal, 104(March), 99–102.

Braidotti, R.; Charkiewicz, E.; Hausler, S.; Wieringa, S. 1994. Women, the environment and sustainable development: towards a theoretical synthesis. Zed Books, London, UK.

Brayman S.E.; Weiss, C., Jr. n.d. Women, technology and microenterprise development. UN Development Fund for Women, New York, NY, USA.

Brophy, J.E.; Evertson, C.M. 1974. Process–product correlations in the Texas teacher effectiveness study: final report. National Institute of Education, Washington, DC, USA.

Brouwer, H.; Stokhof, K.; Bunders, J., ed. 1992. Biotechnology and farmers' rights: opportunities and threats for small farmers in developing countries. Free University Press, Amsterdam, Netherlands.

Brouwers, J.H.A.M. 1993. Rural people's response to soil fertility decline: the Adja case (Benin). Wageningen Agricultural University, Wageningen, Netherlands. Paper 93-4.

Brown, C. 1975. Patriarchal capitalism and the female-headed family. Social Scientist (India), 40/41, 28–39.

Brush, L.R. 1985. Cognitive and affective determinants of course preferences and plans. In Chipman, S.F.; Brush, L.R.; Wilson, D.M., ed., Women and mathematics: balancing the equation. Lawrence Erlbaum Association, Hillsdale, NJ, USA. pp. 123–150.

Brush, S.G. 1991. Women in science and engineering. American Scientist, 79(5), 404–419.

Bryceson, D.A. 1985. Women and technology in developing countries: technological change and women's capabilities and bargaining positions. UN International Research and Training Institute for the Advancement of Women, San José, Santo Domingo, Cuba.

Budinic, V. 1993. Enterprise development: lessons leaned from the experience of the women of Tempoal. Report to UN Development Fund for Women, New York, NY, USA.

Buvinic, M. 1993. Promoting women's enterprises: what can Africa learn from Latin America? In Helmsing, A.H.J.; Kolstee, T.H., ed., Small enterprises and changing policies. Intermediate Technology Publications, London, UK.

Callan, J.M. 1994. Attitudes towards computers: the gender gap revisited. Paper presented at The Information Industry in Transition, 22nd Annual Conference of the Canadian Association for Information Science, 25–27 May 1994, Montreal, Canada. Canadian Association for Information Science, Montreal, PQ, Canada. pp. 46–54.

Carnegie Foundation 1992. Adolescent health, a generation at risk. Carnegie Quarterly, 37(4).

Carr, M. 1981. Technologies appropriate for women. In Dauber, R.; Cain, M., ed., Women and technological change in developing countries. Westview Press, Boulder, CO, USA. American Association for the Advancement of Science Symposium 53, 193–203.

———— 1984. Blacksmith, baker, roofing sheet-maker. Intermediate Technology Publications, London, UK.

———— 1985. Technologies for rural women: impact and dissemination. In Ahmen, I., ed., Technology and rural women: conceptual and empirical issues. Allen and Unwin, London, UK.

Carr, M.; Sandhu, R. 1987. Women, technology and rural productivity: an analysis of the impact of time- and energy-saving technologies on women. UN Development Fund for Women and UN Development Programme, New York, NY, USA.

Carroll, J.S.; Johnson, E.J. 1990. Decision research — a field guide. Sage Publications, Newbury Park, CA, USA. Applied Social Research Methods Series, 22.

Caulfield, M.D. 1978. Imperialism, the family, and cultures of resistance. Socialist Revolution, 20(4), 67–85.

Cecelski, E. 1990a. Linking rural electrification with development in Asia (report to the Regional Energy Development Programme). Economic and Social Commission for Asia and the Pacific, Bangkok, Thailand.

———— 1990b. Women and energy, the international network: policies and experience: a resource guide. UN Development Programme and World Bank (Energy Sector Management Program), Washington, DC, USA.

———— 1992. Women, energy and environment: new directions for policy research. International Federation of Institutes for Advanced Study, Toronto, ON, Canada. Working paper GSD-2.

Chambers, R.; Pacey, A.; Thrupp, L.A., ed. 1989. Farmer first: farmer innovations and agricultural research. Intermediate Technology Publications, London, UK.

Chapman, A.R. 1994. Human rights implications of indigenous peoples' intellectual property rights. In Greaves, T., ed., Intellectual property rights for indigenous peoples: a sourcebook. Society for Applied Anthropology, Oklahoma City, OK, USA.

Chee Heng Leng, ed. 1992. Behind the chip: proceedings of the conference on safety and health in electronics. Women's Development Collective and Sahabat Wanita, Petalang Jaya, Selangor, Malaysia.

Chen, M. 1994. Background paper presented at Beyond Credit: Supporting Poor Women's Enterprises, 2–4 May 1994, Ottawa, Canada. Aga Khan Foundation, Geneva, Switzerland.

Chimedza, R. 1993. Women's management of wildlife resources for household food security. Paper prepared for Environment Liaison Centre International by the Women, Environment, and Development Network (WEDNET) project. International Development Research Centre, Ottawa, ON, Canada.

Christopherson, R. 1990. Geosystems: an introduction to physical geography. Maxwell Macmillan, Toronto, ON, Canada.

Clorfene-Casten, L. 1993. The environmental link to breast cancer. Ms, 1993(May/Jun), 52–57.

Collins, P.H. 1991. Black feminist thought: knowledge, consciousness and the politics of empowerment. Routledge, New York, NY, USA.

Colson, E. 1971. The social consequences of resettlement: the impact of the Kariba settlement. Manchester University Press, Manchester, UK.

Commission for the Status of Women. 1994. Draft platform for action: report of the Secretary-General. Preparations for the 4th World Conference on Women: action for equality, development and peace. UN Economic and Social Council, New York, NY, USA. E/CN.6/1994/10/2 March 1994.

Committee on Women in Science, Engineering and Technology. 1993. The rising tide. A report on women in science, engineering and technology. Her Majesty's Stationery Office, London, UK.

Commonwealth of Learning. 1994. Women: key partners in sustainable and equitable development. Commonwealth of Learning, Vancouver, BC, Canada. Resource materials on women and sustainable development.

Commonwealth Secretariat. 1990. Report of the third meeting of Commonwealth ministers responsible for women's affairs, 9–12 October 1990, Ottawa, Canada. Commonwealth Secretariat, London, UK.

———— 1992a. Commonwealth notes — The Ottawa declaration on women and structural adjustment. Commonwealth Secretariat, London, UK.

———— 1992b. Women, conservation and agriculture: a manual for trainers. Commonwealth Secretariat, London, UK.

———— 1993. Beyond planning to implementation: report of the fourth meeting of Commonwealth ministers responsible for women's affairs, 5–9 July 1993, Cyprus. Commonwealth Secretariat, London, UK.

Cornia, G.A. 1987. Economic decline and human welfare in the first half of the 1980s. *In* Jolly, R.; Steward, F., ed., Adjustment with a human face: protecting the vulnerable and promoting growth. Clarendon Press, Oxford, UK.

Dahl, G. 1987. Women in pastoral production: some theoretical notes on roles and resources. Ethnos, 52, 246–279.

Damarin, S.K. 1992. Teaching mathematics: a feminist perspective. *In* Cooney, T.J.; Hirsch, C.R., ed., Teaching and learning mathematics in the 1990s. National Council of Teachers of Mathematics, Reston, VA, USA. pp. 144–151.

Dankelman, I.; Davidson, J. 1988. Women and environment in the Third World: alliance for the future. Earthscan, London, UK.

Davis, G.R. 1990. Energy for planet earth. Scientific American, 263(3), 54–62.

Dessing, M. 1990. Support for microenterprises: lessons for sub-Saharan Africa. World Bank, Washington, DC, USA. Technical Paper 122.

de Treville, D. 1987. Small-scale enterprise assessment: an analysis of renewable energy users and the informal sector — Draft report to FAO. Equity Policy Center, Washington, DC, USA.

Dirar, M. 1991. Fermented foods in Sudan. Appropriate Technology, 20(2), 24.

Downing, J. 1990. Gender and the growth and dynamics of microenterprises. US Agency for International Development, Washington, DC, USA. Gemini Working Paper 5.

———— 1991. Gender and the growth of microenterprises. Small Enterprise Development, 2(1), 4–12.

Downing, J.; Daniels, L. 1992. The growth and dynamics of women entrepreneurs in Southern Africa. US Agency for International Development, Washington, DC, USA. Gemini Technical Report 47.

Drummond, M.F. 1987. Economic evaluation and the rational diffusion and use of health technology. Health Policy, 7(3), 309–324.

Drummond, M.F.; Stoddart, G.L. 1984. Economic analysis and clinical trials. Controlled Clinical Trials, 5, 115–128.

Duncan, O.D. 1984. Notes on social measurement — Historical and critical. Russell Sage Foundation, New York, NY, USA.

Eckholm, E. 1975. The other energy crisis: firewood. World Watch 1, Washington, DC, USA.

ECOSOC (UN Economic and Social Council). 1991. Information submitted by the World Intellectual Property Organization. Commission on Human Rights, Sub-Commission on Prevention of Discrimination and Protection of Minorities, Working Group on Indigenous Populations, 9th session, 28 July–4 August 1991. United Nations, New York, NY, USA.

———— 1993. Discrimination against indigenous peoples: study on the protection of the cultural and intellectual property of indigenous peoples. Commission on Human Rights, Sub-Commission on Prevention of Discrimination and Protection of Minorities, United Nations, New York, NY, USA. E/CN.4/sub.2/1993/28.

———— 1994. Preparations for the 4th world conference on women: action for equality, development and peace — Draft platform for action. United Nations, New York, NY, USA. E/CN.6/1994/10/2.

Edgerton, J.; Viswanath, V. 1992. Back to office report on WEMTOP project design roundtables in India and the Philippines, 11 May 1992. Economic Development Institute, World Bank, Washington, DC, USA.

Eisenberg, J.M. 1989. Clinical economics: a guide to the economic analysis of clinical practice. Journal of the American Medical Association, 262(20), 2879–2886.

Ellis, P. 1990. Measures increasing the participation of girls and women in technical and vocational education and training: a Caribbean study. Commonwealth Secretariat, London, UK.

Enloe, C. 1989. Bananas, beaches and bases: feminist perspectives on international relations. Pandora Publishing, London, UK.

Ensminger, J. 1987. Economic and political differentiation among Galole Orma women. Ethnos, 52, 28–49.

Erinosho, S.Y. 1993. Nigerian women in science and technology. International Development Research Centre, Dakar, Senegal.

Eshiwani, G. 1989. Kenya. In Kelly, G.P., ed., International handbook of women's education. Greenwood Press, Westport, CT, USA.

European Commission. 1994. Proceedings of the conference on equality and total quality, 4–5 June 1994, Como, Italy. Equal Opportunities Unit, Directorate General of Employment, Education and Training, European Commission, Brussels, Belgium.

Ewusi, K. 1987. Improved appropriate technologies for rural women: a case study of the identification, dissemination, monitoring and evaluation of the adoption of five improved technologies for food processing and home-based industries by rural women in Ghana. Adwinsa Publications, Accra, Ghana.

FAO (Food and Agriculture Organization of the United Nations). 1979. World conference on agrarian reform and rural development. FAO, Rome, Italy.

———— 1987. Restoring the balance: women and forest resources. FAO, Rome, Italy.

———— 1989. Household food security and forestry: an analysis of socio-economic issues. FAO, Rome, Italy.

———— 1990a. Women in agricultural development: gender issues in rural food security in developing countries. FAO, Rome, Italy.

———— 1990b. Women in agricultural development: FAO's plan of action. FAO, Rome, Italy.

———— 1991. Case studies in forest based small scale enteprises in Asia: rattan, matchmaking and handicrafts. FAO, Rome, Italy.

Fausto Sterling, A. 1994. Myths of gender: biological theories about women and men. Basic Books, New York, NY, USA.

Feeny, D.; Torrance, G. 1992. Principles of economic evaluation for health care technologies. Centre for Health Economics and Policy Analysis, McMaster University, Hamilton, ON, Canada.

Feldstein, H.; Poats, S., ed. 1990. Working together: gender analysis in agriculture (vol. 1). Kumarian Press, West Hartford, CT, USA.

Fernandez, M.E. 1992. The social organization of production in community-based agro-pastoralism in the Andes. In McCorkle, C.M., ed., Plants, animals and people: agropastoral systems research. Westview Press, Boulder, CO, USA. pp. 99–108.

Feyerabend, P. 1975. Against method. New Left Books, London, UK.

Financial Times. 1990. Survey of Thailand. Financial Times, 5 December 1990, p. 5.

Foley, G. 1991. Energy assistance revisited: a discussion paper. Stockholm Environment Institute, Stockholm, Sweden.

Ford, R.; Lelo, F. 1991. Evaluating participatory rural appraisal: listening to village leaders in Kakuyuni location. Program for International Development and Social Change, Clark University, Worcester, MA, USA. Paper 2.

Forget, G. 1992. Health and the environment: a people-centred research strategy. International Development Research Centre, Ottawa, ON, Canada.

Fortmann, L.; Rocheleau, D. 1985. Women and agroforestry: four myths and three case studies. Agroforestry Systems, 2, 253–272.

Foucault, M. 1980. Two lectures. In Gordon, C., ed., Power/knowledge: selected interviews and other writings 1972–1977. Pantheon Books, New York, NY, USA. Chapter 5.

Frank, A.G. 1967. Capitalism and underdevelopment in Latin America. Monthly Review Press, New York, NY, USA.

Fraser-Abder, P. 1992. How can teacher education change the downhill trend of science education? Journal of Science Teacher Education, 3(1), 21–26.

Frissen, V. 1992. Trapped in electronic cages? Gender and new information technologies in the public and private domain: an overview of research. Media, Culture and Society, 14, 31–49.

Gaio, F. 1995. Women in software programming: the case of Brazil. In Mitter, S.; Rowbotham, S., ed., Women encounter information technology: perspectives of the Third World. Routledge, London, UK.

Gamser, M.; Almond, F. 1989. The role of technology in microenterprise development. *In* Levitsky, J., ed., Microenterprises in developing countries. Intermediate Technology Publications, London, UK.

Gapasin, D.P. 1993. Filipino women scientists: a potential recruitment pool for the IARCs. Consultative Group on International Agricultural Research, Washington, DC, USA. Gender Program Working Paper 6.

Garland, M.J. 1992. Light on the black box of basic health care: Oregon's contribution to the national movement toward universal health insurance. Yale Law and Policy Review, 10(2), 409–430.

Gata, N. 1992. Guidelines for the integration of women into mainstream FAO plant protection programmes in Africa. Department of Research and Specialist Services, Ministry of Lands, Agriculture and Water Development, Harare, Zimbabwe.

Girvan, N. 1994. Information technology for small and medium sized enterprises in small open economies: issues for policy research. International Development Research Centre, Ottawa, ON, Canada.

Global Child Health Society. 1994. Cloning and human reproduction: WHO calls for the establishment of minimum safeguards. Global Child Health News and Review, 2(1), 3.

Gold, R.B. 1984. Ultrasound imaging during pregnancy. Family Planning Perspectives, 16, 240–243.

Goldschmidt, W. 1981. The failure of pastoral economic development programs in Africa. *In* Galaty, J.; Aronson, D.; Salzman, P.C., ed., The future of pastoral peoples: research priorities for the 1980s — Proceedings of a conference held in Nairobi, Kenya, 4–8 August 1980. International Development Research Centre, Ottawa, ON, Canada. pp. 101–118.

Goldsmith, E.; Allen, R.; Allaby, M.; Davoll, J.; Lawrence, S. 1972. A blueprint for survival: by the editors fo the Ecologist. Houghton Mifflin, Boston, MA, USA.

Gordon, J. 1986. Biomass energy devices for income generation at the household or community level (draft report). Intermediate Technology Development Group, London, UK.

Gothoskar, S. 1995. Computerization and women's employment in the banking sector of India. *In* Mitter, S.; Rowbotham, S., ed., Women encounter information technology: perspectives of the Third World. Routledge, London, UK.

Greaves, T., ed. 1994. Intellectual property rights for indigenous peoples: a sourcebook. Society for Applied Anthropology, Oklahoma City, OK, USA.

Guan Tao. 1992. Chinese women as an important driving force in environment and continued progress. Address to the International Symposium on Women's Role in Environment and Continued Progress, September 1992.

Gupta, A.K. 1989. Scientists' views of farmers' practices in India: barriers to effective participation. *In* Chambers, R.; Pacey, A.; Thrupp, L.A., ed., Farmer first: farmer innovations and agricultural research. Intermediate Technology Publications, London, UK. pp. 24–31.

Gustafson, D.H.; Cats-Baril, W.L.; Alemi, F. 1992. Systems to support health policy analysis: theory, models and uses. Health Administration Press, Ann Arbor, MI, USA.

Haddon, L.; Silverstone, R. 1993. Teleworking in the 1990s: a view from the home — Report on the ESRC/PICT study of teleworking and information communication technologies. Science Policy Research Unit, Sussex University, Brighton, Sussex, UK.

Haggblade, S.; Ritchie, N. 1992. Opportunities for intervention in Thailand's silk subsector. US Agency for International Development, Washington, DC, USA. Gemini Working Paper 27.

Halleck, D. 1993. Breaking down barriers for women and minorities in mathematics and sciences. In Gallon, D.P., ed., Regaining the edge in urban education: mathematics and sciences. A report of the Commission on Urban Community Colleges. American Association of Community and Junior Colleges, Washington, DC, USA.

Halos, S.C. 1992. Biotechnology trends: a threat to Philippine agriculture. In Ahmed, I., ed., Biotechnology: a hope or a threat? Macmillan, London, UK.

Haraway, D.J. 1991. Simians, cyborgs and women: the reinvention of nature. Routledge, New York, NY, USA.

Harcourt, W., ed. 1994. Feminist perspectives on sustainable development. Zed Books and Society for International Development, London, UK, USA.

Harding, J. 1992. Breaking the barrier: girls in science education. International Institute for Educational Planning, United Nations Educational, Scientific and Cultural Organisation, Paris, France.

Harding, S. 1986. The science question in feminism. Cornell University Press, Ithaca, NY, USA.

———— ed. 1987. Feminism and methodology: social science issues. Indiana University Press, Bloomington, IN, USA.

———— 1991. Whose science? Whose knowledge? Thinking from women's lives. Cornell University Press, Ithaca, NY, USA.

———— 1992. After the neutrality ideal: science, politics and "strong objectivity." Social Research, 59, 567–587.

———— 1993. The "racial" economy of science: towards a democratic future. Indiana University Press, Bloomington, IN, USA.

Harding, S.; Hintikka, M., ed. 1983. Discovering reality: feminist perspectives on epistemology, metaphysics, methodology and philosophy of science. Reidel/Kluwer, Dordrecht, Netherlands.

Harding, S.; O'Barr, J., ed. 1987. Sex and scientific inquiry. Chicago University Press, Chicago, IL, USA.

Hellinger, M. 1984. Effecting social change through group action: feminine occupational titles in transition. In Kramarae, C.; Muriel, S.; O'Barr, W.M., ed., Language and power. Sage, Beverly Hills, CA, USA.

Henwood, F. 1987. Microelectronics and women's employment: an international perspective. In Davidson, M.; Cooper, C., ed., Women and information technology. John Wiley & Sons, Chichester, Sussex, UK.

Hertel, S. 1990. Gender, development and microenterprise in Latin America: women's productive and reproductive labour reconsidered. Acción International, Bogotá, Colombia.

Hesse, M. 1966. Models and analogies in science. University of Notre Dame Press, Notre Dame, IN, USA.

Hill, C. 1994. Healthy communities, healthy animals: reconceptualizing health and wellness. In Indigenous and local community knowledge in animal health and production systems: gender perspectives — A working guide to issues, networks, and initiatives. World Women's Veterinary Association, Ottawa, ON, Canada. pp. 4–32.

Hill, M.W., ed. 1989. National information policies: a review of the situation in seventeen industrialised countries, with particular reference in scientific information. International Federation for Documentation, The Hague, Netherlands.

Holcomb, B.; Rothenberg, T.Y. 1993. Women's work and the urban household economy in developing countries. In Turshen, M.; Holcomb, B., ed., Women's lives and public policy. Greenwood Press, Westport, CT, USA.

Holloway, M. 1994. A lab of her own. Scientific American, November 1994, 94–103.

Horowitz, M. 1981. Research priorities in pastoral studies: an agenda for the 1980s. In Galaty, J.; Aronson, D.; Salzman, P.C., ed., The future of pastoral peoples: research priorities for the 1980s — Proceedings of a conference held in Nairobi, Kenya, 4–8 August 1980. International Development Research Centre, Ottawa, ON, Canada. pp. 61–88.

Hubbard, R. 1990. The politics of women's biology. Rutgers University Press, New Brunswick, NJ, USA.

Huws, U. 1991. Telework: projections. Futures, January/February 1991.

———— 1993. Teleworking in Britain: a report to the employment department. Department of Employment, London, UK.

Hynes, H.P. 1992. Feminism and engineering: the inroads. In Kramarae, C.; Spender, D., ed., The knowledge explosion: generations of feminist scholarship. Teachers College Press, New York, NY, USA.

IFAD (International Fund for Agricultural Development); IICA (Instituto Interamericano de Cooperación para la Agricultura); UNIFEM (UN Development Fund for Women). 1993. Communications with a gender perspective: toward a strategy for rural women in Latin America and the Caribbean. IICA, Coronado, Costa Rica.

IFIAS (International Federation of Institutes for Advanced Study); IFAN (Institut Fondamentale d'Afrique Noire). 1994. Women, energy and environment: new directions for policy research. IFIAS, Toronto, ON, Canada.

IIED (International Institute for Environment and Development). 1992. Tackling the crisis in Karamoja. Haramatta, 17, 17–18.

ILO (International Labour Organisation). 1957. Convention concerning the protection and integration of indigenous and other tribal and semi-tribal populations in independent countries. ILO, Geneva, Switzerland. Convention 107.

———— 1989a. Convention concerning indigenous and tribal peoples in independent countries. ILO, Geneva, Switzerland. Convention 169.

———— 1989b. Working with visual display units. ILO, Geneva, Switzerland. Occupational Safety and Health Series, 61.

———— 1990a. Conditions of work digest. ILO, Geneva, Switzerland. Telework, 9(1).

———— 1990b. Security of employment and income in the light of structural and technological change in the printing and allied trades, having regard to other media — Report II: Third tripartite technical meeting for the printing and allied trades. ILO, Geneva, Switzerland.

———— 1991a. Proceedings of ILO's national technical workshop on women and wasteland development. Programme on Rural Women, ILO, New Delhi, India.

———— 1991b. The Bankura story: rural women organize for change. ILO, New Delhi, India. Technical Co-operation Report.

———— 1991c. The impact of technological change on work and training: tripartite European meeting on technological change on work and training. ILO, Geneva, Switzerland. TRITEC/1991/1.

———— 1993. World of work (no. 2). ILO, Geneva, Switzerland.

Indian Institute of Management. 1992. Regional workshop on the development of microenterprises by women, 4–9 August 1992. Indian Institute of Management, Ahmedabad, India.

Institute of Medicine. 1985. Assessing medical technologies. A report from the Committee for Evaluating Medical Technologies in Clinical Use, Division of Health Sciences Policy, Division of Health Promotion and Disease Prevention. National Academy Press, Washington, DC, USA.

INSTRAW (International Research and Training Institute for the Advancement of Women). 1989. Water and sanitation: the vital role of women. INSTRAW News, 13(winter), 3.

ITU (International Telecommunication Union). 1984. The missing link: report of the Independent Commission for World Wide Telecommunications Development. ITU, Geneva, Switzerland.

IUCN (International Union for the Conservation of Nature); UNEP (UN Environment Programme): WWF (World Wide Fund for Nature). 1980. World conservation strategy. IUCN/UNEP/WWF, Gland, Switzerland.

———— 1991. Caring for the earth: a strategy for sustainable living. IUCN/UNEP/WWF, Gland, Switzerland.

IWTC (International Women's Tribune Center). 1990. Filling the information gap: how do women get information and technologies appropriate to their needs? — Proceedings of a communications workshop, June 1990, New York. IWTC and UN Development Fund for Women, New York, NY, USA.

———— n.d. Do it herself: women and technological innovation. IWTC, New York, NY, USA. Briefing paper.

IWTC (International Women's Tribune Center); UNIFEM (UN Development Fund for Women). 1990. Reaching rural women with information on technology? — Report of a meeting on strategies for disseminating appropriate technologies to rural women, July 1990. IWTC and UNIFEM, New York, NY, USA.

Jaarsma, R. 1987. A long way: a study on some activities implemented in the Netherlands to promote equality of opportunity for girls and women in scientific, technical and vocational education, UN Educational, Scientific and Cultural Organisation, Paris, France

Jacobson, J. 1991. Women's reproductive health: the silent emergency. Worldwatch Institute, Washington, DC, USA. Paper 102.

———— 1992. Gender bias: roadblock to sustainable development. Worldwatch Institute, Washington, DC, USA. Paper 110.

———— 1993. Women's health: the price of poverty. *In* Koblinsky, M.; Timyan, J.; Gay, J., ed., The health of women: a global perspective. Westview Press, Boulder, CO, USA.

Jansen, S.C. 1989. Gender and the information society: a socially structured silence. Journal of Communication, 39(3), 196–215.

Jeans, A.; Hyman, E.; O'Donnell, L. 1990. Technology — The key to increasing the productivity of microenterprises. US Agency for International Development, Washington, DC, USA. Gemini Working Paper 8.

Johnson, M., ed. 1992. Lore: capturing traditional environmental knowledge. International Development Research Centre, Ottawa, ON, Canada.

Jones, G.M. 1990. Gender differences in teacher–student interactions in science classrooms. Journal of Research in Science Teaching, 27(9), 861–874.

Kabutha, C.B.; Thomas-Slayter, B.; Ford, R. 1991. Assessing Mbusyani: using participatory rural appraisal for sustainable resources management. Program for International Development and Social Change, Clark University, Worcester, MA, USA. Paper 1.

Kammen, D.M.; Lankford, W.F. 1991. Designing better solar cookers. Nature, 351, 21.

Kanno, K. 1987. Women's participation in decision-making in science and technology. *In* Ng, C., ed., Technology and gender: women's work in Asia. Women's Studies Unit and Department of Extension Education, Universiti Pertanian Malaysia and Malaysian Social Science Association, Kuala Lumpur, Malaysia.

Kazanjian, A.; Cardiff, K. 1993. Framework for technology decisions. New reproductive technologies and the health care system: the case for evidence-based medicine. *In* Proceed with care: final report of the Royal Commission on New Reproductive Technologies (vol. 2). Government of Canada, Ottawa, ON, Canada. pp. 69–127.

Kazanjian, A.; Friesen, K. 1993. Defusing technology: a pilot study of low and high technology in British Columbia. International Journal of Technology Assessment in Health Care, 9(1), 46–61.

Kelkar, G.; Nathan, D. 1992. Social impact of new technologies — Background paper for ESCAP all-China youth federation seminar on the effects of new technologies on the working life of young people, 20–24 October, Zhuhai, China. Economic and Social Commission for Asia and the Pacific, Bangkok, Thailand.

Keller, E.F. 1985. Reflections on gender and science. Yale University Press, New Haven, CT, USA.

Kelly, A. 1985. The construction of masculine science. British Journal of Sociology of Education, 6(2), 133–154.

Kelly, G.P. 1984. Women's access to education in the Third World: myths and realities. *In* Acker, S.; Megarry, J.; Nisbet, S.; Hoyle, E., ed., World yearbook of education 1984: women in education. Nicholas Publishing, New York, NY, USA.

———— 1991. Women and higher education. *In* Altbach, P., ed., International higher education: an encyclopedia. Garland, New York, NY, USA.

Kenya, Government of. 1990. Participatory rural appraisal handbook: conducting PRA's in Kenya. National Environment Secretariat, Nairobi, Kenya.

Kerven, C. 1987. Some research and development implications for pastoral dairy production in Africa. International Livestock Centre for Africa, Bulletin, 26, 29–35.

Kettel, B. 1993. Women, health and the environment. Division of Women and Youth Affairs, Commonwealth Secretariat, London, UK.

——— 1995. Gender and environments: lessons from WEDNET. In Blumberg, R.; Rakowski, C.; Tinker, I.; Monteon, M., ed., EnGENDERing wealth and well-being. Westview Press, Boulder, CO, USA.

Kinyanjui, K. 1993. Enhancing women's participation in the science-based curriculum: the case of Kenya. In Ker Conway, J.; Bourque, S.C., ed., The politics of women's education. University of Michigan Press, Ann Arbor, MI, USA.

Koblinsky, M.; Campbell, O.; Harlow, S. 1993. Mother and more: a broader perspective on women's health. In Koblinsky, M.; Timyan, J.; Gay, J., ed., The health of women: a global perspective. Westview Press, Boulder, CO, USA.

Kristoferson, L.A.; Bokalders, J. 1991. Renewable energy technologies: their application in developing countries. Intermediate Technology Publications, London, UK.

Kuhn, T. 1970. The structure of scientific revolutions (2nd ed.). University of Chicago Press, Chicago, IL, USA.

Lane, N. 1994. Women in science: much has been accomplished, but much remains to be done. The Scientist, 1994(Jan 24), 12.

Last, M.; Chavunduka, G.L., ed. 1986. The professionalisation of African medicine. Manchester University Press, Manchester, UK.

Latour, B.; Woolgar, S. 1979. Laboratory life: the social construction of scientific facts. Sage Publications, Beverley Hills, CA, USA.

Leach, G.; Mearns, R. 1988. Beyond the woodfuel crisis. Earthscan, London, UK.

Lee-Smith, D.; Trujillo, C.H. 1992. The struggle to legitimize subsistence: women and sustainable development. Environment and Urbanization, 4(1), 77–84.

Lenssen, N. 1993. A new energy path for the Third World. Technology Review, October 1993, 43–51.

Lewis, N.; Huyer, S.; Kettel, B.; Marsden, L. 1994. Safe womanhood: a discussion paper. International Federation of Institutes for Advanced Study, Toronto, ON, Canada. Gender, Science, and Development Working Paper 4.

Lewis, N.; Kieffer, E.C. 1994. The health of women: beyond maternal and child health. In Verhasselt, V.; Phillips, D., ed., Health and development. Routledge & Kegan Paul, London, UK.

Light, J. 1994. Not the old boys' network: women's groups and global computer networking. Department of History and Philosophy of Science, Cambridge University, UK.

Lindenbaum, S.; Lock, M., ed. 1993. Knowledge, power and practice: the anthropology of medicine and everyday life. University of California Press, Los Angeles, CA, USA.

Linn, M.C.; Hyde, J.S. 1989. Gender, mathematics, and science. Educational Research, 18(8), 17–19, 22–27.

Lloyd, G. 1984. The man of reason: "male" and "female" in Western philosophy. University of Minnesota Press, Minneapolis, MN, USA.

Logue, H.A.; Talapessy, L.M., ed. 1993. Women in science: international workshop proceedings. European Commission, Brussels, Belgium.

Loudiyi, D.; Nagle, B.; Ofosu-Amaah, W. 1989. The African Women's Assembly: women and sustainable development. WorldWIDE, Washington, DC, USA.

Lubell, H. 1991. The informal sector in the 1980s and the 1990s. Development Studies Centre, Organisation for Economic Co-operation and Development, Paris, France.

Luery, A.; Bowman, M.; Akinola, C. 1992. Technology and women: contradictions in the process of economic and social change — The example of cassava processing, West Africa. Technoserve Inc., Norwalk, CT, USA.

Lycklama à Nijeholt, G. 1992. Women and the meaning of development: approaches and consequences. Institute of Development Studies, Brighton, Sussex, UK. Silver Jubilee Paper 7.

MacCormack, C.P. 1988. Health and the social power of women. Social Science and Medicine, 26(7), 677–683.

Mackenzie, F. 1993. Exploring the connections: structural adjustment, gender and the environment. Geoforum, 24, 71–87.

Maldonado, C.; Sethuranan, S.V. 1992. Technological capability in the informal sector: metal manufacturing in developing countries. International Labour Organisation, Geneva, Switzerland.

Marshall-Thomas, E. 1965. Warrior herdsmen. Knopf, New York, NY, USA.

Mattingly, S.S. 1992. The maternal–fetal dyad: exploring the two-patient obstetrical model. Hastings Centre Report, 22, 13–18.

Mausner, J.S.; Bahn, A.K. 1974. Epidemiology: an introductory text. W.B. Saunders, Philadelphia, PA, USA.

McDowell, I.; Newell, C. 1987. Measuring health: a guide to rating scales and questionnaires. Oxford University Press, New York, NY, USA.

McGranahan, G.; Kaijser, A. 1993. Household energy problems: problems, policies, and prospects. Stockholm Environment Institute, Stockholm, Sweden. EED Series 19.

Meadows, D.H.; Meadows, D.; Pot, L.; Randers, J.; Behrens, W.W., III. 1972. The limits to growth. Potomac Associates, Washington, DC, USA.

Meena, R. 1991. The impact of structural adjustment programs on rural women in Tanzania. In Gladwin, C.H., ed., Structural adjustment and African women farmers. University of Florida Press, Gainesville, FL, USA.

Merchant, C. 1980. The death of nature: women, ecology and the scientific revolution. Harper and Row, New York, NY, USA.

Mies, M. 1986. Patriarchy and accumulation on a world scale: women in the international division of labour. Zed Books, London, UK.

Mies, M.; Shiva, V. 1993. Ecofeminism. Zed Books, London, UK.

Mitter, S. 1992. New skills requirements and appropriate programmes for the enhancement of participation of the female labour force in industry in selected economies of the Asian/Pacific region. Paper presented

at the Regional Workshop on Promoting Diversified Skill Requirements for Women in Industry, 23–27 March 1992, Chiang Mai, Thailand. Economic and Social Commission for Asia and the Pacific,
Bangkok, Thailand.

——— 1994. What women demand of technology. New Left Review, 205,
100–110.

Mitter, S.; Pearson, R. 1992. Global information processing: the emergence of
software services and data entry jobs in selected developing countries. International Labour Organisation, Geneva, Switzerland.

Morgall, J.H. 1993. Technology assessment: a feminist perspective. Temple
University Press, Philadelphia, PA, USA.

Morin, A.J. 1993. Science policy and politics. Prentice Hall, Engelwood Cliffs,
NJ, USA.

Moser, C.O.N. 1993. Gender planning and development: theory, practice and
training. Routledge, London, UK, and New York, NY, USA.

Mozans, H.J. 1991. Women in science (reprint). University of Notre Dame
Press, Notre Dame, IN, USA.

Mpande, R.; Mpofu, N. 1991. Coping strategies. Appropriate Technology,
20(2), 22.

Mullis, V.S.; Jenkins, L.B. 1988. The science report card: elements of risk and
recovery, trends and achievement based in the 1986 national assessment. Educational Testing Service, Princeton, NJ, USA.

Munasinghe, M. 1989. Computers and informatics in developing countries.
Butterworths, London, UK.

Muntemba, S. 1977. Rural underdevelopment in Zambia: Kabwe Rural District. University of California, Los Angeles, CA, USA. PhD dissertation.

——— ed. 1985. Rural development and women: lessons from the field (vol.
1 and 2). International Labour Organisation, Geneva, Switzerland.

——— 1988. Women and land in sub-Saharan Africa. Prepared for the
International Labour Organisations's workshop on women and land,
15–17 October 1988, Harare, Zimbabwe. International Labour
Organisation, Geneva, Switzerland.

——— 1989a. By our own bootstraps: women, resource management and
sustainable development. Paper presented at the African Women's
Assembly on Sustainable Development. Ministry of Natural
Resources, Harare, Zimbabwe.

——— 1989b. Women and environment in Africa: towards a conceptualization. In Rathgeber, E.; Kettel, B., ed., Women's role in natural
resource management in Africa. International Development
Research Centre, Ottawa, ON, Canada. Manuscript Report 238e.

Mureithi, L.P.; Ndiritu, S.K. 1991. Information technology in Kenya's financial
sector. International Labour Organisation, Geneva, Switzerland.
WEP Research Working Paper 217.

Nandy, A., ed. 1990. Science, hegemony and violence: a requiem for moder-
nity. Oxford University Press, New Delhi, India.

NABST (National Advisory Board on Science and Technology). 1988. Participation of women in science and technology. Government of
Canada, Ottawa, ON, Canada.

———— 1993. Winning with women in trades, technology, science and engineering. Government of Canada, Ottawa, ON, Canada.

Ng, C. 1995. Information technology, gender and employment: a case study of the telecommunications industry in Malaysia. *In* Mitter, S.; Rowbotham, S., ed., Women encounter information technology: perspectives of the Third World. Routledge, London, UK.1995.

Ng, C.; Munro-Kua, A., ed. 1994. Keying into the future: the impact of computerization on office workers. Women's Development Collective, Selangor, Malaysia.

Noble, D.F. 1992. A world without women: the Christian clerical culture of Western science. Oxford University Press and Knopf, New York, NY, USA.

Oakes, J.; Rand Corporation. 1990. Opportunities, achievement, and choice: women and minority students in science and mathematics. *In* Cazden, C.B., ed., Review of research in education. American Educational Research Association, Washington, DC, USA. pp. 153–222.

Oakley, A. 1986a. Ultrasound in obstetrics: telling the truth about Jerusalem. Blackwell, New York, NY, USA.

———— 1986b. The captured womb: a history of the medical care of pregnant women. Blackwell, New York, NY, USA.

OECD (Organisation for Economic Co-operation and Development). 1989. Major R&D programmes for information technology. OECD, Paris, France.

———— 1993a. New directions in donor assistance to microenterprises. Development Assistance Centre, OECD, Paris, France.

———— 1993b. Small and medium-sized enterprises: technology and competitiveness. OECD, Paris, France.

Office of Science and Technology. 1994. The rising tide: a report on women in science, engineering and technology. Office of Science and Technology, London, UK.

Ofusu-Amaah, W.; Philleo, W. 1993. Women and the environment: an analytical review of success stories. WorldWIDE, Washington, DC, USA.

Ojeda, M. 1994. Potato production in the Andes. *In* Ilkkaracan, I.; Appleton, H., ed., Women's roles in the development of food cycle technologies. Intermediate Technology Publications, London, UK.

Okuneyo, C.; Nwosu, A. 1988. Women's access to land and its implication: the Nigerian case. Women's Programme, Rural Employment, International Labour Organisation, Geneva, Switzerland.

Olivares, M. 1989. A methodology for working with the informal sector. Acción International, Bogotá, Colombia. Discussion Paper 1.

Østergaard, L., ed. 1992. Gender and development: a practical guide. Routledge, New York, NY, USA.

OTA (Office of Technology Assessment). 1976. Development of medical technology: opportunities for assessment. Government Printing Office, Washington, DC, USA.

Overholt, C. 1984. Gender roles in development projects. Kumarian Press, West Hartford, CN, USA.

Packard, R. 1989. Industrial production, health and disease in sub-Saharan Africa. Social Science and Medicine, 28(5), 475–496.

PAHO (Pan American Health Organization). 1993. Resolution V — Health of indigenous peoples, development and strengthening of local health systems. PAHO, Washington, DC, USA.

Parker, A.; Russo, M.; Sommer, D.; Yaeger, P., ed. 1992. Nationalisms and sexualities. Routledge, New York, NY, USA.

Patel, V.G. 1985. Entrepreneurship development program in India and its relevance for developing countries. World Bank, Ahmedabad, India.

Payne, J.W.; Braunstein, M.L.; Carroll, J.S. 1978. Exploring pre-decisional behavior: an alternative approach to decision research. Organizational Behavior and Human Performance, 22, 17–34.

Payne, S. 1991. Women, health and poverty: an introduction. Harvester Wheatsheaf, New York, NY, USA.

Pearson, R. 1993. Gender and new technology in the Caribbean: new work for women? In Moresem, J., ed., Women and change in the Caribbean. James Currey, London, UK.

Pearson, R. 1995. Health hazards of new technology experiences from developed and developing countries. In Mitter, S.; Rowbotham, S., ed., Women encounter information technology: perspectives of the Third World. Routledge, London, UK.

Pearson, R.; Mitter, S. 1993. Employment and working conditions of low-skilled information-processing workers in less developed countries. International Labour Review, 132(1), 49–64.

Petchesky, R.P. 1987. Fetal images: the power of visual culture in the politics of reproduction. In Stanworth, M., ed., Reproductive technologies: gender, motherhood and medicine. University of Minnesota Press, Minneapolis, MN, USA.

Pfafflin, S.M. 1982. Some reflections on women in science and technology after UNCSTD. In D'Onofrio, P.; Pfafflin, S., ed., Scientific and technological change and the role of women in development. Westview Press, Boulder, CO, USA.

Pickering, A. 1984. Constructing quarks. University of Chicago Press, Chicago, IL, USA.

——— ed. 1992. Science as practice and culture. University of Chicago Press, Chicago, IL, USA.

PIP (Population Information Program). 1992. The reproductive revolution: new survey findings. PIP, Johns Hopkins School of Hygiene and Public Health, Baltimore, MD, USA. Population Reports, Series M, 11.

Posey, D.A.; Goeldi, M.P.E. 1994. International agreements and intellectual property right protection for indigenous peoples. In Greaves, T., ed., Intellectual property rights for indigenous peoples: a sourcebook. Society for Applied Anthropology, Oklahoma City, OK, USA. pp. 225–251.

Quine, W.V.O. 1953. From a logical point of view: two dogmas of empiricism. Harvard University Press, Cambridge, MA, USA.

Raikes, A. 1989. Women's health in east Africa. Social Science and Medicine, 28(5), 447–459.

Rathgeber, E. 1990. Knowledge production, dissemination and utilization in Zimbabwe. International Development Research Centre, Ottawa, ON, Canada. Unpublished.

Rayman, P.; Brett, B. 1993. Pathways for women in the sciences: the Wellesley report (part 1). Wellesley College Center for Research on Women, Wellesley College, Wellesley, MA, USA.

Reyes, L.H.; Padilla, M.J. 1985. Science, math and gender. Science Teacher, 1985(Sep), 47–48.

Rhyne, E.; Holt, S. 1993. Women in finance and enterprise development. World Bank, Washington, DC, USA.

Richards, A. 1932. Hunger and work in a savage tribe: a functional study of nutrition. Routledge, London, UK.

Rocheleau, D. 1992. Gender, ecology and agroforestry: science and survival in Kathama. Clark University, Worcester, MA, USA. ECOGEN Case Study Series.

Roldan, M. 1993. Industrial restructuring, deregulation and new JIT labour processes in Argentina: towards a gender-aware perspective? Institute for Development Studies, University of Sussex, Brighton, Sussex, UK. IDS Bulletin, 24(2), 42–52.

Rose, H. 1987. Hand, brain and heart: a feminist epistemology for the natural sciences. In Harding, S.; O'Barr, J., ed., 1987. Sex and scientific inquiry. Chicago University Press, Chicago, IL, USA.

Rose, H.; Rose, S. 1976. The incorporation of science. In Rose, H.; Rose, S., ed., Ideology of/in the natural sciences. Schenkman Publishing, Cambridge, MA, USA.

Rosell, S.A. 1992. Governing in an information society. Institute for Research on Public Policy, Montreal, PQ, Canada.

Rosenthal, R.; Jacobson, L. 1968. Pygmalion in the classroom: teacher expectation and pupils' intellectual development. Holt, Rinehart and Winston, New York, NY, USA.

Rosser, S.V. 1988. Good science: can it ever be gender-free? Women's Studies International Forum, 11(1), 13–19.

Rothschild, J. 1988. Teaching technology from a feminist perspective: a practical guide. Teachers College Press, New York, NY, USA. Athene Series.

Royal Commission on New Reproductive Technologies. 1993. Proceed with care: final report of the Royal Commission on New Reproductive Technologies (2 vols). Government of Canada, Ottawa, ON, Canada.

Rukuni, M. 1994. Getting agriculture moving in east and southern Africa: a framework for action. Paper presented at the East and Southern African Conference of Agricultural Ministers, 12–15 April 1994, Harare, Zimbabwe. University of Zimbabwe, Harare, Zimbabwe.

RWEDP (Regional Wood Energy Development Programme). 1988. The use of wood fuels in rural industries in Asia and Pacific region. Food and Agriculture Organisation, Bangkok, Thailand.

Sackett, D.L.; Haynes, R.B.; Guyatt, G.H.; Tugwell, P. 1985. Clinical epidemiology: a basic science for clinical medicine (2nd ed.). Little, Brown & Co., Toronto, ON, Canada.

Sadker, M.P.; Sadker, D.M. 1986. Sexism in the classroom: from grade school to graduate school. Phi Delta Kappan, 67, 512–516.

Sagasti, F.R. 1979. Towards endogenous science and technology for another development. Development Dialogue, 1, 68–78.

Sandelowski, M. 1994. Separate, but less unequal: fetal ultrasonography and the transformation of expectant mother/fatherhood. Gender and Society, 8(2), 230–245.

Sandor, M. 1994. Report on opportunities and strategies for developing small enterprises for women. Women in Development, UN Development Programme, New York, NY, USA.

Sardar, Z., ed. 1988. The revenge of Athena: science, exploitation and the Third World. Mansell, London, UK.

Schiebinger, L. 1989. The mind has no sex? Women in the origins of modern science. Harvard University Press, Cambridge, MA, USA.

———— 1993. Nature's body: gender in the making of modern science. Beacon Press, Boston, MA, USA.

Schwass, R.; Banuri, T.; Qutub, A. 1992. Implementation design for the NCS for Pakistan. International Union for the Conservation of Nature, Karachi, Pakistan.

Seager, J. 1993. Earth follies: coming to feminist terms with the global environmental crisis. Routledge, New York, NY, USA.

Secretary-General. 1993. Improvement of the situation of women in rural areas. United Nations, New York, NY, USA. ECOSOC 1/48/187.

Sen, G.; Grown, C. 1987. Development crises and alternative visions: Third World women's perspectives. Monthly Review Press, New York, NY, USA.

Seymour, E. 1992. Undergraduate problems with teaching and advising in SME majors — explaining gender differences in attrition rates. Journal of College Science Teaching, 22(5), 284–292.

Shapin, S.; Schaffer, S. 1985. Leviathon and the air pump. Princeton University Press, Princeton, NJ, USA.

Shapiro, G.; Levy, P.; Mitter, S. 1995. An innovative approach to positive action: the experiences of telecommunications sectors in the EC. Centre for Research in Innovation Management, Brighton University, Brighton, Sussex, UK.

Sherman, J.; Fennema, E. 1977. The study of mathematics by high school girls and boys: related variables. American Educational Research Journal, 14, 159–168.

Shiva, V. 1988. Staying alive: women, ecology and development. Zed Books, London, UK.

———— 1989. Development, ecology and women. In Plant, J., ed., Healing the wounds: the promise of ecofeminism. New Society Publishers, Philadelphia, PA, USA.

Shiva, V.; Dankelman, I. 1992. Women and biological diversity: lessons from the Indian Himalaya. In Cooper, D.; Vellve, R.; Hobbelink, H., ed., Growing diversity: genetic resources and local food security. Intermediate Technology Publications, London, UK. pp. 44–52.

Siddayao, C.M. 1990. Training materials: introductory concepts (energy policy and planning seminars). Economic Development Institute, World Bank, Washington, DC, USA.

Sisk, J. 1987. Discussion — Drummond resources allocation decisions in health care: a role for quality of life assessment? Journal of Chronic Diseases, 40(6), 617–619.

Smith, A.C. 1988. Females in science courses in Swaziland: performance, progress and perceptions. Swazi Journal of Science and Technology, 9(1), 65–82.

Smith, D. 1987. The everyday world as problematic: a sociology for women. Northeastern University Press, Boston, MA, USA.

Sontheimer, S., ed. 1991. Women and the environment: a reader. Monthly Review Press, New York, NY, USA.

Sorensen, K.H. 1992. Towards a feminized technology? Gendered values in the construction of technology. Social Studies of Science, 22(1), 5–31.

Stage, E.K.; Kreinberg, N.; Eccles (Parsons), J.; Becker, J.R. 1985. Increasing the participation and achievement of girls and women in mathematics, science and engineering. In Klein, S.S., ed., Sex equity strategies in the content areas. Handbook for achieving sex equity through education. Johns Hopkins University Press, Baltimore, MD, USA.

Stamp, P. 1989. Technology, gender, and power in Africa. International Development Research Centre, Ottawa, ON, Canada.

Standing, G. 1989. Global feminization through flexible labour. World Development, 17(7), 1077–1095.

Staudt, K. 1978. Agricultural productivity gaps: a case study in male preference in government policy implementation. Development and Change, 9, 398–414.

Steady, F. 1985. Women's work and rural cash food systems: the Tombo and Gloucester development projects, Sierra Leone. In Muntemba, S., ed., Rural development and women: lessons from the field (vol 2). International Labour Organisation, Geneva, Switzerland. pp. 47–70.

Steiner, D.L.; Norman, G.R.; Monroe Blum, H.M. 1989. PDQ epidemiology. B.C. Decker, Toronto, ON, Canada.

Stjernstedt, D. 1985. Successful rural women's projects: the the case of Mupuna multipurpose co-operative society. In Muntemba, S., ed., Rural development and women: lessons from the field (vol. 1). International Labour Organisation, Geneva, Switzerland. pp. 89–98.

Stone, A.; Molnar, A. 1986. Issues: women and natural resource management. Work Program on the Economics of Natural Resource Management, World Bank, Washington, DC, USA.

Suagee, D.B. 1994. Human rights and cultural heritage, developments in the United Nations Working Group on Indigenous Populations. In Greaves, T., ed., Intellectual property rights for indigenous peoples: a sourcebook. Society for Applied Anthropology, Oklahoma City, OK, USA.

Sundal-Hansen, L.S.; Schultz, C. 1984. Eliminating sex stereotyping in schools: a regional guide for educators in North America and Western Europe. UN Educational, Scientific and Cultural Organisation, Paris, France.

Svenson, O. 1979. Process descriptions of decision making. Organizational Behavior and Human Performance, 23, 86–112.

Swaminathan, M.S. 1981. Building a national food security system. Indian Environment Society, New Dehli, India.

Tadesse, Z. 1982. Women and technology in peripheral countries. *In* D'Onofrio, P.; Pfafflin, S., ed., Scientific and technological change and the role of women in development. Westview Press, Boulder, CO, USA.

Taket, A. 1993. Health futures in support of Health for All: report of an international consultation convened by the World Health Organization, Geneva, 19–23 July 1993. World Health Organization, Geneva, Switzerland.

Task Force on Women, Minorities, and the Handicapped in Science and Technology. 1988. Changing America: the new face of science and engineering. US Congress, Washington, DC, USA.

Thapa, R. 1992. Women, health and development: an agenda for public health action. Paper presented at the Annual Meeting of the American Public Health Association, 11 November 1992, Washington, DC, USA. American Public Health Association, Washington, DC, USA.

Thomas-Slayter, B.; Rocheleau, D.; Shields, D.; Rojas, M. 1991. Introducing the ECOGEN approach to gender, natural resources management and sustainable development. Clark University, Worcester, MA, USA.

Thompson, P. 1987. Environment and women: opportunities for improved development. Environment Sector, Canadian International Development Agency, Ottawa, ON, Canada.

Timberlake, L. 1985. Africa in crisis: the causes and cures of environmental bankruptcy. Earthscan, London, UK.

Timyan, J. 1993. Access to care: more than a problem of distance. *In* Koblinsky, M.; Timyan, J.; Gay, J., ed., The health of women: a global perspective. Westview Press, Boulder, CO, USA.

Tinker, A.; Koblinsky, M.A. 1993. Making motherhood safe. World Bank, Washington, DC, USA. Discussion Paper 202.

Ubochi, B. 1988. Women and natural resources in Africa: a bibliography. Prepared for the Conference on Women and Natural Resources in Africa. African Studies Programme, York University, Toronto, ON, Canada.

UN (United Nations) 1979a. Convention on the elimination of all forms of discrimination against women. UN, New York, NY, USA.

———— 1979b. The Vienna programme of action on sciences and technology for development. UN, New York, NY, USA.

———— 1980. Report of the world conference on women: equality, development and peace. UN, New York, NY, USA.

———— 1981. Nairobi program of action for the development and utilization of new and renewable sources of energy. UN, New York, USA.

———— 1984. Report of the ad hoc panel of experts on science and technology and women. UN, New York, NY, USA. A/CN.11/AC.1/IV/4.

———— 1985a. Women's employment and fertility. UN, New York, NY, USA.

———— 1985b. The Nairobi forward-looking strategies for the advancement of women. UN, New York, NY, USA. E.85.IV.10.

———— 1989. 1989 world survey on the role of women in development. Centre for Social Development and Humanitarian Affairs, Vienna, Austria.

———— 1990. World conference on education for all. UN, New York, NY, USA.

———— 1992a. Agenda 21. UN, New York, NY, USA.

———— 1992b. Convention on biological diversity. UN, New York, NY, USA.

———— 1994a. Draft document for the social summit. Social Summit Secretariat, UN, New York, NY, USA.

———— 1994b. Platform for action for the international conference on population and development, Cairo, Egypt. Population Division, UN, New York, NY, USA.

UNDP (UN Development Programme). 1990. Human development report 1990. UNDP, New York, NY, USA.

———— 1993. Human development report 1993. UNDP, New York, NY, USA.

UNEP (UN Environment Programme); WorldWIDE 1991. Partners in life: global assembly of women and environment. WorldWIDE, Washington, DC, USA.

Unesco (UN Educational, Scientific and Cultural Organisation). 1980. Many voices, one world. Report of the International Commission for the Study of Communication Problems (McBride report). Kogan Page, London, UK.

———— 1981. Non-technical obstacles to the use of new energies in developing countries: report of an international workshop, Bellagio, Italy. Unesco, Paris, France.

———— 1987. Statistical yearbook. Unesco, Paris, France.

———— 1993. Project 2000+: science and technology education for all — International forum on science and technology literacy for all. Unesco, Paris, France. ED-93/Conf. 016/LD-14.

UNIDO (UN Industrial Development Organization). 1993. Changing techno-economic environment in the textile and clothing industry: implications for the role of women in Asian developing countries. Regional and Country Studies Branch, UNIDO, Vienna, Austria. PPD.237 (SPEC).

UNIFEM (UN Development Fund for Women). 1993a. The world's women (vol. 2). UNIFEM, New York, NY, USA.

———— 1993b. Women's roles in the innovation of food cycle technologies. UNIFEM, New York, NY, USA. UNIFEM Food Technology Source Book No. 11.

UNSO (UN Statistical Office). 1991. The world's women. UN, New York, NY, USA. p. 83.

Urdang, S. 1979. Fighting two colonialisms: women in Guinea Bisau. Monthly Review, New York, NY, USA.

Van Fraassen, B.; Sigman, J. 1993. Interpretation in science and the arts. In Levine, G., ed., Realism and representation. University of Wisconsin Press, Madison, WI, USA.

van Zoonen, L. 1992. Feminist theory and information technology. Media, Culture and Society, 14, 9–29.

Wajcman, J. 1988. New technology outwork. *In* Willis, E., ed., Technology and the labour process: Australian case studies. Allen and Unwin, Sydney, Australia.

————— 1991. Feminism confronts technology. Pennsylvania State University Press, University Park, PA, USA.

Wakhungu, J.W. 1993. Energy resources management in Kenya: the solution as the problem. Pennsylvania State University, University Park, PA, USA. PhD thesis.

Wallace, T.; March, C., ed. 1991. Changing perceptions — Writings on gender and development. Oxfam, Oxford, UK.

WCED (World Commission on Environment and Development). 1987. Our common future. Oxford University Press, New York, NY, USA.

WEDO (Women's Environment and Development Organization). 1992. Official report: world women's congress for a healthy planet. WEDO, New York, NY, USA.

Wellcome Trust. 1994. Why may women science undergraduates and graduates not be seeking to take up careers as scientists? A scoping study for PRISM. Wellcome Trust, London, UK.

Wertz, D.C.; Fletcher, C. 1993. Prenatal diagnosis and sex selection in 19 nations. Social Science and Medicine, 37(11), 1359–1366.

Westely-Tanaskovic, I. 1985. Guidelines on national information policy: scope, formulation and implementation. UN Educational, Scientific and Cultural Organization, Paris, France.

WETV. 1994. WETV: the Global Access Television Service. WETV Secretariat, International Development Research Centre, Ottawa, ON, Canada.

White, P.E. 1992. Women and minorities in science and engineering: an update. National Science Foundation, Washington, DC, USA.

WHO (World Health Organization). 1982. Report of the second WHO consultation of women as providers of health care. WHO, Geneva, Switzerland.

————— 1986. Health implications of sex discrimination in childhood. WHO/UNICEF, Geneva, Switzerland.

————— 1989a. Report of the 44th World Health Assembly. WHO, Geneva, Switzerland.

————— 1989b. The health of youth. WHO, Geneva, Switzerland.

————— 1991a. Creating common ground. WHO, Geneva, Switzerland.

————— 1991b. Interregional workshop on leadership and participation of women in maternal and child health and family planning, 1991, Cairo. WHO, Geneva, Switzerland.

————— 1991c. Traditional medicine and modern health care: progress report by the Director-General. WHO, Geneva, Switzerland. A/44/10.

————— 1992. Women's health: across age and frontier. WHO, Geneva, Switzerland.

WHO/SEARO (World Health Organization, Southeast Asia Regional Office). 1989a. Concepts of health behavior research. SEARO, WHO, New Delhi, India.

————— 1989b. Mongar project report. WHO/SEARO, New Delhi, India.

WHO (World Health Organization); UNFPA (UN Fund for Population Activities); UNICEF (UN Children's Fund). 1989. The reproductive health of adolescents. WHO, UNFPA, and UNICEF, Geneva, Switzerland.

Whyte, J. 1984. Encouraging girls into science and technology: some European initiatives. UN Educational, Scientific and Cultural Organisation, Paris, France. Science and Technology Education Document Series No. 7.

Wijeyaratne, P.; Jones Arsenault, L.; Hatcher Robers, J.; Kitts, J., ed. 1993. Women and tropical diseases. International Development Research Centre, Ottawa, ON, Canada.

Wilson, F. 1993. Workshops as domestic domains: reflections on small-scale industry in Mexico. World Development, 21, 67–80.

Winner, L. 1986. The whale and the reactor. University of Chicago Press, Chicago, IL, USA.

Winrock International. 1988. Preparing African women for leadership in the agricultural sciences: a concept for development. Winrock International Institute for Agricultural Development, Morrilton, AR, USA.

WACC (World Association for Christian Communication). 1994. Women empowering communication: special report. Women's Programme, WACC, London, UK.

World Bank. 1993. Investing in health. Oxford University Press, New York, NY, USA.

WorldWIDE. 1991. Global assembly of women and the environment: final report. WorldWIDE, Washington, DC, USA.

Yacoob, M.; Brieger, B. 1991. Putting a face on the numbers: the uses of anthropology and epidemiology in guinea worm control among women. Water and Sanitation for Health Project, US Agency for International Development, Washington, DC, USA.

Yoon, S.Y. 1978. Korean rural health culture. Ewha Woman's University, Seoul, Korea.

—— 1982. Asia and the Pacific: children at risk, children at work. In Naidu, U.S.; Kapadia, K.R., ed., Child labor and health: problems and prospects. World Health Organization, Geneva, Switzerland. p. 46.

—— 1993. Water for life. In Steady, F.C., ed., Women and children first. Schenkman Books, Rochester, NY, USA.

Yoxen, E. 1987. Seeing with sound: a study of the development of medical images. In Bijker, W.E.; Hughes, T.P.; Pinch, T.J., ed., The social construction of technological systems: new directions in the sociology and history of technology. MIT Press, Cambridge, MA, USA.

Zimbabwe, Ministry of Natural Resources. 1989. Zimbabwe national report on women and sustainable development. Ministry of Natural Resources, Harare, Zimbabwe.